Instructor's Manual with Test Bank

for

Cultural Anthropology

Instructor's Manual with Test Bank

for

Cultural Anthropology
An Applied Perspective

Sixth Edition

Gary Ferraro
University of North Carolina at Charlotte

THOMSON
WADSWORTH

Australia • Canada • Mexico • Singapore • Spain • United Kingdom • United States

Printed in the United States of America
1 2 3 4 5 6 7 09 08 07 06 05

Printer: Thomson West

ISBN 0-495-00321-2

For more information about our products, contact us at:
Thomson Learning Academic Resource Center
1-800-423-0563

For permission to use material from this text or product, submit a request online at **http://www.thomsonrights.com.**
Any additional questions about permissions can be submitted by email to **thomsonrights@thomson.com.**

Thomson Higher Education
10 Davis Drive
Belmont, CA 94002-3098
USA

Asia (including India)
Thomson Learning
5 Shenton Way
#01-01 UIC Building
Singapore 068808

Australia/New Zealand
Thomson Learning Australia
102 Dodds Street
Southbank, Victoria 3006
Australia

Canada
Thomson Nelson
1120 Birchmount Road
Toronto, Ontario M1K 5G4
Canada

UK/Europe/Middle East/Africa
Thomson Learning
High Holborn House
50–51 Bedford Row
London WC1R 4LR
United Kingdom

Latin America
Thomson Learning
Seneca, 53
Colonia Polanco
11560 Mexico
D.F. Mexico

Spain (including Portugal)
Thomson Paraninfo
Calle Magallanes, 25
28015 Madrid, Spain

CONTENTS

Preface

This Instructor's Manual with Test Bank for Ferraro's *Cultural Anthropology: An Applied Perspective*, 6th edition has been revised with the hope that this manual will ease the burden of preparing lecture outlines and exam questions to make your teaching experience more enjoyable.

Each chapter of the Instructor's Manual includes the following resources:

- Learning Objectives
- Detailed Chapter Outline
- Key Terms
- Critical Thinking Questions
- Class Activities
- Internet Exercises
- *InfoTrac College Edition* Exercises
- Suggested Films*

***Note:** There are several important sources of anthropological films and videos. Seven of the leading ones are:

1. University of California Extension Media Center (UC)
   2176 Shattuck Avenue
   Berkeley, California 94704
   (415) 642-0460

2. Documentary Educational Resources (DER)
   5 Bridge Street
   Watertown, Massachusetts 02172
   (616) 926-0491

3. Pennsylvania State University (PSU)
   Audio-Visual Services
   Special Services Building
   1127 Fox Hill Rd.
   University Park, Pennsylvania 16803-1824
   (800) 826-0132 (or 814-865-6314) for rental, preview
   (800) 826-0132 (or 814-863-3104) for catalog, reference

4. Indiana University (IU)
   Audio-Visual Center
   Bloomington, Indiana 47405
   (812) 337-2103

5. Insight Media (IM)
   2162 Broadway, New York, NY 10024-0621
   Phone: 212-721-6316 / 800-233-9910

6. Films for the Humanities & Sciences
   P.O. Box 2053, Princeton, NJ 08543-2053
   Phone: 800-257-5126

7. Ethnoscope,
   P.O. Box 92353, Rochester, N.Y. 14692.
   Tel: 716-442-5274

Each supplier has a catalog of its holdings, available by writing or calling. Penn State has a special catalog devoted to anthropology entitled *Films: The Visualization of Anthropology*. They are also in the process of acquiring most if not all of the titles in the *Disappearing World Series* (some of which are included in the following listing), which should make them the largest distributor of ethnographic films in this country. The other distributors include their anthropology collections in large catalogs, but occasionally publish specialized supplements updating their holdings. In the list to follow, the source of each film or video is indicated with the abbreviation shown above in parentheses. The length, and if applicable, catalog number are also provided.

Other sources of films and videos are the audio-visual departments of your university, college, or public library. In large cities, it may be possible to acquire a few titles through retail video rental outlets.

Test Bank
Each chapter of the Test Bank includes the following elements:

- Approximately 40 Multiple-choice questions with answers and page references
- 10 True/False questions with answers and page references
- 10 Short Answer questions with answers and page references
- 5 Essay questions

The test bank portion of this manual is available electronically in ExamView® Computerized Testing (Cross-platform ISBN#0495030449), which allows you to create, deliver, and customize tests and study guides (both print and online) in minutes.
ExamView is a registered trademark of FSCreations, Inc. Used herein under license.

Ferraro Online Resources
For additional chapter resources, including quiz questions, Internet exercises, InfoTrac College Edition exercises, and other useful materials, please visit the companion Web site for Ferraro's *Cultural Anthropology: An Applied Perspective*, Sixth Edition at
http://anthropology.wadsworth.com/ferraro6e

Resource Integration Guide

Gary Ferraro's *Cultural Anthropology: An Applied Perspective*, Sixth Edition is available with several well-developed instructor and student resources including dynamic technology tools. All of these resources are described in detail in the visual preface of the text's Instructor's Edition. The purpose of this guide is to show how the rich ancillary materials can be used in conjunction with each chapter.

Chapter 1: What is Anthropology?

Class Preparation and Lecture Tools	Testing Tools and Course Management	Student Mastery, Homework, and Tutorials ~Beyond the Book~
Instructor's Manual with Test Bank Written by the main text author, Gary Ferraro. Contains learning objectives, chapter outlines, key terms, critical thinking questions, class activities, Internet exercises, and suggested films. The test bank offers 40 multiple-choice, 10 true/false, 10 short answer and 5-10 essay questions for each chapter. **Multimedia Manager Instructor's Resource CD-ROM** Includes pre-assembled Microsoft® PowerPoint® lecture slides, video, the Instructor's Manual, and other useful class presentation resources **CNN® Today Videos** Cultural Anthropology Vol. V: *Papua New Guinea Tourism* (6:57) **Wadsworth's Anthropology Video Library** Select a full-length video from the collection of Films for the Humanities	**ExamView®** Computerized version of the Test Bank items for Chapter 1 **WebTutor™ Advantage** Online course management tool for WebCT or Blackboard preloaded with text specific content and media resources for Chapter 1 **Cultural AnthropologyNow™** This program is ready for your students to use without your help. Or, you can choose to incorporate the course management features of the platform to better administer your class and save yourself and your students valuable time. Assign a Pre Test and/or Post Test and students' scores flow into the grade book. The program can be integrated with both WebCT and Blackboard course management platforms.	**Cultural AnthropologyNow™** An online diagnostic study tool. Students take a pretest and receive a *personalized* Study Plan. Within the Study Plan students link to helpful resources (lecture outlines, study videos, and the textbook itself) for material they need to review further. Students assess exactly what they need to know to succeed. An e-book is included! **WebTutor™ Advantage** Quizzing, flashcards, Web links, discussion threads, interactive games and exercises for Chapter 1 **Study Guide** Chapter 1 includes learning objectives, a chapter outline, key terms, Internet and InfoTrac exercises, and practice test questions with multiple choice, true/false, short answer, and essay questions. **Book Companion Website** http://anthropology.wadsworth.com/ferraro6e Tutorial quizzes, Web links, crossword puzzles, flashcards, and much more for learning material from Chapter 1 **InfoTrac® College Edition** *Keywords*: physical anthropology, primatology, archaeology, linguistics, cultural anthropology, ethnocentrism

Chapter 2: The Concept of Culture

Class Preparation and Lecture Tools	Testing Tools and Course Management	Student Mastery, Homework, and Tutorials ~Beyond the Book~
Instructor's Manual with Test Bank Written by the main text author, Gary Ferraro. Contains learning objectives, chapter outlines, key terms, critical thinking questions, class activities, Internet exercises, and suggested films. The test bank offers 40 multiple-choice, 10 true/false, 10 short answer and 5-10 essay questions for each chapter. **Multimedia Manager Instructor's Resource CD-ROM** Includes pre-assembled Microsoft® PowerPoint® lecture slides, video, the Instructor's Manual, and other useful class presentation resources **CNN® Today Videos** Cultural Anthropology, Vol. VII: *Cultural Training for Soldiers in Jordan* (2:43) **Wadsworth's Anthropology Video Library** Select a full-length video from the collection of Films for the Humanities	**ExamView®** Computerized version of the Test Bank items for Chapter 2 **WebTutor™ Advantage** Online course management tool for WebCT or Blackboard preloaded with text specific content and media resources for Chapter 2 **Cultural AnthropologyNow™** This program is ready for your students to use without your help. Or, you can choose to incorporate the course management features of the platform to better administer your class and save yourself and your students valuable time. Assign a Pre Test and/or Post Test and students' scores flow into the grade book. The program can be integrated with both WebCT and Blackboard course management platforms.	**Cultural AnthropologyNow™** An online diagnostic study tool. Students take a pretest and receive a *personalized* Study Plan. Within the Study Plan students link to helpful resources (lecture outlines, study videos, and the textbook itself) for material they need to review further. Students assess exactly what they need to know to succeed. An e-book is included! **WebTutor™ Advantage** Quizzing, flashcards, Web links, discussion threads, interactive games and exercises for Chapter 2 **Study Guide** Chapter 2 includes learning objectives, a chapter outline, key terms, Internet and InfoTrac exercises, and practice test questions with multiple choice, true/false, short answer, and essay questions. **Book Companion Website** http://anthropology.wadsworth.com/ferraro6e Tutorial quizzes, Web links, crossword puzzles, flashcards, and much more for learning material from Chapter 2 **InfoTrac® College Edition** *Keywords*: enculturation, cultural diffusion, civilization, symbol

Resource Integration Guide

Chapter 3: Applied Anthropology		
Class Preparation and Lecture Tools	**Testing Tools and Course Management**	**Student Mastery, Homework, and Tutorials ~Beyond the Book~**
Instructor's Manual with Test Bank Written by the main text author, Gary Ferraro. Contains learning objectives, chapter outlines, key terms, critical thinking questions, class activities, Internet exercises, and suggested films. The test bank offers 40 multiple-choice, 10 true/false, 10 short answer and 5-10 essay questions for each chapter. **Multimedia Manager Instructor's Resource CD-ROM** Includes pre-assembled Microsoft® PowerPoint® lecture slides, video, the Instructor's Manual, and other useful class presentation resources **CNN® Today Videos** Cultural Anthropology, Vol. V: *Muslim Patients* (2:33) **Wadsworth's Anthropology Video Library** Select a full-length video from the collection of Films for the Humanities	**ExamView®** Computerized version of the Test Bank items for Chapter 3 **WebTutor™ Advantage** Online course management tool for WebCT or Blackboard preloaded with text specific content and media resources for Chapter 3. **Cultural AnthropologyNow™** This program is ready for your students to use without your help. Or, you can choose to incorporate the course management features of the platform to better administer your class and save yourself and your students valuable time. Assign a Pre Test and/or Post Test and students' scores flow into the grade book. The program can be integrated with both WebCT and Blackboard course management platforms.	**Cultural AnthropologyNow™** An online diagnostic study tool. Students take a pretest and receive a *personalized* Study Plan. Within the Study Plan students link to helpful resources (lecture outlines, study videos, and the textbook itself) for material they need to review further. Students assess exactly what they need to know to succeed. An e-book is included! **WebTutor™ Advantage** Quizzing, flashcards, Web links, discussion threads, interactive games and exercises for Chapter 3 **Study Guide** Chapter 3 includes learning objectives, a chapter outline, key terms, Internet and InfoTrac exercises, and practice test questions with multiple choice, true/false, short answer, and essay questions. **Book Companion Website** http://anthropology.wadsworth.com/ferraro6e Tutorial quizzes, Web links, crossword puzzles, flashcards, and much more for learning material from Chapter 3 **InfoTrac® College Edition** *Keywords*: applied anthropology, cultural resource management, Ruth Benedict

Chapter 4: The Growth of Anthropological Theory		
Class Preparation and Lecture Tools	**Testing Tools and Course Management**	**Student Mastery, Homework, and Tutorials ~Beyond the Book~**
Instructor's Manual with Test Bank Written by the main text author, Gary Ferraro. Contains learning objectives, chapter outlines, key terms, critical thinking questions, class activities, Internet exercises, and suggested films. The test bank offers 40 multiple-choice, 10 true/false, 10 short answer and 5-10 essay questions for each chapter. **Multimedia Manager Instructor's Resource CD-ROM** Includes pre-assembled Microsoft® PowerPoint® lecture slides, video, the Instructor's Manual, and other useful class presentation resources **Wadsworth's Anthropology Video Library** Select a full-length video from the collection of Films for the Humanities	**ExamView®** Computerized version of the Test Bank items for Chapter 4 **WebTutor™ Advantage** Online course management tool for WebCT or Blackboard preloaded with text specific content and media resources for Chapter 4 **Cultural AnthropologyNow™** This program is ready for your students to use without your help. Or, you can choose to incorporate the course management features of the platform to better administer your class and save yourself and your students valuable time. Assign a Pre Test and/or Post Test and students' scores flow into the grade book. The program can be integrated with both WebCT and Blackboard course management platforms.	**Cultural AnthropologyNow™** An online diagnostic study tool. Students take a pretest and receive a *personalized* Study Plan. Within the Study Plan students link to helpful resources (lecture outlines, study videos, and the textbook itself) for material they need to review further. Students assess exactly what they need to know to succeed. An e-book is included! **WebTutor™ Advantage** Quizzing, flashcards, Web links, discussion threads, interactive games and exercises for Chapter 4 **Study Guide** Chapter 4 includes learning objectives, a chapter outline, key terms, Internet and InfoTrac exercises, and practice test questions with multiple choice, true/false, short answer, and essay questions. **Book Companion Website** http://anthropology.wadsworth.com/ferraro6e Tutorial quizzes, Web links, crossword puzzles, flashcards, and much more for learning material from Chapter 4 **InfoTrac® College Edition** *Keywords*: evolutionism, diffusionism, Franz Boas, Margaret Mead, postmodernism

Resource Integration Guide

Chapter 5: Methods in Cultural Anthropology		
Class Preparation and Lecture Tools	**Testing Tools and Course Management**	**Student Mastery, Homework, and Tutorials ~Beyond the Book~**
Instructor's Manual with Test Bank Written by the main text author, Gary Ferraro. Contains learning objectives, chapter outlines, key terms, critical thinking questions, class activities, Internet exercises, and suggested films. The test bank offers 40 multiple-choice, 10 true/false, 10 short answer and 5-10 essay questions for each chapter. **Multimedia Manager Instructor's Resource CD-ROM** Includes pre-assembled Microsoft® PowerPoint® lecture slides, video, the Instructor's Manual, and other useful class presentation resources **Wadsworth's Anthropology Video Library** Select a full-length video from the collection of Films for the Humanities	**ExamView®** Computerized version of the Test Bank items for Chapter 5 **WebTutor™ Advantage** Online course management tool for WebCT or Blackboard preloaded with text specific content and media resources for Chapter 5 **Cultural AnthropologyNow™** This program is ready for your students to use without your help. Or, you can choose to incorporate the course management features of the platform to better administer your class and save yourself and your students valuable time. Assign a Pre Test and/or Post Test and students' scores flow into the grade book. The program can be integrated with both WebCT and Blackboard course management platforms.	**Cultural AnthropologyNow™** An online diagnostic study tool. Students take a pretest and receive a *personalized* Study Plan. Within the Study Plan students link to helpful resources (lecture outlines, study videos, and the textbook itself) for material they need to review further. Students assess exactly what they need to know to succeed. An e-book is included! **WebTutor™ Advantage** Quizzing, flashcards, Web links, discussion threads, interactive games and exercises for Chapter 5 **Study Guide** Chapter 5 includes learning objectives, a chapter outline, key terms, Internet and InfoTrac exercises, and practice test questions with multiple choice, true/false, short answer, and essay questions. **Book Companion Website** http://anthropology.wadsworth.com/ferraro6e Tutorial quizzes, Web links, crossword puzzles, flashcards, and much more for learning material from Chapter 5 **InfoTrac® College Edition** *Keywords*: fieldwork, participant-observation, culture shock, ethnography
Chapter 6: Language		
Class Preparation and Lecture Tools	**Testing Tools and Course Management**	**Student Mastery, Homework, and Tutorials ~Beyond the Book~**
Instructor's Manual with Test Bank Written by the main text author, Gary Ferraro. Contains learning objectives, chapter outlines, key terms, critical thinking questions, class activities, Internet exercises, and suggested films. The test bank offers 40 multiple-choice, 10 true/false, 10 short answer and 5-10 essay questions for each chapter. **Multimedia Manager Instructor's Resource CD-ROM** Includes pre-assembled Microsoft® PowerPoint® lecture slides, video, the Instructor's Manual, and other useful class presentation resources **CNN® Today Videos** Cultural Anthropology, Vol. VII: *EU Tower of Babel* (2:39) Cultural Anthropology, Vol. VI: *Terror Language* (2:35) Cultural Anthropology, Vol. V: *Language Lineage* (2:18) *Ancient Egyptian Language* (2:18) *Snaps* (2:30) *Singapore Singlish* (2:33)	**ExamView®** Computerized version of the Test Bank items for Chapter 6 **WebTutor™ Advantage** Online course management tool for WebCT or Blackboard preloaded with text specific content and media resources for Chapter 6 **Cultural AnthropologyNow™** This program is ready for your students to use without your help. Or, you can choose to incorporate the course management features of the platform to better administer your class and save yourself and your students valuable time. Assign a Pre Test and/or Post Test and students' scores flow into the grade book. The program can be integrated with both WebCT and Blackboard course management platforms.	**Cultural AnthropologyNow™** An online diagnostic study tool. Students take a pretest and receive a *personalized* Study Plan. Within the Study Plan students link to helpful resources (lecture outlines, study videos, and the textbook itself) for material they need to review further. Students assess exactly what they need to know to succeed. An e-book is included! **WebTutor™ Advantage** Quizzing, flashcards, Web links, discussion threads, interactive games and exercises for Chapter 6 **Study Guide** Chapter 6 includes learning objectives, a chapter outline, key terms, Internet and InfoTrac exercises, and practice test questions with multiple choice, true/false, short answer, and essay questions. **Book Companion Website** http://anthropology.wadsworth.com/ferraro6e Tutorial quizzes, Web links, crossword puzzles, flashcards, and much more for learning material from Chapter 6 **InfoTrac® College Edition** *Keywords*: communication systems, language acquisition, phonology, Sapir-Whorf hypothesis, dialects

Resource Integration Guide

Chapter 7: Getting Food		
Class Preparation and Lecture Tools	**Testing Tools and Course Management**	**Student Mastery, Homework, and Tutorials ~Beyond the Book~**
Instructor's Manual with Test Bank Written by the main text author, Gary Ferraro. Contains learning objectives, chapter outlines, key terms, critical thinking questions, class activities, Internet exercises, and suggested films. The test bank offers 40 multiple-choice, 10 true/false, 10 short answer and 5-10 essay questions for each chapter. **Multimedia Manager Instructor's Resource CD-ROM** Includes pre-assembled Microsoft® PowerPoint® lecture slides, video, the Instructor's Manual, and other useful class presentation resources **Wadsworth's Anthropology Video Library** Select a full-length video from the collection of Films for the Humanities	**ExamView®** Computerized version of the Test Bank items for Chapter 7 **WebTutor™ Advantage** Online course management tool for WebCT or Blackboard preloaded with text specific content and media resources for Chapter 7 **Cultural AnthropologyNow™** This program is ready for your students to use without your help. Or, you can choose to incorporate the course management features of the platform to better administer your class and save yourself and your students valuable time. Assign a Pre Test and/or Post Test and students' scores flow into the grade book. The program can be integrated with both WebCT and Blackboard course management platforms.	**Cultural AnthropologyNow™** An online diagnostic study tool. Students take a pretest and receive a *personalized* Study Plan. Within the Study Plan students link to helpful resources (lecture outlines, study videos, and the textbook itself) for material they need to review further. Students assess exactly what they need to know to succeed. An e-book is included! **WebTutor™ Advantage** Quizzing, flashcards, Web links, discussion threads, interactive games and exercises for Chapter 7 **Study Guide** Chapter 7 includes learning objectives, a chapter outline, key terms, Internet and InfoTrac exercises, and practice test questions with multiple choice, true/false, short answer, and essay questions. **Book Companion Website** http://anthropology.wadsworth.com/ferraro6e Tutorial quizzes, Web links, crossword puzzles, flashcards, and much more for learning material from Chapter 7 **InfoTrac® College Edition** *Keywords*: foraging, food collecting, hunting and gathering, subsistence, horticulture, pastoralism, agriculture

Chapter 8: Economics		
Class Preparation and Lecture Tools	**Testing Tools and Course Management**	**Student Mastery, Homework, and Tutorials ~Beyond the Book~**
Instructor's Manual with Test Bank Written by the main text author, Gary Ferraro. Contains learning objectives, chapter outlines, key terms, critical thinking questions, class activities, Internet exercises, and suggested films. The test bank offers 40 multiple-choice, 10 true/false, 10 short answer and 5-10 essay questions for each chapter. **Multimedia Manager Instructor's Resource CD-ROM** Includes pre-assembled Microsoft® PowerPoint® lecture slides, video, the Instructor's Manual, and other useful class presentation resources **CNN® Today Videos** Cultural Anthropology Vol. VI: *AIDS and Indigenous Peoples in Africa* (4:04) Cultural Anthropology Vol. V: *Papua New Guinea Tourism* (6:57) *South Africa Endangered* (2:27)	**ExamView®** Computerized version of the Test Bank items for Chapter 8 **WebTutor™ Advantage** Online course management tool for WebCT or Blackboard preloaded with text specific content and media resources for Chapter 8 **Cultural AnthropologyNow™** This program is ready for your students to use without your help. Or, you can choose to incorporate the course management features of the platform to better administer your class and save yourself and your students valuable time. Assign a Pre Test and/or Post Test and students' scores flow into the grade book. The program can be integrated with both WebCT and Blackboard course management platforms.	**Cultural AnthropologyNow™** An online diagnostic study tool. Students take a pretest and receive a *personalized* Study Plan. Within the Study Plan students link to helpful resources (lecture outlines, study videos, and the textbook itself) for material they need to review further. Students assess exactly what they need to know to succeed. An e-book is included! **WebTutor™ Advantage** Quizzing, flashcards, Web links, discussion threads, interactive games and exercises for Chapter 8 **Study Guide** Chapter 8 includes learning objectives, a chapter outline, key terms, Internet and InfoTrac exercises, and practice test questions with multiple choice, true/false, short answer, and essay questions. **Book Companion Website** http://anthropology.wadsworth.com/ferraro6e Tutorial quizzes, Web links, crossword puzzles, flashcards, and much more for learning material from Chapter 8 **InfoTrac® College Edition** *Keywords*: economic anthropology, allocation of resources, division of labor, reciprocity, potlatch, market exchange

Resource Integration Guide

Chapter 9: Marriage and Family		
Class Preparation and Lecture Tools	**Testing Tools and Course Management**	**Student Mastery, Homework, and Tutorials ~Beyond the Book~**
Instructor's Manual with Test Bank Written by the main text author, Gary Ferraro. Contains learning objectives, chapter outlines, key terms, critical thinking questions, class activities, Internet exercises, and suggested films. The test bank offers 40 multiple-choice, 10 true/false, 10 short answer and 5-10 essay questions for each chapter. **Multimedia Manager Instructor's Resource CD-ROM** Allows you to create a media lecture for Chapter 9 using this Microsoft® PowerPoint® tool **CNN® Today Videos** Cultural Anthropology Vol. VII: *Gay Marriage* (1:29) *Infidelity & Monogamy* (1:33) *Online Dating (2:25)* Cultural Anthropology Vol. VI: *TV Weddings in India* (3:20) *Bangladesh Dowry* (2:45) Cultural Anthropology Vol. V: *Multiracial Families* (3:45) *Gay Marriage* (7:12)	**ExamView®** Computerized version of the Test Bank items for Chapter 9 **WebTutor™ Advantage** Online course management tool for WebCT or Blackboard preloaded with text specific content and media resources for Chapter 9 **Cultural AnthropologyNow™** This program is ready for your students to use without your help. Or, you can choose to incorporate the course management features of the platform to better administer your class and save yourself and your students valuable time. Assign a Pre Test and/or Post Test and students' scores flow into the grade book. The program can be integrated with both WebCT and Blackboard course management platforms.	**Cultural AnthropologyNow™** An online diagnostic study tool. Students take a pretest and receive a *personalized* Study Plan. Within the Study Plan students link to helpful resources (lecture outlines, study videos, and the textbook itself) for material they need to review further. Students assess exactly what they need to know to succeed. An e-book is included! **WebTutor™ Advantage** Quizzing, flashcards, Web links, discussion threads, interactive games and exercises for Chapter 9 **Study Guide** Chapter 9 includes learning objectives, a chapter outline, key terms, Internet and InfoTrac exercises, and practice test questions with multiple choice, true/false, short answer, and essay questions. **Book Companion Website** http://anthropology.wadsworth.com/ferraro6e Tutorial quizzes, Web links, crossword puzzles, flashcards, and much more for learning material from Chapter 9 **InfoTrac® College Edition** *Keywords*: incest taboo, endogamy, exogamy, monogamy, polygyny, arranged marriages, bridewealth, divorce

Chapter 10: Kinship and Descent		
Class Preparation and Lecture Tools	**Testing Tools and Course Management**	**Student Mastery, Homework, and Tutorials ~Beyond the Book~**
Instructor's Manual with Test Bank Written by the main text author, Gary Ferraro. Contains learning objectives, chapter outlines, key terms, critical thinking questions, class activities, Internet exercises, and suggested films. The test bank offers 40 multiple-choice, 10 true/false, 10 short answer and 5-10 essay questions for each chapter. **Multimedia Manager Instructor's Resource CD-ROM** Includes pre-assembled Microsoft® PowerPoint® lecture slides, video, the Instructor's Manual, and other useful class presentation resources **Wadsworth's Anthropology Video Library** Select a full-length video from the collection of Films for the Humanities	**ExamView®** Computerized version of the Test Bank items for Chapter 10 **WebTutor™ Advantage** Online course management tool for WebCT or Blackboard preloaded with text specific content and media resources for Chapter 10 **Cultural AnthropologyNow™** This program is ready for your students to use without your help. Or, you can choose to incorporate the course management features of the platform to better administer your class and save yourself and your students valuable time. Assign a Pre Test and/or Post Test and students' scores flow into the grade book. The program can be integrated with both WebCT and Blackboard course management platforms.	**Cultural AnthropologyNow™** An online diagnostic study tool. Students take a pretest and receive a *personalized* Study Plan. Within the Study Plan students link to helpful resources (lecture outlines, study videos, and the textbook itself) for material they need to review further. Students assess exactly what they need to know to succeed. An e-book is included! **WebTutor™ Advantage** Quizzing, flashcards, Web links, discussion threads, interactive games and exercises for Chapter 10 **Study Guide** Chapter 10 includes learning objectives, a chapter outline, key terms, Internet and InfoTrac exercises, and practice test questions with multiple choice, true/false, short answer, and essay questions. **Book Companion Website** http://anthropology.wadsworth.com/ferraro6e Tutorial quizzes, Web links, crossword puzzles, flashcards, and much more for learning material from Chapter 10 **InfoTrac® College Edition** *Keywords*: descent, lineage, clan, kinship, kindred, matriarchy

Resource Integration Guide

Chapter 11: Sex and Gender

Class Preparation and Lecture Tools	Testing Tools and Course Management	Student Mastery, Homework, and Tutorials ~Beyond the Book~
Instructor's Manual with Test Bank Written by the main text author, Gary Ferraro. Contains learning objectives, chapter outlines, key terms, critical thinking questions, class activities, Internet exercises, and suggested films. The test bank offers 40 multiple-choice, 10 true/false, 10 short answer and 5-10 essay questions for each chapter. **Multimedia Manager Instructor's Resource CD-ROM** Includes pre-assembled Microsoft® PowerPoint® lecture slides, video, the Instructor's Manual, and other useful class presentation resources **CNN® Today Videos** Cultural Anthropology, Vol. VI: *Bangladesh Dowry* (2:45) *Gender Benders* (2:23) *Caste Killings in India* (2:10) *Tribal Justice in Pakistan* (2:56) Cultural Anthropology, Vol. V: *Women in Afghanistan* (2:41) **Wadsworth's Anthropology Video Library** Select a full-length video from the collection of Films for the Humanities	**ExamView®** Computerized version of the Test Bank items for Chapter 11 **WebTutor™ Advantage** Online course management tool for WebCT or Blackboard preloaded with text specific content and media resources for Chapter 11 **Cultural AnthropologyNow™** This program is ready for your students to use without your help. Or, you can choose to incorporate the course management features of the platform to better administer your class and save yourself and your students valuable time. Assign a Pre Test and/or Post Test and students' scores flow into the grade book. The program can be integrated with both WebCT and Blackboard course management platforms.	**Cultural AnthropologyNow™** An online diagnostic study tool. Students take a pretest and receive a *personalized* Study Plan. Within the Study Plan students link to helpful resources (lecture outlines, study videos, and the textbook itself) for material they need to review further. Students assess exactly what they need to know to succeed. An e-book is included! **WebTutor™ Advantage** Quizzing, flashcards, Web links, discussion threads, interactive games and exercises for Chapter 11 **Study Guide** Chapter 11 includes learning objectives, a chapter outline, key terms, Internet and InfoTrac exercises, and practice test questions with multiple choice, true/false, short answer, and essay questions. **Book Companion Website** http://anthropology.wadsworth.com/ferraro6e Tutorial quizzes, Web links, crossword puzzles, flashcards, and much more for learning material from Chapter 11 **InfoTrac® College Edition** *Keywords*: gender, sexuality, gender stratification, poverty, genderlects, infant mortality, honor killings

Chapter 12: Political Organization and Social Control

Class Preparation and Lecture Tools	Testing Tools and Course Management	Student Mastery, Homework, and Tutorials ~Beyond the Book~
Instructor's Manual with Test Bank Written by the main text author, Gary Ferraro. Contains learning objectives, chapter outlines, key terms, critical thinking questions, class activities, Internet exercises, and suggested films. The test bank offers 40 multiple-choice, 10 true/false, 10 short answer and 5-10 essay questions for each chapter. **Multimedia Manager Instructor's Resource CD-ROM** Includes pre-assembled Microsoft® PowerPoint® lecture slides, video, the Instructor's Manual, and other useful class presentation resources **CNN® Today Videos** Cultural Anthropology Vol. VI: *Indigenous Rights in Mexico* (1:46) *Tribal Justice in Pakistan* (2:56)	**ExamView®** Computerized version of the Test Bank items for Chapter 12 **WebTutor™ Advantage** Online course management tool for WebCT or Blackboard preloaded with text specific content and media resources for Chapter 12 **Cultural AnthropologyNow™** This program is ready for your students to use without your help. Or, you can choose to incorporate the course management features of the platform to better administer your class and save yourself and your students valuable time. Assign a Pre Test and/or Post Test and students' scores flow into the grade book. The program can be integrated with both WebCT and Blackboard course management platforms.	**Cultural AnthropologyNow™** An online diagnostic study tool. Students take a pretest and receive a *personalized* Study Plan. Within the Study Plan students link to helpful resources (lecture outlines, study videos, and the textbook itself) for material they need to review further. Students assess exactly what they need to know to succeed. An e-book is included! **WebTutor™ Advantage** Quizzing, flashcards, Web links, discussion threads, interactive games and exercises for Chapter 12 **Study Guide** Chapter 12 includes learning objectives, a chapter outline, key terms, Internet and InfoTrac exercises, and practice test questions with multiple choice, true/false, short answer, and essay questions. **Book Companion Website** http://anthropology.wadsworth.com/ferraro6e Tutorial quizzes, Web links, crossword puzzles, flashcards, and much more for learning material from Chapter 12 **InfoTrac® College Edition** *Keywords*: authority, tribal societies, nation-state, democracy, autocracy, social control, witchcraft, oath, warfare

Resource Integration Guide

Chapter 13: Social Stratification		
Class Preparation and Lecture Tools	**Testing Tools and Course Management**	**Student Mastery, Homework, and Tutorials ~Beyond the Book~**
Instructor's Manual with Test Bank Written by the main text author, Gary Ferraro. Contains learning objectives, chapter outlines, key terms, critical thinking questions, class activities, Internet exercises, and suggested films. The test bank offers 40 multiple-choice, 10 true/false, 10 short answer and 5-10 essay questions for each chapter. **Multimedia Manager Instructor's Resource CD-ROM** Includes pre-assembled Microsoft® PowerPoint® lecture slides, video, the Instructor's Manual, and other useful class presentation resources **CNN® Today Videos** Cultural Anthropology Vol. VII: *Low Caste Indians* (2:08) Cultural Anthropology Vol. VI: *Caste Killings in India* (2:10) Cultural Anthropology Vol. V: *Ethnic Diversity* (2:59)	**ExamView®** Computerized version of the Test Bank items for Chapter 13 **WebTutor™ Advantage** Online course management tool for WebCT or Blackboard preloaded with text specific content and media resources for Chapter 13 **Cultural AnthropologyNow™** This program is ready for your students to use without your help. Or, you can choose to incorporate the course management features of the platform to better administer your class and save yourself and your students valuable time. Assign a Pre Test and/or Post Test and students' scores flow into the grade book. The program can be integrated with both WebCT and Blackboard course management platforms.	**Cultural AnthropologyNow™** An online diagnostic study tool. Students take a pretest and receive a *personalized* Study Plan. Within the Study Plan students link to helpful resources (lecture outlines, study videos, and the textbook itself) for material they need to review further. Students assess exactly what they need to know to succeed. An e-book is included! **WebTutor™ Advantage** Quizzing, flashcards, Web links, discussion threads, interactive games and exercises for Chapter 13 **Study Guide** Chapter 13 includes learning objectives, a chapter outline, key terms, Internet and InfoTrac exercises, and practice test questions with multiple choice, true/false, short answer, and essay questions. **Book Companion Website** http://anthropology.wadsworth.com/ferraro6e Tutorial quizzes, Web links, crossword puzzles, flashcards, and much more for learning material from Chapter 13 **InfoTrac® College Edition** *Keywords*: wealth, power, prestige, class, caste, race, ethnicity, genocide
Chapter 14: Supernatural Beliefs		
Class Preparation and Lecture Tools	**Testing Tools and Course Management**	**Student Mastery, Homework, and Tutorials ~Beyond the Book~**
Instructor's Manual with Test Bank Written by the main text author, Gary Ferraro. Contains learning objectives, chapter outlines, key terms, critical thinking questions, class activities, Internet exercises, and suggested films. The test bank offers 40 multiple-choice, 10 true/false, 10 short answer and 5-10 essay questions for each chapter. **Multimedia Manager Instructor's Resource CD-ROM** Includes pre-assembled Microsoft® PowerPoint® lecture slides, video, the Instructor's Manual, and other useful class presentation resources **CNN® Today Videos** Cultural Anthropology Vol. VII: *Headscarves Banned in France* (1:50) *Peruvian Shamans* (1:59) *Copts vs. Orthodox* (3:26) *Teaching Evolution* (1:48)	**ExamView®** Computerized version of the Test Bank items for Chapter 14 **WebTutor™ Advantage** Online course management tool for WebCT or Blackboard preloaded with text specific content and media resources for Chapter 14 **Cultural AnthropologyNow™** This program is ready for your students to use without your help. Or, you can choose to incorporate the course management features of the platform to better administer your class and save yourself and your students valuable time. Assign a Pre Test and/or Post Test and students' scores flow into the grade book. The program can be integrated with both WebCT and Blackboard course management platforms.	**Cultural AnthropologyNow™** An online diagnostic study tool. Students take a pretest and receive a *personalized* Study Plan. Within the Study Plan students link to helpful resources (lecture outlines, study videos, and the textbook itself) for material they need to review further. Students assess exactly what they need to know to succeed. An e-book is included! **WebTutor™ Advantage** Quizzing, flashcards, Web links, discussion threads, interactive games and exercises for Chapter 14 **Study Guide** Chapter 14 includes learning objectives, a chapter outline, key terms, Internet and InfoTrac exercises, and practice test questions with multiple choice, true/false, short answer, and essay questions. **Book Companion Website** http://anthropology.wadsworth.com/ferraro6e Tutorial quizzes, Web links, crossword puzzles, flashcards, and much more for learning material from Chapter 14 **InfoTrac® College Edition** *Keywords*: religion, magic, sorcery, witchcraft, myths, conflict resolution, cults, vision quest, shaman, rites of passage, theology

Resource Integration Guide

Chapter 15: Art		
Class Preparation and Lecture Tools	**Testing Tools and Course Management**	**Student Mastery, Homework, and Tutorials ~Beyond the Book~**
Instructor's Manual with Test Bank Written by the main text author, Gary Ferraro. Contains learning objectives, chapter outlines, key terms, critical thinking questions, class activities, Internet exercises, and suggested films. The test bank offers 40 multiple-choice, 10 true/false, 10 short answer and 5-10 essay questions for each chapter. **Multimedia Manager Instructor's Resource CD-ROM** Includes pre-assembled Microsoft® PowerPoint® lecture slides, video, the Instructor's Manual, and other useful class presentation resources **CNN® Today Videos** Cultural Anthropology Vol. VII: *Tracking Antiquities* (2:35) **Wadsworth's Anthropology Video Library** Select a full-length video from the collection of Films for the Humanities	**ExamView®** Computerized version of the Test Bank items for Chapter 15 **WebTutor™ Advantage** Online course management tool for WebCT or Blackboard preloaded with text specific content and media resources for Chapter 15 **Cultural AnthropologyNow™** This program is ready for your students to use without your help. Or, you can choose to incorporate the course management features of the platform to better administer your class and save yourself and your students valuable time. Assign a Pre Test and/or Post Test and students' scores flow into the grade book. The program can be integrated with both WebCT and Blackboard course management platforms.	**Cultural AnthropologyNow™** An online diagnostic study tool. Students take a pretest and receive a *personalized* Study Plan. Within the Study Plan students link to helpful resources (lecture outlines, study videos, and the textbook itself) for material they need to review further. Students assess exactly what they need to know to succeed. An e-book is included! **WebTutor™ Advantage** Quizzing, flashcards, Web links, discussion threads, interactive games and exercises for Chapter 15 **Study Guide** Chapter 15 includes learning objectives, a chapter outline, key terms, Internet and InfoTrac exercises, and practice test questions with multiple choice, true/false, short answer, and essay questions. **Book Companion Website** http://anthropology.wadsworth.com/ferraro6e Tutorial quizzes, Web links, crossword puzzles, flashcards, and much more for learning material from Chapter 15 **InfoTrac® College Edition** *Keywords*: art forms, music, dance, verbal arts, legends, glass art

Chapter 16: Culture Change and Globalization		
Class Preparation and Lecture Tools	**Testing Tools and Course Management**	**Student Mastery, Homework, and Tutorials ~Beyond the Book~**
Instructor's Manual with Test Bank Written by the main text author, Gary Ferraro. Contains learning objectives, chapter outlines, key terms, critical thinking questions, class activities, Internet exercises, and suggested films. The test bank offers 40 multiple-choice, 10 true/false, 10 short answer and 5-10 essay questions for each chapter. **Multimedia Manager Instructor's Resource CD-ROM** Includes pre-assembled Microsoft® PowerPoint® lecture slides, video, the Instructor's Manual, and other useful class presentation resources **CNN® Today Videos** Cultural Anthropology, Vol. VII: *Mideast UAE View of U.S.* (2:54) Cultural Anthropology, Vol. VI: *Peru's Debt for Nature* (1:52) *Latino Immigrants in the U.S.* (3:45) Cultural Anthropology, Vol. V: *Oil Spill Impacts* (2:49) *South Africa Endangered* (2:27)	**ExamView®** Computerized version of the Test Bank items for Chapter 16 **WebTutor™ Advantage** Online course management tool for WebCT or Blackboard preloaded with text specific content and media resources for Chapter 16 **Cultural AnthropologyNow™** This program is ready for your students to use without your help. Or, you can choose to incorporate the course management features of the platform to better administer your class and save yourself and your students valuable time. Assign a Pre Test and/or Post Test and students' scores flow into the grade book. The program can be integrated with both WebCT and Blackboard course management platforms.	**Cultural AnthropologyNow™** An online diagnostic study tool. Students take a pretest and receive a *personalized* Study Plan. Within the Study Plan students link to helpful resources (lecture outlines, study videos, and the textbook itself) for material they need to review further. Students assess exactly what they need to know to succeed. An e-book is included! **WebTutor™ Advantage** Quizzing, flashcards, Web links, discussion threads, interactive games and exercises for Chapter 16 **Study Guide** Chapter 16 includes learning objectives, a chapter outline, key terms, Internet and InfoTrac exercises, and practice test questions with multiple choice, true/false, short answer, and essay questions. **Book Companion Website** http://anthropology.wadsworth.com/ferraro6e Tutorial quizzes, Web links, crossword puzzles, flashcards, and much more for learning material from Chapter 16 **InfoTrac® College Edition** *Keywords*: innovation, diffusion, reciprocity, acculturation, urbanization, multinational corporations, globalization

CNN Today Cultural Anthropology Video Series, Volumes 5-7

The *CNN Today Cultural Anthropology Video Series* is an exclusive series jointly created by Wadsworth and CNN for the cultural anthropology course. Each video in the series consists of approximately 45-minutes of footage originally broadcast on CNN within in the last couple of years. The videos are broken into short two to seven minute segments, which are perfect for classroom use as lecture launchers, or to illustrate key anthropological concepts. An annotated table of contents accompanies each video with descriptions of the segments and suggestions for their possible use within the course.

Volume 5

ISBN: 0-534-54178-X

1. Women in Afghanistan (11/01, 2:41)
For some women in Afghanistan, the Taliban's loss of power signals a time of new hope, while others—including young girls working in sweatshops—see a future of continued poverty. [gender, stratification, labor, politics, culture change]

2. Oil Spill Impacts (3/99, 2:49)
A 1989 oil spill continues to impact the environment and culture of Prince William Sound's native peoples. [native peoples, environment, economics, culture change]

3. South Africa Endangered (11/99, 2:27)
This segment explores the conflict between the preservation of an endangered South African forest and the needs of local people who depend on the forest for their livelihood. [native peoples, environment, overpopulation, economics, culture change]

4. Ancient Egyptian Language (5/97, 2:18)
We can read ancient Egyptian hieroglyphics, but what did the language sound like? Linguists and archaeologists fear that these sounds may be lost forever. [language/linguistics, archaeology]

5. Language Lineage (7/96, 2:18)
This segment looks at the origin of modern languages and linguists' theories about the way different languages developed and spread around the globe. (language/linguistics)

6. Snaps (3/94, 2:30)
This amusing segment looks at snapping, the "art of verbal warfare," and shows how snapping allows kids to trade insults instead of punches. [language/linguistics]

7. Ethnic Diversity (3/01, 2:59)
Welcome to Elmhurst, New York, the most ethnically diverse community in the United States. This segment describes the history and development of this diverse community and the unique challenges faced by the community's teachers and young people. [ethnicity, diversity, language, enculturation]

8. Multiracial Families (3/01, 3:45)
As interracial marriages enter the mainstream in many parts of the United States, parents in mixed-race families look for a balance between their different cultures while their children struggle for acceptance and recognition within their communities. [race, ethnicity, diversity, marriage, family, culture change]

9. Papua New Guinea Tourism (4/01, 6:57)
Tourists visiting Papua New Guinea get a glimpse of a colorful and fascinating culture that has survived into the 21st century. [native peoples, culture continuity, tourism]

10. Gay Marriage (3/00, 7:12)
This thought-provoking segment presents differing opinions on the legal recognition of gay and lesbian unions in the United States, and provides historical context for the current debate over preventing gay marriage. [marriage, family, legal systems, culture change]

11. Singapore Singlish (3/98, 2:33)
A new language is developing in Singapore as English words are incorporated into the country's slang. [language/linguistics]

12. Muslim Patients (5/97, 2:33)
Culturally aware nurses and hospital staff are educating the medical community about traditional Muslim behavior and dietary restrictions in order to help Muslim patients, especially women, receive better health care. [medical anthropology, religion, gender]

Volume 6

ISBN: 0-534-62056-6

1. Terror Language (11/02, 2:35)
The U.S. National Security Agency and FBI are in desperate shortage of linguists proficient in Arabic and other foreign languages. The Bush administration proposes a Linguistics Reserve Corps to help alleviate the crisis. [language/linguistics, politics, war]

2. TV Weddings in India (8/02, 3:20)
Televised arranged marriages are portrayed on modern-day Indian TV. This game show-esque program is watched by millions of conservative Indians and the tradition of arranged marriages is now a burgeoning industry. [ethnicity, marriage, family, cultural tradition]

3. Gay Partnership Rights in Britain (12/02, 2:07)
Rights of a lesbian couple are compared to those of a heterosexual married couple in Great Britain. The two couples discuss their partnerships and differing rights given to them by the government. [diversity, marriage, family, gay rights, politics]

4. Bangladesh Dowry (1/98, 2:45)
More than 25% of violence against women in Bangladesh is the result of the inability to pay dowry—a practice that is illegal but still common. For many families living in poverty, a daughter is a heavy burden. [marriage, family, gender, legal systems, activism]

5. Queen Noor (10/02, 5:40)
CNN news anchor Paula Zahn interviews Queen Noor of Jordan. The Queen discusses the status of women in the world, her fight against honor killings in Jordan, and the war on Iraq and its potential impact upon the region. [culture, marriage, women's rights, war, activism]

6. Gender Benders (8/93, 2:23)
The movie industry stretches gender boundaries with the making of such films as *The Ballad of Little Jo, Normal,* and other movies that include gender-bending characters. How much of gender is experiential and how much is hereditary? Experts discuss. [gender, diversity, genetics, culture]

7. Creationism vs. Evolution (3/00, 2:21)
Rod LeVake no longer teaches biology at Faribault High School because he refuses to teach evolution. This controversy has spawned Creation Clubs in schools across the U.S. that encourage children to challenge the teaching of evolution in the classroom. [creationism, evolution, religion, politics]

8. Peru's Debt for Nature (7/02, 1:52)
Debt for Nature, an agreement between the U.S. and Peru, allows the Peruvian government to give money to environmental conservation groups in exchange for canceling 5.5 million dollars owed to the United States. Conservation groups use this program to protect rainforests and their endangered inhabitants. [environment, conservation, global issues, politics]

9. Latino Immigrants in the U.S. (4/01, 3:45)
In Rogers, Arkansas, the newcomers to the local high schools are Latinos. The results of the sudden influence of Latino culture and the difficulties of Latino assimilation in small town USA are apparent. [ethnicity, diversity, enculturation, culture change]

10. AIDS and Indigenous Peoples in Africa (11/02, 4:04)
Drought and climate changes force a nomadic tribe, the OvaHimba of Southern Africa, to settle in order to feed their flock—both animal and human. Men in search of jobs in the cities are exposed to HIV and are infecting many in their community. The result is a generation of grandparents raising their grandchildren due to the HIV/AIDS-related deaths of parents. [native peoples, disease, economics, culture change]

11. Caste Killings in India (9/01, 2:10)
A boyfriend and girlfriend are hanged because their families are from different castes. Few people in and around the village condemn the killings. Social activists in India say a global forum must act now. [marriage, family, stratification, legal systems, activism]

12. Indigenous Rights in Mexico (5/02, 1:46)
Indian rights activists in Mexico ask the Mexican Supreme Court for help in seeking equality of rights, and controversy ensues. [native peoples, politics, human rights]

13. Tribal Justice in Pakistan (8/02, 2:56)
Four men are accused of gang raping women in Pakistan, and some say a tribal council ordered the rapes. Human rights activists say the federal government turns a blind eye to so-called tribal justice. [women's rights, gender, legal systems, activism]

14. Harry Potter Witchcraft Controversy (12/02, 2:43)
A family fights against readings of *Harry Potter* in the classroom, claiming that it violates the separation of church and state principle and that the popular series teaches witchcraft. [religion, politics, education]

Volume 7

ISBN: 0-534-63010-3

1. Gay Marriage (3/04, 1:29)
Same-sex marriage ceremonies are being performed in Oregon, California, and New York, while legislators in Washington, D.C. debate writing a constitutional amendment banning gay marriage. [gay rights, marriage, politics]

2. Infidelity & Monogamy (11/03, 1:33)
This segment raises the question, "Is monogamy natural for humans?" [marriage, genetics vs. choice]

3. Headscarves Banned in France (02/04, 1:50)
The French government has banned religious symbols from public schools in an attempt to provide equality of opportunity. Opponents insist this will not solve the problem of better integrating Muslims into the community. [culture, diversity, religion, politics]

4. North and South Korean Similarities (8/02, 1:51)
Recent celebration to commemorate Korean independence from Japan more than fifty years ago shows that North and South Koreans have more in common that their heavily guarded border might suggest. [culture, politics]

5. Peruvian Shamans (12/02, 1:59)
Once a year, shamans gather from across Peru to drink hallucinogenic brews that help them to see the future. Predictions for 2003 involved the then war-to-be in Iraq, Latin American politics, North Korea, and Osama bin Laden. [culture, religion, politics, war]

6. Cultural Training for Soldiers in Jordan (1/04, 2:43)
U.S. soldiers on their way to Iraq stop at a Jordanian training facility where scenarios are run to assist them with their upcoming duties. The focus is on cultural awareness—the soldiers' growing respect for the local culture helps them to better communicate with Iraqi civilians. [cultural differences, war]

7. Low Caste Indians (11/01, 2:08)
In a mass ceremony, thousands of Indians known as Untouchables convert to Buddhism to escape lives of discrimination determined by their caste. [religion, economics, politics]

8. Copts vs. Orthodox (7/02, 3:26)
Territory disputes aren't just for Israelis and Palestinians. This segment explores conflict in Jerusalem amongst Christians, this time between the Ethiopian Orthodox and the Egyptian Copts. [religion]

9. EU Tower of Babel (10/03, 2:39)
Exploring the challenges the European Union faces having a multitude of official languages. [language/linguistics, politics]

10. Profile of a Tribal Chief (8/03, 1:52)
A profile of David Laughing Horse Robinson, tribal chief, during his 2003 campaign for Governor of California. [native peoples, politics]

11. Online Dating (2/03, 2:25)
This segment explores matchmaking in the 21st century—the Internet-dating industry. [relationships, internet]

12. Teaching Evolution (4/04, 1:48)
Missouri and other states are voting on how evolution should or should not be taught in public schools as the debate over Intelligent Design continues. [creationism, evolution, religion, education, politics]

13. School in Remote Cambodia (8/02, 2:18)
A profile of a new school in a remote village of Cambodia. [culture, education]

14. Tracking Antiquities (4/04, 2:35)
Antiquities are amongst the casualties of the war in Iraq: treasures from ancient Mesopotamia go missing as museums are looted. Getting them back will be a job for the world market as Iraqi curators' primary concern now is protecting what remains. [war, archaeology, civilization]

15. Gay Bishop (11/03, 2:12)
The 993rd bishop of the Episcopal Church is also the first one to be openly gay. Controversy is sparked once again only a decade after the first woman became bishop. [gay rights, religion]

16. Syria 101 (4/03, 1:40)
A brief introduction to Syria and how it contrasts with Iraq. [culture, politics]

17. Mideast UAE View of US (9/03, 2:54)
Two years after 9/11, a look at how the U.S. is viewed by those in the United Arab Emirates. [culture, economics, war, politics]

18. Religion & Health (10/03, 2:09)
The mind-body connection: a look at how faith can affect health. [medicine, religion]

19. Cross Garden (3/04, 3:11)
A look at how signs throughout the rural south proclaim faith in Jesus. [religion, culture]

20. Shrine Ruling in Japan (4/04, 1:50)
The prime minister's annual visits to a shrine honoring Japan's war heroes—including some from World War II—is declared unconstitutional as it blurs the line between religion and state. [religion, war, politics]

Instructor's Manual with Test Bank

for

Cultural Anthropology

Chapter 1

What is Anthropology?

Learning Objectives

After reading and studying Chapter 1, students should be able to:

1. Define anthropology; understand its breadth, especially its interest in global diversity.
2. Describe the four field approach to anthropology.
3. Understand that the four fields are interrelated and have blurred boundaries.
4. Identify three broad areas of interest to physical anthropologists.
5. Understand why archaeologists analyze material remains of historic and prehistoric cultures.
6. Describe the three types of material remains of interest to archaeologists.
7. Describe the four branches of linguistic anthropology.
8. Explain the difference between ethnography and ethnology.
9. Identify five areas of specialization within cultural anthropology.
10. Understand the guiding principles of holism, ethnocentrism, and cultural relativism.
11. Understand the nature and limitations of ethnocentric reactions and give several examples of their own and others' ethnocentrism.
12. Present a clear explanation of cultural relativism and its importance to anthropology.
13. List four contributions of the holistic, cross-cultural perspective of anthropology to the scientific understanding of humanity.
14. Understand the difference between basic and applied research in anthropology.
15. Distinguish between the emic and the etic approaches to anthropology
16. Understand how the study of anthropology develops skills and competencies necessary for success in the 21st century.

Chapter Outline

I. WHAT IS ANTHROPOLOGY
   - A. The study of the origins, development, and contemporary variations of all humans who have existed anywhere on earth
   - B. A discipline that spans the gap between the humanities, the social sciences, and the natural sciences
   - C. An attempt to understand the human condition
   - D. A very diverse and broad field of interrelated studies

II. FOUR FIELD APPROACH
- A. Physical Anthropology
  1. Paleoanthropology: examining the biological evolutionary record
  2. Primatology: the study of humans' nearest living relatives
  3. Human Physical Variation: racial categories
- B. Archaeology: the study of past cultures by analyzing artifacts left behind
  1. Prehistoric: before written history
  2. Historic: includes written sources
  3. Applied archaeology; Cultural resource management
- C. Anthropological Linguistics
  1. Historical linguistics
  2. Descriptive linguistics
  3. Ethnolinguistics
  4. Sociolinguistics
  5. Applied Linguistics
- D. Cultural Anthropology
  1. Ethnology
  2. Ethnography
  3. Areas of Specialization
     - a. Urban anthropology
     - b. Medical anthropology
     - c. Educational anthropology
     - d. Economic anthropology
     - e. Psychological anthropology

III. GUIDING PRINCIPLES
- A. Holism
  1. Anthropology is comprehensive and includes the study of:
     - a. biological and sociocultural diversity
     - b. a time frame of several million years
     - c. a global perspective
  2. More specialized today and less holistic than in the past, but anthropologists continue to analyze their findings within a wider context
- B. Ethnocentrism
  1. The belief that one's own culture is most desirable and superior to all others
  2. No society has a monopoly on ethnocentrism
  3. Most people raised in a single culture and never learn another, so their ways of life seems to be the most natural
  4. Becoming aware of our own ethnocentrism allows us to temporarily set aside our own value judgments in order to learn how other cultures operate
- C. Cultural Relativism
  1. Early anthropologists recognized a need for dispassionate and objective descriptions of the people they were studying
  2. Cultural relativism is the notion that any part of a culture must be viewed in its proper cultural context rather than from the viewpoint of the observer's culture
  3. Rejects the notion that any culture, including our own, possesses a set of absolute standards by which all other cultures can be judged
  4. There are both methodological and ethical limitations to cultural relativism
- D. The Emic (insider view) and Etic (outsider view) Approaches

IV. CONTRIBUTIONS OF ANTHROPOLOGY
- A. Examines all aspects of humanity during all periods of time in all parts of the world
- B. In a good position to integrate the various disciplines dealing with human physiology and culture
- C. Enhances international/cross-cultural understanding
- D. Corrective to deterministic thinking
- E. Allows us to learn about human nature based on cross-cultural analysis
- F. Helps us to better understand ourselves
- G. Gives a fuller understanding of other cultures
- H. Serves as a bridge to personal development

V. APPLICATIONS
- A. Basic research
  - 1. Gains scientific understanding for its own sake
- B. Applied research
  - 1. Gains scientific understanding for the sake of solving particular social problems
  - 2. Interest has increased over the past decade with a noticeable increase in anthropologists working outside universities and museums
  - 3. Graduate and undergraduate courses in applied anthropology have increased over the past decade

VI. BUILDING SKILLS FOR THE TWENTY-FIRST CENTURY
- A. The process of studying cultural anthropology is valuable because of the skills and competencies that it develops, including
  - 1. Developing a broad perspective
  - 2. Appreciating other perspectives
  - 3. Balancing contradictions
  - 4. Emphasizing global teamwork
  - 5. Developing cognitive complexity
    - a. Differentiation
    - b. Integration
  - 6. Developing perceptual acuity

VII. THE BOTTOM LINE: UNDERSTANDING OTHER CULTURES
- A. Acquiring accurate data about other cultures
- B. Cultural Self Awareness
- C. Knowing how people from other cultures view our culture

Key Terms

These are the anthropological terms introduced in Chapter 1. You may want to ask your students to write definitions of one or more of these terms during class to see how well they understood the reading. Even if you choose not to grade the assignment, the students will take it more seriously if you collect their answers.

ethnocentrism
linguistics
archaeology
artifacts
cultural anthropology
cultural relativism
race
sociolinguistics
etic approach
management
paleoanthropology
ethnography
ethnolinguistics
ethnology
features
glottochronology
descriptive linguistics
ecofacts
epidemiology
emic approach
anthropological
paleopathology
physical anthropology
population biology
primatology
genetics
historical linguistics
holism
cultural resource

Critical Thinking Questions

1. How does anthropology as a discipline differ from other academic disciplines such as history, biology, political science, sociology, or psychology?
2. If anthropology "spans the gap between the humanities, social sciences, and the natural sciences," what is the nature of this gap?
3. What does it mean to say that the global scope of anthropological studies has actually increased in recent years? Why have we begun to study industrialized societies as well as less technologically complex ones? How could anthropologists improve understanding of tension between urban populations in the United States or religious consciousness in the Middle East?
4. What kinds of data are used by each of the subfields of anthropology?
5. How does paleoanthropologists' concern with adaptation to environment and human evolution influence our understanding of what it means to be human?
6. Why is ethnology dependent upon ethnography?
7. How does the holism of anthropology distinguish it from other disciplines that study human nature?
8. Think of instances where you have engaged in ethnocentrism. What was the situation? What cultural trait or practice were you judging? How might you now make a more culturally relative assessment of the situation?
9. Why can we expect applied anthropological research to become increasingly important in the future?
10. Think of the skills necessary for a degree in your major. How will this course in cultural anthropology help you build those skills?

Class Activities

1. Divide the class into small groups and hand out back issues of *Fortune Magazine*, *National Geographic*, *Natural History*, and/or the local newspaper. Assign each group the task of finding three research projects for anthropologists of the various subfields and have the students identify what would interest an archaeologist, a linguistic, a physical, or a cultural anthropologist.
2. According to the text, anthropology has the task of examining all aspects of humanity through all periods of time and in all parts of the world. Ask the students to examine how culture has changed from the time that their grandparents were young until today (from the 1920s forward). Use their examples to discuss how comparing their grandparents' time to today is important for understanding our own culture. Topics such as changes in food, music, or clothing stimulate good discussions).
3. Talk about the limits of cultural relativism using such contemporary practices in the world as infanticide, female circumcision, warfare, "ethnic cleansing," and suicide bombings.
4. In order to get a better idea of the scope of research interests in anthropology, have students do a content analysis of three randomly selected issues of the American Anthropologist over the past five years. Have them classify articles into cultural anthropology, archaeology, physical anthropology, and linguistics. Does one subfield predominate? How many are based on quantitative data and how many on qualitative data? How many examine contemporary aspects of humans versus more diachronic (through time) studies? How many deal with US society as compared to other parts of the world?

The Internet Exercises

Each chapter in this textbook is followed by at least one Internet exercise. These exercises are designed to accomplish two separate objectives. First, they provide students with a chance to practice their computer and internet skills. Second, the exercises are designed to reinforce some of the substantive concepts and insights found in each chapter.

A word of caution is in order before beginning.

Internet addresses have the bad habit of changing. All of the web links listed in the Internet exercises at the end of each chapter were correct at the time of publication. If the site no longer exists, a suitable substitute can often be found by conducting a subject search on one of the search engines.

Internet Exercises

1. The American Anthropological Association (AAA) is the major professional organization for anthropologists in the Americas and in fact is the largest such organization for anthropologists in the world. If you want information on what anthropology is and what anthropologists do, go to the web site of the AAA:

   http://www.aaanet.org

   a. Click on the section "About AAA." Next click on "What is anthropology?" Then, in several sentences for each, answer the following questions: (1) what are the four major subfields of anthropology? (2) What is meant by the term comparative method? (3) What is meant by the statement "Language - hallmark of the human species"? (4) What types of evidence do archaeologists rely on when reconstructing prehistoric cultures?

   b. While you are in the section of the AAA home page titled "About AAA," click on the latest annual "Survey of Anthropology PhDs." According to the latest data, what percentage of anthropologists represent the four traditional fields (and the fifth field of applied anthropology)? Have there been any noticeable changes in the ethnic/racial composition of American anthropologists over the decades? Have there been any significant changes in gender composition over the decades? Roughly what percentage of anthropologists are employed in academic institutions (colleges and universities), and what percentage are employed in nonacademic jobs?

   c. Now go back to "About AAA" and click on the section titles "Sections and Interest Groups." Browse the more than 30 specialized sections and interest groups that are officially recognized by the AAA. Select one such interest group and write a paragraph summary of what you think this group is all about.

2. Go to the web site for the Society for Applied Anthropology, the professional organization supporting the work of applied and practicing anthropologists in the United States and around the world.

   http://www.sfaanet.org

   a. What are the differences between the SfAA and AAA? Are there units or interest groups in this organization? What can you tell about the kinds of research and the fields of anthropology from the publications or employment notices?

Infotrac® Exercises

1. Students will need to access *InfoTrac College Edition* at http://infotrac.thomsonlearning.com/index.html to answer the following questions. Once logged on, type "Ethnocentrism" in the Search field. Next click on "Periodicals." Once the results appear, scroll down to the article "Student Perceptions of the Developing World: Minimizing Stereotypes of the 'Other'" or use the Limit Search function to find the article. Read the selection and answer the following:

    a. How can cultural relativism be taught to students in the classroom?

    b. After this exercise, do you think that your reactions would be similar to the students in the article?

2. In the Search field, type in "Cultural Relativism." Click on "Periodicals." Use the Limit Search function to find the article "Helping Students Deal With Cultural Differences."

    a. Why would an anthropological perspective be helpful for a person's view of another group of people?

    b. How is spatial distance culturally patterned?

Suggested Films

A Man Called Bee: Studying the Yanomamo. Documentary Educational Resources, 1975, 42 minutes. - One of a number of films by filmmaker Tim Asch and anthropologist Napoleon Chagnon depicting the promises and pitfalls of conducting ethnographic research among the Yanomamo of Northern Brazil and Southern Venezuela.

Who Owns the Past? University of California Extension, 2002, 56 minutes. - An outstanding documentary on Native Americans' struggle for control of their ancestral remains.

The Trail of the Neanderthal. Insight Media, 1998, 30 minutes. - Examines the basic questions asked by physical anthropologists about Neanderthals, including what was their relationship to humans.

Chapter 2

The Concept of Culture

Learning Objectives

After reading and studying Chapter 2, your students should be able to:

1. Give a clear definition of the anthropological concept of culture and recognize what is included in this concept.
2. Explain the significance of the shared nature of culture.
3. Define culture shock and explain when it is likely to be experienced.
4. Understand how the three basic components of culture are interrelated
5. Explain the importance of learning for culture acquisition.
6. Give several examples of how humans do things because of what they have learned from their culture.
7. Understand the symbolic nature of culture.

   Be able to distinguish between a culture and a subculture.
8. Explain how culture can affect our physical bodies and biological processes.
9. Understand that cultures are constantly changing and give examples of cultural innovation and diffusion.
10. Understand why anthropologists are interested in the similarities as well as the differences among human cultures.
11. Understand what cultural universals are and be able to give several examples of such universals.
12. Describe how, for all human societies, culture is an important form of adaptation to environment.
13. Explain what it means to say culture is integrated and what that implies about the process of culture change.
14. Understand the difference between ideal and real behavior.
15. Be able to distinguish between the concepts of culture and race.
16. Be able to differentiate between the concepts of culture and civilization.

Chapter Outline

I. THE CONCEPT OF CULTURE
   A. Culture is most precisely and thoroughly defined by the discipline of anthropology
II. CULTURE DEFINED
   A. Culture is everything that people have, think, and do as members of a society
   B. Components of culture
      1. All cultures are comprised of material objects; ideas, values and attitudes; and patterned ways of behaving
III CULTURE IS SHARED
   A. Behavior and thought in a society are predictable because of shared culture
   B. There is always some deviation from cultural norms
      1. Due to biological reasons
      2. Due to personal history
      3. Due to differentiation based on class or ethnicity
      4. Because societal rules are never adhered to strictly
   C. Subculture - subsets of the wider mainstream that retain a certain level of cultural uniqueness that sets them apart
   D. Pluralistic Societies - composed of a number of subcultural groups
IV. CULTURE IS LEARNED
   A. Culture is acquired through the process of interacting with one's cultural environment
   B. Enculturation is the process of acquiring culture
   C. Learning Versus Instincts
      1. Humans are born with relatively little predetermined behavior
      2. Culture is not transmitted genetically
      Humans must learn most of their coping skills from others in their culture
   D. Learning Different Content
      1. Although there is a range of variation in cultural behavior throughout the world, all people acquire their culture by the same process
      2. People in different cultures learn different culture content
      3. People learn (with relatively equal efficiency) what they need to know in order to best adapt to their environments
      4. No other animal has greater capacity for learning than humans
      5. Because human behavior is learned, it can be changed
V CULTURE IS TAKEN FOR GRANTED
VI. CULTURE INFLUENCES BIOLOGICAL PROCESSES
   A. As animals, we have biological needs, but it is culture that determines how we satisfy those needs
      1. How, when, and where we satisfy needs is determined by culture
      2. Ideas, values, and norms can have a physical effect on the body
      3. Even our body stature is related to our cultural ideas
      4. Extreme Makeovers
VII. CULTURE CHANGES
   A. Despite the wide variation in the speed by which cultures change, one thing is certain: No cultures remain completely static year after year
   B. The Processes of Change
      1. Internal changes, innovations
         a. Innovations can occur independently in different times and places
         b. Not all innovations lead to a change in the culture

c. Innovations depend upon the recombination of already existing elements in a culture
d. Internal changes possible in any given culture are usually limited to what already exists in a culture
e. Innovations occur more frequently in technologically complex societies than in less developed ones

2. External changes, cultural diffusion
   a. Cultural elements commonly spread from one culture to another
   b. Cultural diffusion is responsible for the greatest amount of change that occurs in a society
3. Causes of Cultural Change
   a. No agreement on primary causes of cultural change
   b. Some argue it is technology and economies
   c. Others argue the prime mover is ideology
   d. Still others suggest that cultures change in response to changes in the physical and social environment.

VIII. CULTURAL UNIVERSALS
A. Anthropology has been more effective at documenting cultural differences than similarities
B. Result, in part, of wanting to move away from the premature generalizing about "human nature" prevalent at the end of the 1800s
C. Each culture has developed its own set of solutions to the universal human problems facing all societies
D. The significant number of cultural differences illustrates how flexible and adaptable humans are
E. Basic Needs
   1. Physiological needs must be met
   2. Despite many differences in details, all cultures share a number of common features related to meeting the basic physiological needs of members of society including:
      a. economic system
      b. system of marriage and family
      c. educational system
      d. social control system
      e. system of supernatural beliefs (religion, witchcraft, magic, sorcery)
      f. system of communication (verbal, nonverbal)

IX. CULTURE IS ADAPTIVE OR MALADAPTIVE
A. Humans rely more heavily upon cultural than biological adaptations
   1. It is possible for some features of a culture to be maladaptive or dysfunctional
   2. Features adaptive in some cultures are maladaptive or neutral in others
   3. The adaptability of a cultural item varies over time within any culture

X. CULTURES ARE GENERALLY INTEGRATED
A. Cultural components are interconnected with one another
   1. The organic analogy means that culture is systemic in a way similar to a living body made up of a number of systems that function together to maintain life
   2. A cultural anthropologist's task is to describe the various parts of a culture, show how they function, and how they are interconnected
   3. Cultures are logical and coherent systems
   4. Because the parts of a culture are interrelated, a change in one part influences other parts
   5. Not all parts of a culture are interrelated

XI. "PRIMITIVE" CULTURES
- A. Anthropologists are interested in the entire range of human societies
  1. "Primitive" is a term no longer used in cultural anthropology because of its connotation of inferiority
- B. "Small-scale" describes a society:
  1. Relatively small population
  2. Technologically simple
  3. Usually pre-literate
  4. Little labor specialization
  5. Unstratified

XII. CULTURE AND THE INDIVIDUAL
- A. Lives of individuals are less complicated because they have learned their culture and know, within broad limits, what to expect from one another
  1. Lives of individuals are constrained or influenced by their culture
  2. Deviance from the cultural norms is found in all societies
  3. All people have the option of doing things different from what is culturally expected
  4. Cultural anthropologists distinguish between ideal behavior (what people are expected to do) and real behavior (what people actually do)

Key Terms

These are the anthropological terms introduced in Chapter 2. You may want to ask your students to write definitions of one or more of these terms during class to see how well they understood the reading. Even if you choose not to grade the assignment, the students will take it more seriously if you collect their answers.

adaptive nature of culture
civilization
cultural diffusion
cultural universals
small scale society
subculture
symbol
organic analogy
pluralistic society
polychronic
culture shock
enculturation
innovations
monchronic

Critical Thinking Questions

1. Some anthropologists define culture as "learned and shared ways of thinking." How would using this definition, rather than Ferraro's, change how you would study people's behavior and their material culture?

2. What does it mean to say that "culture is shared" for a society like the United States with its regional differences, or the former Yugoslavia with its ethnic conflict?

3. When does a culture begin to influence the learning process? At birth? Before birth? Discuss whether a culture has more influence on a child's learning process through the influence of his or her parents or peers.

4. Does cultural learning have greater or less influence on our biological processes as societies become more complex technologically?

5. In what parts of our culture does change occur most rapidly, most slowly? Do ideas about food and clothing change rapidly or slowly?

6. Describe some extreme environments where people live and tell how culture has made human habitation possible there.

7. What are some of the drawbacks of the organic analogy? How is culture a different type of system from a living body?

8. How would the use of the term "primitive" be ethnocentric?

Class Activities

1. Have small groups of students work together to develop a list describing the culture of the United States to someone in another country. Then ask questions such as: What is typical American food? (religion?, politics?, education?). This will indicate whether students understand the part culture plays in determining their responses.

2. Ask students to make a list of three aspects of American culture that are innovations unique to this society, and three aspects that are the result of diffusion from another culture. How many students cite examples of technology? How many cite ideology (knowledge)? Do disagreements develop over what is an innovation and what is imported?

Internet Exercises

1. The concept of culture has been defined in a number of different ways over the years. Washington State University has a web site devoted to exploring some of the ways by which scholars have defined the concept. Using one of the major search engines, search the web for a site called "What is culture?" You may do a subject search using the name of the site or you can use the URL:

   http://www.wsu.edu:8001/vcwsu/commons/topics/culture/culture-index.html

   a. Once there, click on "a baseline definition of culture." According to the authors what is the "essential feature" of culture?

   b. Read over the brief definitions of culture presented by Matthew Arnold, Raymond Williams, and Clifford Geertz. In a single paragraph, how do these three definitions differ from each other?

2. Have students go to web sites of universities in other countries and gather information that allows them to discuss the culture/s of American universities and contrast them with foreign universities. Doing a preliminary search and providing a few sites in advance may help the students' search.

Infotrac® Exercises

1. Students will need to access InfoTrac at **http://infotrac.thomsonlearning.com/index.html** to answer the following questions. Once logged on, type "Culture" in the Search field. Next click

on "Periodicals." Once the results appear, use the Limit Search function to find the article "Two or Three Things That I Know About Culture." Read the selection and answer the following:

a. How does British anthropology differ from American anthropology?

b. Based on this overview of different theoretical perspectives, can there be an agreed upon definition of culture?

Suggested Films

The Nature of Culture, in the *Faces of Culture* series, (PSU), 30 min. - Shows that human beings are dependent upon cultural customs and pattern not only for survival but for order and tranquility.

The Hutterites. (PSU), 28 min. - Anabaptist religious communitarian society in Alberta is portrayed. Covering the history of sect, resistance of outside influences, and communal ideology, this film is an excellent example of a subculture within a larger, more complex society.

Stoney Knows How. Ethnoscope, P.O. Box 92353, Rochester, N.Y. 14692. Tel: 716-442-5274. 29 min. - This video interviews and watches Stoney St. Clair, disabled by arthritis since the age of four, as he goes about his art of tattooing.

Chapter 3

Applied Anthropology

Learning Objectives

After reading and studying Chapter 3, your students should be able to:

1. Understand the differences and similarities between applied and pure anthropology as well as recognize their mutually supportive relationship.
2. Understand the history of contemporary applied anthropology and the cultural anthropologist's involvement in applied projects.
3. Discuss the special features of anthropology that contribute to applied science: participant-observation, holistic perspective, regional expertise, emic view, etic view, and cultural relativism.
4. Differentiate between the various specialized roles played by applied anthropologists

Chapter Outline

I. APPLIED ANTHROPOLOGY
   - A. Grew out of experience in participant-observation and close contact with people with serious societal problems
   - B. Research aimed explicitly at practical application
   - C. Applies anthropological data, concepts, and strategies to the solution of social, economic, and technological problems at home and abroad
   - D. Characterized by problem-oriented research among the world's contemporary populations
   - E. While this book focuses on applied cultural anthropology, the other three sub-fields of anthropology also have applied components (forensic anthropology, cultural resource management, and applied linguistics)
   - F. Supported by large public and private organizations seeking to better understand the cultural dimension of their sponsored programs

II. APPLIED VERSUS PURE ANTHROPOLOGY
   - A. Pure anthropology traditionally was seen as the advancement of the theories and methods of the discipline
   - B. Applied anthropology was characterized as being primarily aimed at changing human behavior in order to ameliorate contemporary problems
   - C. Not mutually exclusive types of anthropology - both approaches (1) share training and methods and (2) developed along side one another
   - D. Applied anthropologists take into account the theories, methods, and data that have been developed by the discipline as a whole

E. More theoretically oriented anthropologists are indebted to applied anthropologists for stimulating interest in new areas of research and contributing to the development of new theory

F. Because pure and applied anthropologists share a wide variety of both theoretical and practical concerns, the task of defining the behavioral dimensions of applied anthropologists is difficult

III. APPLIED ANTHROPOLOGY IN THE TWENTIETH CENTURY

A. The real stimulus for applying anthropology came in the 1940s when cultural anthropologists were asked to participate in efforts related to World War II
   1. National Research Council national morale studies
   2. National character studies on our adversaries - the Germans, Italians, and Japanese

B. After the war anthropologists left government service and returned to positions in colleges and universities. Also returned to more theoretical concerns
   1. Trend continued through the 1950s and 1960s.
   2. Whatever applied research conducted was carried out by academic anthropologists engaged in short-term projects outside the university setting

C. Since the 1970s, more applied anthropologists became full-time employees of research agencies
   1. American Anthropological Association - approximately 30 per cent of all anthropology Ph.D.s work outside an academic setting
   2. Result of two major trends
      a. Market for academic jobs has declined drastically over the past two and a half decades
      b. Increase in federal legislation mandating policy research that can be accomplished effectively by cultural anthropologists

D. Increase in number of MA programs in applied anthropology and the membership of applied anthropology organizations
   1. Society for Applied Anthropology (SfAA)
   2. National Association of Practicing Anthropologists (NAPA)

E. Much variation in the extent to which an applied anthropologist becomes involved in any given project
   1. Provide information for planners and decision makers
   2. Use collected data to construct a plan for bringing about a desired change in a particular population
   3. Become involved in actual implementation and evaluation of particular projects

IV. SPECIAL FEATURES OF ANTHROPOLOGY

A. Participant-observation
   1. Can lead to a fuller understanding of the sociocultural realities
   2. Develops rapport that can be drawn on in the implementation stage of the applied project

B. Holistic perspective
   1. Looks at multiple variables and sees human problems in their historical, economic, and cultural contexts
   2. Sees the various parts of a sociocultural system as interconnected
   3. Encourages us to look at the problems in terms of both the short run and the long run

C. Regional expertise
   1. Long term association with a cultural region provides a depth of geographic coverage that most policymakers lack

- D. Emic view
  1. Linguistic and cultural differences invariably exist between project planners and the local client populations
  2. Uses the mental categories and assumptions of the local people (emic) rather than the technical/professional view (etic)
- E. Cultural relativism
  1. Tends to foster tolerance
  2. Can help anthropologists cross class lines and relate to a wide range of people
- F. Topical expertise
  1. Studies done in one part of the world often have policy relevance in other parts
- G. Anthropology has some drawbacks that limit its effectiveness in solving societal problems
  1. Long term participant-observation is not particularly well suited to the accelerated time schedules of applied programs of change
  2. Long tradition of qualitative research methods is not balanced by sophistication in use of quantitative data

V. SPECIALIZED ROLES OF APPLIED ANTHROPOLOGISTS

- A. The roles are not mutually exclusive. An applied anthropologist may play two or more roles as part of the same job.

Policy researcher	Trainer
Evaluator	Advocate
Impact assessor	Expert witness
Planner	Administrator-Manager
Research analyst	Cultural broker
Needs assessor	

VI. SOME EXAMPLES OF APPLIED ANTHROPOLOGY

- A. Nestle baby formula controversy
- B. Working with minority prison inmates
- C. Adolescent drug dealers
- D. Marital patterns and population growth
- E. Mediating between the government and Trukese villagers

VII. THE GREAT USE OF ANTHROPOLOGICAL KNOWLEDGE

- A. Despite advances in applied anthropology, much more must be done to ensure that anthropological data is actually put to use.
- B. Anthropology must be more attentive to policy rather than simply supplying data.
- C. Anthropologists need to be better cultural brokers of already existing data.

Key Terms

These are the anthropological terms introduced in Chapter 3. You may want to ask your students to write definitions of one or more of these terms during class to see how well they understood the reading. Even if you choose not to grade the assignment, the students will take it more seriously if you collect their answers.

applied anthropology
holistic perspective
participant-observation
problem-oriented research

Critical Thinking Questions

1. Ferraro argues that pure anthropology benefits from applied anthropology. Discuss some of the conflicts between these two approaches within the discipline in terms of research methods and contributions to theory.
2. What are the similarities and differences between working for an applied research organization and a university?
3. To what degree do the various specialized roles of applied anthropologists create conflict with the value orientation of cultural relativism?
4. What are the contributions to applied research of participant-observation methods, regional expertise, and an emic perspective?
5. How would you characterize the change in applied anthropology after 1970?
6. Why is it difficult to distinguish between pure and applied anthropology?
7. In what ways did anthropologists contribute to the war effort in WWII?
8. What types of contributions can an applied anthropologist make to our system of corrections?

Class Activities

1. Ask several of the students to bring to class the abstract of an article from a recent issue of *Human Organization.* Have them discuss how the particular research in each article makes a contribution to the solution of a particular societal problem.
2. Have students select any one of the 39 readings from APPLYING CULTURAL ANTHROPOLOGY by Gary Ferraro (ed.), Belmont, CA: Wadsworth Publishing, 1998. The assignment is for students to write a 300 word synopsis of the article dealing with (1) a statement of the problem, (2) who are the players, (3) methods used, (4) findings, and (5) what was the anthropological difference?
3. Have students read a major US newspaper (e.g., New York Times, Washington Post, Los Angeles Times) and identify ten contemporary societal problems that could be the subject of studies by applied anthropologists.

Internet Exercises

1. A leading journal in the field of applied anthropology is called *Human Organization* and is published by the Society for Applied Anthropology. Go to the web site of the Society for Applied Anthropology by doing a subject search on any major search engine or by using the URL for the society:

   http://www.sfaa.net/

   Once there, click on "publications" and then "Human Organization," which is the society's major professional journal containing scholarly articles on applied anthropology. This file contains summaries (abstracts) of recent and forthcoming research in applied anthropology. Browse the sections on forthcoming issues and recent and back issues. Read over the first 20 research summaries. Make a list of the range of social problems that have been addressed in these applied studies.

2. Using any major search engine, find a site called ANTHAP (The Applied Anthropology Computer Network). Once there, click on "Applied Anthropology Documentation Project at the University of Kentucky." What is the purpose of this site. Give some examples of the type of information found on the site.

Infotrac® Exercises

1. Students will need to access InfoTrac at **http://infotrac.thomsonlearning.com/index.html** to answer the following questions. Type in "Anthropology" in the Search field. Click on "Periodicals." At the results list, use the Limit Search function to find the article "North Dakota Diary."

   a. How can anthropological methods be applied to rural towns in the U.S.?

   b. Do "outside influences" in this society have the same effects as those of native populations?

Suggested Films

Anthropologists at Work: Careers Making a Difference. - National Association for the Practice of Anthropology, 1994, 36 minutes. This very excellent film which captures applied anthropologists working at home and abroad in such areas as health, development, education, and business.

Chapter 4

The Growth of Anthropological Theory

Learning Objectives

After reading and studying Chapter 4, your students should be able to:

1. Give a precise definition of theory and explain what issues anthropological theories attempt to address.
2. Describe the cultural evolutionary theory of Tylor and Morgan, recognize its limitations and the significance of their distinction between cultural and biological processes.
3. Recognize the limitations of both the diffusion theories and the importance of the questions, "Why do some traits arise in the first place?" and "Why do certain ones spread throughout a geographical region while others do not?"
4. Understand the significance of Boas' emphasis on the importance of history and ethnographic fieldwork and his contribution to methodological.
5. Describe functionalist theory and distinguish between Malinowski's and Radcliffe-Brown's approaches to the meaning of function.
6. Comprehend the concepts of universal functions and functional unity and Merton's criticisms of those concepts.
7. Summarize psychological anthropologists' positions on the connections between personality, the individual, and culture and recognize the theoretical contributions of Sapir and Margaret Mead.
8. Understand the neoevolutionary theories of Leslie White and Julian Steward.
9. Understand the meaning of structure for French structuralist theory, the contributions of Levi-Strauss to that theory and the importance it gives to the structure of the human mind.
10. Recognize the importance of the linguistic model and the emic view for ethnoscience.
11. Explain the focus of cultural materialism, the significance of etic research methodology for it, and why it is not a Marxist theory.
12. Understand the basic tenets of postmodernism and why it is not viewed as a scientific enterprise.
13. Discuss the importance of self-knowledge ideas, and values for interpretive anthropology and its humanistic approach.

Chapter Outline

I. ANTHROPOLOGICAL THEORY
  A. A theory is a statement that allows us to both explain and predict phenomena and enables us to represent reality as an abstract set of principles
  B. A good theory is one that can both explain and predict
  C. Hypothesis is an unproven proposition that can provide a basis for further investigation
  D. Anthropological theory changes constantly as new data come forth
  E. Attempts to answer questions like
    1. Why do people behave as they do?
    2. How do we account for human diversity
  F. Some of the earlier theoretical orientations no longer attract much attention (diffusionism)
  G. Others have been refined and reworked into something new (evolutionism)
  H. Others continue to command popularity (functionalism)
  I. Contemporary anthropological theories that may appear plausible today were built on what was learned from the older theories

II. EVOLUTIONISM
  A. The first group of early anthropologists, writing during the mid-nineteenth century, suggested the theory of cultural evolutionism. Basic premise was that all societies pass through a series of distinct evolutionary stages
  B. Edward B. Tylor in England and Lewis Henry Morgan in the United States
  C. Euro-American cultures were at the top of the evolutionary ladder and "less developed" cultures occupied the lower stages
  D. Replaced the prevailing theory that explained the existence of small-scale, preliterate societies by claiming that they were people whose ancestors had fallen from grace
  E. Criticisms
    1. Ethnocentricity - concluded that Western societies represented the highest levels of human achievement
    2. Armchair speculators
  F. Contributions
    1. Tried to establish what Tylor called "the science of culture" whereby human behavior was explained in terms of secular evolutionary processes rather than supernatural causes
    2. Firmly established the notion that differences in human lifestyles are the result of cultural processes
    3. Morgan's use of techno-economic factors to distinguish between different types of cultures remains a viable concept
  G. Evolutionism in Brief
    1. All cultures pass through the same developmental stages in the same order.
    2. Evolution is unidirectional and leads to higher (better) levels of culture.
    3. A deductive approach is used to apply general theories to specific cases.
    4. Evolutionism was ethnocentric because evolutionists put their own societies at the top.

III. DIFFUSIONISM
  A. Developed during the late nineteenth and ran its course after the first several decades of the twentieth century
  B. Diffusionists held that humans were essentially uninventive
  C. Certain cultural features were invented originally in one or several parts of the world and then spread, through the process of diffusion, to other cultures

D. Represented by Grafton Elliot Smith and W.J. Perry in England and Fritz Graebner and Wilhelm Schmidt in Germany and Austria
E. Criticisms
    1. Started with a sound anthropological concept and either took it to its illogical extreme or left too many questions unanswered
    2. Smith and Perry suggested that everything found in the world could be traced back to the early Egyptians
    3. Diffusionists were not able to prove primary centers or invention
    4. Diffusionists were not able to answer questions concerning the process of cultural diffusion
    5. Failed to raise questions about the reasons certain traits arise in the first place
    6. Like the evolutionists, the diffusionists took a deductive approach to the discipline (reasoning fro the general to the specific). Started off with a general principle to explain specific cases
    7. Based their theories on inadequate data at best because of armchair speculation
F. Contributions
    1. First to point out the need to develop theories dealing with contact and interaction among cultures
G. Diffusionism in Brief
    1. All societies change as a result of cultural borrowing from one another.
    2. A deductive approach is used by applying general theories to explain specific cases.
    3. The theory overemphasized the essentially valid idea of diffusion.

IV. AMERICAN HISTORICISM
A. A reaction to the deductive approach of evolutionists and diffusionists led primarily by Franz Boas at the beginning of the twentieth century
B. Emphasized inductive reasoning, starting with data collection and moving to general theories
C. Emphasized careful collection of empirical data from specific cultures
D. Called for a moratorium on theorizing
E. Criticisms
    1. Anti-theoretical stance was responsible for retarding the discipline of anthropology as a science
F. Contributions
    1. Brought the young discipline of anthropology both methodological rigor and a sense of how to define problems in scientific terms
    2. Trained the first generation of American anthropologists
    3. Purposeful about attracting women in order to describe all of a culture
    4. Took a strong stance against racism
G. American Historicism in Brief
    1. Collection of ethnographic facts must precede development of cultural theories (induction).
    2. Any culture is partially composed of traits diffused from other cultures.
    3. Direct fieldwork is absolutely essential.
    4. Each culture is, to some degree, unique.
    5. Ethnographers should try to get the view of those being studied, not their own view.

V. FUNCTIONALISM
A. Bronislav Malinowski established a tradition of firsthand data collection in the United Kingdom at the same time Boas was developing American anthropology.
    1. Like Boas, Malinowski was a strong advocate of fieldwork

2. Both men insisted on learning local language and trying to understand a culture from the perspective of the native
3. Concentrated on how contemporary cultures operated or functioned (functionalism)

B. Assumed that cultures provided various means for satisfying both societal and individual needs

C. Each cultural item had a meaning and performed some useful function for the well-being of the individual or the society. Fieldworker had to become sufficiently immersed in the culture and language to be able to identify the functions

D. All aspects of a culture are related to one another
Kula ring system of trade

E. A. R. Radcliffe-Brown
1. Viewed functions in terms of how they contributed to the well-being of the society (structural functionalism)
2. Based on two fundamental principles
    a. The notion of universal functions holds that every part of a culture has a function
    b. The principle of functional unity states that a culture is an integrated whole composed of a number of interrelated parts. If cultural parts are interconnected, a change in one part is likely to result in changes in other parts

F. Robert Merton
1. Most effective revisions of functionalist theory have come from sociologists
2. Suggests that although every cultural item may have a function, it is incorrect to assume that every item must have a function
3. Proposed the notion of dysfunction, which tends to cause stress of imbalance in a cultural system
4. Whether a cultural trait is functional or dysfunctional can be resolved only by empirical research
5. Warns against applying extreme functionalist assumptions (which may be more valid for small-scale societies) to the large, complex societies

G. Functionalism in Brief
1. Through direct fieldwork, anthropologists seek to understand how the parts of contemporary culture work for the well-being of the individual and the society.
2. Society is like a biological organism with all of the parts interconnected.
3. With this high level of integration, societies tend to be in a state of equilibrium; a change in one part of the system brings change in other parts.
4. Empirical fieldwork is absolutely essential.
5. The existing institutional structure of any society contains indispensable functions without which the society could not continue.

VI. PSYCHOLOGICAL ANTHROPOLOGY

A. Boas' students in the 1920s and 19302 became interested in the relationship between culture and the individual

B. Focus on the relationship between culture and the individual
Is personality a part of the cultural system?
1. How can personality variables be causally related to the cultural system?

C. Looked to child-rearing practices and personality from a cross-cultural perspective

D. Interactive relationship between child-rearing practices, personality structure, and culture.

E. Edward Sapir
1. Individuals learn their cultural patterns unconsciously, much as they learn their language

2. The true locus of culture was in the interaction of individuals
3. Writing and lectures stimulated interest in others (Mead and Benedict)

F. Margaret Mead
1. Questioned whether the period of adolescence is universal in its experience or varies from one culture to another
2. *Coming of Age in Samoa* (1928) - concluded that the emotional turbulence found among U.S. adolescents was culturally, not biologically, based
3. Gender roles (1935) - our own Western conception of masculine and feminine are not sex-linked but rather are culturally determined
4. Work criticized on the basis of both accuracy and methodology
5. Greatest contribution to anthropological theory was her demonstration of the importance of cultural rather than biological conditioning
6. Popularized the discipline of cultural anthropology
7. Served as a pioneer for many women who became anthropologists
8. Was severely criticized by Derek Freeman in 1983

G. Psychological Anthropology in Brief
1. Anthropologists need to explore the relationships between psychological and cultural variables.
2. Personality is largely the result of cultural learning.
3. Universal temperaments associated with males and females do not exist

VII. NEOEVOLUTIONISM

A. Although critical of nineteenth-century evolutionists, no researcher, including Boas, was able to demonstrate that cultures do not develop or evolve in certain ways over time

B. Leslie White
1. Resurrected the theories of the nineteenth century evolutionists in the 1930s. Like Tylor and Morgan, believed that cultures evolve from simple to increasingly more complex forms and that cultural evolution is as real as biological evolution
2. Suggested that culture evolves when people are able to increase the amount of energy under their control
3. Culture = Energy x Technology Cultural evolution is caused by advancing levels of technology and a culture's increasing capacity to "capture energy"

C. Julian Steward
1. Interested in the relationship between cultural evolution and adaptation to the environment
2. Interested in developing propositions about specific cultures or groups of cultures
3. Distinguished among three types of evolutionary thought
   a. Unilinear evolution - Tylor and Morgan
   b. Universal evolution - White
   c. Multilinear evolution - Steward
4. Focused on evolution of specific cultures without assuming that all cultures follow the same evolutionary process

D. Criticisms
1. Steward thought White's approach was too general
2. White's theory could not explain why some cultures evolve by "capturing energy" and others do not

E. Contributions
1. By focusing on the relationship among people, environment, and culture, Steward was the first and leading proponent of the study of cultural ecology

F. Neoevolutionism in Brief
1. Cultures evolve in direct proportion to their capacity to harness energy.
2. Culture is shaped by environmental conditions.

3. Through culture, human populations continuously adapt to techno-environmental conditions.
4. Because technological and environmental factors shape culture, individual (personality) factors are de-emphasized.

VIII. FRENCH STRUCTURALISM

A. No single theoretical orientation is as closely associated with a single person as French structuralism is associated with Claude Lévi-Strauss

B. Concentrates on identifying the mental structures that support social behavior

C. Sees ethnology as more psychological or cognitive than sociology

D. Draws heavily on the science of linguistics

F. Argues that certain codes programmed into the human mind are responsible for shaping cultures

G. Although there are differences in the codes because of environment and history, in the final analysis the mental structure of all humans is essentially the same

H. The structure of cultural elements is limited by the very nature of the human mind

I. Basic tenet - the human mind is programmed to think in binary oppositions, or opposites. These dichotomies give shape to culture

J. Criticisms

Overly abstract theories are not susceptible to empirical testing

K. Contributions

1. Directed our attention to the relationship between culture and cognition
2. Focused on the grand questions that anthropologists, questing for specialization, have largely abandoned: How does the human mind work? Is there a psychic unity for all of human kind?
3. Prodded other researchers to generate more imaginative hypotheses that can be tested through empirical research

L. French Structuralism in Brief

1. Human cultures are shaped by certain preprogrammed codes of the human mind.
2. Theory focuses on the underlying principles that generate behavior rather than the observable empirical behavior itself.
3. Theory emphasizes repetitive structures rather than sociocultural change.
4. Rather than examining attitudes, values, and beliefs, structural anthropologists concentrate on the unconscious level.
5. It is assumed that the human mind categorizes phenomena in terms of binary oppositions.

IX. ETHNOSCIENCE

A. Theory is similar to French structuralism

1. Both approaches draw on a linguistic model, seek explanations in the human mind, and view human behavior from a logical or rational perspective

B. Methods are different

1. Attempts to understand a culture from the point of view of the people themselves

C. Proponents were a small group of American cultural anthropologists during the 1950s and 1960s and include Ward Goodenough and William Sturtevant

D. Try to describe a culture in terms of how it is perceived, ordered, and categorized by the members of that culture rather than by imposing the categories of the ethnographer

E. Distinguishes between the emic and the etic approaches to methodology. Strongly advocates the emic approach

F. Criticisms

1. Some anthropologists feel that one's own conditioning and preconceptions make it impossible to get into the mind of someone from another culture

2. There is a question about how the researcher can communicate findings to others in the researcher's own linguistic/cultural group
3. If every ethnographer describes specific cultures using native categories, there would be little or no basis for comparing different societies
4. Ethnoscience is extremely time-consuming

G. Contributions
1. The ethnoscientific approach has served as a useful reminder of the anthropological principle that people from different cultural and linguistic backgrounds organize and categorize their world in essentially different ways

H. Ethnoscience in Brief
1. Theory attempts to make ethnographic description more accurate and replicable.
2. Ethnoscience describes a culture by using the categories of the people under study rather than by imposing categories from the ethnographer's culture (emic approach).
3. Because of the time-consuming nature of their methodology, ethnoscientists have been confined to describing very small segments of a culture.
4. It is difficult to compare data collected by ethnoscientists.

X. FEMINIST ANTHROPOLOGY

A Developed along with the women's movement of the 1960s and 1970s.

B. Basic premise is that anthropology for most of the 20th century has had a male bias.
1. Women in societies studied were often neglected.
2. When studied, women were often viewed as passive players in society.

C. Called for the re-analysis of ethnographies "as if gender really mattered" by studying how gender relates to economic, political, and social power.

D. Basic principles of Feminist Anthropology
1. Gender is an important cultural variable.
2. Rejects scientific positivism because it supports the elites.
3. Tends to be subjective and collaborative between ethnographer and subjects
4. Emphasis on qualitative methods.
5. It does not assume to be value-free.

E. Annette Weiner is a good example of a feminist anthropologist reinterpreting Trobriand society from a gender perspective.

XI. CULTURAL MATERIALISM

A. The theoretical position based on the concept that material conditions or modes of production determine human thoughts and behavior

B. Most closely associated with Marvin Harris in the 1960s and 1970s

C. Primary task of anthropology is to provide causal explanations for the similarities and differences in thought and behavior found among human groups

D. Study material constraints which arise from the universal needs of producing food, technology, tools, and shelter

E. See material constraints as the primary causal factors accounting for cultural variation

F. Relies heavily on an etic research methodology - assumes the viewpoint of the anthropologist rather than the native informant

G. Rejects the Marxist notion of dialectic materialism, which calls for destroying capitalism and empowering the working class

H. Cultural materialism is committed to the scientific study of culture

I. Criticisms
1. Devalues the importance of ideas and political activities as sources of cultural change
2. Critical of cultural idealists, anthropologists who rely on an emic approach and use ideas, values, and ideologies as the major explanatory factors

J. Cultural Materialism in Brief
   1. Material conditions determine human thoughts and behavior.
   2. Theorists assume the viewpoint of the anthropologist, not the native informant.
   3. Anthropology is seen as scientific, empirical, and capable of generating causal explanations.
   4. Cultural materialism de-emphasizes the role of ideas and values in determining the conditions of social life.

XII. POSTMODERNISM
   A. In the 1970s and 1980s a number of anthropologists questioned the very scientific nature of anthropology
   B. Grew out of the traditions of the structuralists, interpretative anthropology, and feminist anthropology
   C. Postmodernists dispute the possibility that anthropology can construct a grand theory of human behavior
   D. Claims that the modernists' enterprise for much of the twentieth century was based on the privileged status of science and reflected the basic power imbalances between the wealthy, colonial countries and those developing countries where much anthropological research was conducted
      1. It is impossible for predominantly White, male, Euro-American anthropologists to step outside of their own culture so as to produce an objective view of another culture
   E. Holds that all ethnographic accounts are subjective because they are conditioned by the experiences and personal histories of the ethnographer
   F. Calls for a more collaborative approach to the study of culture
   G. Rejects generalizing and developing predictable theories
      1. By emphasizing the uniqueness of every culture, views culture as a changing set of individual meanings that require continual reinterpretation
   H. More interested in describing and interpreting particular cultures
   I. Interpretive anthropology
      1. Major force in postmodernism led by Clifford Geertz
      2. Cultures can best be understood by listening and recording the ways in which the natives explain their own customary behavior
      3. Strongly wedded to the emic approach to the discipline
      4. Admittedly relativistic and designed to sensitize anthropologists to their own views and values as well as those of the informant
      5. Advocates combining self-knowledge with knowledge of the people under study so anthropologists learn about themselves as they learn about the culture of the informant
   J. Postmodernism in Brief
      1. Postmodernism called on anthropologists to switch from cultural generalization and laws to description, interpretation, and the search for meaning.
      2. Ethnographies should be written from several voices - that of the anthropologist along with those of the people under analysis.
      3. Postmodernism involves a distinct return to cultural relativism.

XIII. CONCLUDING THOUGHTS ON ANTHROPOLOGICAL THEORY
   A. Few anthropologists today would tie themselves to a single school or theoretical orientation
   B. Contemporary anthropologists tend to be more eclectic and problem oriented, focusing on explaining cultural phenomena while drawing on a wide variety of methods and sources of data
   C. Many of the theoretical schools are not mutually exclusive

Key Terms

These are the anthropological terms introduced in Chapter 4. You may want to ask your students to write definitions of one or more of these terms during class to see how well they understood the reading. Even if you choose not to grade the assignment, the students will take it more seriously if you collect their answers.

American historicism
barbarism
binary opposition
civilization
cultural ecology

cultural materialism
deductive
diffusionism
dysfunction
ethnoscience
evolutionism
Feminist anthropology
French structuralism
functional unity
functionalism

hypotheses
inductive
interpretive anthropology
multilinear evolution
neoevolutionism
positivism
postmodernism
psychic unity
psychological anthropology
savagery
structural functionalism

theory
unilinear evolution
universal evolution
universal functions

Critical Thinking Questions

1. How has ethnocentrism influenced anthropological theory?
2. Describe the concept of culture used by Morgan and Tylor.
3. What was the basis, in unilinear evolution, for determining the evolutionary stage to which a society belonged?
4. Which theories were the most important in fostering anthropology's reliance on extensive first-hand ethnographic fieldwork for data collection?
5. How does the anthropological concept of culture provide an important argument against racism and genetic determinism?
6. Explain the following quote by Ruth Benedict about Franz Boas: "Boas found anthropology a collection of wild guesses and a happy hunting ground for the romantic lover of primitive things. He left it a discipline in which the theories could be tested."
7. Do the neoevolutionary theories of Leslie White and Julian Steward contradict one another?
8. Why was it so important (from a methodological perspective) for Boas to attract women into the field of cultural anthropology?
9. What were the basic issues in the controversy between Margaret Mead and Derek Freeman?
10. Is there any way to test French structuralism empirically?
11. In what way are cultural materialism and interpretive anthropology almost opposites?

12. What contributions did Annette Weiner make to Feminist anthropology?

Class Activities

1. Select three or four of the theoretical perspectives discussed and assign each to a group of students. Then show an ethnographic film and have each group interpret the significance of an aspect of subsistence, technology, or ideology according to "their" theory. It is a good idea to include unilineal evolutionary and diffusionist theories because they are more common in popular culture than may be expected.
2. Ask students to bring articles to class from a newspaper or a magazine such as *Time* or *National Geographic*. Instruct them to reinterpret the data presented in the article using one of the anthropological theories they studied.
3. Select any one of the following anthropologists and discuss his/her contributions to socio-cultural theory:

Leslie White	Marvin Harris
Margaret Mead	Bronislav Malinowski

Internet Exercises

1. By using any major search engine, conduct a subject search for some of the founders of anthropological theory, such as Franz Boas, Marvin Harris, Margaret Mead, Clifford Geertz, and Bronislav Malinowski. What additional information (not mentioned in the chapter) can you find about these giants of anthropology?

2. The University of Indiana has a web site dealing specifically with anthropological theory:
http://www.indiana.edu/~wanthro/theory.htm#sub
Once there, select "psychological anthropology" from the section on subdisciplines. Write a one-page paper on what you consider to be the most distinctive feature of psychological anthropology.

3. Minnesota State University at Mankato has a web site devoted to biographies of famous cultural anthropologists. This site can be found at the following URL:
http://kroeber.anthro.mankato.msus.edu/information/biography/index.shtml

   What information can you find on the professional careers of Franz Boas, Clifford Geertz, Marvin Harris, Margaret Mead, and Bronislav Malinowski that was not mentioned in the chapter?

Infotrac® Exercises

1. Students will need to access InfoTrac at **http://infotrac.thomsonlearning.com/index.html** to answer the following questions. Type in "Postmodernism" in the Search field. Click on "Periodicals." Use the Limit Search function to find the article "Logical and Moral Dilemmas of Postmodernism."

   a. Is a postmodernist view beneficial to anthropological research?

b. Should anthropology continue to regard itself as a science?

Suggested Films

Anthropology on Trial. (UC), 50 min., #11116 - Critique of ethnographers, using Margaret Mead's work on Manus as a case study. Manus people talk about her, her work, and its biases and inadequacies. (Originally shown on NOVA)

Bronislaw Malinowski: Off the Verandah. (IM), 52 min., video #39AC1003 - Examines Malinowski's work, especially in the Trobriands and his pioneering methodology.

Franz Boas (1858 - 1942). (PSU), 59 min., #50511 - A portrait of Boas, showing his ethnographic work among the Kwakiutl and discussing his influence on American anthropology.

Margaret Mead: Taking Note. (DER), 59 min. - Tells the story of Mead's personal and professional life. Shows her in many field situations, her activities during WWII, and the many causes with which she became concerned the rest of her life.

Chapter 5

Methods in Cultural Anthropology

Learning Objectives

After reading and studying Chapter 5, your students should be able to:

1. Discuss the importance of experiential fieldwork to cultural anthropology.
2. Understand all aspects of preparing for and carrying out anthropological fieldwork.
3. Describe the difference between a generalized ethnography and the more focused, problem oriented research usually conducted in recent decades.
4. Recognize the importance of hypotheses, independent variables, and dependent variables for research design in anthropology.
5. Discuss the five stages of field research as they were carried out in the Kenya Kinship Study.
6. Distinguish among the stages of data collection, analysis, and interpretation in field research and recognize the significance each has for the others.
7. Understand the importance, as well as the limitations, of participant-observation in fieldwork.
8. Evaluate the appropriate use of both structured and unstructured interviews and be able to suggest ways to determine the validity of the data gathered.
9. Describe anthropologists' use of mapping, document analysis, genealogies, and photography in fieldwork and recognize that a variety of types of data allows for cross-checking of information.
10. Understand the nature of culture shock and appreciate the benefits of biculturalism.
11. Describe how the scientific objectivity of ethnographic fieldwork is different from research in a chemistry or biology laboratory.
12. Explain "narrative ethnography", the theoretical approach to which it is associated, and its impact on anthropological fieldwork.
13. Describe the Human Relations Area Files (HRAF) and its impact on statistical, cross-cultural comparative studies in anthropology.
14. Describe the major ethical issues confronting applied anthropologists.
15. Understand the importance of Project Camelot and its consequences for the development of ethics in cultural anthropology.

Chapter Outline

I. EXPERIENTIAL FIELDWORK
- A. Cultural anthropologists are interested in explaining *how*, *with what*, and *why* people in different parts of the world behave and think the way they do
  1. To answer questions of both description and explanation, they collect data and test hypotheses by means of fieldwork
- B. Fieldwork Strategy
  1. Live with the people being studied
  2. Ask them questions
  3. Survey their environments and material possessions
  4. Spend long periods of time observing them in everyday interaction in their natural setting
- C. Has not always been an integral part of the discipline
  1. Much of nineteenth-century anthropological theorizing based on secondhand data and writings of untrained observers
  2. Franz Boas influenced the acceptance of experiential fieldwork as a research methodology
  3. Before 1960s anthropologists produced a book on "his" or "her" people several years after returning from a fieldwork experience with little explanation of field methods or of the fieldwork experience itself
  4. Since the 1960s anthropologists have been producing accounts of their own fieldwork experiences
  5. Recent articles explore the methodological issues involved in designing a fieldwork study, collecting the data, and analyzing the results
  6. Often traditional ethnographic methods are blended with survey methods.
- D. No two fieldwork experiences are the same, but all fieldworkers have concerns, problems, and issues in common
  1. Preparing for fieldwork
  2. Gaining acceptance into the community
  3. Selecting the most appropriate data-gathering techniques
  4. Understanding how to operate within the local political structure
  5. Taking precautions against investigator bias
  6. Choosing knowledgeable informants
  7. Coping with culture shock
  8. Learning a new language
  9. Willingness to reevaluate findings in the light of new evidence

II. PREPARING FOR FIELDWORK
- A. The popular image of the field anthropologist tends to be overly romanticized
- B. Fieldwork is hard work with serious demands on one's time, patience, and sense of humor
- C. Requirements:
  1. A minimum of a year's lead time
  2. Funding from an agency that supports anthropological research
  3. Proper health precautions
  4. Governmental clearance or permission from the host government
  5. Proficiency in the local language
  6. Taking care of personal details before leaving home

III. STAGES OF FIELD RESEARCH

A. Even though no two fieldwork experiences are ever the same, every study should progress though the same basic stages:
   1. Selecting a research problem
   2. Formulating a research design
   3. Collecting the data
   4. Analyzing the data
   5. Interpreting the data
   6. There are often many theoretical and methodological issues that interfere with this neat five-fold scheme of doing research.

B. Selecting a research problem
   1. Fieldworkers have moved away from general ethnographies
      a. More focused
      b. More specific
      c. More problem-oriented
   2. Shift has resulted in the formulation of hypotheses (stating the predicted relationship between two or more variables) that are tested in a fieldwork setting
   3. Kenya Kinship Study hypothesis: As Kenya becomes more urbanized, extended family interaction will be replaced by more nuclear family interaction

C. Formulating a Research Design
   1. Fieldworker must decide how to measure the two major variables in the hypothesis
   2. KKS variables - urbanization and family interaction
   3. Independent variable (urbanization) is the variable that is capable of affecting change in the other variable
   4. Dependent variable (family interaction) is the variable whose value is dependent on the other variable
   5. Dependent variable must be defined more specifically so that it can be measured quantitatively
      a. Residence patterns
      b. Visitation patterns
      c. Mutual assistance
      d. Formal family gatherings
   6. Important to control for any extraneous factors that might interfere with the testing of the hypothesis. In the KKS - controlled for ethnic group (tribal affiliation) by using only one ethnic group for both rural and urban samples

D. Collecting the Data
   1. Appropriate data-gathering techniques for measuring the variable must be determined
   2. The KKS used three principal data-gathering techniques
      a. Participant-observation
      b. Structured interviews
      c. Day histories - a technique modified for the study. Generated specific quantitative data on family interaction. Designed to determine
         1) who people were with
         2) what relationship they had
         3) how much time they spent together
         4) how long they had known each other
         5) what they did together

E. Analyzing the Data
   1. The data collected must be analyzed, categorized, and measurements compared.
   2. Data analysis for the KKS

a. Analyzed contents of day histories
b. Various time segments were categorized into one of nine types of social interaction
c. Counted the number of minutes per 24-hour period that each interviewee spent in family interaction
d. Calculated the mean number of minutes spent in each type of family interaction for both rural and urban samples
1) No significant differences in family interaction emerged between the rural and urban sample

F. Interpreting the Data
1. Involves explaining or interpreting the findings
2. Questions to ask are:
a. Has the original hypothesis been confirmed or rejected?
b. What factors can be identified that will help explain the findings?
c. How do these findings compare with the findings of similar studies?
d. How can the findings be generalized to wider populations?
e. Have these findings raised methodological or theoretical issues that have bearing on the discipline?
3. The key to understanding the KKS findings lies in the general socioeconomic status of the people under study
4. The wide range of family interaction found among both rural and urban populations in Kenya can be understood largely in terms of a lack of money and economic security
a. The maintenance of strong kinship ties among both rural and urban Kikuyu populations is a rational choice which provides for their welfare in an environment lacking economic security and access to any type of public welfare program

IV. DATA GATHERING TECHNIQUES
A. Data-collection methods that work in one culture might not work in another
B. Anthropologists must be flexible in order to find the most appropriate techniques and use more than one to verify the findings from others
C. Use of a variety of techniques is recommended
D. Participant-observation
1. Anthropologists use this technique more than any other technique and more extensively than any other social science discipline
2. Means becoming involved in the culture under study while making systematic observations of what is going on
3. Involves establishing rapport in a new community
4. Guidelines for Participant-Observation Fieldwork
a. It is advisable to work one's way down the political hierarchy.
b. When introducing oneself, select one role and use it consistently
c. Proceed slowly. Ethnographers must invest a considerable amount of time and energy establishing their credibility by allowing the local people to get to know them
d. Communicate to the local people, in a genuine way, that one is a *student*, wanting to learn more about a subject on which they are the experts
5. Advantages of Participant-Observation
a. People in most cultures appreciate any attempt by the anthropologist to live according to rules of their culture
b. Enables the fieldworker to distinguish between normative and real behavior (what people should do and what people actually do)

c. Data-gathering is more accurate

6. Disadvantages of Participant-Observation
   a. Only a small sample size can be used because the technique is time consuming
   b. It is often hard to categorize the data, which makes synthesizing and comparing the data difficult
   c. Sometimes difficult to record experiences as they happen.
   d. Details are lost in the time between the event and its recording

E. Interviewing
1. Used for obtaining two kinds of information:
   a. What people think or feel (attitudinal data)
   b. What people do (behavioral data)
2. Unique in several respects
   a. The interviewer and the subject may speak different first languages
   b. The ethnographic interview is often much broader in scope because it elicits information on the entire culture
   c. Cannot be used alone but must be used in conjunction with other data-gathering techniques

F. Structured and Unstructured Interviews
1. Unstructured interviews
   a. Involve a minimum of control
   b. Interviewer asks open-ended questions on a general topic and allows interviewees to respond at their own pace using their own words
   c. Usually used early in the data-gathering process
   d. Have the advantage of allowing informants to decide what is important to include in their information
2. Structured interviews
   a. Interviewer asks all informants exactly the same set of questions, in the same sequence, and preferably under the same set of conditions
   b. Have the advantage of producing large quantities of data that are comparable and lend themselves well to statistical descriptions
3. Guidelines for conducting interviews
   a. Field guides available but may force one's thinking into Western categories that have little relevance for the culture being studied
   b. Take precautions to minimize distortions in the data
   c. Phrase questions positively
   d. Avoid two-pronged questions
   e. Leave more controversial questions for last
   f. Keep recording as unobtrusive as possible
   g. Pre-test questions asked as part of a structured interview to eliminate ambiguous or misleading questions
   h. Be aware of the social situation in which the interview takes place
4. Validity of Data Collected
   a. Ask a number of people the same question
   b. Ask a person the same question over time
   c. Compare responses with behavior

G. Additional Data-Gathering Techniques
1. Census Taking - involves the collection of basic demographic data
2. Mapping - ethnographic mapping is the attempt to locate people, material culture, and environmental features in space

3. Document Analysis - supplements the information collected through interviewing and observation. Provides large quantities of data, is inexpensive, and is totally unobtrusive
4. Genealogizing - writing down all of the relatives of a particular informant
5. Photography - both still and motion pictures are important aids to data collection
    a. Allows proxemic analysis or event analysis
    b. Still camera has many uses as a research tool
    c. Can produce a lasting record
    d. Can use photographs as a probe in the interview process
    e. Can be used for sociometric tracking
    f. Often an easier and less time-consuming mode of data collection than written description
    g. Drawbacks - some people object to being photographed

H. Choosing a technique
1. Which techniques will be used depends largely on nature of the problem being investigated
2. Receptivity of the people being studied also influences the choice of techniques
3. Should be used in conjunction with other techniques

V. THE PAINS AND GAINS OF FIELDWORK

A. The anthropologist in the field is faced with a number of anxiety-producing situations that can be both stressful and growth inducing

B. Despite careful research design and preparations, fieldwork is full of unanticipated difficulties

C. Sometimes cultural anthropologists in the field can be in life-threatening situations
1. Contagious diseases
2. Social violence, including civil wars, intergroup warfare, muggings, and other forms of crime

D. Culture Shock
1. The psychological disorientation caused by trying to adjust to major differences in lifestyles and living conditions
2. Term introduced in 1960
3. The very success or failure of an anthropological field project depends largely on how well the ethnographer can make the adjustment to the new culture and overcome the effects of culture shock

E. Biculturalism
1. Total immersion experience of fieldwork provides opportunities for personal growth and increased understanding
2. Learn about one's own culture as well
3. Develop a much broader view of human behavior

VI. RECENT TRENDS IN ETHNOGRAPHIC FIELDWORK

A. Cultural anthropology must strive toward objectivity by being sensitive to methodological issues

B. Tension between subjectivity of participating and objectivity of observation has traditionally been resolved by reporting findings in scientific terms

C. Reflexive Methods/Narrative ethnography
1. Interested in co-producing ethnographic knowledge by focusing on the interaction between the researcher and the informant
2. Dialogue between ethnographer and informant becomes an integral part of the field experience as well as of the written ethnography

3. Emergence has stimulated a debate among anthropologists as to whether anthropological fieldwork is an objective scientific enterprise or more of a dialogue or co-production between the ethnographer and the informant
4. Has raised questions including, What is the best way to represent cultural reality?

D. Statistical Cross Cultural Comparisons
1. Made possible in the 1940s by George Peter Murdock and colleagues at Yale University
2. Developed a coded data retrieval system known as the Human Relations Area Files (HRAF)
3. Largest anthropological data bank in the world
4. Information organized according to over 300 different cultures and over 700 different cultural subject headings
5. Opened up the possibility for making statistical comparisons among large numbers of cultures
6. HRAF data bank must be used carefully and in full recognition of potential methodological pitfalls
    a. Variation in quality of data
    b. Uneven coverage, with a greater amount of material from non-Western cultures
    c. Questionable comparability of units of analysis
7. Remains a powerful tool for testing universal theories and identifying causal relationships among cultural phenomena

VII. THE ETHICS OF APPLIED ANTHROPOLOGY

A. Researchers are faced with a number of ethical dilemmas, often involving conflicting values
1. All anthropologists (applied and theoretical) find themselves in social situations that are varied and complex because they work with people in a number of different role relationships
2. Applied anthropologists work in an even more complex situation, for their work often is aimed at facilitating change in the culture of the local population

B. Each member of the profession is ultimately responsible for anticipating ethical dilemmas and resolving them in such a way as to do damage neither to their subjects nor to other scholars

C. Concern for ethics is not a recent phenomenon
1. 1919 - Franz Boas spoke out against the practice of anthropologists engaging in spying activities while allegedly conducting scientific research
2. 1971 - AAA adopted its “Principles of Professional Responsibility” and established its Committee on Ethics
3. 1975 - SfAA published its “Statement on Professional and Ethical Responsibilities”

D. Project Camelot
1. In the 1960s administrators of Project Camelot were accused of using anthropologists to act as a cover for U.S. Army intervention in the internal political affairs of other sovereign nations
2. Enormous repercussions on the social sciences in general and anthropology in particular. Debate revolved around two questions:
    a. Was Project Camelot a legitimately objective attempt to gather social science data?
    b. Were the participating anthropologists misled into thinking that scientific research was the project’ sole objective?

3. For years afterward, many U.S. anthropologists experienced difficulties trying to prove that they were not engaged in secret research sponsored by the CIA or the Department of Defense

E. Major areas of responsibility for anthropologists are outlined in the codes of professional ethics adopted by the AAA (revised 1998) and by the SfAA. Codes are not appreciably different.
   1. the people studied
   2. the public
   3. the discipline
   4. students
   5. sponsors
   6. their own and their host governments

F. Field ethnographers in the United States have little legal protection in maintaining the confidentiality of their sources

Key Terms

These are the anthropological terms introduced in Chapter 5. You may want to ask your students to write definitions of one or more of these terms during class to see how well they understood the reading. Even if you choose not to grade the assignment, the students will take it more seriously if you collect their answers.

analyzing data
attitudinal data
behavioral data
bicultural perspective
census taking
collecting data
culture shock
data analysis
dependent variable
document analysis
ethnographic mapping
event analysis
fieldwork
genealogical method
Human Relations Area Files (HRAF)
independent variable
informant
interpreting data
narrative ethnography
participant-observation
photography
proxemic analysis
reflexive ethnography
research clearance
research design
research proposal
sociometric tracking
structured interview
survey methods
unstructured interview

Critical Thinking Questions

1. What are the most important ways doing experiential fieldwork will change an anthropologist's understanding of a culture?
2. What are some of the uses to which still photography can be put when conducting fieldwork?
3. Does the Kenya Kinship Study suggest that comparable results might be found in a study of people living in poverty in the United States?

4. During the course of his or her research, an anthropologist using participant-observation will frequently alternate between data collection and data analysis in order to understand what she or he is doing. What will be the impact of the integration of these two aspects of research?

5. Under what circumstances would participant-observation be a poor methodological choice for an anthropologist?

6. What is lost to an anthropologist who does fieldwork among a people who do not allow photographs? Are there any advantages to such a situation?

7. Why would a goal of developing some degree of biculturalism in all students in an introductory anthropology class be important in today's world?

8. Do you think an anthropologist can really become bicultural? Explain your answer. Are there any people in our society who are bicultural, even without taking an anthropology class?

9. What kind of dialogue does an anthropologist and the informant have in a narrative ethnography?

10. In what ways can an anthropologist doing fieldwork actually harm the people being studied?

Class Activities

1. Require that all members of your class do fieldwork in the same setting, but allow (or require) individuals to use more than one method of data collection. Have them discuss what difference it made to their understanding of the situation and to the data they collected.

2. Ask students to attempt "narrative ethnography." Suggest they talk with another student about something they themselves know little about and then write a narrative on how they learned the other's cultural knowledge.

3. Have students interview a grandparent or someone in their grandparent's generation about the cultural changes that have occurred over the course of their lifetime.

Internet Exercises

1. Anthropologist Laura Zimmer Tamakoshi has developed an excellent web site that illustrates how she conducted fieldwork in Papua New Guinea. The site contains personal descriptions (complete with color photos) of such topics as preparation for the fieldwork experience, developing rapport without he local people, coping with culture shock, participating in the culture, taking field notes, and coming home again. Read over the material on this site to get a good feel for the types of challenges and rewards derived from anthropological fieldwork. You can find the site, entitled "Fieldwork: The Anthropologist in the Field," at

   http://www.truman.edu/academics/ss/faculty/tamakoshil/index.html

2. Using any major search engine, type in the term "Human Relations Area Files." What can you learn about this vast anthropological data source that is not mentioned in the chapter?

3. Assume that your employer has asked you to take a two-year assignment abroad. To increase your chances for success in your overseas assignment, you will need a lot of information in a

hurry about your host country. Select a country where you would like to work for several years. Now start your Internet search for relevant *cultural* information that will enable you to make as smooth an adjustment as possible

Starting with any major search engine, locate as much cultural information about your host country and culture as you can. Then, write a several-page paper identifying the features of the host culture that will be most relevant to your making a satisfactory adjustment to working and living in the country.

Infotrac® Exercises

1. Students will need to access InfoTrac at **http://infotrac.thomsonlearning.com/index.html** to answer the following questions. Type in "Ethnology" in the Search field. Click on "Periodicals." Find the article "Anthropology and Cultural Studies: Difference, Ethnography and Theory."

   a. How does ethnography affect the fieldworker's view of a culture?

   b. Why are anthropologists concerned about creating meaning within their ethnographies?

Suggested Films

Franz Boas (1858 - 1942). (PSU), 59 min., #50511 - A portrait of Boas, showing his ethnographic work among the Kwakiutl and discussing his influence on American anthropology.

Franz Boas: The Shackles of Tradition. (IM), 52 min., #39AC1001 - Examines his influence on anthropology including his challenge of the concept of race.

A Man Called Bee: Studying the Yanomamo. (PSU), 40 min., #40237 - Film about Chagnon's experiences as an ethnographer. Insights on the difficulties, both personal and professional, of fieldwork. Presents some methods of collecting information.

Margaret Mead. Coming of Age. (IM), 52 min., #39AC1004 - An examination of her fieldwork and her contribution to anthropology.

Chapter 6

Language

Learning Objectives

After reading and studying Chapter 4, your students should be able to:

1. Discuss the importance of language in human culture, especially as it relates to humans' ability to adapt to a wide variety of environments.
2. Distinguish between human and nonhuman communication in terms of closed and open systems, physical ability, and the characteristic of displacement.
3. Recognize the differences between phonology, morphology, and grammar.
4. Understand the symbolic nature of language.
5. Appreciate the diversity of languages in the world.
6. Understand that no language is superior to others in expressing abstract ideas.
7. Recognize that size of and specialization in vocabulary reflects adaptive importance to a culture.
8. Discuss the Sapir-Whorf hypothesis and the difficulties of testing it.
9. Comprehend the speed with which some languages are becoming extinct.
10. Recognize that languages are constantly changing.
11. Understand that linguists use the notion of family to show relationships between languages.
12. Understand how language is acquitted by children.
13. Discuss how a language reveals a culture's basic value structure.
14. Recognize that different cultural groups have different linguistic styles.
15. Explain the meaning of diglossia, describe when it occurs, and contrast diglossia with the use of dialects.
16. Recognize the symbolic role of language in the development of national and ethnic identities.
17. Explain the importance of non-verbal communication, including hand gestures, posture, and touching, for humans and the possibilities of cross-cultural misunderstanding.

Chapter Outline

The ability to create and use language is the most distinctive feature of humans. The capacity to adapt to the physical environment is made possible by language and it is largely through language that our cultural heritage is passed from one generation to the next.

I. THE NATURE OF LANGUAGE
    A. Language is a symbolic system of sounds that, when put together according to a certain set of rules, conveys meanings to its speakers
    B. Diversity of Language
        1. Criterion for a language is mutual unintelligibility, but there are differing degrees of intelligibility
        2. Considerable variation in the number of languages of the world and in the size of the different language communities
        3. 95 per cent of the world's people speak fewer than 100 of the approximately 6,000 different languages
        4. Linguists concerned about the last 5 percent of the world's languages, which are in danger of disappearing
        5. Perhaps as many as 90 percent of all world languages will be extinct or moribund within a hundred years
        6. Others become moribund - spoken only by a few older people and unknown to children
        7. Power of strong state governments can discourage the use of certain traditional languages
        8. The Linguistics Department at the University of California at Berkeley is attempting to revive some threatened American Indian languages.
        9. An entire way of thinking is lost each time a language becomes extinct
    C. Communication: Human versus Nonhuman
        1. Communication is not unique to humans
        2. Primate communication is complex
        3. Nonhuman primates have a closed call system
            a. sounds unique in form and message
            b. sounds are mutually exclusive
        4. Humans have open call systems
            a. Starting with limited number of sounds, are capable of producing an infinite number of meanings by combining sounds and words into new meanings
            b. Can send messages that have never been sent before
        5. Nonhuman primate communication
            a. Previously suggested that humans were endowed with certain genetically based mental capacities found in no other species
            b. Now claim certain species such as chimpanzees and gorillas have latent capacity for language
            c. Do not have the physical vocal equipment to produce speech
            d. Degree of difference between human and nonhuman forms of communication remains immense
    D. Displacement
        1. Human capacity to convey information about a thing or an event that is not present
        2. Enables humans to speak of purely hypothetical things
        3. Transmitted largely through tradition rather than through experience alone

   4. Specific language that a person speaks is passed from one generation to another through the process of learning

II. LINGUISTIC ACQUISITION AMONG CHILDREN
- A. Language acquisition involves more than the mastery of a list of words
  1. Child needs to master the system of grammatical rules with all of its complexities
  2. How languages are learned
  3. Mastery of vocabulary possible through imitation
  4. Imitation of sounds also helps children learn the specific language spoken in their immediate environment
- B. Parents and child caretakers throughout the world modify their normal speech when talking to small children
  1. Attention-getting devices
     - a. Talking in simple sentences only about the here and now
     - b. Avoiding abstractions in conversations
     - c. Tending to exaggerate certain vowel sounds
     - d. Using a form of baby talk to help children grasp the meaning of words
     - e. Repeating themselves in their speech to small children
- C. Chomsky - believes that language is more than the accumulation of words, sounds, and rules
  1. All languages share a limited set of organizing principles
  2. Universal grammar - all humans are born with a blueprint or basic linguistic plan
  3. As children learn to speak, they master a specific grammar system that has been imbedded in a universal grammar

III. THE STRUCTURE OF LANGUAGE
- A. Every language has a logical structure
  1. All languages have rules and principles governing what sounds are to be used and how those sounds are to be combined to convey meaning
- B. Two aspects of structure:
  1. A sound structure - phonology
  2. A grammatical structure
  3. Descriptive linguist studies both the sound system and the grammatical system of as many human languages as possible
- C. Phonology
  1. No single language uses all possible sounds
  2. Phonemes - the minimal units of sound that signal a difference in meaning
     - a. English language - 46 phonemes
     - b. Other languages vary from 15 to 100 phonemes
  3. The manner in which sounds are grouped into phonemes varies from one language to another
- D. Morphemes
  1. Two or more phonemes can be combined to form a morpheme
  2. Should not equate morphemes with words
  3. The majority of words in any language are made up of two or more morphemes
  4. Free morphemes - can stand alone
  5. Bound morphemes - have no meaning except when attached to other morphemes
- E. Grammar
  1. A highly complex set of rules for combining sounds into phonemes, phonemes into morphemes, morphemes into words, and words into sentences
  2. Grammatical systems consist of two parts:
     - a. Morphology - set of rules governing how morphemes are formed into words

b. Syntax - a set of principles guiding how words are arranged into phrases and sentences

IV. LANGUAGE CHANGE

A. Synchronic analysis (single point in time) - linguistic investigation of the sound system or structure of a language

B. Diachronic analysis (through time) - study of how languages change over time

C. Historical linguists are interested in studying both the changes that have occurred in a single language through time as well as the historical relationship of languages to one another

D. Historical linguistics seeks to discover not only how languages change, but also why they change

1. Change from internal sources
2. Change from external forces, or linguistic borrowing
3. The introduction of new words into a language parallels the events that shape that language community's history

E. Language Families

1. Study of historical linguistics dates back to the 1880s - Sir William Jones noticed similarities between Sanskrit and classical Greek and Latin
   a. Assumed that languages evolve much as do biological organisms
   b. Suggested that languages had family trees
2. A language family is composed of all of the languages that derive from its common protolanguage
   a. Diagrams of language families show the direction of linguistic change and how various languages of a region are interconnected
   b. Can be misleading in their simplicity
3. In reality, languages split apart very slowly. Gradual fission makes it difficult to tell exactly when a language becomes a separate entity

V. ARE SOME LANGUAGES SUPERIOR TO OTHERS?

A. Until the start of the twentieth century, European linguists were convinced that Western languages were superior to all others

B. Now anthropologists have shown that people from technologically simple societies are not less capable of expressing a wide variety of abstract ideas

C. No one language is more efficient at expressing abstract ideas than another

VI. LANGUAGE AND CULTURE

A. Anthropologists routinely learn to communicate in another language in order to do fieldwork because of the close relationship between language and culture

B. Important relationship between language and culture (the subject of cultural linguistics) recognized by Franz Boas

C. How Culture Influences Language

1. Cultural emphasis - the vocabulary found in any language tends to emphasize the words that are considered to be adaptively important in that culture
2. Reflected in the size and specialization of vocabulary
3. In small-scale cultures where most of people's lives revolve around hunting or herding, areas of cultural emphasis are obvious. Not always easy to identify in complex societies
4. Technology also affects language (e.g., cell phones are now used to send "disinformation."

D. How Language Influences Culture

1. Major concern of linguistic anthropology since the 1930s has been the question of whether language influences or perhaps even determines culture
2. The Sapir-Whorf Hypothesis

a. Different cultures see the world differently because of their different linguistic categories
b. Language establishes mental categories that predispose people to see things in a certain way
c. Testing of the hypothesis has shown that speakers of different languages do have different world views
d. Drawbacks to the hypothesis
1) Linguistic determinism- people are virtual prisoners of their language
2) It is possible that culture determines language rather than that language determines culture

E. Language Mirrors Values
1. A language also reveals a culture's basic value structure
2. North American English reflects the importance of individualism in the culture
3. Japanese reflects the importance of group harmony

VII. LINGUISTIC STYLE
A. Languages vary not only in terms of vocabularies, grammars, and syntax, but also in terms of linguistic styles
1. Some language groups are very direct and straightforward
2. Others tend to be very indirect, relying on implicit messages

VIII. SOCIOLINGUISTICS
A. Concentrates on variations in language use depending on the social situation or context in which the speaker is operating
B. Bilingualism and multilingualism are examples of adaptation to changing language circumstances
C. Code switching - selectively using a totally different language or variations on the same language
D. Major focus is on the relationship between language and social structure
E. Diglossia
1. Linguistic situation where two varieties of the same language are spoken by the same person at different times and under different social circumstances
2. In cases of diglossia, one form is considered to be high and the other low
3. Generally agreed that high forms are superior to low forms
4. Often the high form is associated with elites and the religious literature
F. Specialized vocabularies ("communities of practice")
G. Dialects - minority dialects are often assigned an inferior status by the majority for the purpose of maintaining the political, economic, and social subordination of the minority
H. Nonstandard forms of English are fully efficient languages with their own unique set of grammatical rules that are consistently applied
I. Language, Nationalism, and Ethnic Identity
1. Language plays an important symbolic role in the development of national and ethnic identities
2. A national language can unify a society
3. Official languages may not prevent conflict within countries
4. Linguistic tolerance within the European Union.
5. The French "language police."

IX. NONVERBAL COMMUNICATION
A. Helps in interpretation of linguistic messages
B. Frequently carries messages of its own
C. As much as 70 per cent of all human communication is nonverbal

D. Misunderstanding can occur when the same nonverbal cue has different meanings in different cultures

E. Nonverbal communication includes:
   1. Hand gestures
   2. Posture (body stance) - often communicates information about social status, religions practices, social distance
   3. Touching - each culture defines who can touch whom and under what circumstances

Key Terms

These are the anthropological terms introduced in Chapter 6. You may want to ask your students to write definitions of one or more of these terms during class to see how well they understood the reading. Even if you choose not to grade the assignment, the students will take it more seriously if you collect their answers.

arbitrary nature of language
bound morpheme
closed system of communication
code switching
cultural emphasis
diachronic analysis
diglossia
displacement
free morphemes
grammar
cultural linguistics
dialects
historical linguistics
language family
morphemes
morphology
nonverbal communication
open system of communication
phonemes
phonology
Sapir-Whorf hypothesis
synchronic analysis
syntax
descriptive linguistics
doublespeak

Critical Thinking Questions

1. How is human communication different from that of chimps or gorillas?
2. How difficult is it for a native English speaker to hear and recognize non-English phonemes?
3. How do people modify their speak when conversing with small children?
4. How important are the morphological, as compared to the syntactical, features of English?
5. How is the vocabulary of a language affected by culture?
6. What other examples of specialized vocabularies are found in various "communities of practice" in the United States and Canada?
7. How is sociolinguistics important to the analysis of communication on college campuses today?
8. What are some common uses of non-verbal communication in the college classroom?
9. What hand gestures and touches are used in public situations and what do we learn about status from that usage?'

10. How does language affect a person's perception? Be specific.

Class Activities

1. Invite someone to your class who speaks a language none of your students understand. After the class listens to five or ten minutes of speech in your guest's language, instruct them to write a brief report on what they understood. Ask your speaker to help you discuss such topics with your class as the significance of non-verbal as well as verbal communication for understanding and which phonemes and morphemes were recognized by your English-speaking class.
2. Instruct each student to interview a bilingual or multilingual individual. Ask them to focus on the benefits, as well as any negative experiences, their interviewee has had because of his or her language ability.
3. What would a sociolinguist say about the recent controversy in California over Ebonics? Have your students gather opposing positions on the topic and debate their merit.
4. Have students make systematic observations on nonverbal communication in various public places, such as basketball games, buses, restaurants, etc. Can the students observe nonverbal responses to overcrowding or flirting?
5. Have students watch a segment of a sit-com or a drama with the sound turned off. How much of the story line can they get from just watching the nonverbal cues?

Internet Exercises

1. The Summer Institute of Linguistics maintains an interesting web site filled with information about the different languages of the world"

   http://www.sil.org

   The Ethnologue database has information on thousands of different languages found in the world. Go to the section entitled "Language Name Index" and look up information on the Kikamba language. In what country is it spoken? How many speakers are there? What are several related languages? And what can you learn about the way of life of the speakers of this language?

2. In our very fast-paced world, it is not unlikely that during your career you will be asked to take a foreign assignment. In such an event, where would you turn to learn quickly at least some of the language of your host country? Select a language you would like to learn. By using any search engine, conduct a subject search on that language. What can you learn about the language from the Internet? Are there nearby language courses or schools of which you can take advantage? Are there self-instruction tutorials that you can take directly off the internet?

3. The Center for Applied Linguistics is an organization devoted to developing effective educational practices for linguistic and cultural minority students. By using any major search engine, go to the center' web site:

   http://www.cal.org/crede/

By browsing the different parts of the site, describe how the organization actually goes about applying linguistics to help in the educational process for linguistically and culturally different people.

Infotrac® Exercises

1. Students will need to access InfoTrac at **http://infotrac.thomsonlearning.com/index.html** to perform the following exercise. Conduct a subject search of the topic "nonverbal communication." Browse through the first 10 hits. What can you learn about different forms of nonverbal communication? What can you find about differences in nonverbal communication in other cultures? Write a one-page paper on cross-cultural differences in nonverbal communication.

Suggested Films

A Definition of Language. (IU), 30 min. - Shows the impact of culture on language, mainly through vocabulary. Good in illustrating the cultural bias of language, and why one language cannot be considered "better" than another.

Dialects. (IU), 30 min. - Dialect differences in English are documented.

Language and Communication. (part of Faces of Culture series), PSU, 30 min. - Discusses the structure of language and its relationship to thought, body language, and dialectic speech.

A World of Gestures. (UC), 28 min. - Explores gestures from cultures around the world in an entertaining fashion.

Chapter 7

Getting Food

Learning Objectives

After reading and studying Chapter 7, your students should be able to:

1. Identify five major food-procurement categories found among the world's populations.
2. Understand how people in other parts of the world use culture to adapt to their environment.
3. Discuss the impact of a culture's environment and technology on its food acquisition strategies.
4. Explain the concept of carrying capacity, the consequences of exceeding it, and the theory of optimal foraging.
5. Describe four generalizations about food collecting societies.
6. Recognize the different degrees of reliability of food collection strategies and the relative success of groups in environments with stable food supplies.
7. Compare Ju/'hoansi and Inuit food collection strategies.
8. Understand the positive and negative cultural changes brought about by the Neolithic Revolution.
9. Be able to define horticulture and explain the limitations and the advantages of slash and burn cultivation.
10. Describe the differences between transhumance and nomadic pastoralism.
11. Understand how the change from horticulture to agriculture allowed the development of peasantry.
12. Recognize the expenses, as well as the benefits, of industrialized agriculture, especially in terms of environmental impact.
13. Explain the scientific rationality which people have developed because of the systematic observations required by their successful adaptation to their environments.

Chapter Outline

I. GETTING FOOD
   A. The most critical of the cultural universals
   B. Food-getting strategies vary widely from one society to another
   C. Five major categories
      1. Food collection
      2. Horticulture
      3. Pastoralism
      4. Agriculture

5. Industrialization

II. HUMAN ADAPTATION
- A. Human populations adapt to cold environments both culturally and biologically
- B. Small-scale societies usually make very satisfactory adaptations to their environments
- C. Archaeologists now have evidence that certain prehistoric societies used their environmental resources wisely.

III. ENVIRONMENT AND TECHNOLOGY
- A. Food getting strategy developed by any culture depends on the culture's environment and technology
  1. Environment does not determine food-getting patterns but rather sets broad limits on possible alternatives
  2. Technology helps people adapt to their specific environment
  3. Variation in technological adaptation does not imply less ability to cope with the environment
- B. Carrying capacity
  1. The environmentally-determined upper limit on the productivity of any food-getting system and the size of the population it can support
- C. Consequence of exceeding the carrying capacity is damage to the environment
  1. Optimal foraging theory suggests that foragers maximize their caloric return for the time they spend in food-getting

IV. MAJOR FOOD-GETTING STRATEGIES
- A. Five forms of food procurement are not mutually exclusive
- B. Can expect to find considerable variation within each category
- C. Food collection
  1. Exploits wild plants and animals
  2. Only strategy available to humans until the Neolithic Revolution 10,000 years ago
  3. Very few societies still exist
  4. Originally found in a wide range of environments
  5. Generalizations
     - a. Have very low population densities
     - b. Are usually nomadic or semi-nomadic rather than sedentary
     - c. Basic social unit is the family or band
     - d. Contemporary food-collecting peoples occupy the remote and marginally useful areas of the earth
  6. In prehistoric times may have had greater social complexity
  7. Collecting wild vegetable matter provides the greatest amount of food
  8. Food collectors are capable of adapting to harsh environments with creativity and resourcefulness - "original affluent society"
  9. Examples of hunters and gatherers
     - a. The Ju/'hoansi of the Kalahari Region
       - 1) Inhabit area too dry to support either agriculture or the keeping of livestock
       - 2) Totally dependent on foraging for their food
       - 3) Food-gathering techniques are both productive and reliable - not starving
       - 4) Selectively consume edible plants - only about one-third are eaten
       - 5) Survival rate and life expectancy are high
       - 6) Number of hours spent procuring food is low
       - 7) Have experienced enormous changes in recent decades.

b. The Inuit of the Arctic
1) Like Ju/'hoansi, the Inuit inhabit one of the least hospitable regions of the world
2) Rely almost entirely on fishing and hunting of sea and land mammals
3) Adapt by organizing their economic and social lives around the availability of different types of game and the strategies required for hunting them.
4) Nunavut - new territory created April 1, 1999. Gives the Inuit a measure of control over their own lives and opportunity to preserve traditional culture

10. Important to acknowledge that foragers have always had contact with non-foraging peoples through trade, employment, and, in some cases, marriage
11. Contact has resulted in a wide variety of cultural patterns found among people generally classified as food collectors
12. Modern fishing industry illustrates the classic dilemma of foraging societies; that is, being so successful that you ultimately destroy your means of livelihood. This commercial fishing is particularly detrimental to poorer countries.

D. Food-producing Societies
1. Food production is the domestication of plants and animals
2. Approximately 10,000 years ago humans made transition from food collecting to food production
a. Humans gained a measure of control over their food supply
b. Shift is known as the Neolithic Revolution
1) Occurred in several different areas independently of one another
2) Fertile Crescent - 10,000 years ago
3) China - 8,000 years ago
4) Thailand - 8,800 years ago
5) sub-Saharan Africa - 5,000 years ago
6) Produced the first population explosion and allowed humans to be more sedentary
7) Allowed specialization and a more complex social structure
c. Changes resulting from food production
1) Increased food supply to support larger populations
2) Fertility rates are higher - children are more useful economically for farmers and herders
3) Populations become more sedentary
4) Stimulated a greater division of labor
5) Led to a decline in overall health as compared to foraging
6) Egalitarianism replaced by increasing social inequality, poverty, crime, environmental degradation

E. Horticulture
1. Simplest type of farming that uses basic hand tools (hoe or digging stick) rather than plows or other machinery driven by animals
2. Land is neither irrigated nor enriched by use of fertilizers
3. Insufficient surpluses to develop extensive market systems
4. Major technique is shifting cultivation (swidden cultivation or the slash and burn method)
5. Crops can be divided into three categories
a. Tree crops

   b. Seed crops
   c. Root crops
6. Many horticulturalists supplement cultivation with other food-getting strategies
7. Cannot support high densities of population that can be sustained by intensive agriculture
8. Reasonably efficient form of food production
9. Slash and burn system was criticized late 1990s by environmental groups and governments
   a. Destroys large tracts of both forests and grasslands
   b. Air pollution
   c. Soil erosion reduces long-term productivity of land
10. The Bemba of Zambia
   a. Shifting cultivation of fairly wide range of crops, seeds, and roots
   b. Supplement diet by some hunting, gathering, and fishing
   c. Power, status, and authority of chiefs based not on the accumulation of material wealth but rather on the amount of service they could extract from their subjects
   d. Common feature of diet is the alternation between scarcity and plenty
   e. Food and diet occupy a prominent place in Bemba culture

F. Pastoralism
1. First appeared in the Neolithic period
2. Involves the keeping of domesticated herd animals
3. Found in areas of the world that cannot support agriculture
4. Associated with geographic mobility
5. Two types of movement patterns
   a. Transhumance - men move livestock seasonally while women, children, and the other men remain in permanent settlements
   b. Nomadism - no permanent villages and the whole social unit moves the livestock
   c. Not a unified phenomenon - wide variety in ways animals are herded
   d. Take advantage of seasonal variations in pasturage in order to maximize the food supply of the herds
6. Pure pastoralists are either extremely rare or nonexistent -- combine keeping of livestock with some form of cultivation or maintain trade relations with agriculturalists
7. Livestock play vital economic role. Also may influence social relationships among people in pastoral societies
8. The Maasai of East Africa
   a. They are part of the East African "cattle complex," numbering 400,000.
   b. Traditional reputation as the best example of East African pastoralists.
   c. Maasai have been very successful in managing their environment by preventing agriculturalists from coming in and by controlled burning.
   d. Key to ecological adaptation was the open access to land.
   e. Today the government is forcing the Maasai onto permanent settlements because (a) they will be easier to control, (b) selling cattle will help the national economy, and (c) their herds will not compete with wildlife.
   f. Today open pastoralism is becoming increasingly more scarce.

G. Agriculture
1. Intensive cultivation
2. Relies on animal power and technology rather than human power alone
3. Characterized by the use of the plow, draft animals, fertilizers, irrigation, and other technological innovations
4. Greater use of technology enables the support of many times more people per unit of land
5. Requires a greater investment of capital and labor
6. Closely associated with both higher levels of productivity and more settled communities
7. A fully efficient system of food production, brought about by intensive agriculture, is a necessary, if not sufficient, condition for the rise of civilization
8. Enabled development of a more complex specialization of labor
9. Peasantry
a. Peasant farmers developed with intensification of agriculture and rise of civilization
b. Not isolated or self-sufficient societies
c. Tied to the larger unit (the city or state) politically, religiously, and economically
d. Usually make up a large percentage of the total population and provide most of dietary needs of city dwellers
e. Peasants have low social status, little political power, and scant material wealth
f. Urbanites extract labor and products in the form of taxation, rent, or tribute

H. Industrialized Food Getting
1. Major revolution in capacity for feeding the population occurred during seventeenth and eighteenth centuries with the coming of the Industrial Revolution
2. Industrialization relies on technological sources of energy rather than human or animal energy
3. Uses motorized equipment, chemicals to increase productivity
4. Commercialized - majority of food today is sold by food producers to non-producers for some form of currently
5. Requires complex systems of market exchange because of its highly specialized nature
6. Rise of agribusiness (large-scale agricultural enterprises accompanied by decline of family farms. Decrease in percentage of world's population engaged in food production
7. Costs of industrialization
a. Machinery and technology are expensive
b. Fuel costs are high
c. Expenses of processing, transporting, and marketing products
d. Environmental destruction

V. FOOD COLLECTING STRATEGIES AND SCIENCE
A. Foragers, pastoralists or horticulturalists require processing large amounts of information about the environment over long periods of time - not inefficient or irrational.
B. People's scientific understanding allows successful adaptation to the environment
C. Traditional scientific wisdom must be incorporated into development planning
D. Easter Island society is a good example of what can happen when natural resources are not managed effectively.

Key Terms

These are the anthropological terms introduced in Chapter 7. You may want to ask your students to write definitions of one or more of these terms during class to see how well they understood the reading. Even if you choose not to grade the assignment, the students will take it more seriously if you collect their answers.

agriculture
carrying capacity
food collecting
horticulture
hunting and gathering
industrialization
Neolithic Revolution
nomadism
optimal foraging theory
pastoralism
peasantry
shifting cultivation
slash and burn method
swidden cultivation
social functions of cattle
transhumance

Critical Thinking Questions

1. How important is the influence of shared knowledge and social organization on a society's ability to secure food?
2. If hunting and gathering requires the lowest expenditure of energy, then why are there not more hunters and gatherers in the world?
3. Is the carrying capacity of an environment as important for an agricultural society as it is for food collectors?
4. Could a society, such as the !Kung in the 1960s, be considered an affluent society because of the amount of leisure time they had? Why would it be impossible to consider the Inuit affluent?
5. What types of means of livelihood are associated with desert terrain? Tropical forests? Savannas?
6. What has happened to food collecting societies during the last thirty years?
7. Why did some populations switch over to horticulture from foraging?
8. Are there peasants in the United States today? Do peasants provide any of the food or drink consumed by the people of the United States?
9. In what countries do peasants provide most of the food for the urban populations?
10. Considering the environmental damage done by industrialized agriculture, is the argument valid that it is more productive than other forms of plant cultivation?

Class Activities

1. Assign a particular country, including industrialized nations as well as Third World countries, to each of your students. Ask the students to find out what percentage of the food in "their" country is produced by local farmers, produced by national industrialized agriculture, and imported.

2. Divide your class into groups and assign each a food common in the American diet. Ask them to investigate when humans began to consume the food, where it usually comes from and how it is produced, processed, and distributed.

3. Organize a debate on the relative affluence of food collecting societies versus that of industrialized nations. Have them focus on work load and leisure time.

4. People in different social classes and/ethnic groups within the United States often have different diets. Have students discuss in a one page paper how the diets of the following people would differ: a Mexican migrant worker in California; an IBM manager from New York City; an elementary school teacher from Burlington, Vermont; and a tobacco farmer from rural North Carolina.

Internet Exercises

1. As a way of learning more about foraging (hunting and gathering) societies, consult a web site entitled "Hunting and Gathering:"

   http://www.mc.maricopa.edu/academic/cult_sci/anthro/lost_tribes/asb222sg.html

   This well-illustrated and attractive site, sponsored by Mesa Community College, provides excellent information on many of the topics discussed in this chapter, including foraging societies, pastoralists, the beginnings of agriculture, and the growth of sedentary lifeways. What can you learn from this site that supplements the knowledge gained from this chapter?

2. An excellent source of information on how the peoples of the world are feeding themselves is the web site provided by the Food and Agriculture Organization (FAO), a branch of the United Nations. Go to the FAO home page:

   http://www.fao.org

   Click on "FactFile." What can you learn from this site about world hunger and malnutrition? What is meant by the "feminization of agriculture" and where does it most frequently occur? How do developing countries and developed countries differ in terms of the mechanization of agriculture?

Infotrac® Exercises

1. Students will need to access InfoTrac at **http://infotrac.thomsonlearning.com/index.html** to answer the following questions. Once logged on, type "Swidden" in the Search field. Next click on "Periodicals." Once the results appear, use the Limit Search function to find the article "Swidden, Sawah, and In-Between: Agricultural Transformation in Borneo." Read the selection and answer the following.

   a. What are some of the environmental concerns for swidden horticulture?

   b. How are outside forces pressuring traditional populations?

2. In the Search field, type in "Pastoralism." Click on "Periodicals." Find the article "On Pastoralism and Inequality."

a. Describe the differences between wealth distinctions and stratification.

b. How is pastoral leadership different from the leadership found in industrial societies like the U.S.?

Suggested Films

Bakhtiari Migration: The Sheep Must Live. (PSU), 51 min. - Half a million Bakhtiari push millions of livestock across the Zagros mountains of Iran twice a year during migration. This film documents the movement with all its hardships for humans and beasts.

Nomads of the Rainforest. (UC), 59 min. video - Visually pleasing overview of the Waorani, a tropical forest people of eastern Ecuador. Much of the video is monkey-hunting scenes, using blowguns with poisoned darts. Shows preparation of curare and manufacture of a blowgun. Also deals with family life and relations between men and women and young and old in this highly egalitarian society. (Originally shown on NOVA)

Faces of Culture: Patterns of Subsistence: Hunter-Gatherers and Pastoralists. (PSU), 30 min. - Describes the earliest forms of subsistence, how people adapted to their environments, and the relationship of subsistence to cultural patterns.

Millennium: Tribal Wisdom and the Modern World: An Ecology of Mind. (PSU), 60 min. - Series hosted by David Maybury-Lewis in 1992. Studies ecological perspectives of three cultures: the Gabra of Kenya who live in a harsh environment, the Makuna of Colombia whose rituals and myths reveal sophisticated ecological awareness, and a modern gardener who resists the West's passion to control nature.

Chapter 8

Economics

Learning Objectives

After reading and studying Chapter 8, your students should be able to:

1. Explain the focus of cross-cultural studies of economics.
2. Understand questions raised by economic anthropologists about the universal nature of economic behavior.
3. Recognize there are alternative ways of allocating natural resources other than the principle of private property.
4. Describe the advantages of community control of resources for food collectors, pastoralists, and horticulturalists.
5. Explain the significance of the concepts of production, distribution, and consumption for anthropological economics.
6. Recognize the importance of the study of division of labor, especially in non-industrialized societies.
7. Explain the universal use of gender and age for allocation of economic tasks.
8. Distinguish among three types of reciprocity.
9. Understand the difference between redistribution and market economy.
10. Explain the differences between the economic roles of big men and chiefs.
11. Present a clear description of the variety of markets that exist and their distinct functions.
12. Understand both the positive and the negative effects of globalization on world economies.

Chapter Outline

I. ECONOMICS
    A. All societies
        1. Have a limited amount of vital resources
        2. Must develop systems of production, distribution, and consumption
II. ECONOMICS AND ECONOMIC ANTHROPOLOGY
    A. Economics focuses on production, distribution, and consumption as observed in the industrialized world
    B. Economic anthropology studies the three areas comparatively in all societies of the world, both industrialized and nonindustrialized
    C. Much of formal economic theory based on assumptions derived from observing Western, industrialized societies

D. Long-standing debate is how applicable economic theories are to the understanding of small-scale, nonindustrialized societies
   1. Western economists assume that individuals as well as corporations are motivated by desire to maximize material well-being
   2. Other societies' economic principles may be based on reciprocity or redistribution which emphasize cooperation and generosity
   3. Even in the United States there is an increase in the extent to which people fail to maximize their economic well-being

E. Cross-cultural Examination of Economic Systems
   1. Possible to examine economic systems cross-culturally along key dimensions
      a. Regulation of resources
      b. Production
      c. Exchange

III. THE ALLOCATION OF NATURAL RESOURCES

A. Every society has developed a set of rules governing allocation and use of resources

B. The degree to which humans are territorial varies widely throughout the world

C. Notion of personal property is absent in most societies that base livelihood on food collecting, pastoralism, or horticulture

D. Food Collectors
   1. Land is not owned
   2. Follow migratory patterns of animals
   3. Claiming and defending territory requires time, energy, and technology that foragers choose not to expend
   4. Territoriality can lead to conflict
   5. Amount of communal control of land varies cross-culturally
   6. Will have open or flexible boundaries if animals are mobile and supplies are unpredictable
   7. More likely to live in permanent settlements and maintain greater control over land in areas where supplies are plentiful and predictable

E. Pastoralists
   1. Require extensive territory and access to water and pasturage for livestock
   2. Must work out arrangements among themselves and with nonpastoralists to gain access to pasturage
   3. Corporate (nonindividual) control of pastures is general rule
   4. Allocation of land and resources depends on ecological variables, types of animals herded, size of population relative to land, relationship of pastoralists to larger society

F. Horticulturalists
   1. Tend to live on land that is communally controlled, usually by an extended kinship group
   2. Small family units retain rights as long as they work the land and are in good standing with larger family
   3. No advantage to owning land that can't be used permanently

G. Intensive Agriculturalists
   1. Resources are allocated according to the principle of private individual ownership
   2. Western concept of individual property rights has affected research with non-Western peoples
   3. Most westerners believe that commonly held property will be destroyed or degraded because people will lack an individual incentive to naintain it (The

tragedy of the commons). However, there are examples from around the world where this is not the case.

IV. PRODUCTION

A. The process of obtaining goods from the natural environment and transforming them into usable objects

B. Vast range of systems of production

C. Why any society produces certain items is determined by economic factors and cultural values

1. Accessibility of certain resources
2. Technology available for processing resources
3. Abundance of energy supplies

D. Most societies fail to exploit all of the resources at their disposal

E. Units of Production

1. All societies have some type of productive unit comprising people with specific tasks to perform
2. Production in the Household
    a. In most nonindustrialized societies, basic unit of production is the household
    b. Most, if not all, of the goods and services consumed are produced by members of the household (either nuclear or extended)
    c. Structural differences between business firm and household
        1) Firm is primarily just a unit of production; household performs a number of overlapping functions
        2) Household is far more self-sufficient
        3) Business firm concentrates exclusively on its economic function and is a more productive unit than the household
        4) Family unit less likely to use highly productive, progressive, or innovative methods than business firm
        5) During times of economic downturn family businesses often increase

F. Division of Labor

1. Every society distinguishes to some degree between work appropriate for men and women (gender) and adults and children (age)
2. Gender specialization
    a. Theories to explain common, if not universal, division of labor by gender
        1) Men's greater body mass and strength makes them better equipped for hunting, warfare, and land clearing
        2) Women's tasks compatible with child care
        3) Men tend to be more expendable so they engage in dangerous activities
    b. Men and women are often assigned roles because of social, political, and historical forces operating in individual societies
3. Age Specialization
    a. Because of lack of knowledge and physical strength, children are often excluded from certain tasks
        1) In a growing number of countries children under 14 are working full time in the global economy
        2) Negative effects of child labor include working long hours under deplorable condition for low wages
    b. Elderly, because of waning physical strength, often prohibited from certain tasks or are expected to engage in different activities from earlier years

4. Labor Specialization
    a. Another term for division of labor and an important descriptive characteristic of any society
    b. Continuum
        1) Extremes are little specialization beyond gender and age (subsistence societies) to industrialized specialization
    c. Major consequence of Neolithic Revolution has been the increasing amount of labor specialization in the world
    d. More complex division of labor provided a basis for social solidarity
    e. Durkheim - organic and mechanical solidarity

V. DISTRIBUTION OF GOODS AND SERVICES
- A. Systems of exchange are essential for every economy
- B. Allow people to dispose of surpluses
- C. Maximize diversity of goods and services consumed
- D. Goods and services are allocated in all societies according to three different modes of distribution
    1. Reciprocity
    2. Redistribution
    3. Market exchange
- E. Even though more than one mode of distribution can operate in any given society at a time, usually only one mode predominates
- F. Reciprocity
    1. Exchange of goods and services of roughly equal value between two parties without the use of money
    2. Generalized reciprocity
        a. An exchange system based primarily on generalized reciprocity is common among food collectors and contributes to their very survival
        b. Generosity is the highest ideal
        c. Hoarding and stinginess are seen as antisocial
        d. Usually between family members or close friends
        e. Involves the highest level of moral obligation
        f. No expectation of immediate return
        g. Common among foragers
        h. Best illustrated by the type of giving that takes place between parents and children in U.S. society
        i. Reciprocal gift giving in U.S. society takes a number of different forms
        j. Consciously or unconsciously give gifts with the expectation of getting something in return
    3. Balanced Reciprocity
        a. An exchange system involving the expectation that goods and services of equivalent value will be returned within a specified period of time
        b. Involves more formal relationships, greater social distance, and strong obligation to repay the original gift
        c. Major economic motivation is to exchange surplus goods and services for those in short supply
        d. Semang - silent trade
        e. Kula Ring - Trobriand Island ritualized exchange of shell bracelets and shell necklaces that pass (in opposite directions) between a ring of islands
    4. Negative Reciprocity

a. A form of exchange between equals in which the parties attempt to take advantage of each other
b. Based on the principle of trying to get something for nothing
c. Involving the most impersonal (possibly hostile) social relations
d. Sense of altruism and social obligation is at its lowest
e. Incompatible with close, harmonious relations
f. Most often practiced against strangers and enemies

5. Redistribution
    a. Goods are given to a central authority and then given back to people in a new pattern
    b. Involves two stages: an inward flow of good sand services to a social center, followed by an outward dispersal of these goods and services back to society
    b. Most common in societies that have political hierarchies
    c. Can take a number of different forms
        1) Tribute
            a) Serves social functions by dispensing goods within a society and affirming political power of the chief and value of solidarity among the people
            b) Equitable distribution is rarely found in most situations where tribute is given
        2) Big Men/Feast Givers
            a) Self made leaders who are able to convince their relatives and neighbors to contribute surplus goods for the sake of community wide feasting
            b) Economic entrepreneurs
            c) Found widely throughout Melanesia and New Guinea
            d) Work hard to produce surpluses and encourage followers to do the same, all for the sake of giving it away
            e) Growing evidence that there are also big women in Melanesia
        3) Bridewealth
            a) Involves the transfer of valuable commodities from the groom's lineage to the bride's lineage as a precondition for marriage
            b) Mechanism for maintaining the roughly equitable distribution of goods within a society
        4) Potlatch
            a) Chiefs or prominent men announce rights, privileges, and high social status within their communities.
            b) Claims accompanied by elaborate feasting and gift giving.
            c) Host would either give away or destroy all of his personal possessions
            d) Serves as a mechanism for allocating social status
            e) Important mechanism for the dispersal of material goods
            f) Also serves many socio-political functions
        5) Prestige Economies
            a) The institutions of the Kula, potlatch, and Big Men/Women are not only mechanisms of distribution, but also ways of allocating prestige and social status

6) Market Exchange
   a) Goods and services are bough and sold, often through the use of a standardized currency
   b) Less personal than exchanges based on reciprocity or redistribution
   c) Exchanges predominantly economic in nature
   d) People more interested in maximizing profits than in maintaining a long-term relationship
   e) Most likely found in sedentary societies that produce appreciable surpluses and have a complex division of labor
   f) Increase in division of labor brings proliferation of specialized commodities and increased dependency on market exchange

6. Standardized currency
   a. Defined as a generally accepted medium of exchange that also measures the value of a particular item
   b. Highly flexible medium of exchange
   c. Serves as a form of deferred payment
   d. Most often found in societies with high levels of economic development
   e. Market economies do not always involve money - barter,
   f. Relative value (or price) of any good or service determined by market principle of supply and demand
7. Variety of Markets
   a. Extent to which markets are responsible for distribution of goods and services varies widely
   b. Every economy is a blend of both government control and free markets
   c. U.S. market - there is virtually nothing that cannot be bought or sold in the market
   d. Small-scale economies - little labor specialization, small surpluses, and limited range of goods and services exchanged
   e. All societies have both formal and informal(unregulated) economies
   f. Societies with well-developed market economies struggle with question of how much to rely on forces or the market or on government to regulate the economy
   g. Globalization of World Markets
      1) The spread of free market economies to all parts of the world
      2) Basic assumption is that economies will be healthier and growth will occur more rapidly if market forces are allowed to rule
      3) Has encouraged the participation of many new players in the markets
      4) Various types of jobs are moving all over the world
   h. Globalization has increased, not reduced, poverty

Key Terms

These are the anthropological terms introduced in Chapter 8. You may want to ask your students to write definitions of one or more of these terms during class to see how well they understood the reading. Even if you choose not to grade the assignment, the students will take it more seriously if you collect their answers.

allocation of resources
balanced reciprocity
barter
big men/women
bridewealth
chiefly redistribution
division of labor
economic anthropology
economics
generalized reciprocity
globalization
kula ring
labor specialization
market exchange
mechanical solidarity
negative reciprocity
organic solidarity
particularism
potlatch
prestige economies
production
property rights
reciprocity
redistribution
silent trade
standardized currency
tribute
universalism

Critical Thinking Questions

1. How does this chapter on economics force you to integrate the information you learned in the last chapter on food-getting?
2. What is the relationship between the unpredictability of resources and the level of sharing in a society?
3. In the United States, when a home is mortgaged or a car purchased with a bank loan, is it really private property?
4. While Ferraro says that a business firm is a more productive unit than a household, what are some of the advantages of the household as a productive unit?
5. Is a gender-based division of labor necessary in an industrialized society?
6. Why do industrialized societies still use age to determine division of labor?
7. Are there similarities in the ways in which a "big man" and a CEO or other head of an American corporation operate?
8. What do the institutions of the Kula, the Potlatch, and Big Men/women have in common?
9. What are some of the negative consequences of the globalization of world economies?

Class Activities

1. Have each student write as complete a list as he or she can of holiday gifts received from a relative or a friend. Ask them to include the following:
   - age at the time they received the gift
   - if they gave a gift in return
   - when they gave a gift in return (if applicable)
   - what they gave (if applicable).

   Use this exercise as a basis for a discussion of the significance of reciprocity within the United States' market economy.

2. Ferraro remarks that markets serve social as well as economic functions in other societies. What are some of the social functions of marketing in our society? Two examples that come to mind are the significance of shopping centers for teenagers and that of flea markets for both buyers and sellers. Use this discussion to reinforce the idea of the integration of economy with other aspects of culture.

3. Find the current figures on the expense of raising a child today in the United States. Use that information to discuss the economic value of a child in an industrialized versus a non-industrialized country.
4. Have students research and discuss some of the problems that countries from the former Soviet Union are experiencing in their change-over from state-controlled economies to market economies.

Internet Exercises

1. The nature of markets in the world is changing very rapidly. Just several decades ago, it was expected that the buyer and the seller of most goods and services would have some face-to-face contact. Today, however, it is possible to buy things over the phone, through mail-order catalogues, and via fax. Moreover, within the last several years it has become possible to order a wide range of goods and services almost instantaneously over the Internet. To really appreciate how widely the Internet is now used for marketing goods and services, use any major search engine to identify how you can find and order the following items:
   a. A book of photographs by William Wegman
   b. Tickets to your favorite professional sports team
   c. A Doberman pinscher puppy
   d. A Roger Maris baseball card
   e. A glass sculpture by Dante Marioni

   Alternative list of items
   a. A book of photographs by Gordon Parks
   b. Tickets to your favorite musical event
   c. A piece of Haitian art
   d. A Reggie Jackson baseball card
   e. A print by Romaire Bearden

Infotrac® Exercises

1. Students will need to access InfoTrac at **http://infotrac.thomsonlearning.com/index.html** to perform the following exercise. In the Search field, type in "Mali." Click on "Periodicals." Locate the article "Garden Money Buys Grain: Food Procurement Patterns in a Malian Village."

   a. Describe the process of cash cropping practiced by the Mali.

   b. What role do women have in the subsistence of this society?

Suggested Films

Faces of Culture: The Aymara: A Case Study in Social Stratification. (PSU), 30 minutes, 1983. - Documents the inequities of a sharp class division between the Spanish-speaking mestizos and the subordinate Aymara Indians of the northern Bolivian Andes.

The Kawelka. (PSU), 52 min. video - In Papua New Guinea, status is earned by giving things away rather than acquiring them. In the moka ceremonies, people, and sometimes whole tribes, give gifts to other tribes. The larger the gift, the greater the victory over the recipient.

Kula: Argonauts of the Western Pacific. (UC), 19 min. - Trobriand men undertake a kula voyage. Produced in Japan, but narration is in English.

Chapter 9

Marriage and the Family

Learning Objectives

After reading and studying Chapter 9, your students should be able to:

1. Give a cross-culturally valid definition of family.
2. Give a cross-culturally valid definition of marriage.
3. Explain three functions of marriage.
4. Define incest and summarize four theories explaining why the incest taboo is universal.
5. Explain and give examples of endogamy and exogamy.
6. Describe how unilineal descent systems make cousin marriages possible and often preferable.
7. Understand the circumstances that foster the practice of polygyny.
8. Explain the circumstances in which polyandry occurs and the ways in which it is adaptive.
9. Understand the practice of bridewealth and why it is important to recognize its social, as well as economic, aspects.
10. Understand the factors leading to the high divorce rate in the United States
11. Understand the variety of residence patterns after marriage.
12. Explain under what circumstances nuclear families are found and why they are not more common in the United States.
13. Explain under what circumstances extended families are found and in which economies they are most beneficial.
14. Describe modern-day family structure and its functions.

Chapter Outline

I. MARRIAGE AND THE FAMILY: SOME DEFINITIONS
    A. In all known societies, people recognize a certain number of relatives who make up the basic social group called the family
    B. Family is a social unit characterized by
        1. Economic cooperation
        2. Management of reproduction and child rearing
        3. Common residence
        4. Includes both male and female adults who maintain a socially approved sexual relationship

5. Family members recognize certain rights and obligations toward one other
6. Distinct from the institution of marriage
    a. A series of customs formalizing the relationship between male and female adults within the family
    b. A socially approved union that regulates the sexual and economic rights and obligations between two people
    c. Involves explicit contract or understanding entered into with the assumption that it will be a permanent union

C. Sexual Union
1. Marriage is a socially legitimate sexual union
2. In some societies, there may be specified periods during which sexual relations with one's spouse may be taboo

D. Permanence
1. Permanence of marriage varies widely
2. In no societies do all marriages last until death

E. Common Residence
1. Definitional problems with common residence
2. 94 of 240 African Societies in Murdock's *Ethnographic Atlas (*1967) are characterized by wives and their children living in separate houses from the husband.

II. MARRIAGE AND THE FAMILY: FUNCTIONS

A. Creates fairly stable relationships between men and women that regulate sexual mating and reproduction.
B. Provides a mechanism for regulating sexual division of labor
C. Creates a set of family relationships that can provide for material, educational, and emotional needs of children for a long period of time

III. MATE SELECTION: WHO IS OUT OF BOUNDS?

A. Every society has established rules regulating mating (sexual intercourse)
B. Incest Taboo - Most common form of prohibition against mating with certain types of kin defined by the society as inappropriate sexual partners
1. Most universal form of incest taboo involves mating between members of the immediate (nuclear) family
    a. Invariably extends beyond the scope of the immediate or nuclear family
2. Explanations for the incest taboo
    a. Natural Aversion Theory (early twentieth century)
        1) There is a natural aversion to sexual intercourse among those who have grown up together
        2) Theory does not explain why we even need a taboo if people already have a natural aversion to incest
    b. Inbreeding Theory (late nineteenth century)
        1) Focuses on potential harmful effects of inbreeding on the family
        2) Mating between close kin tends to produce a higher incidence of genetic defects
        3) Prehistoric populations would not have understood a genetic argument
        4) Taboo may simply have been adaptively advantageous
    c. Family Disruption Theory - Malinowski
        1) Mating between a mother and son, father and daughter, or brother and sister would disrupt family functioning as a unit of economic cooperation and socialization
        2) Would create role ambiguity

d. Theory of Expanding Social Alliances
   1) Marrying out of the immediate family creates a wider network of interfamily alliances
   2) Creates a larger gene pool

IV. MATE SELECTION: WHOM SHOULD YOU MARRY?

A. People in all societies are faced with rules either restricting one's choice of marriage partners or strongly encouraging the selection of other people as highly desirable mates
   1. Rules of exogamy - marrying outside of a certain group
   2. Rules of endogamy - marrying within a certain group

B. Rules of Exogamy
   1. Requires marrying outside of a certain group of kin
   2. Rules of exogamy based on kinship do not appear to be based on genealogical proximity

C. Rules of Endogamy
   1. Requires mate selection from within a certain group
   2. General social segregation by class results in a high level of endogamy in many complex Western societies
   3. Rules of exogamy and rules of endogamy are not opposites or mutually exclusive.
   4. Can coexist in the same society
   5. Possible to have an endogamous ethnic group while at the same time having an exogamous lineage

D. Arranged Marriages
   1. In many societies, the interests of the families are so strong that marriages are arranged
   2. Marriage is a union of two kin groups rather than two individuals
   3. Found in societies with elaborate social hierarchies
   4. Contemporary matchmakers fit in with the pressures of the modern business world, and many singles today use internet matchmaking websites

E. Preferential Cousin Marriage
   1. Occurs in societies that specify a preference for choosing certain categories of relatives as marriage partners
   2. Is practiced in one form or another in most of the major regions of the world
   3. Cross cousins - children of siblings of the opposite sex
   4. Parallel cousins - children of siblings of the same sex
   5. Most common form is between cross cousins because it functions to strengthen and maintain ties between kin groups established by previous marriages
   6. Parallel cousin marriage is less common. Can prevent the fragmentation of family property

F. The Levirate and Sororate
   1. Levirate - the custom whereby a widow is expected to marry the brother (or some close male relative) of her dead husband
   2. Serves as a form of social security for widow and children and preserves the rights of the husband's family to her sexuality and future children
   3. Closely associated with placing high value on male heirs
   4. Sororate - practice of a widower's marrying the sister (or some close female relative) of his deceased wife

V. NUMBER OF SPOUSES

A. Cultural anthropologists have identified three major types of marriage based on the number of spouses permitted
   1. Monogamy - marriage of one man to one woman at a time

2. Polygyny - marriage of a man to two or more women at a time
3. Polyandry - marriage of a woman to two or more men at a time

B. Monogamy
1. Allows only one spouse at a time
2. Extramarital affairs or serial monogamy may be allowed
3. Serial monogamy common in the United States, Canada, and much of western Europe

C. Polygyny
1. Found in 70 per cent of the world's cultures
2. Male sex drive as an explanation is problematic
a. No evidence that male sex drive is stronger than female sex drive
b. Less complicated to gain sexual access through extramarital liaisons than choosing multiple wives
c. Most men in polygynous societies have neither the inclination, family power base, nor social skills needed to achieve the high status of being a polygynist
3. Economic Status of Women in Polygynous Societies
a. Critical factor influencing incidence of polygyny is extent to which women are seen as economic assets of liabilities
1) Common where women are assets
2) Unusual where women are liabilities
4. Sex Ratio in Polygynous Societies - excess women needed for a polygynous marriage created by postponing the age at which men can marry
5. Advantages of Polygyny
a. Symbol of prestige for older men and their wives and children
b. Multiple wives may be economic and political assets
c. Newer research does not support the idea that women favor polygyny over monogamy
6. Competition Among Wives
a. Problem in polygyny is jealousy among the wives
b. Ways to minimize friction
1) Sororal polygyny - a man marries two or more sisters
2) Separate living quarters
3) Clearly outlined rights and obligations among wives
4) Establishing a hierarchy among the wives
c. Some ethnographic reports reveal considerable harmony and cooperation among wives

D. Polyandry
1. Involves the marriage of a woman to two or more men at a time
2. Found in less than one per cent of societies in the world - Tibet, Nepal, and India
3. Can be fraternal (where the husbands are brothers) or nonfraternal
4. May be due to a shortage of females
5. Junior husbands augment the manpower of the household
6. Alleviates the problem of land shortage in a family

VI. ECONOMIC CONSIDERATIONS OF MARRIAGE

A. Marriage is a binding contract between individuals or their families that often includes the transfer of some type of economic consideration

B. Four categories
   1. Bridewealth
   2. Bride service
   3. Dowry
   4. Reciprocal exchange

C. Bridewealth
   1. Compensation given upon marriage by the family of the groom to the family of the bride
   2. Approximately 46 per cent of all societies give bridewealth payment as a normal part of the marriage process
   3. Paid in a wide variety of currencies, but the commodity used for payment is highly valued in the society
   4. Performs functions for the well-being of the society
      a. Security of insurance for the good treatment of the wife
      b. Mechanism to stabilize marriage by reducing the possibility of divorce
      c. Form of compensation to bride's lineage for loss of her economic potential and her childbearing capacity
      d. Symbol of the union between two large groups of kin
      e. Mechanism to legitimize traditional marriage
      f. Transfer of rights over children
   5. Monetization of bridewealth - use of money as the medium of exchange
      a. Reported since mid-1980s
      b. Transition from subsistence-based economies to cash-based economies has had a profound effect on traditional bridewealth practices and on the institution of marriage
      c. Close interdependence of family members (and their sanctioning of the marriage) becomes less important
      d. Bridewealth remains popular today, even among the younger adults.

D. Bride Service
   1. Men give their labor to the bride's family instead of material goods in exchange for wives
   2. Found in approximately 14 per cent of world societies
   3. May last from several weeks to several years

E. Dowry
   1. Involves a transfer of goods or money from the bride's family to the groom or to the groom's family
   2. Not widely practiced - confined to Eurasia
   3. May be used to marry daughter into higher status family

F. Woman Exchange
   1. Two men exchange sisters or daughters as wives for themselves, their sons, or their brothers
   2. Limited to small number of societies in Africa and the Pacific
   3. The number of wives a man can obtain is limited to the number of sisters and daughters at his disposal

G. Reciprocal Exchange
   1. Most prominent in the Pacific region and among traditional Native Americans
   2. Involves the roughly equal exchange between families of both the bride and the groom

VII. DIVORCE
  A. All cultures have ways of dealing with divorce as well as marriage
  B. Divoce is less likely in societies with strong kin groups and systems of bridewealth
  C. Divorce in the U.S. has increased dramatically in last half century for many reasons:
    1. Industrialization and urbanization have undermined traditional family functions
    2. Rise of individualism has led people to be less willing to make sacrifices for family
    3. Romantic love makes marriage vulnerable when sexual passion subsides
    4. Much less of a stigma attached to divorce today
    5. Divorce has become relatively easy to obtain

VIII. RESIDENCE PATTERNS: WHERE DO WIVES AND HUSBANDS LIVE?
  A. Societies set guidelines regarding where couples will live when they marry
  B. Patrilocal residence
    1. Married couple lives with or near husband's father
    2. 69 percent of societies
  C. Matrilocal residence
    1. Married couple lives with or near relatives of the wife
    2. 13 percent of societies
  D. Avunculocal residence
    1. Married couple lives with or near the husband's mother's brother
    2. 4 percent of societies
  E. Ambilocal (bilocal) residence
    1. Married couple has a choice of living with either relatives of wife or relatives of husband
    2. 9 percent of societies
  F. Neolocal residence
    1. Married couple forms an independent place of residence away from the relatives of either spouse
    2. 5 percent of societies

IX. FAMILY STRUCTURE
  A. Two fundamentally different types of family
    1. Nuclear family - based on marital ties
    2. Extended family - larger social unit based on blood ties among three or more generations of kin
  B. Nuclear Family
    1. Consists of husband and wife and their children
    2. A two-generation family formed around the conjugal or marital union
    Most likely found in societies with greatest amount of geographic mobility
    3. Declining in the United States
      a. Women are delaying marrying and having children
      b. Increased cost of maintaining a middle-class household has caused couples to opt for remaining childless
      c. Increasing divorce rate has contributed to increase in nonnuclear families in recent decades
  C. The Extended Family
    1. Blood ties more important than ties of marriage
    2. Consists of two or more families that are linked by blood ties
    3. Based on parent-child linkages
    4. Obligations to lineage may be more important than relationship to spouse

5. Rough correlation exists between extended family systems and an agricultural way of life
    a. Provide large numbers of workers
    b. Prevent subdivision of land
    c. Exist where there is a lack of man or woman power to simultaneously carry out subsistence and domestic tasks

D. Modern-Day Family Structure
    1. Progressive nuclearization of the family in the face of modernization
    2. Extended family ties may be preserved
    3. No longer a "typical" family in the United States

Key Terms

These are the anthropological terms introduced in Chapter 9. You may want to ask your students to write definitions of one or more of these terms during class to see how well they understood the reading. Even if you choose not to grade the assignment, the students will take it more seriously if you collect their answers.

ambilocal (bilocal) residence
arranged marriage
avunculocal residence
bridewealth
bride service
cross cousins
divorce
dowry
endogamy
exogamy
extended family
incest taboo
kibbutz
levirate
matrilocal residence
monogamy
neolocal residence
nuclear family
parallel cousins
patrilocal residence
polyandry
polygyny
post partum sex taboo
preferential cousin marriage
reciprocal exchange
role ambiguity
serial monogamy
sororate

Critical Thinking Questions

1. How important is gender definition in determining what marriages and families are like in any society?
2. Which is more important in marriages across cultures, sexual activity or economic obligations?
3. What are the differences between bridewealth, bride price, and dowry?
4. How has the study of the genetics of small groups influenced our understanding of the effects of cross-cousin marriages?
5. What contributes to the high divorce rate in the U.S.?
6. How could an arranged marriage benefit a bride and groom?
7. Based on what you know about U.S. culture, why are marriages based so heavily on romantic love?

8. When is polygyny advantageous to women?

9. Does the term "bridewealth" stress the economic implications of the marriage exchange over more important social implications?

10. How wouldmarriage based on sister exchange be viewed from the female perspective? Is the social structure the same as seen from the male point of view?

Class Activities

1. Ask your students to write a paper comparing the importance of the extended family for their parents and for themselves. Has the extended family gained or lost importance between these two generations? What factors seem to be involved in families where extended kin seem more intimate? Are they social, economic, or political?

2. Have members of the class interview a foreign exchange student on the topic of what it takes to get married in his/her culture.

3. Have students discuss the topic of mate selection in the United States. Are people really free to choose anyone they like? What are the constraints that limit our choice?

Internet Exercises

1. Starting with any search engine, conduct a subject search for the name Brian Schwimmer, an anthropologist who has developed an interactive tutorial entitled "Kinship and Social Organization." Click on the section of the tutorial titled "Marriage Systems" and answer the following questions:

   a. What is the difference between exogamy and endogamy?

   b. In reference to marriage, what are the three ranges of social distance mentioned in this tutorial?

   c. How many ranges of social distance are found in Yanomamo society? What are they?

   d. What is the difference between cross cousin and parallel cousins?

   e. What is meant by "avunculocal residence?"

2. As was discussed in this chapter, people in the Western world, although not generally favoring arranged marriages, often get some help in finding Mr. or Ms. Right. Using any search engine, conduct a subject search for "matchmaker" and answer the following questions:

   a. Roughly how many different web sites did you find that offer matchmaking services for single people?

   b. How many of these sites specialize in finding a specific type of partner, such as Christians, Russians, or vegetarians?

   c. Select any one site and describe the services provided and the procedures one follows to find the perfect "soul mate

3. Wedding customs vary all over the world. Either enter "wedding wire" in any search engine or go to the link below to learn about customs (both historical and contemporary) in cultures other than the United States.

http://www.jmts.com/wedding/customs.htm

You can link to the home page for Wedding Wire from this page. Write a two page paper comparing wedding customs cross-culturally.

Infotrac® Exercises

1. Students will need to access InfoTrac at **http://infotrac.thomsonlearning.com/index.html** to answer the following questions. Type in "Cross-Cousin Marriage" in the Search field. Click on "Periodicals." Find the article "Netting in Nepal: Social Change, the Life Course, and Bride Service in Sangila."

   a. How are cross-cousin marriages and bride service connected in Nepal?

   b. Are there any connections between economics and marriage patterns in the United States that can compare with those in Nepal?

2. Type "Coresidence" in the Search field. Next, click on "Periodicals." Once the results appear, lcoate the article "Family Values and Coresidence with Married Children in Urban China." Read the selection and answer the following:

   a. What are the benefits obtained by parents and their children in this living situation?

   b. How does the living arrangement described in the article compare with most of those in the United States?

Suggested Films

Faces of Culture: The Yucatec Maya: A Case Study in Marriage and the Family. (PSU) #10, 30minutes. - Follows the life-style of an extended Mayan agricultural family.

Millennium: Tribal Wisdom and the Modern World: Strange Relations. (PSU), 60 min. - Hosted by David Maybury-Lewis in 1992, this film studies marriage in three cultures: Nepalese who practice polyandry, the Wodaabe of Niger who have arranged marriages but also marry for love, and a Canadian couple.

A Wife among Wives. (UC), 70 min. - Turkana (northern Kenya) women recount their ideas about marriage and polygyny, showing two sides of this custom.

Chapter 10

Kinship and Descent

Learning Objectives

After reading and studying Chapter 10, your students should be able to:

1. Explain how the complexity of human social organization differs from that of any other species.
2. Contrast the importance of kinship as a factor in social structure of small-scale societies with its importance in industrialized societies.
3. Give a clear definition of kinship.
4. Recognize the importance of cultural rules for kinship classification that may not account for biological factors.
5. Diagram their own or another's kinship systems.
6. Describe how sex and age are important in determining kinship relationships.
7. Explain the structure of both patrilineal and matrilineal descent systems.
8. Understand the organizational hierarchy of moieties, phratries, clans, and lineages.
9. Describe the three types of cognatic descent and explain what is a bilateral system's kindred.
10. Explain the six basic systems of classification of kin.

Chapter Outline

Human social organization is more complex than that of the rest of the animal world. Human social groups are formed on the basis of:

Occupation
Kinship
Social class
Sex
Age
Ethnic affiliation
Education
Religion

I. KINSHIP DEFINED
   A. Kinship refers to the relationships - found in all societies - that are based on blood or marriage

B. Every society defines the nature of kinship interaction by determining which kin are more socially important than others, terms to classify kin types, and expected forms of behavior between them
C. Fictive kinship - people who are not related by either blood or marriage
D. Some societies define kinship in predominantly biological terms
E. Some societies like the Bari believe in "partible paternity," the notion that a child can have more than one biological father.

II. CULTURAL RULES REGARDING KINSHIP
A. All kinship systems are founded on biological connections
1. Each society classifies its kin according to a set of cultural rules that may or may not account for biological factors
2. The ways in which societies sort and categorize kinship relationships is as much a matter of culture as it is a matter of biology

III. FUNCTIONS OF KINSHIP SYSTEMS
A. Vertical function - provides social continuity by binding together a number of successive generations
B. Horizontal function - tend to solidify or tie together a society across a single generation through the process of marriage

IV. USING KINSHIP DIAGRAMS
A. Cultural definitions of kinship vary widely
B. EGO - the person from whose point of view the relationships are traced
C. Standard symbols used to make kinship charts
1. Female
2. Male
3. Non-specific gender
4. Married to
5. Divorced from
6. Connect parents and children
7. Connect siblings
8. Deceased
9. Female ego
10. Male ego

V. PRINCIPLES OF KINSHIP CLASSIFICATION
A. All kinship systems group relatives into certain categories
B. Refer to relatives by the same term
D. Generation
1. In some cultures distinctions between kin depend on generation
2. In other cultures kinship systems do not confine a kin category to a single generation
E. Sex or Gender
1. Some societies allow for the possibility of both males and females occupying a single kin category
F. Lineality Versus Collaterality
1. Lineality refers to kin related in a single line, such as son, father, grandfather
2. Collaterality refers to kin related through a linking relative, such as the relationship between EGO and his or her parents' siblings
G. Consanguineal Versus Affinal Kin
1. Distinctions in kinship categories based on whether people are related by blood or marriage
H. Relative Age

1. Kinship terms based on relative age carry with them different behavioral expectations

I. Sex of the Connecting Relative
   1. Cross Cousins
   2. Parallel Cousins
   3. These first cousins are considered to be different by virtue of the sex of their parents

J. Social Condition
   1. Distinctions made based on a person's general life condition - married, unmarried, deceased

K. Side of the Family
   1. Distinctions in kin terms for EGO's mother's side of the family and father's side of the family

VI. THE FORMATION OF DESCENT GROUPS

A. Kinship systems encompass all of the blood and marriage relationships that
   1. Distinguish among different categories of kin
   2. Create rights and obligations among kin
   3. Serve as the basis for the formation of certain types of kin groups

B. Descent
   1. The rules a culture uses to establish affiliations with one's parents
   2. Often provide the basis for the formation of social groups
   3. In societies with descent groups, members:
      a. Have a strong sense of identity
      b. Often share communally held property
      c. Provide economic assistance to one another
      d. Engage in mutual civic and religious ceremonies
      e. Serve as a social and political mechanism for
         1) Inheriting property and political office
         2) Controlling behavior
         3) Regulating marriages
         4) Structuring primary political units
      f. Rules of descent can be divided into two distinct types
         1) Unilineal descent
         2) Cognatic (nonunilineal descent)

C. Unilineal Descent Groups
   1. Trace descent through either mother's or father's line, but not both
   2. Approximately 60 percent of all kinship systems found in the world are based on the unilineal principle
   3. Provide clear-cut and unambiguous social units
   4. Patrilineal Descent
      a. Found on all major continents and a wide range of societies
      b. The most common unilineal descent system
      c. Females marry outside patrilineage and their children belong to their father's patrilineage
      d. Traditional Chinese families
         1) Were patrilineal and patrilocal
         2) Practiced sim pua, a form of adoption
         3) Children had strong obligations to families and elders
         4) Males were very conscious about their place in their patrilineage
      e. Description of uterine family in patrilineals societies indicates that women have their own (different) kinship structure

5. Matrilineal Descent
    a. A matrilineal descent group comprises a woman, her siblings, her own children, her sisters' children, and her daughters' children
    b. Make up about 15 percent of the unilineal descent groups found among contemporary societies
    c. Different from matriarchy, a situation known only in myth, whereby women have greater authority and decision-making prerogatives than men
    d. Men retain power and authority but inherit it through women
    e. Zuni of New Mexico are a good example of matrilineal kinship
        1) Household comprised of grandmother, and her sisters, and daughter
        2) Husband divides time between wife's and mother's lineage
        3) Men perform lineage ceremonies at mother's lineage, not wife's
        4) Marriage is more fragile than in most patrilineal societies

D. Types of Unilineal Descent Groups
    1. Categorized by increasing levels of inclusiveness
    2. Four major types - lineages, clans, phratries, and moieties
    3. Lineages
        a. Unilineal descent groups of up to approximately 10 generations in depth
        b. Members can trace their ancestry back (step by step) to a common founder (matrilineages or patrilineages)
        c. Can undergo segmentation - subdivision into smaller units depending on the social situation
    4. Clans
        a. A group of kin usually comprising ten or more generations whose members believe they are all related to a common ancestor but are unable to trace their connections
        b. When clans and lineages are found together, the clan is usually made up of a number of different lineages
        c. Tend to be larger and more loosely structured categories with which people identify
        d. Often associated with animals or plants (totems) that provide a focal point for group identity
    5. Phratries
        a. Unilineal descent groups composed of two or more clans
        b. Actual connections among the various clans usually are not recognized
        c. Generally rare and do not serve important social functions
    6. Moieties
        a. Societies that are divided into two unilineal descent groups
        b. Excellent example of social reciprocity
        c. Can play important roles in the society but are not a part of the political structure as are lineages or clans
    7. The Corporate Nature of Unilineal Descent Groups
        a. Clearly define who is a member and who is not
        b. Endure over time
        c. Shape a person's identity
        d. Regulate marriage
        e. Regulate property, rather than individual control
        f. Strong corporate focus in social control

E. Cognatic (Nonunilineal Descent Groups)
   1. Approximately 40 percent of the world's population
   2. Three basic types - double descent, ambilineal descent, and bilateral descent
   3. Double Descent
      a. Kinship is traced both matrilineally and patrilineally
      b. Only about 5 percent of the world's cultures practice double descent
      c. The patrilineal groups and the matrilineal groups are active in different spheres of the culture
   4. Ambilineal Descent
      a. Parents have a choice of affiliating their children with either kinship group
      b. More flexible system - allows for individual choice concerning group affiliation
      c. The greater the flexibility of choice concerning membership, the weaker the group's loyalties, cohesiveness, and impact on the lives of its members
   5. Bilateral Descent
      a. A person related equally to mother's and father's side of the family
      b. Practiced in the United States
      c. Creates links from both sides of the family but usually include only close kin from a small number of generations
      d. Kindred - a group of closely related relatives connected through both parents to one living relative (or to EGO)
      e. No two individuals (except siblings) have the same kindred
      f. The kindred is not a group at all but a network of relatives
      g. Loosely structured network of relatives works well in a society that highly values personal independence and geographic mobility

VII. SIX BASIC SYSTEMS OF CLASSIFICATION
   A. Every society has a coherent system of labeling various types of kin - six basic systems
   B. It is both internally logical and consistently applied
   C. Eskimo System
      1. Associated with bilateral descent
      2. Found in one-tenth of the world's societies
      3. Emphasizes the nuclear family
      4. Found where economic conditions favor a relatively independent nuclear family (United States society)
   D. Hawaiian System
      1. Associated with ambilineal descent
      2. Found in one-third of the world's societies
      3. Uses the same term for all relatives of the same sex and generation
      4. Nuclear family is submerged into a larger kin group
   E. Iroquois System
      1. Emphasizes the importance of unilineal descent groups by distinguishing between members of one's own lineage and those belonging to other lineages
      2. Makes a basic distinction between the sex of one's parents' siblings
      3. Associated with parallel and cross cousins
   F. Omaha System
      1. Emphasizes patrilineal descent
      2. Merging of generations does not occur on EGO's father's side of the family but does on the mother's side

G. Crow System
1. Mirror image of the Omaha system
2. Emphasizes matrilineal descent

H. Sudanese System
1. Most descriptive system because it makes the largest number of terminological distinctions
2. Generally associated with patrilineal descent
3. Found in societies wirh considerable differences in wealth, occupation, and social status

VIII. KINSHIP AND THE MODERN WORLD

A. The revolution in information technology now enables people to learn more about their distant relatives.
B. Research on kinship generalizes from systems and relationships that are not neat and tidy in real life
C. Kinship systems are constantly experiencing changes through contact with external forces
D. Kinship systems are the most intimate, intense, and long-lasting set of social relationships
E. Even well-integrated kinship groups are changed by external pressure
F. Today reproductive technologies (e.g., in vitro fertilization, sperm banks, surrogate mothers) are causing us to rethink kinship theoretically, legally, and ethically

Key Terms

These are the anthropological terms introduced in Chapter 10. You may want to ask your students to write definitions of one or more of these terms during class to see how well they understood the reading. Even if you choose not to grade the assignment, the students will take it more seriously if you collect their answers.

affinal relatives
ambilineal descent
bilateral descent
clans
cognatic descent
collaterality
consanguineal relatives
Crow system
descent
double descent
EGO
Eskimo system
fictive kinship
Hawaiian system
horizontal function of kinship
Iroquois system
kindred
kinship system
lineages
lineality
matriarchy
matrilineal descent
moieties
Omaha system
patrilineal descent
phratries
reproductive technology
segmentation
Sudanese system
unilineal descent
uterine family
vertical function of kinship

Critical Thinking Questions

1. How have language and learning influenced the complexity of human social organization?
2. It is often said that kinship is not important in societies such as the United States. However, how do our kinship relationships still have significance?
3. Which is more important in defining kinship - biology or culture?
4. Which sub-cultural groups in the United States tend to live in extended families rather than nuclear families? How do you explain this?
5. How important are a person's age and sex for determining kinship relations in the United States?
6. Is there any tendency toward either patrilineality or matrilineality in the United States?
7. What examples of "fictive kinship" can you cite from your own society?
8. What ethical questions are raised by the new reproductive technologies?
9. How is a double descent system different from the bilateral descent system of the United States?
10. Which of our kin would we categorize differently if the Hawaiian system of classification were used in the United States, rather than the Eskimo system?

Class Activities

1. Have each student interview a foreign student and diagram his or her kin. Have the students compare the number of kin and the number of generations known. Discuss which cultures have the most elaborate kinship diagrams.
2. Have each student interview a person over age sixty on the importance of kinship in their life. Have them analyze whether kinship appears to be gaining or losing importance.
3. Since kinship influences inheritance rules, have students conduct library research on how different states in the US regulate the inheritance of property. What are some differences between states (legally) regarding who inherits property when a person dies without a will.

Internet Exercises

1. Go to the same web site you visited for the Internet Exercise in Chapter 9: Brian Schwimmer's interactive tutorial "Kinship and Social Organization." Start the tutorial and answer the following questions:
   - A. How does the author distinguish between matrilineal, patrilineal, and bilateral kinship systems?
   - B. Are the kinship symbols used in the tutorial different from those used in your textbook? If yes, what is different about them?
   - C. What is the difference between consanguineal and affinal relations?
   - D. In such matrilineal societies as the Ashanti kingdom of West Africa, who is the heir to the throne?

2. There are many resources for conducting genealogical research in the internet. Using any search engine, look for "Heritage Quest," one such resource. You can try to link to the site using this URL:

http://www.heritagequest.com/index.html

You can also search under terms such as "genealogy" or "kinship research." Think about the steps you would need to begin genealogical research on your immediate family. Do resources already exist? What would be your first steps in creating a family genealogy?

Infotrac® Exercises

1. Students will need to access InfoTrac at **http://infotrac.thomsonlearning.com/index.html** to answer the following questions. Once logged on, type "Mosuo" in the Search field. Read the article "Land of the Walking Marriage" and answer the following:

   a. Describe the matrilineal kinship practiced by the Mosuo.

   b. How do the marriage and family patterns of the Mosuo differ from those of the United States?

2. In the Search field, type in "Kinship." Click on "Periodicals." Locate and read the article "New Directions in Kinship Study: A Core Concept Revisited."

   a. How is the study of kinship changing in anthropology?

   b. Why is kinship described as a system of classification?

Suggested Films

Faces of Culture: Kinship AND Descent, Parts I and 2. (Numbers 11 and 12), (PSU), 30 min. each video - Illustrates methods of determining descent, defines kindred, and diagrams some of the 6 major ways of classifying kin.

Her Name Comes on Arrows: A Kinship Interview with the Baruya of New Guinea. (DER) - French anthropologist Maurice Godelier invites five of his Baruya friends and informants to discuss Baruya kinship and rules of marriage. Their kinship rules are brought to life, and abstract terms are given practical meaning.

Chapter 11
Sex and Gender

Learning Objectives

After reading and studying Chapter 11, your students should be able to:

1. Explain why anthropologists discuss gender differences rather than sex differences.
2. Discuss how research on gender in other cultures demonstrates that it is not biology alone that is responsible for differences in women's and men's behavior.
3. Understand the large variation in human sexual behavior across cultures.
4. Recognize that the universal presence of gender role definitions does not mean the roles are identical in all societies.
5. Understand the meaning of gender stratification and the difficulties involved in its measurement.
6. Discuss the relative sexual equality in food collecting societies and suggest two reasons why that equality exists.
7. Discuss whether or not women are universally subordinate and the dimensions in which women's status varies.
8. Explain what gender ideology is and be able to argue whether those ideologies represent only a male perspective.
9. Give examples of male gender bias and the impact it has on women in our culture and in other cultures.
10. Discuss the controversy about genital mutilation and female infanticide.
11. Explain when there is a period of breadwinner/housewife households in the U.S. and why that type of household came to prevail and then became less common.
12. Describe the characteristics of occupational segregation along gender lines in the United States and the negative impact that has on relations of women and men.

Chapter Outline

I. SEX AND GENDER
   A. There are biological differences between males and females
   B. Humans are sexually dimorphic
   C. The definition of femaleness and maleness varies widely from society to society
   D. Gender
      1. The way members of the two sexes are perceived, evaluated, and expected to behave

2. Biological differences influence social definitions of maleness or femaleness to varying degrees
3. Not all cultures limit humans to two genders
4. Not always possible to determine the extent to which culture or biology determines differences in behaviors or attitudes between the sexes

II. HUMAN SEXUALITY
A. Before the 1960s there was little research on comparative sexuality
B. Although no society fails to regulate sexual conduct, some are permissive and some more restrictive
C. There are a wide variety of attitudes and behaviors concerning male homosexuality
D. Sexual behavior in the U.S. is becoming more permissive
1. Young people are becoming more sexually active at an earlier age
2. The percentage of sexually active youngsters is increasing
3. Sexual activity is becoming more frequent for those who are sexually active
E. Today erectile dysfunction drugs are being used recreationally by young male adults

III. GENDER ROLES
A. All societies make some distinctions between what men are expected to do and what women are expected to do
B. Some gender roles are rigidly defined while others overlap
C. There is some uniformity in gender role definition around the world
D. Theories to explain division of labor by gender
1. Males' body mass and strength better prepare them for certain tasks
2. The constraints of childbirth and infant care create the division of labor by task
E. In the U.S. "stay at home dads" are becoming more common

IV. SEXUAL ASYMMETRY IN LANGUAGE
A. Some languages allow men and women to use different languages
B. Genderlects (linguistic gender differences in the United States)---women and men have different linguistic styles and communication goals
C. Basic speech differences in the United States result from childhood games and socialization

V. GENDER STRATIFICATION
A. Gender stratification exists to some degree in all societies
B. Difficult to measure stratification
1. Number of important indicators of women's status
2. Status of women is not static
3. The age of women influences their status
4. Although possible to identify societies where gender distinctions are minimal, overwhelming evidence suggests that in many critical areas of life women are subordinate to men
C. Apartheid of gender
1. Two-thirds of all illiterate people in the world today are women
2. World's women are concentrated in lowest-paid occupations and receive less pay and fewer benefits than men
3. Increasing number of women are being pushed into the informal economy
4. The "feminization of poverty"
5. Reproductive health issues are problems in developing countries
6. Women do not have access to credit
7. Women, approximately half the world's population, do two-thirds of the work, earn one-tenth of the world's income, and own less than one percent of the world's property

VI. GENDER IDEOLOGY
- A. Gender ideology is a system of thoughts and values that legitimize gender roles, statuses, and customary behavior
  1. Religion - women excluded from holding major leadership roles or participating in certain ceremonies
  2. Women associated with pollution
  3. Foods procured by men are more highly valued than those procured by women
  4. Women treated legally as minors
  5. There are rare societies that prefer female children, but the dominant trend is toward male-biased parental favorites
- B. Question now is whether women accept the ideological justifications for their subjugation
  1. Male ethnographers may have distorted interpretations of gender ideology
  2. Recent studies, written from a woman's perspective, are important because they serve as a corrective to male gender bias in previous work

VII. EXPLOITATION CAUSED BY GENDER IDEOLOGY
- A. Gender ideology can lead to women suffering harsh consequences
- B. Females missing in census counts in parts of the world (India and China)
  1. Selective abortions - India
  2. Underreporting or hiding of female births - China
  3. Female infanticide
  4. Nutritional deprivation which, if not fatal, can retard learning, physical development, or social adjustment
  5. Honor Killings - a woman's purity is the most important part of the family's reputation. An unchaste woman is killed in order to restore family honor
  6. Dowry Deaths in India
  7. Female genital mutilation, although condemned by WHO as dangerous and medically indefensible, continues to be practiced
     - a. Girls subjected to pain, infection, and death to an extent that their brothers are not. Leads to differential levels of subjugation between men and women
  8. Gender based violence also occurs in U.S. society
     - a. Physical violence, wife-battering and homicide, and sexual assault against women are a direct consequence of extreme gender ideology

VIII. GENDER IN THE UNITED STATES
- A. The breadwinner/housewife gender roles were only valid for a relatively brief period in the nation's history (1860-1950)
- B. The change to manufacturing from agriculture separated work life from family life
- C. With industrialization some women became confined to the home
- D. Women made contributions to factory production
  1. Women of the poor and working classes as well as members of minority or immigrant groups or single mothers entered the work force
  2. Clerical workers were needed
  3. Having fewer children made it easier for women to work outside the home
  4. Women were thought to be more suited for the textile industry
  5. A rising divorce rate forced women to support their families
  6. The baby bottle enabled women to work outside the home
  7. Two salaries often needed to make ends meet
- E. Nature of women working outside the home has changed over past 30 years
  1. Percentage of working women between 25 and 54 increased from 50% in 1970 to 76% in 1995

2. Married women carry a double workload by being both wage employed and primarily responsible for housework and child care
3. Occupational segregation along gender lines - women concentrated in certain lower-paying jobs
4. Wages for full-time female employees are only 70% of wages for full-time male employees

F. The cost to men of gender stratification is also high (stress, poor health, and higher mortality rates)

Key Terms

These are the anthropological terms introduced in Chapter 11. You may want to ask your students to write definitions of one or more of these terms during class to see how well they understood the reading. Even if you choose not to grade the assignment, the students will take it more seriously if you collect their answers.

breadwinner
double workload
dowry death
extramarital activity
female genital mutilation
female infanticide
femininity
feminization of poverty
gender
gender ideology
gender roles
gender stratification
genderlects
heterosexual
homosexual
honor killings
housewife
human sexuality
infant mortality
male gender bias
masculinity
matriarchy
nutritional deprivation
occupational segregation
postpartum sexual abstinence
purdah
sex drive
sexual asymmetry
sexual dimorphism
universal male dominance

Critical Thinking Questions

1. In the U.S., less than 25 percent of all doctoral degrees in mathematics, computer science, and engineering are award to women. How do you account for this?

2. How rigidly are gender roles defined in the United States? Where is there overlap in the definitions of these roles?

3. In what circumstances, and for what jobs, would men's body mass and strength or women's childbearing not have great significance for gender role definition? How has the sexual division of labor in the United States changed over the last 50 years?

4. What factors are the most important influence eon gender stratification in one culture? How do those factors compare with those that determine stratification among the Ju/'hoansi?

5. Ferraro states that in 99 percent of societies it is men who hunt and that women overwhelmingly do child care. What is the importance of the exceptions to these rules?

6. Discuss two major ways by which contemporary women in India are exploited.

7. Is it fair to categorize rape and spouse abuse as a form of male gender bias or are they criminal activities concerned with power?

8. Why is it important to society to regulate sexual conduct?

9. Do you think that women in the U.S. military should serve on the front lines in combat situations? Why or why not?

10. Is the feminization of poverty found in the United States? What can improve the supply of resources available to women and children??

Class Activities

1. Divide the class into two groups and assign one the task of generating reasons why being in a polygynous household could benefit a woman. Have the second group developing reasons why such a household could be disadvantageous to women. Ask how gender definition in the United States makes it difficult to do this assignment.

2. Have each student interview two women and two men. Have them prepare an interview schedule of the same questions asking about gender roles in the United States. In class have them present the results of the interviews of women and men separately without identifying gender. The class should discuss if it was possible to accurately identify which are female and which are male responses.

3. Have the class discuss the following questions: "Should western nations put pressure on African cultures to stop the practice of female genital mutilation? Would it be any different than if Africans tried to stop westerners from having breast enhancements, liposuction, or "nose jobs" because these operations violated their values?

Internet Exercises

1. Using any search engine, find the home page entitled "Gender in Development: UNDP." What is meant by the term *gender mainstreaming*?

   Go to the section of the site called "Gender Good Practice." Select any single case study (from any part of the world) and describe its essential features in no more than 250 words.

2. This chapter has mentioned the general gender discrimination that exists in North America as well as in other parts of the world. It would be interesting to see what our legislators are doing about this problem in the United States and in Canada. For U.S. students, consult the home page of the United States Senate:

   http://www.senate.gov

   Canadian students can do the same by consulting the home page of the Canadian Parliament"

   http://www.parl.gc.ca

   Select a woman from the directory of U.S. senators or the directory of Canadian MPs. Find as much information on this female legislator as possible concerning the topic of eliminating discrimination against women in the workplace. Read her speeches and public statements that are part of her own home page. Once you have familiarized yourself with this legislator's public positions, write her a letter via email asking her what specific pieces of legislation she is sponsoring or supporting that will help eliminate or minimize gender discrimination in the workplace.

3. Use any search engine to find "female genital mutilation" or go to

   http.//www.fgm.org

   What can you learn about the prevalence and incidence of this practice on a world wide basis? Use the various links to inform yourself about this practice. Think about the connections between male and female circumcision - are there any? Are the practices the same? How does female circumcision reflect extreme gender ideology? Why is the practice being perpetuated by the females in many of the cultures where it is prevalent?

Infotrac® Exercises

1. Students will need to access InfoTrac at **http://infotrac.thomsonlearning.com/index.html** to answer the following questions. Once logged on, type "Cook Islands" in the Search field. Next click on "Periodicals." Once the results appear scroll down to the article "Dragging Drag: The Performance of Gender and Sexuality in the Cook Islands." Read the selection and answer the following.

   a. Are there any similarities between the Kia Orana performance and western drag?

   b. How are sexuality and gender related to the residents of the Cook Islands notions of personhood?

2. In the Search field, type in "Sex roles." Click on "Periodicals." At the results list, find the article "Gender and Preferences for Job Attributes: A Cross Cultural Comparison."

   a. Consider the results of this study. Does gender play any role in a person's attitudes toward a job?

   b. Do you think that the results of this study might be different in a non-western, non-industrialized society?

Suggested Films

Asante Market Women. (PSU), 52 min. - Although the women in the Asante tribe of Ghana are subordinate in all domestic matters to their polygynous husbands, in the marketplace they reign supreme. Shows the intricacies of the powerful matrilineal society and the noise and color of the Kumasi Central Market.

Becoming a Woman in Okrika. (PSU), 27 min. video - Documents a coming-of-age ritual among the women of a village in the Niger Delta. The rite of passage, iria, includes elaborate body painting, public scrutiny, and a race in which they are pursued by young men, all designed to prepare the women for marriage and childbearing.

Masai Manhood. (PSU), 53 min. video - Focuses on the lives of these young East African warriors until the time of eunoto, the four-day ceremony that marks their transition from warrior to elder.

Masai Women. (PSU), 52 min. video - Looks at the women of this East African group from childhood through marriage to old age, and their role in a completely male-dominated society. Shows ceremonies at significant stages, including "female circumcision," and gives the women's view of co-wives in this polygynous society.

Secret of the Sexes. (PSU), 58 min. video - A study of the socialization process that modifies a child's behavior according to common assumptions about what is "masculine" or "feminine."

Women in a Changing World. (UC), 48 min. - Impact of modernization of women in Bolivian highlands, Kenya, Afghanistan, and Hong Kong islands. Shows how traditional women's roles are changing due to new opportunities and ideas.

Women of the Toubou. (UC), 25 min. - Sexual egalitarianism among a nomadic people of the Sahara.

Chapter 12

Political Organization and Social Control

Learning Objectives

After reading and studying Chapter 12, your students should be able to:

1. Define political organization.
2. Define and identify three dimensions of political organization.
3. Recognize that all types of political organization have more complex state political systems superimposed over them.
4. Describe the characteristics of political organization in band societies.
5. Recognize the significance of pan-tribal associations for tribes and the similarities and differences between tribes and bands.
6. understand how the increased social and technological complexity of chiefdoms over bands or tribes is reflected in their political organization.
7. Understand the differences between nation, state, and nation-state.
8. Describe the political organization of state societies and the basis for the authority of the state.
9. Contrast the four types of political structures discussed by Ferraro in his description of the continuum of variation from acephalous societies to state systems.
10. Explain three theories that account for the formation of state societies and recognize that independent cases of state formation might require more than one theory for adequate explanation.
11. Understand how state systems have changed over the millennia, particularly in light of globalization.
12. Recognize the great importance of informal means of social control for complex state organizations as well as for bands and tribes.
13. Understand the great diversity in formal means of social control and the significant difference in the objectives of legal systems in more and less complex societies.
14. Understand how state systems deal with the unauthorized uses of force such as crime, rebellion, and revolution.
15. Understand how warfare serves as a mechanism of social control outside one's own group or society.

Chapter Outline

I. POLITICAL ORGANIZATION AND SOCIAL CONTROL
  A. Every society must develop a set of customs and procedures for
    1. Making and enforcing decisions
    2. Resolving disputes
    3. Regulating the behavior of its members
  B. The cultural arrangements by which societies maintain social order, minimize chances of disruption, and cope with disruptions vary
  C. Political organization is a set of customary procedures that accomplish decision making, conflict resolution, and social control

II. TYPES OF POLITICAL ORGANIZATION
  A. Political organization can be found in all societies, but degree of specialized and formal mechanisms varies
  B. Differ along three dimensions
    1. The extent to which political institutions are distinct from other aspects of the social structure
    2. The extent which authority is concentrated in specific political roles
    3. The level of political integration ranked as band, tribe, chiefdom, or state
  C. Today nonstate forms of political organization have complex state political systems superimposed over them
  D. Band Societies
    1. Small and usually nomadic populations of food collectors
    2. Most number between 30 and 50 people
    3. Actual size of particular bands is directly related to food-gathering methods
    4. Little or no concept of individual property ownership
    5. Place a high value on sharing, cooperation, and reciprocity
    6. Very little role specialization
    7. Highly egalitarian
    8. Closely associated with a foraging technology
    9. Generally thought to be the oldest form of political organization
    10. Common traits of band societies
    11. Least amount of political integration
    12. Political decisions often embedded in the wider social structure
    13. Leadership roles tend to be informal
    14. Band leadership stems from the recognized personal traits admired by the others in the group
    15. The !Kung of the Kalahari
  E. Tribal Societies
    1. Found most often among food producers (horticulturalists and pastoralists)
    2. Tend to have populations that are larger, denser, and somewhat more sedentary in nature
    3. No marked differences in status, rank, power, and wealth
    4. Have local leaders but do not have centralized leadership
    5. Pan-tribal mechanisms cut across and integrate all of the local segments of the tribe into a larger whole
      a. Clan - a group of kin who consider themselves descended from a common ancestor
      b. Segmentary lineage system - individuals belong to a series of different descent units that function in different social contexts

c. Segmentary lineage effective for the mobilization of a military force
d. The Nuer of the southern Sudan

6. The term "tribal" is often equated with "uncivilized."

F. Chiefdoms
1. Political authority is likely to reside with a single individual, acting alone or in conjunction with an advisory council
2. Integrate a number of local communities in a more formal and permanent way
3. Differing levels of prestige and power
4. Chiefships are often hereditary
5. Chiefs are centralized and permanent officials with higher rank, power, and authority than others in the society
   a. Authority to make judgments, punish wrongdoers, and settle disputes
   b. Authority to distribute land, recruit people into military service, and recruit laborers for public works projects
   c. Authority usually reinforced by alleged supernatural powers
6. Control a redistributive system
7. Some societies with no former tradition of chiefs have had chiefships imposed on them by European colonial powers (Nigeria, Kenya, Australia)
   a. Precolonial Hawaiian political system embodied the features of an indigenous chiefdom

G. State Systems
1. Hierarchical form of political organization that governs many communities within a large geographic area
2. Power organized on a suprakinship basis - a person's membership in a state is based on place or residence and citizenship rather than on kinship affiliation
3. Authority rests on two foundations
   a. State holds exclusive right to use force and physical coercion
   b. State maintains its authority by means of ideology
4. First appeared 5,500 years ago in association with civilizations
5. Supported by intensive agriculture which allows considerable labor specialization
6. Complex internal distribution mechanism
7. Foreign trade
8. Stratified with specialized political roles
9. Laws and regulations needed to control population give rise to the need for writing, record keeping, and weights and measures
10. Nation and State are two distinct concepts
   a. Nations are groups of people who share common symbolic identity, culture, history, and often religion
   b. State is a particular type of political structure distinct from a band, tribal society or chiefdom
   c. When combined, nation-state refers to a group of people sharing a common cultural background and unified by a political structure that they all consider to be legitimate
   d. Few nation-states today fit this definition because of culturally heterogeneous populations

H. Variations in Political Structures
1. Fourfold typology of political systems is not universally accepted
2. May distinguish only between state systems and acephalous (headless) societies
3. May recognize simple, intermediate, and complex political structures
4. All schemes are ideal types

5. All political systems vary along a continuum of political and socioeconomic dimensions
    a. State is the predominant form of government in the world
6. Explanations for the formation of state societies
    a. Hinge on question of what induces people to surrender at least a portion of their autonomy to the power and control of the state
    b. Voluntaristic Theory of State Formation
        1) V. Gordon Childe
        2) Development of intensive agriculture created increase in occupational specialization.
        3) Necessitated wider form of political integration to mediate between and protect special interest groups and to provide the economic superstructure to enable them to work in an efficient manner
    c. Hydraulic Theory of State Formation
        1) Karl Wittfogel
        2) Small-scale irrigation farmers came to see economic advantages to surrendering their autonomy and merging into a larger political entity capable of large-scale irrigation
    d. Coercive Theory of State Formation
        1) Robert Carniero
        2) Force is the mechanism by which political evolution has moved to the state.
        3) Operates only under certain environmental conditions
    e. State systems have changed in the last 100 years
        1) Democratization of many nation states
        2) Technological advances in communication mean that governments can no longer control the flow of information
        3) The information revolution - and the Internet specifically - is significantly impacting political and electoral processes

III. THE MODERN NATION-STATE
    A. A nation refers to a group of people with a common symbolic identity, culture, and history; a state refers to a bureaucratic form of government structure.
    B. Ethnic Diversity within Contemporary Nation-States
    C. Ethnic populations pushing for greater autonomy (Kurds, Chechens, French Canadians)
    D. Gender and Leadership
        1. In all societies, women do not hold the majority of positions of political leadership
        2. With over 90 million missing women, Asia has the potential for increases in domestic crime and external warfare.
    E. Recent Trends Toward Greater Democracy
    F. Role of Internet in Changing Government Structures
    G. Role of Multinational Corporation in Dealing with International Conflicts (India/Pakistan)

IV. SOCIAL CONTROL
    A. Ensures that members of society behave in appropriate ways most of the time
    B. Less deviation from acceptable behavior in most band societies than in more complex political organizations
    C. Social norms define normal. proper, or expected ways of behaving
        1. Take a number of forms - ranging from etiquette to formal laws
        2. Deviance from social norms is relative and culturally defined

3. Sanctions - patterned or institutionalized ways of encouraging people to conform to the norms
    a. Both positive and negative
    b. May also be formal or informal

D. Informal Means of Social Control
1. Socialization
    a. Every society, if it is to survive, must pass on social norms from one generation to the next
    b. When people learn their cultural norms they also usually internalize the moral necessity to obey them
2. Public Opinion
    a. In all parts of the world most people want the approval of other members of their society
    b. Gossip, ostracism, rumor, sarcasm, and derision are all powerful corrective measures for reforming social behavior
    c. Degradation ceremonies refer to formal societal mechanisms to publicly humiliate a deviant
3. Corporate Lineages
    a. Play a dominant role in most small-scale societies
    b. Exert economic control over their members
    c. Act of mechanisms because of their scale - localized communities whose members know what everyone else is doing
    d. Exert social control because of diffuse roles
    e. Exert social control due to collective capacity to control marriage
4. Supernatural Belief Systems
    a. Belief in supernatural forces such as gods, witches, and sorcerers
    b. Ancestor Worship
        1) Dead ancestors are fully functioning members of the descent group
        2) Ghost invocation brings the wrath of the ancestor gods against the sinner
        3) Ghost vengeance is the belief that ancestor-gods inflict sickness on their own without having to be invoked
        4) The belief that implications for social control rather than the ability to be scientifically verified
    c. Witchcraft
        1) Common in acephalous societies
        2) People reject the idea that misfortunes result from natural causes
        3) A deviant runs the risk of being labeled a witch, and fear of being accused of witchcraft encourages conformity
    d. Witches often identified by ritual specialist, a shaman, then community takes action
5. Age Organizations
    a. Age set - group of people initiated during a periodic ceremony
        1) Usually men
        2) Strong sense of group identity with one another
        3) Lasts from its inception until its last member has died
    b. Age Grades
        1) Categories through age sets pass as a group
        2) Associated with a well-understood set of social roles and statuses

c. Control behavior in a number of ways
   1) Establish a clear set of role and statuses
   2) Effective channels for the distribution of authority
   3) Rites of passage are almost always preceded by intense periods of training in the norms and values of society
   4) Bonds of camaraderie are so strong that age sets tend to take on the characteristics of a corporate group
d. Neither self-perpetuating nor property owning

E. Formal Means of Social Control
   1. The violation of social norms often results in disputes among people in the society
   2. When disputes become violent conflicts, they are called crimes
      a. Crime more likely in large, heterogeneous, stratified societies than in small-scale societies
      b. Little or no anonymity in small scale societies
      c. More concern with negative public opinion in small-scale societies
      d. Heterogeneity of complex societies means more groups with different, and probably conflicting, interests
      e. Lower classes or castes in complex societies may be more likely to violate the rights of the more privileged
   3. Song Duels
      a. Inuit of Canada, Alaska, and Greenland
      b. A derisive song contest
      c. Used to settle disputes that frequently involved wife stealing
      d. Alternative to murder
   4. Intermediaries
      a. the Nuer of Sudan
      b. Help resolve serious conflicts
      c. Nuer's Leopard-skin chief has no authority to determine guilt or enforce settlement between parties
      d. Uses personal and supernatural influence to bring the disputing parties to some type of agreed-upon settlement
   5. Moots: Informal Courts
      a. the Kpelle of Liberia and Guinea
      b. Found in many African societies
      c. Effective mechanism for conflict resolution
      d. Informal airings of disputes involving kinsmen and friends of litigants
      e. Generally deal with the resolution of domestic disputes
      f. Attempt to reintegrate the guilty party back into community, restore normal social relations, achieve reconciliation without bitterness and acrimony
   6. Oaths and Ordeals
      a. Ashanti of West Africa
      b. Religiously sanctioned
      c. Oath - a formal declaration to some supernatural force that what you are saying is truthful or that you are innocent
      d. Almost always accompanied by a ritual act
      e. Ordeal is means of determining guilt by submitting the accused to a dangerous test
      f. Most likely to be found in complex societies where the political leadership lacks the power to enforce judicial decisions

7. Courts and Codified Law
    a. State systems possess a monopoly on the use of force
    b. Through system of codified law, state both forbids individuals from using force and determines how it will use force to require certain behaviors from citizens
    c. When legal prescriptions are violated, state has the authority to fine, imprison, or even execute the wrongdoer
    d. Unauthorized use of force happens - crime, rebellion, revolution
    e. Three basic features of codified law
        1) Involves the legitimate use of physical coercion
        2) Allocate official authority to privileged people who are able to use coercion legitimately
        3) Based on regularity and a certain amount of predictability
    f. Emphasis on punishment in order to avoid a threat to the legitimacy of political and legal authority
8. Warfare
    a. Systematic, organized, and institutionalized fighting between different groups
    b. Enormous cultural variability in the extent to which societies use warfare
    c. Only a human activity since the Neolithic period, starting about 10,000 years ago
    d. Reasons foraging societies were not warlike
        1) Had no centralized governments that could finance and coordinate number of people needed for military campaigns
        2) Absence of food surpluses precluded prolonged combat
        3) Did not control land or territorial boundaries - major motivations for warfare
        4) Exogamous bands not likely to become hostile toward other bands into which relatives have married
    e. General factors that contribute to warfare
        1) Social problems
        2) Perceived threats
        3) Political motivations
        4) Moral objectives

Key Terms

These are the anthropological terms introduced in Chapter 12. You may want to ask your students to write definitions of one or more of these terms during class to see how well they understood the reading. Even if you choose not to grade the assignment, the students will take it more seriously if you collect their answers.

acephalous society
age grade
age organizations
age set
ancestor worship
authority
band society

oath
ordeal
pan-tribal mechanisms
political coerciveness
political integration
positive sanctions
public opinion

chiefdoms
coercive theory of state formation
corporate lineages
crime
degradation ceremony
democracy
deviance
ghost invocation
ghostly vengeance
hydraulic theory of state formation
intermediaries
law
Leopard-skin Chief
moots
nation
negative sanctions
rebellion
revolution
sanctions
social control
social norms
socialization
song duel
specialized political roles
state
state system of government
supernatural belief system
tribal societies
voluntaristic theory of state formation
warfare
witchcraft

Critical Thinking Questions

1. Is Western anthropologist's emphasis on political organization ethnocentric because of their own experiences in state societies where authorities have a difficult time maintaining social control?
2. Is it accurate to identify an institution as political if it is hardly distinguishable from economic, kinship, or religious structures?
3. How do we understand the position of a headman in a band society such as the Ju/'hoansi when he has very little authority?
4. How is the leader of a tribe different from that of a band?
5. Did the creation of chiefs by colonial administrations really facilitate administration of local groups, or did it create problems that the colonial powers could not have foreseen?
6. What impact did incorporation into state society have on the lives of agricultural people?
7. In what ways are multinational corporations influencing foreign policy?
8. If belief in witchcraft increases conformity because of fear of being accused, could it also threaten social control by recognizing that witches' behavior is possible?
9. In what contemporary nation-states do women have the greatest number of positions of political leadership?
10. What are the advantages and disadvantages of the Internet in fostering democratization?

Class Activities

1. Ask the students to look for examples of music in American society that may be used in a way similar to the Inuit song duels. For example, isn't rap music (including some hard-core rap) used in a way derisive to mainstream society, perhaps deflecting the need for violence? What about heavy metal? Is conflict a theme in country music?

2. There are both advantages and disadvantages to living in a state society. Have students discuss in class both the advantages and disadvantages.

3. Divide the students into two groups and have one role play a moot and the other a court hearing. Ask them to compare the experiences of the accused party/ies and of the families and neighbors. You might want to discuss how the O.J. Simpson murder trial might have been different if a moot hearing had taken place rather than a formal courtroom trial.

Internet Exercises

1. State systems of government are complex organizations with many branches and many layers. The United States federal government is divided into three major branches: the legislative, the executive, and the judicial. Perhaps the most poorly understood branch of the U.S. government is the judiciary. To learn more about how the federal judiciary operates, start with the Yahoo search engine (**www.yahoo.com**).

   Click on "government," then "law," then "federal," and then "federal courts."

   Now go to "United States Federal Judiciary" and then click on the section titled "About the U.S. Courts." Then go to "Understanding the Federal Courts" and click on "structure." Examine the various descriptions of the federal district courts, courts of appeals, and the Supreme Court. Describe the path a civil case takes as it works its way through the federal system. Now do the same for a criminal case. Writs a one-page paper on what you learned from this exercise.

Infotrac® Exercises

1. Students will need to access InfoTrac at **http://infotrac.thomsonlearning.com/index.html** to answer the following questions. In the Search field, type in "Nuu-chah-nulth." Again click on "Periodicals." At the results list, click on the article "Whales, Chiefs, and Giants: An Exploration into Nuu-chah-nulth Political Thought."

   a. What is the connection between chiefs and whales in this society?

   b. What characteristics distinguish the chief as different from his constituents?

2. In the Search field, type in "Kanak." Click on "Periodicals." At the results list, click on the article "The Political Order and Corporal Coercion in Kanak Societies of the Past (New Caledonia)."

   a. Describe the differences between the Kanak chief and the bigman.

   b. What is the connection between cannibalism and political power?

Suggested Films

Cows of Dolo Ken Paye: Resolving Conflict among the Kpelle. (UC), 32 min. - Case of conflict and its resolution in a Liberian village. Relates the conflict over the killing of a cow to economic inequalities in the village.

Dead Birds. (UC), 83 min. - Classic film on the Dani of West New Guinea, now Irian Jaya. Shows scenes of warfare, interpreted as revenge killings necessary because the ghosts of people killed on both sides make trouble for their own side until the death is avenged. Also has good scenes of gardens, manufacture and exchange of wealth objects, and funeral feasts.

Little Injustices: Laura Nader Looks at the Law. (DER), 50 min. - Contrasts the legal process in a Zapotec village in Oaxaca, Mexico with that in the contemporary United States. The impersonal nature of the American system is documented, with its concomitant frustration due to our inability to get at powerful decision-makers. (Originally part of Odyssey series)

Chapter 13

Social Stratification

Learning Objectives

After reading and studying Chapter 13, your students should be able to:

1. Explain three factors involved in social ranking.
2. Describe the social and economic organization of egalitarian societies.
3. Understand how access to power and wealth does not correlate with access to prestige in rank societies.
4. Recognize the range of socio-economic organization that occurs within stratified societies.
5. Explain the difference between class and caste societies.
6. Discuss the contradictions between the ideology and the actual experience of social mobility in the United States.
7. Understand the distinction between race and ethnicity.
8. Discuss the revival of ethnic consciousness in the contemporary United States and its implications for the Hispanic/Latino population.
9. Describe the range of ways in which racial and ethnic groups relate to one another.
10. Discuss the functionalist interpretation of social stratification.
11. Understand conflict theory's interpretation of stratification as exploitation by the upper levels of hierarchy.
12. Appreciate the idea of global stratification between the rich and poor countries of the world.

Chapter Outline

I. SOCIAL STRATIFICATION
   A. All people are socially differentiated on some sort of criteria
   B. Societies confer a larger share of wealth, power, and prestige on those possessing more admired characteristics
   C. All complex societies are stratified
   D. Simpler societies do not have clear-cut division into hierarchically ranked strata

II. DIMENSIONS OF SOCIAL INEQUALITY
   A. Max Weber delineated three basic criteria for measuring levels of social inequality that can operate independently of one another
   B. Wealth
      1. Forms of wealth vary

2. Extent of economic inequality varies
3. Range of wealth in the U.S. is great
4. Ranges from unemployed individuals to Bill Gates who is worth $46.6 billion

C. Power
1. The ability to achieve goals and objectives even against the will of others
2. Does not necessarily overlap with wealth
3. Theory in U.S. is power is in hands of the people
4. Reality is the belief that the real power resides with an unofficial power elite (C. Wright Mills)

D. Prestige
1. Social respect, esteem, or admiration that society confers on certain people
2. Sources vary from one culture to another
3. Based on norms and values of a particular group
4. Rankings of occupation in U.S. have remained stable for much of the twentieth century
5. U.S. rankings are consistent with those from other parts of the world

III. TYPES OF SOCIETIES

A. Based on levels of social inequality

B. Egalitarian societies
1. Food collectors
2. No individual or group has more wealth, power, or prestige than any other
3. Esteemed individuals cannot transform skills into power or wealth
4. High status positions constantly change to reflect the number of qualified candidates
5. As many positions of prestige as there are persons capable of filling them
6. Are usually transformed to non-egalitarian when contact with stratified societies occurs

C. Rank societies
1. Oceania and among Native Americans of the Northwest Coast
2. Unequal access to prestige or status but not unequal access to wealth or power
3. Fixed number of high-status positions
4. High prestige positions are largely hereditary
5. Kinship plays an important role
6. Basic standard of living of chief is not significantly different from ordinary people
7. Chief has no real power or control over land and maintains position by virtue of generosity
8. Redistribution is not only economic but validates rank

D. Stratified societies
1. Inequality in power, wealth, and prestige
2. Inequality is permanent and formally recognized
3. Access to resources is inherited
4. Arose approximately 5500 years ago with the rise of civilization
5. Population is highly differentiated into role specialization
6. Two different types of stratified societies: those based on class and those based on caste
   a. Class versus caste
   b. Differ in social mobility
   c. Class is associated with achieved status
   d. Caste is associated with ascribed status
   e. Caste and class systems may overlap each other

7. All stratified societies are along continuum from perfect class to perfect caste system
8. Class societies
    a. Social classes are population segments
    b. Members share relatively similar life styles
    c. Share levels of wealth, power, and prestige
    d. United States recognizes six social classes
    e. 1990s economic expansion contradicted by increasing inequality in wealth (average corporate CEO pay is $22,000/day!)
    f. According to U.S. national mythology there is a good deal of social mobility
    g. Reality is that most people do not change class in lifetime
    h. Members of a class share economic level, experiences, education, politics, values, and social memberships
9. Caste societies
    a. Members are ranked according to birth
    b. Membership is unchangeable
    c. Usually associated with specific occupation
    d. Are ranked hierarchically
    e. Higher castes have more and do less
    f. Members of caste share same social status and are socially segregated
    g. Caste exclusiveness is furthered by rituals
    h. Higher castes have most interest in maintaining the system
    i. Hindu caste system
        1) Four sacred categories, *varnas*, associated with occupations
        2) Dalits (outcastes) are below these four
        3) Each *varna* is subdivided and stratified (jati)
            a) *Jati* are subgroups
            b) Local family groups that are strictly endogamous
            c) Ranking varies regionally
            d) Social interaction within *jati* is egalitarian
            e) Avoid egalitarian socializing with other *jati*
        4) Hindu religion sanctions caste system
        5) Castes are economically interdependent
        6) Politics in contemporary India are becoming increasingly caste oriented
        7) Sanskritization involves moving up the caste ladder

IV. RACIAL AND ETHNIC STRATIFICATION
A. Anthropology studies physical and cultural diversity throughout the world
B. Some differentiation among members in all societies
C. Terms race and ethnicity are sometimes used synonymously in everyday speech, but have different meanings for anthropologists
D. Race means an inbreeding population whose members share a greater number of traits with one another than they do with people outside the group
    1. Different societies have different categories of classification (U.S. and Brazil)
    2. Race is only a statistical statement about the occurrence of physical traits
    3. There are no pure races because recessive traits are not lost but can reappear in future generations
    4. Racial classifications all differ depending on the traits on which they are based
    5. Populations have been interbreeding for thousands of years, producing a continuum of human physical types

6. Race gives little insight into human behavior
7. People use race socially even without a scientific basis for their beliefs

E. Ethnicity refers to cultural traits that are passed on from generation to generation
1. Ethnic group members define themselves and members of their group as "us"
2. Ethnic groups tend to cut across socioeconomic lines
3. Certain groups may be both racially and ethnically distinct from their neighbors

V. RACE AND ETHNICITY IN THE UNITED STATES

A. There are enormous problems when measuring race and ethnicity in the U.S.

B. U.S. image of an ethnic melting pot has not been realized
1. U.S. has experienced a revival of ethnic consciousness in recent decades, particularly in urban areas
2. Should think of contemporary American society more as a salad bowl, in which the individual ethnic groups are mixed together but retain their own distinctiveness and identity

C. Fastest growing ethnic group is not really an ethnic group at all - Hispanics
1. Composed of a number of different subcultural groups (17 groups) that share a common language
2. By 2050 will represent one-quarter of the total U.S. population
3. Backlash in U.S. based on myths about the Hispanic population affects relations between ethnic groups

D. Forms of Intergroup Relations
1. Pluralism - two or more groups live in harmony while retaining their own ethnic identity (Swiss)
2. Assimilation - a racial or ethnic minority is absorbed into the society (Hawaii)
3. Legal protection for a minority group -may be necessary in a society where groups are hostile toward one another (Australia)
4. Population transfer - may physically remove a minority group to another location (Native Americans in the U.S.)
5. Long-term subjugation - experience of many minority groups around the world for indefinite period of time (South Africa)
6. Genocide - the actual killing of a group (Rwanda)

VI. THEORIES OF STRATIFICATION

A. Inequitable distribution of wealth, power, and prestige appears to be a fundamental characteristic of societies with complex, highly differentiated economies

B. There have been some unsuccessful attempts at establishing classless societies (former Soviet Union, Albania, People's Republic of China)

C. The Functionalist Interpretation
1. Stratification contributes to the overall well-being of the society
2. Stratification adequately rewards the most important jobs in society
3. Fills society's key jobs with the best people
4. Weaknesses
   a. Greatest rewards not always given to those filling the most vital positions
   b. Puts barriers in the way of certain segments of the society
   c. Incorrectly assumes that people in all societies are motivated by the desire to maximize wealth, power, and prestige

D. The Conflict Theory Interpretation
1. The natural tendency of all societies is toward change and conflict
2. Stratification exists because people at the upper levels are willing and able to use wealth, power, and prestige to exploit those below them
3. Derived from writings of Karl Marx
4. Economic forces are the main factors shaping a society

5. There is a classic struggle between those who control the means of production and those who provide labor
6. A false consciousness is created to keep workers from revolting
    a. A class consciousness would allow workers to recognize their own exploitation as well as their collective power to change their situation

E. Functionalists Versus Conflict Theorists
1. Functionalists emphasize the positive benefits of social stratification for the total society
2. Conflict theorists emphasize the negative aspects of such systems
3. Neither theory explains the existence of all types of stratification

VII. GLOBAL STRATIFICATION

A. Not only are people stratified within a society, but societies themselves are stratified
1. Per capita gross national income varies from \$100 (Ethiopia) to \$34,000 (U.S.)
2. Poor countries have a number of negative characteristics:
    a. Highest birth rates
    b. Lowest life expectancy
    c. Poorest health facilities
    d. Poorest education

Key Terms

These are the anthropological terms introduced in Chapter 13. You may want to ask your students to write definitions of one or more of these terms during class to see how well they understood the reading. Even if you choose not to grade the assignment, the students will take it more seriously if you collect their answers.

achieved status
ascribed status
assimilation
bourgeoisie
caste
class
conflict theory
Dalit
egalitarian societies
ethnic group
functional theory
genocide
jati
nouveau riche
pluralism
population transfer
power
prestige
proletariat
race
rank societies
Sanskritization
social mobility
stratified societies
varnas
wealth

Critical Thinking Questions

1. Does power lead to wealth or does wealth lead to power?

2. Why do egalitarian societies change so much when they come into contact with stratified societies?

3. How is the destruction of wealth one way of controlling wealth?

4. Since there is little social mobility in a class society, does it really differ from a caste society?

5. Are people of color in the United States treated as though they are members of a caste society?
6. What factors limit social mobility in the United States?
7. Is wealth, power, or prestige most important in the stratification of race and ethnic groups in the United States?
8. Why is race not considered to be an important scientific concept today?
9. What do functionalists mean when they say that some jobs require more talent and hard work than others?
10. How would a conflict theorist argue that the people at upper levels of the hierarchy are harmed by their own exploitation of the workers?
11. List as many examples as possible of Latinos making an impact on U.S. culture.
12. Are there political parties in the United States which use either the functionalist or conflict theory to support their political policy?

Class Activities

1. Divide the class into two teams and, allowing time for preliminary discussion, ask them to debate the functionalists' and conflict theorists' positions.
2. Have students discuss the following question: "Which requires the most hard work and talent, surgery, teaching, or staying at home raising a child?" What is the basis for the assignment of wealth, power, and prestige in the United States in the 21st century?
3. Make a list of 25 common professions in the United States. Have students rank order them in terms of their levels of prestige. To what extent do class members agree on the rankings?

Internet Exercises

1. A problem that is becoming increasingly widespread in North America is that of homelessness, particularly in urban areas. Many people have a poor understanding of the dimensions of the problem. Using any search engine, conduct a subject search on homelessness.

   You will find a web site titled "54 Ways You Can Help the Homeless" by Rabbi Charles A. Kroloff. Which of the 54 ways do you think are the most realistic? Can you suggest any others?
2. As part of your subject search on homelessness, find a site called "Homeless in America." According to the data found on this site, how many people in the United States are homeless? What are the major causes of homelessness? Write your reaction to this information.
3. Conduct a subject search for a site called "United for a Fair Economy." Visit the section entitled "The Racial Wealth Gap: Left Out of the Boom." What data are provided to suggest that racial minorities have not gained economically during the relatively good economic years of the 1990s?

Infotrac® Exercises

1. Students will need to access InfoTrac at **http://infotrac.thomsonlearning.com/index.html** to answer the following questions. Once logged on, type "Beta Israel" in the Search field. Next click on "Periodicals." Once the results appear, find the article "Caste and Class in Historical North-West Ethiopia: The Beta Israel (Falasha) and Kemant, 1300-1900." Read the selection and answer the following:

   a. What is the distinction between caste and class systems in these societies?

   b. How is caste related to religious ideology?

2. In the Search field, type in "Class system." Click on "Periodicals." Use the Limit Search function to find the article "Who's Afraid of the Class System?"

   a. Besides finances, what other characteristics determine a person's social class?

   b. According to the author, what are some of the negative consequences of class distinctions?

Suggested Films

Another American. (PSU), 27 min. - Projections indicate that by the end of the 20th century Hispanics may make up the largest minority group in the United States. Interviews with well-known Hispanics underline the individualism of the Hispanic people.

Canada: True North - The Immigrants. (PSU), 57 min. - Explains that in Canada, unlike the U.S. "melting pot" concept, people with different backgrounds tend to retain their cultural identities and ties.

Caste and Class. (PSU), 24 min. film or video - Demonstrates how the caste system of India is changing to a system based on social class. The film argues that the change in the system is a result of modern capitalism's effects on traditional relationships.

Chapter 14

Supernatural Beliefs

Learning Objectives

After reading and studying Chapter 14, your students should be able to:

1. Define and critically evaluate the concept of religion.
2. Explain the focus of anthropological interest in the functions of religion and acknowledge that anthropologists are not interested in proving which religion is the best.
3. Distinguish between religion and magic.
4. Explain the difference between sorcery and witchcraft.
5. Recognize the differences between the Wicca movement in North America and witchcraft in traditional societies.
6. Describe what myths are and what they do.
7. Understand the social and the psychological functions of religion.
8. Describe Wallace's four categories of religious organization.
9. Give an example of an individualistic cult.
10. Explain the difference between shamanistic cults and communal cults.
11. Evaluate the relationship between ecclesiastical cults and state societies.
12. Describe how religion can play an important role in transforming a society.
13. Give examples and describe the functions of revitalization movements.
14. Understand the way religion is affected by contemporary globalization.

Chapter Outline

I. DEFINING RELIGION
  A. Forms of religion vary but are all alike to the extent that they are founded on a belief in the supernatural
  B. Religion is a set of beliefs and patterned behaviors concerned with supernatural beings and forces
  C. Humans manipulate supernatural forces to solve important life problems that cannot be resolved through the application of science and technology
  D. All societies have a recognizable set of beliefs and behaviors that can be called religions
  E. Natural tendency for people to see their own religion as the best while viewing all others as inferior

F. Anthropologists are interested in
   1. What beliefs are
   2. How they function
   3. Their effect on human behavior
G. Problems of Defining Religion
   1. No universal agreement among anthropologists as to how to distinguish between religious and nonreligious phenomena
   2. May be embedded in the total social structure
   3. Different societies have different ways of distinguishing between the natural world and the supernatural world
   4. Archaeological evidence suggests that people have believed in an afterlife for as long as 300,000 years
   5. It is important to distinguish between animism (belief in spiritual beings) and animatism (belief in a generalized impersonal power over which people have some control
H. Religion and Magic
   1. Important to examine both the similarities and differences between magic and religion because they are most often found in some combined or compound form
   2. Share features
      a. Both are systems of supernatural belief
      b. Nonrational - not susceptible to scientific verification
      c. Both are practiced as a way of coping with the anxieties, ambiguities, and frustrations of everyday life
      d. Elements of both are often found together
   3. Religion
      a. Deals with major issues of human existence
      b. Uses prayer and sacrifices to appeal to or petition supernatural powers for assistance
      c. Tends to be a group activity
      d. Is usually practiced at a specific time
      e. Usually involves officially recognized functionaries such as priests
   4. Magic
      a. Is directed toward specific, immediate problems
      b. Magical practitioners believe they can control or manipulate nature or other people by their own efforts
      c. Is more individually oriented
      d. Is practiced irregularly in response to specific and immediate problems
      e. May be performed by a wide variety of practitioners - not always recognized as having supernatural powers
      f. Involves the manipulation of supernatural forces for the purpose of intervening in a wide range of human activities and natural events
      g. Can be directed to cause evil
      h. Imitative Versus contagious magic

II. Sorcery and Witchcraft
   A. According to the author, witchcraft is inborn, involuntary, often unconscious capacity to cause harm
      1. Virtually impossible to prove or disprove because of absence of visible evidence of its existence
      2. How witches are conceptualized varies widely, but, in all cases, witches are viewed negatively
      3. Often associated with certain animals

- B. Sorcery is the deliberate use of supernatural powers to bring about harm and often involves use of materials, potions, and medicines
  1. Sorcerers generally believed to direct malevolence purposefully rather than acting randomly
  2. Accusations of sorcery are patterned to the extent that they reflect conflicts, rivalries, and antagonisms that already exist among people in any given society
- C. Both are found in both small scale societies and highly industrialized parts of the world
  1. Distinction found in the Western world is between the forms of magic used for beneficial purposes and those used for malevolent purposes
- D. Basic distinction exemplified by modern-day witches and Satanists
  1. Contemporary witches call their belief system **Wicca** (Old English term meaning "witch").
     - a. Practiced largely in urban areas
     - b. Involves worship as a central part of its activities
     - c. Most practitioners are women, and Wicca has a matriarchal character
     - d. May involve the practice of magic - bringing about changes by concentrating on one's natural powers
     - e. As a neo-pagan movement, contemporary Wiccans view themselves as rediscovering ancient lost magical powers
     - f. A reflection of contemporary religious pluralism
  2. Satanists worship the Judeo-Christian devil
     - a. View themselves as the antithesis of Christianity, in league with the devil
     - b. Suggested modern Satanism is a direct outgrowth of the Christian churches' strong stance against witchcraft
     - c. Use evil magic to curse their enemies
  3. No evidence that these forms of supernatural belief are dying out
  4. Witchcraft and Satanism, like other belief systems, can be empowering in that they offer a sense of control, provide an explanation for personal failure and inadequacy, and allow the individual social acceptance into a group

III. MYTHS

- A. Every society has a sacred literature called myth that states certain religious truths
- B. Myths, embodying a specific world view, contain stories of the gods, their origins, their activities, and the moral injunctions they teach
  1. Serve to explain the large questions surrounding human existence
  2. A culture's mythology is closely connected to its moral and social order
- C. Common form is the myth of origin, which provides answers to questions about how things began.
- D. Trickster myths - less serious in tone but carry important messages about the history and morality of the culture

IV. FUNCTIONS OF RELIGION

- A. Studies of religion no longer dominated by the search for origins
  1. More recently focused on how religious systems function for both the individual and the society as a whole
  2. New questions related to explaining the universal existence of religion

B. Social Functions of Religion
  1. Social Control
    a. Encourages socially acceptable behavior
    b. Religion is an ethical system with social sanctions
  2. Anthropologists are interested in whether and to what extent people actually believe in the power of the supernatural forces because the belief determines the level of conformity to socially prescribed behavior.
  3. Conflict Resolution
    a. Reduces stress and frustrations that often lead to social conflict
    b. Used by disenfranchised or powerless people in stratified societies as a way to diffuse anger and hostility that might otherwise be directed against the total social system
    c. Serves as a s mechanism to reduce conflict between differing economic groups
  4. Group Solidarity
    a. Intensifies the group solidarity of practitioners
    b. Enables people to express their common identity
    c. Excludes those who do not practice it
    d. Strengthens a person's sense of group identity and belonging

C. Psychological Functions of Religion
  1. Cognitive function - provides an intellectual framework for explaining parts of the world that we don't understand
    a. Helps people to maintain world view even when it is contradicted
  2. Emotional function - helps to reduce anxiety by prescribing straightforward ways of coping with stress
    a. Allows people to act with confidence

V. TYPES OF RELIGIOUS ORGANIZATIONS

A. Anthony Wallace identified four principal patterns of religious organizations based on cults
  1. Cult - forms of religion that have their own set of beliefs, rituals, and goals (individualistic, shamanistic, communal and ecclesiastical)
  2. Correspond roughly to different levels of socioeconomic organization

B. Individualistic Cults
  1. No religious specialists and represent most basic level of religious structure
  2. Each person has relationship with one or more supernatural beings whenever he or she has a need for control or protection
  3. No distinctions between specialists and laypersons
  4. Some small scale band societies practice it as a predominant mode
  5. Plains Indian vision quest is an example

C. Shamanistic Cults
  1. Have part-time religious specialists who are thought to have supernatural powers by virtue of birth, training or inspiration
  2. Powers used for healing, diving and telling fortunes during times of stress
  3. Represent simplest form of religious division of labor
  4. Term *shaman* encompasses variety of specialists - men/women, diviners, spiritualists, palm readers, and magicians
  5. Shamans have access to supernatural spirits that they contact on behalf of their clients
  6. Reputation rests on power of the shaman's spirit helpers and ability to contact them at will while in an altered state of consciousness
  7. Reindeer Tungus of Siberia are example of shamanistic cult

D. Communal Cults
   1. Involve a more elaborate set of beliefs and rituals
   2. Operate at a higher level of organizational complexity
   3. Groups of ordinary people conduct religious rites and ceremonies for the larger community
   4. Rites considered vital to the well-being of both individuals and society as a whole
   5. Fall into two broad categories - rites of passage and rites of solidarity
   6. Rites of passage
      a. Ceremonies mark a change in a person's social position
      b. Important public rituals recognize a wider set of altered social relationships
      c. Van Gennep - three phases (Separation, Transition, and Incorporation)
      d. Kikuyu of Kenya practice rites of passage
   7. Rites of solidarity
      a. Directed toward the welfare of the community rather than the individual
      b. Serve to restore social harmony with group
      c. Ancestral cults foster group solidarity
E. Ecclesiastical Cults
   1. Most complex form of religious organization
   2. Found in societies with state systems of government
   3. Characterized by full-time professional clergy who are formally elected or appointed and devote all or most of time performing priestly functions
   4. Conduct rituals that occur at regular intervals
   5. Organized into hierarchical organization under control of centralized church or temple
   6. Often controlled by central government or closely associated with it
   7. Prevailing myths and beliefs used to support supremacy of ruling class
   8. Priests often part of ruling class
   9. Role not traditionally given to women
   10. Lay population spiritually dependent on priests for their ritual supernatural well-being
   11. Ecclesiastical cults in the United States
      a. Church membership has grown, not declined, over last several hundred years
      b. Not a secular society - places a very high value on organized religion
      c. Roman Catholics are the largest single denomination
      d. Islam is the fastest growing religious group
      e. Also an increase in non-Christian religious practices
      f. The role of religious ideas in the 2004 presidential election
F. Globalization of World Religions
   1. Revolution in information and communications has had far reaching effects on various ecclesiastical religions of the world
   2. Traditional world religions are cross-pollinating at a rapid rate
   3. Causing dilemma for leaders of world religions who see this as a threat to their very identity
   4. There is a growing number of ideas working their way into the secular world of business
   5. American Catholics are now outsourcing their religious rituals to India

VI. RELIGION AND SOCIAL CHANGE
A. Religion is a conservative force within society and supports the status quo

1. Keeps people in line through supernatural sanctions
2. Relieves social conflict
3. Provides explanations for unfortunate events

B. Religion has also played major role in global social change over the past several decades
   1. Liberation theology - a militant form of Catholicism that merged Catholic theology with an activism for social justice for the poor
   2. Religion can play important role in transforming society
      a. Under high levels of societal stress and strain, new religions or sects spring up to create a new social order
      b. Role of African-American churches in social change
      c. Revitalization movements
         1) Include nativistic movements, cargo cults, separatist Christian churches, mahdist movements, and millenarian movements
         2) Common thread is that they tend to occur during times of cultural stress brought about by rapid change, foreign domination, and perceived deprivation
         3) Widespread among Native American groups - Handsome Lake, Ghost Dance, and Peyote cults

C. Revitalization in the Age of Globalization
   1. Possible to find revitalization movements in today's world (Indonesia's Muhammadiya Islamic organization)
   2. Religious nationalism rejects the idea that religion and government should be separate
      a. Calls for an absolute merging of traditional religious beliefs into government institutions and leaders (Islamic nationalism)

D. The Changing Nature of Religion
   1. The continued power and influence of TV evangelists
   2. The growing influence of the Internet for spreading religious ideas

Key Terms

These are the anthropological terms introduced in Chapter 14. You may want to ask your students to write definitions of one or more of these terms during class to see how well they understood the reading. Even if you choose not to grade the assignment, the students will take it more seriously if you collect their answers.

cargo cults
communal cults
contagious magic
covens
cults
ecclesiastical cults
imitative magic
individiualistic cults
liberation theology
magic
mahdist movements
millenarian movements
myths
nativistic movements
religion
religious nationalism
revitalization movements
rites of passage
rites of solidarity
Satanists
separatist Christian church
shamanistic cults
sorcery
vision quest
Wicca
witchcraft

Critical Thinking Questions

1. There are many cultural variations in distinguishing between the natural and the supernatural. What exactly is meant by the supernatural? Is it a cross-culturally valid concept?

2. Do religions ever deal with the more immediate and specific problems that are said to be the domain of magic?

3. What is the difference between superstition and religion?

4. Do societies that have witches usually have sorcerers as well? Is there a difference between traditional and industrialized societies when it comes to the practice of witchcraft?

5. Has the rise of science over the past 150 years caused people to abandon their religious (non-rational) beliefs?

6. What religions would provide greater psychological than social support?

7. Are there examples of individualistic cults in modern American society?

8. Are there ritualistic rites of passage in industrialized society?

9. Do major sports events serve as rites of solidarity in the United States?

10. Can revitalization movements occur when there is rapid culture change but no foreign domination?

Class Activities

1. Assign each student to study the death ritual of a non-Western society. Have each student report how the particular ritual they studied provides emotional comfort and helps to reduce the stress of the afflicted. An alternative would be to assign birth rituals.

2. Invite a medical practitioner with non-Western training, such as someone who works in herbal medicine, to your class to discuss her or his experiences practicing in the United States. What types of health-related beliefs are the most difficult to understand?

3. Referring to the Contemporary Issues Box in Chapter 14 ("Religious Freedom in Florida"), have students discuss other areas of everyday life in the U.S. which can come up against the exercise of religious freedom.

Internet Exercises

1. Shamans and shamanism are usually associated with small-scale, non-Western societies, but shamanism is also found in the industrialized world. Conduct an Internet subject search on the topic of **shamanism**. As strange as it may seem, many contemporary shamans have their own web sites. What can you learn from these web sites about the practice of shamanism in the Western, industrialized world?

2. Use any search engine to conduct a subject search on cargo cults on the Internet. Locate the **Jon Frum** home page, which describes a particular cargo cult located in Vanuatu, Melanesia. Melanesia in the southwest Pacific has experienced a number of revitalization movements called cargo cults.

Write a one-page paper (written for someone who has never had a course in anthropology) describing the general features of cargo cults.

3. Rastafari is a contemporary religion that contains the elements of a revitalization movement. Link to information about Rastafari from any search engine, or go to

http://www.swagga.com.

Write a one-page paper on the history and essential elements of this belief system. How does the information you gained confirm or change your knowledge of this New World system of religious expression?

Infotrac® Exercises

1. Students will need to access InfoTrac at **http://infotrac.thomsonlearning.com/index.html** to answer the following questions. Once logged on, type in "Reichel-Dolmatoff" in the Search field. Click on "Periodicals." Locate the article "Rainforest Shamans—A Feature Review of Gerardo Reichel-Dolmatoff's anthropological essays."

   a. How are creation myths codes of instruction?

   b. How do the native peoples described in the article connect with their supernatural spirits?

2. In the Search field, type in "Tolai." Read the article "Tolai Sorcery and Change."

   a. How has Tolai sorcery been affected by colonial rule?

   b. What are some of the social and psychological functions of witchcraft and sorcery?

Suggested Films

Bali. The Mystical Land. Films for the Humanities, 56 min. - Focuses on religion and life-cycle rituals in Bali.

Eduardo the Healer. (PSU), 54 min., #50469 - Eduardo Calderon, a Peruvian shaman, is shown using spells and drugs to heal villagers.

Holy Ghost People. (PSU), 53 min., #50249 - Church service and testimonies of rural white Pentecostals in West Virginia. Scenes include speaking in tongues, singing and dancing, snake handling, informal "preaching". Excellent counterpoint to view that Westerners are less ecstatic and "more rational" than others in their religious beliefs and practices.

Pomo Shaman. (PSU), 22 min., #21780 - A shaman goes into a trance and cures her patient by sucking. An edited version of Sucking Doctor.

Chapter 15

Art

Learning Objectives

After reading and studying Chapter 15, your students should be able to:

1. Give a clear definition of art while recognizing that art is integrated into the whole of culture.
2. Explain why such activities as carving, weaving, or telling folktales can be art.
3. Describe the significance of both process and product for the definition of art.
4. Understand the forms of art most common in nomadic or semi-nomadic societies and how they differ from those of complex societies.
5. Recognize the psychological functions of art for the artist as well as for the audience.
6. Describe the contribution of art to the social integration of a society.
7. Recognize how distinct the creation of art is across cultures.
8. Explain the ways in which art can preserve the status quo of a society both symbolically and mechanically.
9. Understand the importance of culture in determining what a person actually hears in music.
10. Explain how dance and verbal arts can be integral aspects of socialization.
11. Recognize how new art forms, such as the glass art movement since the 1970s, can develop with considerable rapidity.
12. Understand how art functions as a social control mechanism and works to preserve the status quo.
13. Recognize the impact of globalization on the preservation of traditional art forms.

Chapter Outline

Artistic expression is found in every society and aesthetic pleasure is felt by all humans.

I. WHAT IS ART?
   A. Definitions of art vary with the purposes of the definers
   B. Includes certain basic elements
      1. Artistic process that is creative and not concerned with usefulness
      2. Produces some type of emotional response, either positive or negative
      3. Should be transformational
      4. Should communicate information by being representational
      5. Artists develop a certain level of technical skill not shared by all people in a society
   C. Art is both the process and the products of applying certain skills to any activity that transforms matter, sound, or motion into a form that is deemed aesthetically meaningful to people in a society

- D. Various types of artistic expression
  1. Graphic or plastic arts
  2. Creative manipulation of sounds and words (verbal arts)
  3. Application of skill and creativity to body movement (dance)
  4. Sometimes include forms not familiar to Westerners
- E. Every society has a set of standards that distinguish between good and bad art or between more and less satisfying aesthetic experiences

II. DIFFERENCES IN ART FORMS

- A. The term *primitive* has fallen out of fashion when referring to societies. Still used when associated with art, but is misleading
- B. Art is part of small-scale societies (preferred term)
- C. Differences between art in small-scale and complex societies
  1. Art in small-scale societies is highly portable
  2. Art in complex societies has full time specialists
  3. Aesthetic standards are less elaborate, more implicit, and more widely diffused in small-scale societies
  4. Art in complex societies becomes associated with the elite
  5. Art in small-scale societies tends to be more democratic
  6. Art in small-scale societies is embedded to a greater degree in other aspects of the culture
  7. Art can reflect the political system of a society in some parts of the world (Melanesia and Polynesia)

III. THE FUNCTIONS OF ART

- A. Emotional Gratification for the Individual
  1. A source of personal gratification for both the artist and the viewer
  2. Provides a temporary break from pursuits related to meeting basic survival needs
  3. Psychological functions for the artist - permits the release of emotional energy in a concrete or visible way
  4. Psychological functions for viewer - portrays events that conjure up positive emotions that contribute to mental well being
  5. Can also elicit negative emotions for both artist and viewer
- B. Art Contributes to Social Integration
  1. Functions to help sustain the longevity of the society in which it is found
  2. Is connected to other parts of the social system
  3. Has been used in many societies to evoke positive sentiments for systems of government and individual political leaders
  4. Art forms found in a society reflect the major cultural themes and concerns of the society
  5. Function to help integrate the society by making the dominant cultural themes, values, and beliefs more visible
  6. Cultural values are passed from generation to generation using the media of song and dance
  7. Music also used to solidify a group of people
- C. Social Control
  1. Much art functions to reinforce the existing sociocultural system
  2. Mano masks in Liberia embody the spiritual forces that actually control human behavior
  3. State-sponsored monumental architecture used to control the behavior of citizens in more complex societies

D. Preserving or Challenging the Status Quo
   1. All societies make distinctions between levels of power and prestige
   2. One way to display power is symbolically through the control of valuable items in the society
      a. Accumulation of art objects serves as a symbol of high prestige
      b. Association of art with status seen in ranked societies
   3. Art also used as a vehicle of protest, resistance, or revolution
      a. Arpilleristas in Chile
      b. Liberation theater from 1960s Peru
   4. Works of art can be the focal point of controversy between those who would defend, as opposed to those who would oppose, the existing thinking in a society (Mel Gibson versus Russell Biles)

IV. GRAPHIC AND PLASTIC ARTS
A. Include a number of forms of expression and a wide variety of skills
   Painting
   1. Sculpture
   2. Printmaking
   3. Architecture
   4. Weaving
   5. Embroidery
   6. Jewelry making
   7. Tattooing and other forms of body decorating
   8. Metalworking
   9. Carving
B. Cross-cultural Variations
   1. Nature of the creative process varies cross-culturally
   2. Graphic/plastic arts received greatest attention from anthropologists
   3. Analysis was the most manageable
   4. Are very physical and can be removed from their cultural contexts, displayed in museums, and compared with ease
   5. Has a permanence of form not found in music, dance, or drama

V. MUSIC
A. All people have same physiological mechanisms for hearing, but what is actually heard is influenced by culture
B. Ethnomusicology
   1. Cross-cultural study of music involving the cooperative efforts of anthropologists and musicologists
   2. Study of music in its cultural context
C. Four major concerns
   1. Ideas about music
   2. Social structure of music
   3. Characteristics of the music itself
   4. Material culture of music
D. Two approaches
   1. Search for musical universals - elements found in all musical traditions
   2. Demonstration of musical diversity around the world

VI. DANCE
A. Defined as purposeful and intentionally rhythmical nonverbal body movements that are culturally patterned and have aesthetic value
B. Forms vary widely from society to society

C. Functions of dance
   1. Psychological - helps people cope more effectively with tensions and aggressive feelings
   2. Political - expresses political values and attitudes, shows allegiance to political leaders, and controls behavior
   3. Religious - methods of communicating with supernatural forces
   4. Social - articulates and reinforces relationships between members of society
   5. Educational - passes on cultural traditions, values, and beliefs from one generation to the next

D. Dance and Other Aspects of a Culture
   1. Tends to reflect and reinforce work patterns
   2. Netsilik Eskimos are an example
   3. Capoeira is a combination of dance, acrobatics, and martial arts

VII. VERBAL ARTS

A. Creative forms of expression using words
   1. Folklore - unwritten verbal arts
   2. Many types including myths, legends, folktales, jokes, folk medicine, folk poetry, games, prayers, sounds used to summon animals or to give them commands
   3. Myths and folktales have received the most attention

B. Myths
   1. Specific types of narratives that involve supernatural beings and designed to explain some of the really big issues of human existence
   2. Stories of our search for significance, meaning, and truth
   3. Generally thought in the Western world that myths are symptomatic of small-scale, non-Western peoples.
   4. Entire history of Western civilization has witnessed a demythologization, but much of Western culture has been molded by the power of myth.

C. Folktales
   1. More secular in nature, have no particular basis in history, and exist largely for the purposes of entertainment
   2. Have a moral and are important for socialization
   3. Seen as an art form from two perspectives
   4. Are creative expressions that can be analyzed in terms of plot, character development, and structure
   5. Involve artistry - teller retains right to embellish and dramatize the story through rhythm, emotions, and use of nonverbal gestures

VIII. FILM: A RECENT ART FORM

A. Excellent films have been made outside of Hollywood for decades

B. Filmmakers from small scale societies (Inuit) and large scale societies (Bollywood)

IX. ART: CONTINUITY AND CHANGE

A. The various forms of expressive arts are subject to both internal and external forces of change

B. The twentieth century witnessed many more changes than occurred in the two previous centuries

C. Possibilities for quick and widespread cultural diffusion are increasing (glass art)

D. Pure art forms, either Western or non-Western, will become increasingly difficult to find as the world becomes more interdependent

E. Reason to be concerned that traditional art forms in small-scale cultures may be globalized out of existence

Key Terms

These are the anthropological terms introduced in Chapter 15. You may want to ask your students to write definitions of one or more of these terms during class to see how well they understood the reading. Even if you choose not to grade the assignment, the students will take it more seriously if you collect their answers.

Capoeira
dance
ethnomusicology
folklore
folktales
graphic arts
hija
legends
liberation theater
plastic arts
transformational

Critical Thinking Questions

1. Cross-culturally, is process or product more important in art?
2. What are the limits to understanding the symbolic communication of art from another society?
3. When does body decoration become art instead of good grooming?
4. Why are art historians and others so resistant to giving up the use of the term "primitive" in connection with art?
5. Is the art of small-scale societies less durable than that of complex societies?
6. How do you account for the fact that in museums displaying art from small scale societies, the collector is identified, but the artist is not?
7. Are there universal elements found in all musical traditions?
8. Why is solo singing found in stratified societies and not in egalitarian ones?
9. How important are the political functions of dance to complex societies?
10. What can be done to preserve the art forms of small-scale societies in the face of globalization and cultural diffusion?

Class Activities

1. Assign students to study body decoration in a variety of societies. Are there any universals in the aesthetics of decorating bodies? Do the social functions of this art form limit the aesthetics?
2. Assign students to attend a dance concert of one of the cultures in your community or on your campus. Have them discuss the experience from the perspective of the audience and to reflect on the differences in this experience between performer and viewer.

Internet Exercises

1. Starting with Yahoo (**http://www.yahoo.com**), click on "Arts and Humanities," then "Cultures and Groups." You will find a list of approximately 45 countries. Select a country that you are interested in by clicking on it. By browsing through the various sites, what can you learn about the artistic tradition of that country? What forms of art are most prominent? What connections can you find between this country's art forms and other parts of the culture? After considering these questions, write a two-page paper on the art of this country.

2. Glass sculptural art is a relatively new art form that has developed in the United States and Canada over the last 30 years. One of the glass artists in the United States is Dante Marioni. Using the name "Dante Marioni," conduct a search on the Internet to see if you can locate any of his art for sale. By which gallery is he represented? Select a piece of Marioni's glass sculpture that you find appealing. How would you describe this piece of sculpture? How much does it cost?

3. Masks take many forms, from the ceremonial types described in your text to contemporary artistic productions. Link to the following URL to view contemporary masks, or search for "goddess magic masks."

   http://www.maui.net/~love/index.html

   Contrast ceremonial mask work and that used for social control with the masks on this site.

Infotrac® Exercises

1. Students will need to access InfoTrac at **http://infotrac.thomsonlearning.com/index.html** to answer the following questions. Once logged on, type "Anthropology" in the Search field. Next click on "Periodicals." Once the results appear, use the Limit Search function to find the article "Dancing the Past Into Life: The Rasa, Nrtta and Raga of Immigrant Existence." Read the selection and answer the following.

   a. How are gender and caste distinctions established through Indian dance?

   b. How are the roles represented through dance altered by colonialism?

Suggested Films

Behind the Mask. (UC), 52 min. - The Dogon of Mali make impressive sacred masks, which this film shows being used in rituals, songs, and dances. Also shows the influence of Dogon sculpture on European artists. (Part of Tribal Eye Series)

The Spirit of the Mask. 60 mins.(1992) Gryphon Productions. Dist. By Atlas Video, Bethesda, MD. - Wade Davis hosts this program on the Northwest Coast Indians. This video explains myths, rituals and ceremonies behind their art.

Stoney Knows How. Ethnoscope, P.O. Box 92353, Rochester, N.Y. 14692. Tel: 716-442-5274 - This video interviews and watches Stoney St. Clair as he goes about his art of tatooing.

Tatau: What One Must Do. (UC), 27 min. - Examines the art of Samoan tattooing.

Chapter 16

Culture Change and Globalization

Learning Objectives

After reading and studying Chapter 16, your students should be able to:

1. Understand how change is essential to all cultures.
2. Describe the two processes that cause cultures to change internally.
3. Explain the difference between invention and innovation and recognize the greater impact of the latter.
4. Recognize that diffusion is a two-way process and understand what is involved in the selection of characteristics that are diffused.
5. Explain how acculturation is distinct from diffusion.
6. Describe why change in one part of culture is likely to bring about changes in other parts.
7. Explain three reasons why a society might resist cultural change.
8. Describe the anthropological concern with the survival of indigenous peoples.
9. Explain why the dichotomous rural-urban model is simplistic and the concept of circulation of labor is more realistic.
10. Describe the stratification of economic development.
11. Understand the contrast between modernization and world system theory.
12. Explain the role of multinational corporations in economic development and the process of neocolonialism.
13. Explain the impact of globalization and modernization on small-scale cultures.

Chapter Outline

I. CULTURE CHANGE
   A. Nothing is as constant as change in culture
   B. Change as a result of internal mechanisms such as inventions or innovations
   C. Change as a result of external mechanisms through the process of cultural diffusion or borrowing
   D. Diffusion is responsible for the greatest amount of cultural change

II. INVENTIONS / INNOVATIONS
  A. Any new thing, idea, or behavior pattern that emerges from within the society
    1. Some are deliberate and purposeful; others are unconscious and unintentional
    2. Unconscious inventor had had a greater impact on cultural change
    3. Deliberate inventor tends to receive the greatest rewards and recognition
  B. Innovation and invention are not synonymous
    1. Innovator - first people to adopt or use a new thing or idea
    2. Suggested that both inventors and innovators tend to be marginal people living on the fringes of society
    3. Not bound by tradition, can see problems and their solutions with a fresh perspective
    4. Innovators and early adopters likely to come from upper-class, wealthy, and well-educated segments of society

III. DIFFUSION
  A. Diffusion - the spreading of a thing, an idea, or a behavior pattern from one culture to another
  B. General Patterns of Diffusion
    1. Selectivity
      a. Only a small number of cultural elements are ever diffused
      b. Item's utility and compatibility to existing traits is influential
      c. Adoption of innovation is affected by
        1) Whether it is seen to be superior to what already exists
        2) Whether it is consistent with existing cultural patterns
        3) Whether it is easily understood
        4) Whether it can be tested on a trial basis
        5) Whether its benefits are clearly visible
    2. Reciprocity
      a. Cultural traits are diffused in both directions
    3. Modification
      a. Once a cultural element is accepted into new culture, may undergo changes in form or function
      b. Partial diffusion (yachts in the PRC)
    4. Likelihood
      a. Some parts of culture more likely to be diffused
      b. Items of material culture more likely to be diffused than ideas or behavior patterns
    5. Variables
      a. Duration and intensity of contact
      b. Degree of cultural integration
      c. Similarities between donor and recipient cultures

IV. ACCULTURATION
  A. A special type of diffusion that takes place as a result of sustained contact between two societies, one subordinate to the other
  B. Involves the widespread reorganization of one or both cultures over a short period of time
  C. Subordinate culture always changes most dramatically
    1. Could become extinct
    2. Could be incorporated as a distinct subculture of the dominant group
    3. Could be assimilated (blended) into the dominant group
  D. Involves forced borrowing under conditions of external pressure
  E. Ranges from "freely chosen" to brutal exploitation

F. May occur because people think certain technologies or behavior will increase adaptation to the environment

V. LINKED CHANGES
  A. Cultures are systematic wholes, the parts of which are interconnected
  B. Linked changes - changes in one part of the culture likely to bring about changes in other parts

VI. OBSTACLES TO CULTURAL CHANGE
  A. Every culture has opposing forces
    1. Those promoting the status quo
    2. Those promoting change
    3. Barriers to cultural change are important to understand
  B. Cultural Boundary Maintenance
    1. Create and maintain cultural boundaries to keep people separate from other groups
    2. Boundaries strengthen and glorify cultural traditions
    3. Boundaries discourage cultural borrowing from other groups
    4. Aspects such as language, eating habits, clothing, folklore, and humor used to both emphasize a culture's uniqueness and to exclude outsiders
  C. Language
    1. An embodiment of the people's values - reflective of a people's ethos or world view
    2. Use own language exclusively
    3. Forbid the use of other languages
    4. Discourage outsiders from speaking their language
    5. Swahili in Tanzania or French in Quebec are examples
  D. Clothing
    1. To maintain unique cultural identity, people (particularly when away from home) are likely to wear their own ethnic or national dress
  E. Eating Styles
    1. Every culture uses the sharing of food in one way or another to maintain social ties and group solidarity
  F. Relative Values
    1. Change may be resisted because it is not compatible with the existing value system
  G. Cultures as Organic Wholes
    1. Functional interrelatedness of parts of culture can serve as conservative force discouraging culture change
    2. Small-scale cultures have reached a state of equilibrium
    3. To change one part of such a culture is likely to threaten existing social and economic relationships
    4. Resisting change may be the sensible response

VII. CULTURAL SURVIVAL OF INDIGENOUS PEOPLES
  A. Indigenous population - any people living in countries which have populations composed of different ethnic or racial groups who are descendants of the earliest populations which survive in the area, and who do not, as a group, control the national government of the countries within which they live.
  B. Indigenous populations negatively affected by the onslaught of civilization
    1. Cultural patterns (and sometimes the people themselves) have been eradicated
    2. Industrial revolution and the explosions in population and consumerism had negative effects - needed to control and exploit natural resources

3. Major motivation for colonization of non-Western world was economic in that natural resources in Asia and Africa were needed to fuel European factories
4. Conference of Berlin in 1884 divided up African continent's natural resources for European nations but did not protect the rights of indigenous populations
    a. Land and resources were appropriated
    b. Landless people forced to become laborers
    c. Resistance met with force
    d. Economic exploitation
    e. Forced to give up their traditional identities
    f. Historical examples (Tasmania; Brazilian Amazon)
    g. Exploitation waiting to happen (Wnnemem Wintu of California)

VIII. URBANIZATION AND CHANGE
- A. Cities have existed for more than 5000 years
    1. Rate of urbanization has accelerated over last century
    2. By 2025 approximately 60% of world's population will be urban (increase from 37% in 1990)
    3. Most rapid urbanization in less-developed countries (LDCs)
    4. LDCs do not have a strong industrial base for population looking for work
- B. The Sociocultural Nature of Cities
    1. Fundamental structural differences between cities and rural societies have been recognized by social scientists since id-nineteenth century
        a. Tonnies - *Gemeinschaft* versus *Gesellschaft*
        b. Durkheim - mechanical versus organic solidarity
        c. Morgan - *societas* versus *civitas*
    2. Recent research shows dichotomous rural-urban model is overly simplistic
    3. Circulation of labor - movement between urban and rural areas
    4. Rural and urban areas should be viewed as complex fields of social relationships comprising criss-crossing peoples, ideas, and resources
    5. Occupational duality - the simultaneous management of a cash-cropping farm at home and some type of wage employment in the city
- C. Adaptation to City Life
    1. Urban anthropologists interested in how migrants meet economic, social, and emotional needs once they come to town
    2. One common strategy is to rely on connections, usually kin-based, from the rural homeland
    3. Beachhead theory of migration - migrants contact relatives or people from home who are established in town.
       Operates with both rural-to-urban migration and international migration
    4. Also use social groups based on voluntary membership as adaptive mechanisms
        a. Voluntary associations serve a variety of purposes
        b. Voluntary associations provide individuals with a sense of belonging

IX. CHANGE AND DEVELOPMENT
- A. Today's world divided into two broad categories of countries - the haves and the have-nots
    1. The industrialized versus the nonindustrialized world
    2. The developed versus the undeveloped world
- B. Theories to explain stratification in economic development
    1. Modernization Theory
        a. Based on a dichotomy of traditional versus modern that serves both as an attempted description of reality and as a planning strategy for bringing about economic development

b. Assumes that in order for undeveloped nations to become developed, they must engage in activities that would make them more like the developed ones
c. Process of economic development would occur through mechanism of foreign aid from wealthy nations
d. Includes many of the same assumptions as the culture of poverty notion (Lewis 1996)
e. Blames poverty on the poor by suggesting that their cultural characteristics keep them undeveloped

2. World System Theory
   a. Rich and poor nations of the world are really part of the world system
   b. Wealthy countries achieved development by exploiting other regions, plundering natural resources, using people as cheap labor, and dominating their markets
   c. Economic development is not the result of an enlightened or progressive population but rather the result of one group purposefully increasing wealth at the expense of others
3. Neocolonialism
   a. Process by which wealthy (former colonial) nations continue to exercise political, economic, financial, and military power over less developed nations.
   b. Debt can be a major form of control
   c. Increasing power and influence of multinational corporations also maintains gap between rich and poor nations
4. Modernization approach suffers from ethnocentric assumptions
   a. Take as a given the fact that all peoples in the world want to become modern
   b. Overestimates extent to which some nonwestern people resist modernization
   c. Assumes that traditional people will be better off if they become modern
5. Studies suggest that economic growth and development do not always lead to an improvement in people's lives
   a. May lower the quality of life through greater poverty, longer working hours, overpopulation, poorer health, more social pathology, and environmental degradations
   b. Increase in diseases found in developed nations - diabetes, heart disease, obesity, hypertension, gout, high blood pressure
   c. Certain bacterial or parasitic diseases also increase
   d. Rapid urbanization creates health-related problems - contagious diseases, poor nutrition, unsanitary conditions
   e. Natural environment negatively affected by development
6. Negative results occur most often when development programs are introduced without full participation and understanding of the peoples they are designed to help

X. GLOBALIZATION AND WORLD CULTURES

A. Globalization

1. Rapid cultural change and interconnection between countries and cultures since later 1980s
2. With demise of world communism, the world is experiencing a new type of integration of markets, technology, and information that is oblivious to both national and cultural borders

3. Driven by free-market capitalism and idea that the more a country opens up its markets to free trade, the healthier its economy will become
4. In actual fact, the way globalization has worked so far is that largely American products have been exported to other cultures on a global scale
5. Concomitant revolution in the world of information technology that facilitate the exchange of ideas across national and cultural boundaries

B. Changes that have defined globalization
1. Revolution in computer technology, which has made communication faster and cheaper
2. Fundamental changes in way money is invested
3. Fundamental change in flow of information - availability of Internet permits spread of ideas (and ideologies) across national boundaries without governmental interference
4. Differences in responses to globalization (India versus Saudia Arabia)

D. Long-term effects on 5,000 plus cultures of the world has yet to be fully realized
1. Suggest that globalization will eventually lead to a general homogenization of cultures into a single global culture
2. Suggest that globalization, rather than totally changing cultures, can stimulate local cultures to redefine themselves in the face of external forces - creating various hybrid cultures

E. The positive and negative aspects of globalization

Key Terms

These are the anthropological terms introduced in Chapter 16. You may want to ask your students to write definitions of one or more of these terms during class to see how well they understood the reading. Even if you choose not to grade the assignment, the students will take it more seriously if you collect their answers.

acculturation
marginal people
culture of poverty
diffusion
globalization
invention
modernization theory
multinational corporations
neocolonialism
world systems theory
linked changes
less developed countries (LDCs)

Critical Thinking Questions

1. Do we discuss culture change as a separate topic because theoretically we have a static view of what culture is? Why can't we incorporate change into all our discussions of culture?
2. If we view culture as a process, do we begin to see more clearly the connections between what is internal to and external to culture?
3. What is the difference between innovation and diffusion?
4. What does it take to make one culture's ideas or ways of behaving diffuse into another society?
5. Are changes in ideas or changes in material goods more significant to acculturation?

6. Are there parts of culture for which it is fairly easy to predict the nature of changes that will occur?
7. Why do so many groups demonstrate at the meetings of the World Trade Organization (WTO)?
8. Is the concept of modernization ethnocentric? Why or why not?
9. What aspects of culture does world systems theory focus on? How does that compare with the focus of modernization theory?
10. Are harmful effects of globalization inevitable? What are harmful effects that people have experienced? How does that compare to the benefits they receive?

Class Activities

1. Divide the class into a number of groups and assign some to research products that are imported from the tropical forests of South America and consumed in the United States. Assign others to research information on native peoples from the same region. After they present their findings to the class, ask students to evaluate the impact that United States consumers have on indigenous South Americans.
2. Divide the class into two groups for a debate on the importance of native language retention for immigrants. Ask them to consider the following question: When immigration requires learning a new language, should it also require that native languages be given up?

Internet Exercises

1. Many industrialized countries have foreign assistance programs that provide economic development funds for poorer, less developed nations. For example, the United States administers foreign assistance programs through the United States Agency for International Development (USAID); in Canada the same function is performed by the Canadian International Development Agency (CIDA).

   Students in the United States should contact the USAID home page

   http://www.info.usaid.gov/

   Canadian students should contact the CIDA home page

   http://www.acdi-cida.gc.ca/

   After selecting the appropriate agency, browse the site and make a list of the various accomplishments of the agency over the years. Make a list of the types of economic assistance programs USAID and CIDA have sponsored around the world over the past several decades.

   Both USAID and CIDA have devoted a substantial amount of money in the last five years in the NIS countries. What are the NIS countries? What has been the justification for this large amount of assistance? What types of specific projects have USAID and CIDA sponsored in the NIS countries since 1990?

2. Conduct a subject search for the organization known as **Cultural Survival**. Once on the home page, write a one-page paper answering the following questions"

   a. What is the purpose of the organization?
   b. What types of projects does the organization sponsor?
   c. After consulting the section dealing with the organization's published journal *Cultural Survival Quarterly*, what are some themes for upcoming issues of the journal?

INFOTRAC® EXERCISES

1. Students will need to access InfoTrac at **http://infotrac.thomsonlearning.com/index.html** to answer the following questions. In the Search field, type in "Papua." Click on "Periodicals." Locate and read the article "Anthropology and the Professionalisation of Colonial Administration in Papua and New Guinea."

   a. What is the relationship between colonialism and anthropology?

   b. How can the fact that some anthropologists are government appointed affect their relationship with aboriginal peoples.

2. In the Search field, type in "Indigenous Knowledge." Click on "Periodicals." Find and read the article "The Development of Indigenous Knowledge: A New Applied Anthropology."

   a. How can we benefit from indigenous knowledge?

   b. Compare indigenous knowledge with Western and industrialized techniques.

SUGGESTED FILMS

Controlling Interest: The World of the Multinational Corporation. (IU), 45 min. - Shows the corporate expansion that has brought productive resources and economic decision-making throughout the world under the control of a small number of giant multinational corporations. Examines the corporation's search for cheap labor, causing "running" industries in developed areas and exploitation of the industrial work force in the Third World.

Edge of Survival. (PSU), 57 min. - Survey of world food problems, focusing on India, Brazil, Ecuador. Examples of dams and other large-scale projects that impact on local communities.

Extinction: The Last Tasmanian. (UC), 60 min. - Documents the genocide of Tasmanians by British colonists.

The Kayapo. (PSU), 53 min. - Documents how dramatically life changed for the Amazonian Kayapo after 1982, when outsiders invaded following the discovery of gold.

Mr. Ludwig's Tropical Dreamland: Parts 1 & 2. (PSU), 57 min. - Billionaire Daniel Ludwig floated a giant pulp mill into the Amazon, planted fast-growing trees in monoculture, and constructed a large settlement for his laborers. The environmental and social impacts of this project are explored. (Originally shown on NOVA)

Test Bank

Chapter 1

What is Anthropology?

Multiple-Choice

1. Anthropology includes the study of all of the following except:

   a. how humans vary biologically
   b. why contemporary people have different cultures
   c. when humans first appeared on earth
   d. how insect cultures vary biologically
   e. how cultures change over time
   ANS: D
   PG: 2

2. Medical anthropology most often draws upon research from

   a. linguistic and cultural anthropology.
   b. archaeology.
   c. physical anthropology.
   d. archaeology and physical anthropology.
   ANS: C
   PG: 12

3. Primatology is the study of

   a. the origin of life on earth.
   b. the culture of early humans.
   c. the first tools used by humans.
   d. the anatomy and social behavior of apes, monkeys, and prosimians.
   ANS: D
   PG: 5-6

4. A holistic approach to the study of humans means that anthropologists

   a. concentrate only on the social customs of the group under study.
   b. study all varieties of people and all aspects of their existence.
   c. limit themselves to the study of religious leaders.
   d. only study literate societies.
   ANS: B
   PG: 14-15

5. The anthropological attitude that a society's customs and ideas should be viewed in the context of that society's culture is called

   a. cultural relativism.
   b. the etic approach.
   c. ethnocentrism.
   d. holism.

   ANS: A
   PG: 15-16

6. A linguistic anthropologist studying the situational use of language is working in the field of

   a. ethnolinguistics.
   b. descriptive linguistics.
   c. historical linguistics.
   d. sociolinguistics.

   ANS: D
   PG: 10

7. An anthropologist studying the relationship between language and culture is working in the field of

   a. ethnolinguistics.
   b. descriptive linguistics.
   c. historical linguistics.
   d. sociolinguistics.

   ANS: A
   PG: 10

8. Studying sound and grammatical systems in a specific language is the work of a/an

   a. ethnologist.
   b. historical linguist.
   c. sociolinguist.
   d. descriptive linguist.

   ANS: D
   PG: 10

9. Prehistoric archaeologists work with which of the following?

   a. artifacts, ecofacts, and features
   b. artifacts, features, and grammar systems
   c. contemporary religious systems, artifacts, and ecofacts
   d. artifacts, grammar systems, and contemporary religious systems

   ANS: A
   PG: 8

10. An example of an ethnography is a/an

a. study of chimpanzee language.
b. excavation of an archaeological site.
c. description of the residents of a retirement home in southern California.
d. study of rates of disease in prehistoric populations.
ANS: C
PG: 11

11. Ethnographic research usually involves

a. many months of fieldwork.
b. talking to a number of people.
c. observing people's behavior.
d. all of the above
ANS: D
PG: 11-12

12. The discipline of anthropology looks at both the biological and sociocultural aspects of human behavior because of its

a. relativistic nature.
b. holistic nature.
c. comparative nature.
d. simplistic nature.
ANS: B
PG: 14-15

13. Because anthropology is holistic, research within the discipline involves

a. only European populations.
b. all human populations, both living and dead.
c. only prehistoric populations which developed state societies.
d. only prehistoric populations which did not develop state societies.
ANS: B
PG: 14-15

14. Urban anthropology

a. has focused research in suburbs.
b. ignored the existence of violent gangs and the marketing of drugs.
c. grew out of research which followed rural people into cities.
d. has been important since the earliest days of anthropology.
ANS: C
PG: 12

15. Educational anthropology is

a. concerned with anthropological theories but not with case studies in education and culture.
b. anthropology taught at the grade school level only.
c. used only to study formal school systems.
d. the study of the process of learning in its proper cultural context.
ANS: D
PG: 13

16. The author of your textbook argues that the best way to gain self-knowledge is to learn about one's own culture. The best way to accomplish this is

a. to do anthropological research in your own society.
b. through psychoanalysis.
c. to read as much as possible about your own culture.
d. to learn something about other cultures.
ANS: D
PG: 22

17. An important goal of this textbook is to

a. teach about exotic cultures.
b. show how anthropology has relevance for all of our lives.
c. focus on the importance of basic research in ethnology.
d. demonstrate the superiority of basic research over applied research.
ANS: B
PG: 17-23

18. Which of the following is NOT a sub-branch of cultural anthropology?

a. medical anthropology
b. primatology
c. economic anthropology
d. educational anthropology
ANS: B
PG: 5-6

19. Economic anthropology studies how goods and services are

a. produced within the total cultural context of which they are a part.
b. distributed within the total cultural context of which they are a part.
c. consumed within the total cultural context of which they are a part.
d. all of the above
ANS: D
PG: 13-14

20. Which of the disciplines that study humans is the broadest in scope?

a. psychology
b. anthropology
c. political science
d. economics
ANS: B
PG: 2

21. Which statement about psychological anthropology is false?

a It looks at how culture affects personality, cognition, and emotions.
b. Since 1990, it has focused on broad national character studies.
c. It is associated with such names as Margaret Mead and Franz Boas.
d. It examines the relationship between culture and the psychological makeup of individuals and groups.
ANS: B
PG: 14

22. Physical anthropologists are interested in

a. how and why the physical traits of contemporary humans vary.
b. reconstructing the evolutionary record of all forms of life.
c. reconstructing the evolutionary record of all humans.
d. a and c only
ANS: D
PG: 4

23. Paleopathology

a. is a primary focus of research in linguistic anthropology.
b. is the analysis of disease in ancient populations.
c. examines language from the time period before the invention of writing.
d. is the analysis of disease in contemporary populations.
ANS: B
PG: 12

24. Ethnocentrism is the belief that

a. one's culture is no better or no worse than any other.
b. other cultures are inferior to one's own.
c. other cultures are superior to one's own.
d. to understand another cultural feature, you must look at it from within its proper cultural context.
ANS: B
PG: 15

25. Historical archaeology

a. deals with that vast segment of the human record prior to writing.
b. analyzes the first stone tools used by humans.
c. contributes significantly to our understanding of colonial American cultures.
d. none of the above
ANS: C
PG: 8

26. Ecofacts are

a. objects found in the natural environment that were used by people but not made or altered by them.
b. objects that have been made by people and are portable.
c. objects that have been made by people but are not portable.
d. objects found in the natural environment that were formed by natural occurrences such as exposure to great heat or cold.
ANS: A
PG: 8

27. Which statement about applied anthropology is <u>false</u>?

a. It is considered by some to be the fifth sub-branch of anthropology.
b. All four fields of anthropology have applied components.
c. The author of this textbook takes a strong stance against applied anthropology.
d. In recent decades, there has been a significant increase in the percentage of applied anthropologists in the discipline of anthropology.
ANS: C
PG: 19-20

28. Applied anthropology

a. does not include forensic anthropology.
b. examines specific societal problems only in the United States but never in other societies.
c. is a specialization not yet practiced in cultural anthropology.
d. cuts across most specializations within cultural anthropology.
ANS: D
PG: 19-20

29. The comparative tradition in cultural anthropology has revealed

a. that all great works of art come from European societies.
b. that all morality does not stem from Judeo-Christian ethics.
c. that social order cannot be maintained without a centralized, bureaucratic government.
d. all of the above
ANS: B
PG: 18-19

30. The study of anthropology develops all of the following skills except:

a. developing cognitive complexity
b. appreciating other perspectives
c. responsible money management
d. building emotional resilience
ANS: C
PG: 21

31. Some of the topics discussed in a leading anthropological journal in the 1990s were

a. the health of a medieval population in the Sudan.
b. the distribution of religious paraphernalia.
c. speech patterns among the Creek Indians.
d. all of the above
ANS: D
PG: 2-3

32. Which of the following principles guide the discipline of anthropology?

a. genocide
b. cultural relativism
c. assimilation
d. holism
e. b and d only
ANS: E
PG: 14-17

33. Anthropologists suspended their cultural relativism when studying the practices of

a. the custom of the Dani who cut off a finger from the hand of any close female relative of a man who dies.
b. the Kikuyu custom of female circumcision.
c. the Inuit custom of leaving the aged out in the cold to die.
d. none of the above
ANS: D
PG: 16

34. Physical anthropology's primary concern(s) and focus is/are

a. paleoanthropology.
b. primatology.
c. contemporary human physical variation.
d. all of the above
ANS: D
PG: 4-7

35. The major subdivisions of anthropological linguistics are

a. historical linguistics.
b. descriptive linguistics.
c. ethnolinguistics.
d. sociolinguistics.
e. all of the above
ANS: E
PG: 9-11

36. In the early 1900s, anthropologists concentrated on

a. the industrial societies of the world.
b. non-Western, preliterate societies.
c. technologically simple societies.
d. b and c
ANS: D
PG: 3

37. One of the techniques anthropological linguists use to study historical linguistics is

a. bilingualism.
b. paralanguage.
c. glottochronology.
d. none of the above
ANS: C
PG: 10

38. Ethnology is to ethnography as

a. bilingualism is to description.
b. comparison is to description.
c. description is to comparison.
d. comparison is to archaeology.
ANS: B
PG: 11

39. The major purpose of cultural anthropology is to understand other cultures. This can be accomplished most effectively if we:

a. have as much specific data as possible about other cultures in the world
b. understand our own culture
c. understand how people from other cultures view us.
d. all of the above
ANS: D
PG: 22

40. A difficulty in taking the concept of cultural relativism too literally is that

a. we would have to conclude that no behavior in the world is immoral.
b. we would have to accept all behaviors found in cultures if the people who practice them concur that they are morally acceptable.
c. we would have to view all cultural practices as morally equivalent.
d. all of the above

ANS: D
PG: 16

True-False

1. Anthropologists are concerned with all humans, both past and present, as well as humans' behavior patterns, thought systems, and material possessions.
ANS: T
PG: 2

2. All anthropologists excavate the material remains of prehistoric societies.
ANS: F
PG: 2

3. Anthropologists recognize non-human primates as important research subjects because they can be studied in environments similar to those our human ancestors lived in several million years ago.
ANS: T
PG: 5-6

4. Ethnocentrism is declining all over the world due to globalization.
ANS: F
PG: 15

5. Educational anthropology addresses issues that bridge the gap between cultural anthropology and linguistics.
ANS: T
PG: 13

6. Anthropology draws on theories and data from a number of other disciplines in the humanities, the social sciences, and the physical sciences.
ANS: T
PG: 2

7. The study of cultural anthropology can build the skill of perceptual acuity.
ANS: T
PG: 21-22

8. An important skill for the twenty-first century will be the ability to balance contradictory needs and demands rather than trying to eliminate them.
ANS: T
PG: 21

9. An important skill in today's world (which can be strengthened by the study of cultural anthropology) is the ability to work effectively in cross-cultural teams.
ANS: T
PG: 21

10. The current head of NATO is Kofi Annan.
ANS: F
PG: 18

Short Answer

1. What does the term anthropology mean?
ANS: the study of humans
PG: 2

2. What are the sub-fields of anthropology?
ANS: physical anthropology, archaeology, anthropological linguistics, and cultural anthropology
PG: 3

3. What is ethnography?
ANS: the descriptive study of specific contemporary cultures
PG: 11

4. What is ethnocentrism?
ANS: the belief that one's own culture is most desirable and superior to all others
PG: 15

5. What three broad areas of investigation concern physical anthropologists?
ANS: reconstructing the evolutionary record of the human species, primate behavior, and human physical variation
PG: 4

6. What is cultural relativism?
ANS: the notion that any part of a culture must be viewed in its proper cultural context rather than from the viewpoint of the observer's culture
PG: 15-16

7. With what three types of material remains do archaeologists work?
ANS: artifacts, features, and ecofacts
PG: 8

8. What are the four branches of linguistic anthropology?
ANS: historical linguistics, descriptive linguistics, ethnolinguistics, and sociolinguistics
PG: 9-10

9. What does the holistic approach in anthropology involve?
ANS: both biological and sociocultural aspects of humanity, the deepest possible time frame, study of all people wherever they may be found, studying many different aspects of the human experience
PG: 14-15

10. What does applied research in anthropology seek to do?
ANS: gain scientific knowledge for the sake of solving particular social problems
PG: 19-20

Essay

1. Describe the four-field approach to anthropology. List the principal concerns of specialists in each field.

2. What is the difference between applied and basic research in anthropology? Explain how both of these types of research help us to better understand ourselves.

3. Describe how anthropology is holistic. How does holism help us to learn about human nature?

4. Why is it important for anthropologists to study contemporary human differences? What does it mean to say that all humans are a single species? How important are physical differences in human populations?

5. Why have modern cultural anthropologists not conducted first hand studies of upper middle class Americans living in the suburbs?

6. Discuss five major skills/competencies that should be developed while studying cultural anthropology.

7. By citing specific examples, discuss how people from other parts of the world might look unfavorably on certain aspects of U.S. culture.

Chapter 2

The Concept of Culture

Multiple-Choice

1. The anthropological concept of culture includes

a. the ideas people learn.
b. the material things people share.
c. the ways people behave.
d. all of the above
ANS: D
PG: 28

2. Which statement about the concept of culture is true?

a. Culture is symbolic.
b. Culture is learned.
c. Culture is always changing.
d. all of the above
ANS: D
PG: 28, 30-33; 36-37

3. The central concept in anthropology is the concept of

a. distribution.
b. power.
c. culture.
d. artifact.
ANS: C
PG: 27

4. People from the same culture can predict one another's behavior because

a. culture determines behavior.
b. culture conditions behavior.
c. all people in any given society accept exactly the same rules for behavior.
d. all people in any given society have exactly the same ideas.
ANS: B
PG: 29

5. Trying to operate in an unfamiliar culture

a. often leads to the experience of culture shock.
b. is never difficult for an educated person.
c. is never hard if you have read a book about that culture.
d. may lead to physical distress but not psychological distress.
ANS: A
PG: 29

6. Despite many differences in details, all cultures share a number of common cultural features including

a. marriage systems
b. a system of distribution
c. a system of communication
d. all of the above
ANS: D
PG: 37-39

7. Children in the United States and Uganda are

a. likely to marry one spouse at a time.
b. born knowing the best solution for situations in daily life, if they are healthy at birth.
c. likely to learn the ways of thinking and acting determined by their own cultures.
d. likely to have the same set of values.
ANS: C
PG: 30-31

8. A majority of our behavioral responses are

a. simple expressions of an individual's original thoughts.
b. instinctive.
c. acquired at birth.
d. the result of complex learning processes.
ANS: D
PG: 31

9. The process by which people acquire their culture is

a. enculturation.
b. genetically based.
c. more rapid in industrialized societies than in less technologically developed ones.
d. slowest in industrialized societies and most rapid in less technologically developed ones.
ANS: A
PG: 30-31

10. The three basic components of culture are

a. things, artifacts, and blood types.
b. things, ideas, and behavior patterns.
c. religions, values, and attitudes.
d. music, painting, and dance.
ANS: B
PG: 28

11. Which statement about the term civilization is true?

a. Civilization is synonymous with culture.
b. All cultures are civilizations, but all civilizations are not cultures.
c. Civilizations are characterized by monumental architecture, writing and centralized government.
d.. all of the above
ANS: C
PG: 29

12. Some people in the world have tattoos, use scarification or wear bones in their noses because

a. they don't understand the harm they do to their bodies.
b. they have a distorted concept of beauty.
c. they do it as part of their religious practice.
d. their culture tells them that it looks good.
ANS: D
PG: 34-36

13. Ferraro's wife was considered unattractive by the Kikuyu because

a. of the color of her skin.
b. she was too thin.
c. she had pierced ears.
d. they wore lipstick.
ANS: B
PG: 35

14. Internal cultural changes occur most often in

a. small-scale, non-western societies.
b. highly Catholic societies.
c. Asian societies.
d. technologically complex societies.
ANS: D
PG: 36

15. What types of cultures remain completely static year after year?

a. small-scale cultures
b. non-western cultures
c. no culture remains completely static
d. western cultures
ANS: C
PG: 36

16. The spread of a cultural element from one society to another is called

a. innovation.
b. tabula rasa.
c. ethnocentrism.
d. cultural diffusion.
ANS: D
PG: 36

17. Which statement about the Amish culture is false?

a. They live in Pennsylvania.
b. They are at the forefront of change in the United States.
c. They are hard-working farmers.
d. They infrequently send their children to public schools.
ANS: B
PG: 30

18. Cultural diffusion is very important in cultural change because

a. people are essentially uninventive and unimaginative.
b. all important elements of culture came from European societies.
c. all important elements of culture came from Asian and African societies.
d. it is easier to borrow a thing or idea than it is to invent it.
ANS: D
PG: 36

19. Cultural universals include

a. division of labor
b. marriage
c. monogamy
d. a and b
ANS: D
PG: 37-39

20. Which statement about the concept of culture is <u>false</u>?

a. Culture influences biological processes.
b. Culture is learned.
c. Cultures change over time.
d. none of the above
ANS: D
PG: 34, 29, 36-37

21. When we describe a culture as being polychromic, we mean that people

a. feel comfortable engaging in a number of activities simultaneously.
b. tend to be extremely punctual.
c. prefer to engage in only one activity at a time.
d. believe in the saying "time is money."
ANS: A
PG: 34

22. The integration of a culture means

a. that all its parts are tightly connected to all other parts.
b. that its parts are somewhat interconnected with one another.
c. that Blacks and Whites attend school together.
d. a culture is exactly like the body of a living organism.
ANS: B
PG: 42-46

23. The task of the cultural anthropologist is to

a. describe the various parts of the culture he or she studies.
b. study aspects of a culture in isolation from the rest of the cultural system.
c. show how parts of a culture are independent from one another.
d. determine if one culture is more moral than another.
ANS: A
PG: 42

24. The process by which culture traits are spread from one culture to another is called

a. parallel evolution.
b. cultural diffusion.
c. racism.
d. ethnocentrism.
ANS: B
PG: 36

25. The anthropological attitude that a society's customs and ideas should be viewed in the context of that society's culture is called

a. ethnocentrism.
b. cultural relativism.
c. cultural constraint.
d. cultural diffusion.
ANS: B
PG: 46

26. Civilizations are generally characterized by

a. cities.
b. monumental architecture.
c. state systems of government.
d. all of the above
ANS: D
PG: 29

27. In the applied perspective dealing with Apache house preferences,

a. Esber found that people preferred to have separate rooms for family members.
b. Esber's work led to house designs that were much preferred to designs used on other Apache reservations.
c. Esber used only traditional anthropological research method of interviewing.
d. the Payson Project was unable to keep any Apaches in the new homes because they all moved back into their old homes.
ANS: B
PG: 32-33

28. Subcultures

a. are subsets of the wider culture.
b. enjoy all the benefits of the mainstream culture.
c. retain a level of cultural uniqueness that sets them apart.
d. a and c
ANS: D
PG: 29-30

29. The "organic analogy" refers to the idea that

a. the parts of a culture are interconnected much as are the organs of a living animal.
b. only the fittest members of a species will survive.
c. humans evolved directly from non-human primates.
d. culture helps people adapt to their environments.
ANS: A
PG: 42

30. The study of comparative cultures has taught us that people in different cultures

a. learn different cultural content.
b. learn essentially the same content in similar ways.
c. learn cultural content with similar efficiency.
d. a and c
ANS: D
PG: 32

31. Culture is changed by

a. technology.
b. ideas and values.
c. changes in the physical and social environment.
d. all of the above
ANS: D
PG: 36-37

32. Cultural anthropologists no longer use the term "primitive" because

a. it erroneously implies that a culture is earlier in time.
b. it erroneously implies that a culture is inferior.
c. it is politically incorrect.
d. all of the above
ANS: D
PG: 46

33. Saying that every society has an economic system means

a. that every society has a system of standardized currency.
b. that every society has markets.
c. that each receives goods and services based on his or her capacity to pay.
d. that every society has worked out a patterned way of ensuring that people get what they need for survival.
ANS: D
PG: 39

34. When Ferraro used "small-scale society," he is referring to societies with relatively

a. small populations.
b. simple technologies.
c. little labor specialization.
d. all of the above
ANS: D
PG: 46

35. In terms of how close people get to one another in different cultures, we know that
- a. middle class North Americans get closer than Cubans
- b. Cubans tend to get closer to one another than do people from New York City
- c. Cubans and New Yorkers tend to keep the same distance during normal conversations
- d. People from New York City get closer to one another than people from all other cultures

ANS: B
PG: 43

36. Cross cultural coaching is appropriate in which setting?

- a. factory
- b. public high school
- c. the United States Army
- d. all of the above

ANS: D
PG: 44-45

37. Which statement about culture change is false?

- a. Cultures are always changing.
- b. Cultures change through the processes of diffusion and innovation.
- c. Cultures change more through invention than through diffusion.
- d. Anthropologists do not agree on the single most important cause of culture change.

ANS: C
PG: 36

38. A Hindu who vomits after inadvertently eating beef illustrates which cultural principle?

- a. Culture is learned.
- b. Cultures are always changing.
- c. Culture influences biological processes.
- d. The parts of a culture are interrelated.

ANS: C
PG: 34

39. Which statement about the learned nature of culture is true?

- a. Humans are born with very few predetermined behaviors.
- b. People learn what they need to know in order to adapt to their environment.
- c. There are no dumb cultures.
- d. all of the above

ANS: D
PG: 30-33

40. A pluralistic society

a. is composed of a number of subcultural groups.
b. has a great potential for misunderstandings or hostilities.
c. is found in the United States and the United Kingdom.
d. all of the above
ANS: D
PG: 30

True-False

1. Culture refers to the people living in a society.
ANS: F
PG: 29-30

2. Culture is acquired through learning rather than encoded in genes or DNA.
ANS: T
PG: 30-33

3. A subculture refers to an inferior cultural group
ANS: F
PG: 29

4. It is ethnocentric for a member of an African tribe to think an anthologist's wife is too thin in comparison to his own wives.
ANS: T
PG: 35

5. Few cultural universals have to do with meeting the basic physiological needs of humans.
ANS: F
PG: 37-39

6. Cultural adaptations have little importance in humans' adaptation to the sub-Arctic.
ANS: F
PG: 39-41

7. The American Anthropological Association has taken the official position that humans are born with a built-in culture.
ANS: F
PG: 31-32

8. In the last decade there has been a reduction in the extent to which Americans alter their appearance through plastic surgery.
ANS: F
PG: 35-36

9. Taiwanese men are prevented from wearing green hats because it violates their religious beliefs.
ANS: F
PG: 37

10. People in French-speaking Africa tend to view their language as an art form.
    ANS: T
    PG: 45

Short Answer

1. What are the two basic processes of cultural change within a society?
   ANS: innovations and cultural diffusion
   PG: 36

2. What is a social control system?
   ANS: a set of mechanisms that coerce people to obey the social norms of a society
   PG: 39

3. Why is the word "primitive" ethnocentric?
   ANS: It implies that something primitive is both inferior and earlier in a chronological sense.
   PG: 46

4. How does the author define the concept of culture?
   ANS: everything that people have, think, and do as members of a society
   PG: 28

5. What is culture shock?
   ANS: a form of psychological distress that can result in depression, overeating, or irritability brought on when trying to operate in an unfamiliar culture
   PG: 29

6. Define the organic analogy made popular by some of the early functionalist anthropologists.
   ANS: A comparison between a culture and a living organism such as the human body that has systems that work together to maintain the overall health of the organism
   PG: 42

7. What are pluralistic societies?
   ANS: societies composed of a number of subcultural groups
   PG: 30

8. What was the preferred housing design for the Apache people in the Payson Project?
   ANS: an open design similar to that of traditional Apache houses, with a minimum of partitions in the general living space
   PG: 32-33

9. Give examples of variations in cultural attitudes concerning male and female attractiveness.
   ANS: Burmese women elongating their necks with brass rings, Chinese foot binding, scarification, tattooing, ear piercing
   PG: 35

10. List five cultural universals
    ANS: see pages 37-40
    PG: 37-40

Essay

1. One of the most important technological changes that took place in the United States was the mass use of television during the 1950s. How has the introduction of that one new gadget influenced or changed other parts of American culture, such as politics, education, religion, and family life?

2. Write an essay illustrating how the concept of "culture influencing biological processes" has affected American culture.

3. In your own words, how would you define the concept of culture? What general statements hold true for all cultures of the world?

4. Write an essay illustrating the concept of the interrelatedness of the parts of culture.

5. What is ethnocentrism and how would you illustrate it from a number of different cultures?

6. How many things that you do during your waking hours are purely biologically based?

7. What types of problems of cultural adjustment would a Japanese teenager face when enrolling in a public high school in the suburbs of Chicago? What advice could you offer this student if you were his/her cross-cultural coach?

Chapter 3

Applied Anthropology

Multiple-Choice

1. Anthropologists for the most part have conducted fieldwork in parts of the world experiencing

   a. poor health.
   b. inadequate food production.
   c. high infant mortality.
   d. all of the above
   ANS: D
   PG: 50

2. Applied anthropology includes which of the following?

   a. advocacy anthropology
   b. development anthropology
   c. post-modern anthropology
   d. a and b only
   ANS: D
   PG: 50

3. Applied and theoretical anthropology have
   a. never had much to contribute to one another.
   b. developed alongside one another.
   c. always used distinctive methods.
   d. a and c
   ANS: B
   PG: 51-53

4. Applied and pure anthropologists have

   a. for the most part, received the same form of training.
   b. always had very different training programs.
   c. almost never involved the same personnel.
   d. both avoided participant-observation as a research method.
   ANS: A
   PG: 51-53

5. Supporters of applied anthropological research

   a. seldom include international agencies.
   b. never include private corporations.
   c. rarely include nonprofit organizations.
   d. often include international and national agencies.
   ANS: D
   PG: 51

6. A specialized role, in which an applied anthropologist interprets research findings so that policy makers, planners, and administrators can make more culturally sensitive decisions is that of

   a. research analyst.
   b. expert witness.
   c. impact assessor.
   d. trainer.
   ANS: A
   PG: 58-59

7. A specialized role, in which an applied anthropologist conducts a fairly specialized type of research designed to determine ahead of time the need for a proposed program or project is that of

   a. advocate.
   b. a needs assessor.
   c. an impact assessor.
   d. an expert witness.
   ANS: B
   PG: 58-59

8. A feature of anthropology that contributes to its potential as a policy science and allows a fuller understanding of sociocultural realities is

   a. an emic view.
   b. an etic view.
   c. ethnocentrism.
   d. the use of survey methodology.
   ANS: A
   PG: 54-57

9. Understanding of the multiple variables involved in human problems is fostered by which special feature of anthropology?

   a. anthropology's holistic perspective
   b. ethnocentrism
   c. an outsider's perspective
   d. a narrow specialization within the discipline of anthropology
   ANS: A
   PG: 55-56

10. During WWII anthropologists helped with the war effort in which of the following ways?

a. studying national morale during wartime
b. studying about food preferences and rationing
c. conducting national character studies of Japanese and Germans
d. all of the above
ANS: D
PG: 53

11. Which group is most likely to hold an emic view?

a. government bureaucrats
b. local clients
c. evaluation researchers
d. planners
ANS: B
PG: 58-59

12. Cultural relativism tends to foster

a. prejudice in anthropologists.
b. inaccuracy in ethnographies.
c. tolerance in anthropologists, a characteristic which can be important for working with diverse populations.
d. ethnocentrism.
ANS: C
PG: 56-57

13. A common methodological problem that applied anthropologists encounter is that

a. they must always use quantitative (statistical) methods.
b. they have a natural bias to side with urban populations rather than with rural populations.
c. participant-observation is time-consuming because it is carried out over a year or more.
d. a and b
ANS: C
PG: 57

14. U.S. anthropologists during World War II

a. performed national character studies on our adversaries.
b. refused to have anything to do with research on the relocation of Japanese-American interns on the West Coast.
c. were recruited by the National Research Council.
d. a and c
ANS: D
PG: 53

15. Many anthropologists, after World War II, left government service for positions in higher education because

a. there was a return to theoretical concerns.
b. there were more academic opportunities.
c. there was increasing disenchantment with government service.
d. all of the above
ANS: D
PG: 49-50

16. How is the applied anthropology since 1970 different from that of the 1950s and 1960s?

a. Since 1970, 90% of all anthropological Ph.D.s work outside an academic setting.
b. More of the new applied anthropologists are full-time employees of government or non-profit agencies.
c. In the last two decades, most applied work has been conducted by professors in academic settings.
d. Applied anthropologists are now more likely to be academics.
ANS: B
PG: 53

17. Which statement about applied anthropology is false?

a. Applied anthropology is a rapidly growing specialty within anthropology in recent decades.
b. Applied anthropology played an important role during WWII.
c. Applied and pure anthropology are sometimes hard to distinguish.
d. All applied anthropologists play the role of advocate by taking public positions on controversial issues.
ANS: D
PG: 59

18. Forensic anthropology involves

a. using traditional physical anthropology methods to help identify crime scene victims.
b. the study of different races.
c. conducting quick research on archaeological sites before they are destroyed for building projects.
d. the study of non-human primates.
ANS: A
PG: 5

19. When compared to societies which allow only one wife at a time, societies which practice polygyny (a man having more than one wife at a time) tend to have

a. higher birth rates.
b. lower birth rates.
c. similar birth rates.
d. two to three times as high a birth rate.
ANS: B

PG: 62-63

20. Which statement about applied anthropology is true?

a. It is problem-oriented.
b. It is less popular than it was 20 years ago.
c. It is primarily aimed at testing new theories.
d. It has always been more prestigious than pure or academic anthropology.
ANS: A
PG: 50

21. The result of the Nestle corporation selling instant baby formula to Third World mothers was

a. infant mortality was sharply reduced.
b. infants developed a higher rate of diarrhea.
c. infants suffered much less from dehydration.
d. infants were generally healthier with the baby formula than they were before drinking it.
ANS: B
PG: 59-60

22. Applied anthropologist Penny Esterik played what role when dealing with the Nestle controversy?

a. trainer
b. advocate
c. expert witness
d. planner
ANS: B
PG: 59-60

23. In her role as advocate against the Nestle corporation, anthropologist Penny Esterik engaged in which activities?

a. used her personal research data from Thailand in public debates
b. helped organize educational forums and local boycotts of Nestle products
c. headed up a large scale research project on the effects of instant baby formula in Colombia, Kenya, Indonesia, and Thailand
d. all of the above
ANS: D
PG: 59-60

24. Elizabeth Grobsmith worked in which area of applied anthropology?

a. homeless shelters
b. medical anthropology
c. prisons and corrections
d. educational anthropology
ANS: C
PG: 60-61

25. In her work with Native American inmates in Nebraska prisons, Grobsmith played which applied anthropological role(s)?

a. cultural broker
b. expert witness
c. prison administrator
d. a and b only
ANS: D
PG: 60-61

26. Problems emerge when central governments institute programs of planned change

a. because governments and local populations frequently have different values and interests.
b. because local populations seldom recognize when projects are in their best interest.
c. but almost never result in hostilities.
d. and usually lead to hostilities, which make it fruitless for anthropologists to intervene.
ANS: A
PG: 63-64

27. The original plans for expanding an airport on the island of Truk

a. were developed by the local population and submitted to the government for approval.
b. angered the local population even though there was no significant impact on fishing or living conditions.
c. were recognized as an important expansion of local employment opportunities.
d. were made without consultation with the local villagers.
ANS: D
PG: 63-64

28. Parker and King, serving as cultural mediators between the government and the local Trukese villagers

a. were unable to get the government to change its plans for the airport.
b. helped the villagers protect their fishing grounds but were unable to save the cultural/historical landmarks.
c. were able to work out an agreement satisfactory to all parties concerned.
d. helped the government build the airport at half the originally proposed cost.
ANS: C
PG: 63-64

29. Cultural Resource Management is an applied form of which sub-field of anthropology?

a. anthropological linguistics
b. physical anthropology
c. cultural anthropology
d. archaeology
ANS: D
PG: 9

30. A specialized role in which an applied anthropologist presents culturally relevant research findings as part of a judicial proceeding is called

a. an administrator
b. a needs assessor
c. a policy researcher
d. an expert witness
ANS: D
PG: 59

31. Anthropology aimed very purposefully at practical results is referred to as

a. modernization anthropology
b. applied anthropology
c. new age anthropology
d. theoretical anthropology
ANS: B
PG: 50

32. Which statement about applied anthropology is true?

a. It is considered by many to be the fifth sub-field of anthropology.
b. It is highly theoretical.
c. It is problem-oriented.
d. a and c only
ANS: D
PG: 50, 52

33. The first important stimulus for applying anthropological insights came

a. in the 1950s, after the Korean War.
b. as a result of the Vietnam War.
c. in the 1940s, when researchers were asked to work in efforts related to World War II.
d. during the great depression of the 1930s.
ANS: C
PG: 53

34. Dembo's study of crack cocaine in West Central Florida found that

a. teenagers were dealing drugs to support their cocaine addiction.
b. teenage dealers were using most of their income to support their families.
c. teenage dealers were using most of their income on luxury items for themselves.
d. all of the above
ANS: C
PG: 61-62

35. Dembo's ethnographic study of adolescent crack dealers suggested strategies such as

a. improving the vocational and educational skills of teenage dealers.
b. treating the dealers for their drug dependency.
c. using former dealers who have gone legitimate as role models.
d. a and c
ANS: D
PG: 61-62

36. Which statement about nuclear testing in the Marshall Islands is true?

a. Most nuclear testing after WWII was conducted by the Japanese.
b. The U.S. government did not ask permission of the Marshall Islanders before testing.
c. Testing on the Marshall Islands resulted in no adverse effects on the local people.
d. The US government published the results of their nuclear testing as soon as they were available.
ANS: B
PG: 56-57

37. When Christian missionaries put pressure on small-scale societies to give up polygyny, they

a. argued it was immoral.
b. unknowingly contributed to the world-wide problem of population growth.
c. contributed to the overall lowering of birth rates.
d. a and b only
ANS: D
PG: 62-63

38. In the specialized role of trainer, an applied anthropologist

a. uses his or her skills to determine if a program has succeeded in its objectives.
b. becomes an active supporter of a particular group of people.
c. imparts cultural knowledge about certain populations to groups working in cross-cultural situations.
d. serves as a liaison between the program planner and administrators and the local ethnic communities.
ANS: C
PG: 59

39. The Japanese word "aizuchi" refers to

a. a traditional ethnic group living in northern Japan.
b. conversational replies that indicate you are listening.
c. the Japanese work ethic.
d. the Japanese word for anthropologist.
ANS: B
PG: 60

True-False

1. It is difficult for cultural anthropologists to ignore the enormity of the social problems faced on a daily basis by the people with whom they work.
ANS: T
PG: 50

2. Unlike cultural anthropologists, archaeologists and physical anthropologists do not conduct applied work.
ANS: F
PG: 50

3. Applied anthropologists work only in the least industrialized parts of the world.
ANS: F
PG: 51

4. The emic view and the value orientation of cultural relativism are unique contributions that anthropology can make to policy decisions.
ANS: T
PG: 56-57

5. Teenagers become crack cocaine dealers in Florida in order to support their families.
ANS: F
PG: 61-62

6. The line between pure and applied anthropology is not clear cut because both groups receive similar training and use similar methods.
ANS: T
PG: 51-53

7. During the 1990s, applied anthropological associations' memberships have shrunk.
ANS: F
PG: 53

8. Societies that practice polygyny have a higher birth rate than those societies that practice monogamy.
ANS: F
PG: 62-63

9. The benefits from the proposed changes for the people being studied are of great importance to an applied anthropologist.
ANS: T
PG: 65-66

10. The country of Taiwan is an integral part of the Peoples Republic of China (Mainland China).
ANS: F
PG: 58

Short Answer

1. What two trends have stimulated the movement of applied anthropologists out of the academic setting?
   ANS: the market for academic jobs has declined and there has been an increase in federal legislation mandating policy research
   PG: 53-54

2. Name three organizations that support applied anthropological research.
   ANS: U. S. Agency for International Development, the world Bank, the World Health Organization, the Ford Foundation, the Population Council, the Bureau of Indian Affairs, the U.S. Department of Agriculture, private corporations
   PG: 51

3. In Dembo's research, adolescent crack cocaine dealers reported what kinds of behaviors?
   ANS: They had killed or hurt someone through their association with cocaine, had spent most of their income on personal luxury items, had contributed less than 10 per cent of their income to families, had sold cocaine to gain higher status among their peers.
   PG: 61-62

4. Why is it difficult to distinguish between pure and applied anthropology?
   ANS: They have same training, often use same theories and methods, and at times are in fact the same people.
   PG: 51-53

5. List the negative effects of nuclear testing on the people of the Marshall Islands.
   ANS: Displacement from land, illness, genetic damage, and death.
   PG: 56-57

6. List four special features of applied anthropology.
   ANS: participant-observation, the holistic perspective, regional expertise, the emic view, cultural relativism, and topical expertise
   PG: 54-57

7. List five specialized roles of applied anthropologists.
   ANS: policy researcher, evaluator, impact assessor, planner, research analyst, needs assessor, trainer, advocate, expert witness, administrator/manager, cultural broker
   PG: 58-59

8. In what specific ways did anthropology contribute to the war effort in WWII?
   ANS: Rationing programs, national morale, and national character studies of Germans and Japanese
   PG: 53

9. In which areas do applied linguists work?
   ANS: Teaching ESL, advising on language policy, helping preserve languages from extinction, and pre-departure training programs for people working overseas.
   PG: 10-11

10. What is a key characteristic of applied anthropology?
ANS: problem-oriented research among the world's contemporary populations
PG: 50

Essay

1. How can applied anthropologists make a contribution to the area of international business?

2. Based on the Applied Perspective concerning nuclear testing in the Marshall Islands, what type of restitution, if any, would you recommend be given to the Marshallese people?

3. How do the other three branches of anthropology (other than cultural anthropology) apply their insights to the solution of practical problems?

4. How can applied anthropology be distinguished from "pure" or "academic" anthropology? How are they the same?

5. Explain why an applied anthropologist might become involved in the actual implementation and evaluation of particular change projects. Who would benefit from such involvement?

6. In what specific ways could applied anthropologists be used to facilitate the stabilization and reconstruction of Iraq in the aftermath of the 2003 war?

Chapter 4

The Growth of Anthropological Theory

Multiple-Choice

1. Anthropological theories in the 21st century are

   a. developed entirely independently of the theories of the earliest anthropologists.
   b. merely hypotheses.
   c. often built upon what was learned from earlier theories.
   d. entirely new concepts due to rapid modernization of the United States.
   ANS: C
   PG: 70

2. Nineteenth century evolutionary theory was developed by

   a. Clifford Geertz.
   b. Margaret Mead.
   c. Ruth Benedict.
   d. Edward Tylor and Lewis Henry Morgan.
   ANS: D
   PG: 70

3. In nineteenth century evolutionary theory, the stages of __________ were proposed.

   a. savagery, barbarism, and civilization
   b. primitive, transitional, and modern
   c. small-scale, traditional, and complex
   d. European, Asiatic, and American
   e. none of the above
   ANS: A
   PG: 71

4. Tylor's and Morgan's theories of evolution presented a

   a. theological interpretation of human differences.
   b. biological interpretation of human differences.
   c. cultural interpretation of human differences.
   d. all of the above
   ANS: C
   PG: 72

5. Morgan proposed that the three stages of savagery were associated with

a. monumental architecture.
b. food collecting.
c. the domestication of plants and animals.
d. a and c
ANS: B
PG: 71

6. Diffusionism stresses how

a. inventive Egyptians are.
b. distinctive different cultures are.
c. inventive Europeans are.
d. uninventive people are.
ANS: D
PG: 72

7. The diffusionists concentrated on

a. the principle of evolution as the major explanatory reason for cultural variability.
b. different levels of cultural borrowing to explain cultural diversity.
c. inductive methodology.
d. a and c
ANS: B
PG: 72

8. The school of Diffusionism could not explain

a. why some traits diffused when others did not.
b. what conditions bring about diffusion of a cultural item.
c. what determines the rate of cultural diffusion.
d. all of the above
ANS: D
PG: 72

9. Diffusionism and evolutionism had in common

a. the idea of a deductive approach.
b. the idea of a single center for the invention of culture.
c. the idea of a straight line of cultural evolution that was universal.
d. the same explanation for cultural diversity.
ANS: A
PG: 74

10. American historicism was developed by

a. Melville J. Herskovits.
b. Claude Lévi-Strauss.
c. Ruth Behar.
d. Franz Boas.
ANS: D
PG: 73-75

11. Franz Boas argued that the discipline of anthropology needed

a. the careful collection of empirical data on as many specific cultures as possible.
b. the development of complex theory as soon as possible.
c. theory that clarified how contact with other people was the single most important factor in shaping any society's culture.
d. theory that emphasized the environment as the single factor determining a culture.
ANS: A
PG: 73-75

12. Boas trained nearly the entire first generation of American anthropologists, including

a. Ruth Benedict.
b. Edward Tylor.
c. Alfred Radcliffe-Brown.
d. Marvin Harris.
ANS: A
PG: 74-75

13. Functionalist theory that focused on how cultures met the needs of individuals was developed by

a. Claude Lévi-Strauss.
b. Alfred Radcliffe-Brown.
c. Bronislaw Malinowski.
d. Franz Boas.
ANS: C
PG: 76

14. Nineteenth century evolutionary theory was developed by

a. Claude Lévi-Strauss.
b. Franz Boas.
c. Bronislaw Malinowski.
d. Edward Tylor and Lewis Henry Morgan.
ANS: D
PG: 70-71

15. The two theorists (one in England and one in the U.S.) who gave the greatest importance to fieldwork were

a. Tylor and Morgan.
b. Boas and Morgan.
c. Malinowski and Radcliffe-Brown.
d. Boas and Malinowski.
ANS: D
PG: 75-76

16. The functionalist concept of universal function means

a. that every component of a culture has a function.
b. that social structure is universal.
c. that individual needs are universal.
d. that culture is an integrated whole.
ANS: A
PG: 77

17. Functional unity means

a. that every component of a culture has a function.
b. that social structure is universal.
c. that individual needs are universal.
d. that culture is an integrated whole.
ANS: D
PG: 77

18. The notion of dysfunction was

a. proposed by Merton to refer to stress or imbalance in a cultural system.
b. proposed by Radcliffe-Brown to refer to stress or imbalance in a cultural system.
c. proposed by Merton to refer to unintended or unrecognized functions of culture.
d. proposed by Radcliffe-Brown to refer to unintended or unrecognized functions of culture.
ANS: A
PG: 77

19. Psychological anthropology was developed

a. by psychologists rather than anthropologists.
b. by anthropologists interested in the relationship between personality and employment.
c. by students of Boas interested in the question of the relationship of personality and culture.
d. by individuals with no interest in the impact of child-rearing on human societies.
ANS: C
PG: 78-79

20. Leslie White and Julian Steward developed the theory of

a. ethnoscience.
b. psychological anthropology.
c. neoevolutionism.
d. diffusionism.
ANS: C
PG: 80-81

21. The Functionalists and the American Historicists were similar in that both

a. encouraged direct fieldwork.
b. were inductive rather than deductive.
c. were associated with the 20th century.
d. all of the above
ANS: D
PG: 73-77

22. Leslie White, in his theory, focused on the harnessing of energy and

a. the relationship of ideology to environment.
b. the relationship between the structure of the human brain and the development of technology.
c. humans' use of technology to "capture energy."
d. all of the above
ANS: C
PG: 80

23. French structuralism concentrates on

a. human adaptation to the environment.
b. level of technological achievement.
c. the identification of mental structures that undergird social behavior.
d. the political and economic structures of societies.
ANS: C
PG: 81-83

24. Ethnoscience, like French structuralism,

a. draws upon a linguistic model.
b. seeks explanation in the human mind.
c. views human behavior from a logical or rational perspective.
d. all of the above
ANS: D
PG: 84-85

25. The primary aim of ethnoscience is to

a. understand a culture from the point of view of the people themselves.
b. identify the universal rules found in all the societies of the world.
c. describe a culture in terms of the categories of the ethnographer.
d. do a complete ethnoscientific study of every aspect of a culture.
ANS: A
PG: 84

26. Most anthropologists today

a. utilize evolutionary theory.
b. utilize neoevolutionary theory.
c. do not tie themselves to a single theoretical orientation.
d. utilize ethnoscience theory.
ANS: C
PG: 90-91

27. In *Coming of Age in Samoa*, Margaret Mead's first book

a. reported on the divorce rate of that society and compared it to the United States.
b. tried to determine if the strains of adolescence are universal.
c. found that Samoan youth are equally stressed as youth of the United States.
d. found that Derek Freeman had not portrayed Samoan adolescents accurately.
ANS: B
PG: 79

28. Margaret Mead, in her research in Samoa,

a. concluded that the emotional turbulence of adolescents in the United States is culturally rather than biologically based.
b. has definitely been proved inaccurate due to poor quality fieldwork.
c. has definitely been proved inaccurate in spite of the superior quality of her fieldwork.
d. demonstrated the importance of genes rather than cultural conditioning.
ANS: A
PG: 79

29. Leslie White argued that the driving force of cultural evolution was

a. the complexity of language.
b. political complexity.
c. the amount of energy harnessed per capita.
d. ideological progress.
ANS: C
PG: 80

30. Lévi-Strauss' approach emphasizes the importance of

a. certain codes, programmed into the human mind, which make it impossible for humans to learn more than one culture.
b. certain codes, programmed into the human mind, which are responsible for shaping cultures.
c. cultural traits which universally have the same function.
d. all of the above
ANS: B
PG: 81-83

31. The interpretive approach

a. sensitizes anthropologists to their own views and values.
b. is wedded to the etic approach.
c. sensitizes anthropologists to the views and values of the informant.
d. a and c
ANS: D
PG: 89

32. Murray, in his USAID reforestation project in Haiti, recommended that the local farmers

a. learn about the ecological need for conserving trees.
b. clear cut trees to open more land for agriculture.
c. own the trees they grow.
d. grow trees rather than food crops.
ANS: C
PG: 74-75

33. The theory that people are inherently uninventive and prefer to borrow the inventions of other cultures, rather than inventing them for themselves, is a tenet of which of the following schools of thought?

a. Evolutionists
b. Diffusionists
c. Functionalists
d. Psychological Anthropologists
ANS: B
PG: 72-73

34. Postmodernists emphasize

a. solitary research by one ethnographer.
b. the rejection of generalizing and developing predictable theories.
c. their close relation to biology.
d. the etic approach.
ANS: B
PG: 88-91

35. Cultural materialism
    a. is wedded to the emic approach.
    b. emphasizes the etic approach.
    c. avoids participant-observation.
    d. was created by Ruth Benedict.
    ANS: B
    PG: 87-88

36. Cultural materialism

    a. holds that material conditions determine human thoughts and behavior.
    b. assumes the viewpoint of the native informant.
    c. de-emphasizes the role of ideas and values in determining the conditions of social life.
    d. a and c
    ANS: D
    PG: 87-88

37. Postmodern anthropology

    a. is similar to the Cultural Materialist School.
    b. is wedded to the etic point of view.
    c. should be written from several perspectives, that of the anthropologist and that of the local people.
    d. aims at the construction of laws and generalizations.
    ANS: C
    PG: 88-89

38. One of the primary advocates for the theory of French structuralism is

    a. Franz Boas.
    b. Ruth Benedict.
    c. Claude Lévi-Strauss.
    d. Marvin Harris.
    ANS: C
    PG: 81

39. Which of the following anthropologists is not associated with the school of Feminist Anthropology which emerged in the 1960s and 1970s?:

    a. Annette Weiner
    b. Ruth Benedict
    c. Micaela di Leonardo
    d. Sherry Ortner
    ANS: B
    PG: 85-87

40. Which statement best describes Feminist Anthropology?:

a. It takes an objective/scientific approach to the study of society
b. Gender should not be considered as a major variable influencing cultural behavior.
c. It strongly embraces a value-free orientation.
d. It calls for the long-overdue correction to male bias in traditional ethnographies.
ANS: D
PG: 85-87

True-False

1. Anthropological theory attempts to explain the great cultural diversity in the world.
ANS: T
PG: 70

2. Tylor and Morgan, as nineteenth-century evolutionists, based their theories on fragmentary data.
ANS: T
PG: 70-72

3. The British diffusionists maintained that all cultural features, wherever they may be found, had their origins in Britain.
ANS: F
PG: 72

4. Boas called for a moratorium on theorizing.
ANS: T
PG: 74

5. The study by Gibson and Weisner of the New Hope Antipoverty Program in Milwaukee, WI, was significant because it illustrates how theory can be useful to applied anthropology.
ANS: T
PG: 82-83

6. Some 50 years after Margaret Mead published *Coming of Age in Samoa*, the book's findings were challenged by Derek Freeman.
ANS: T
PG: 79

7. Margaret Mead became interested in the study of culture and personality because of the writings and lectures of Edward Sapir and Ruth Benedict.
ANS: T
PG: 78

8. Lévi-Strauss' theory maintains that the human mind thinks in binary oppositions.
ANS: T
PG: 82

9. Ethnoscience attempts to describe a culture as it is perceived and categorized by the ethnographer.
ANS: F
PG: 84

10. Postmodernists emphasize that ethnographies should be written from several voices.
ANS: T
PG: 88

Short Answer

1. Define theory.
ANS: a statement that suggests a relationship among phenomena
PG: 70

2. What is the basic premise of the theory of evolutionism?
ANS: All societies pass through a series of distinct evolutionary stages.
PG: 70-71

3. What seven stages did Morgan define in evolutionary theory?
ANS: lower savagery, middle savagery, upper savagery, lower barbarism, middle barbarism, upper barbarism, civilization
PG: 71

4. Which anthropologist trained virtually the entire first generation of American anthropologists?
ANS: Franz Boas
PG: 75

5. In addition to performing the function of distributing goods within the society, what other areas of Trobriand culture are related to the kula ring?
ANS: political structure, magic, technology, kinship, social status, myth, and social control
PG: 76

6. What are the two fundamental principles upon which the functionalist approach is based?
ANS: the notion of universal functions and the principle of functional unity
PG: 77

7. What was Margaret Mead attempting to demonstrate in her research among the Arapesh, Tchambuli, and Mundugumor of New Guinea?
ANS: there were no universal temperaments that were exclusively masculine or feminine
PG: 79

8. To which school of anthropological theory does this formula relate - $C = E \times T$?
ANS: neoevolutionism (Leslie White)
PG: 80

9. What is the task of an ethnoscientist?
ANS: to describe a culture in terms of how it is perceived, ordered, and categorized by the members of that culture rather than by imposing the categories of the ethnographer
PG: 84

10. What three aspects do cultural materialists consider the most important parts of cultural systems?
ANS: tools, technology, and material well-being
PG: 87

Essay

1. How is Margaret Mead's portrayal of Samoa different from that of Derek Freeman's? What has anthropology learned from this controversy? Is either anthropologist right or wrong?

2. How are the preordained evolutionary stages of Tylor's and Morgan's theories of cultural evolution ethnocentric? What effect did limited empirical data on non-Western societies have on the development of this theory?

3. What are the most important contributions of Boas' American historicism approach? Why was ethnographic fieldwork important to him? Why did he want women trained as anthropologists?

4. Select any two of the following schools of anthropology and discuss its assumptions, methods, and theories. Who were its leading proponents and opponents? Discuss in a critical way the schools' major contributions and shortcomings.

Evolutionists	Diffusionists
American Historicists	Functionalists

5. What is cultural materialism? How does its position and methodology differ from the postmodern approach?

Chapter 5

Methods in Cultural Anthropology

Multiple-Choice

1. Anthropologists rely on fieldwork to

   a. describe and explain diverse cultures.
   b. study how people think rather than how they behave.
   c avoiding having to test hypotheses.
   d. all of the above
   ANS: A
   PG: 94

2. Anthropological fieldwork involves

   a. living with the people being studied.
   b. asking questions, and observing the every day behaviors of the people being studied.
   c. surveying the environment and material possessions of the people being studied.
   d. all of the above
   ANS: D
   PG: 94

3. Collecting, analyzing, and interpreting data are all part of

   a. selecting a research problem.
   b. formulating a research design.
   c. the preliminary preparation for anthropological fieldwork.
   d. concluding field research.
   ANS: D
   PG: 96

4. Learning another language is

   a. seldom part of the anthropologist's preparation for fieldwork.
   b. always accomplished before the anthropologist enters the field site.
   c. necessary only when an interpreter cannot be found.
   d. an important part of the tradition of anthropological fieldwork.
   ANS: D
   PG: 96

5. Anthropologists usually obtain funding from agencies that give research grants

a. awarded on a highly competitive basis.
b. to all students in graduate programs of anthropology.
c. but few anthropologists actually do research overseas today.
d. b and c
ANS: A
PG: 96

6. Permission or clearance from a host government must be obtained for fieldwork,

a. although anthropologists are always allowed to work in any part of the world.
b. although few countries pay much attention to the research interests of anthropologists.
c. because most countries want to make sure the research will not be embarrassing or politically sensitive.
d. a and b
ANS: C
PG: 96

7. Anthropological fieldwork in recent decades has

a. produced mostly general ethnographies.
b. been more focused and specific than in earlier times.
c. been more problem-oriented than in earlier times.
d. b and c
ANS: D
PG: 97

8. The theory that was tested in the Kenya Kinship Study was

a. neoevolutionary.
b. that urbanization lessens ties with distant kin and emphasizes the nuclear family.
c. that urbanization leads to high rates of crime.
d. that urbanization strengthens ties to distant kin.
ANS: B
PG: 97

9. In the Kenya Kinship Study, the dependent variable was

a. rural to urban migration.
b. urbanization.
c. family interaction.
d. urban employment.
ANS: C
PG: 97

10. Principle method(s) of collecting data in the Kenya Kinship Study included

a. day histories.
b. focus groups.
c. participant-observation.
d. a and c
ANS: D
PG: 98

11. Factors responsible for the importance of extended kinship interaction in Nairobi, Kenya include the

a. security of land tenure in rural areas.
b. uncertainty of urban employment.
c. easy availability of jobs for well-educated Kenyans.
d. a and b only
ANS: D
PG: 99

12. According to Ferraro, family interaction in both urban and rural Kenya can be understood largely in terms of lack of

a. knowledge of modernization.
b. political knowledge.
c. both money and economic security.
d. knowledge about employment and social security.
ANS: C
PG: 99

13. The Kenya Kinship Study allowed anthropologists to conclude that

a. urban life in Nairobi does not by itself lead to the truncation of extended kinship ties.
b. the extended kinship ties of rural Kenyans are stronger than those of urban residents.
c. urban experience in Nairobi leads to the truncation of extended kinship ties.
d. rural life in Kenya itself eventually led to the truncation of extended kinship ties.
ANS: A
PG: 99

14. When conducting fieldwork among the Kikuyu, Ferraro

a. never told the local people about his profession in the United States.
b. told them he was interested in farming practices when he really was studying kinship.
c. told them he was a government official.
d. told them he was a teacher, wanting to learn more about Kikuyu culture so he could teach his students.
ANS: D
PG: 101

15. Which statement about data collection used in anthropology is correct?

a. Participant-observation always is appropriate for cross-cultural research.
b. Methods that work in one culture might not be appropriate for a neighboring culture.
c. Photography is always appropriate in public settings.
d. Structured interviews should always be used early in the fieldwork.
ANS: B
PG: 99

16. The data-gathering technique used most often by anthropologists is

a. structured interview.
b. mailed questionnaires.
c. participant-observation.
d. document analysis.
ANS: C
PG: 100

17. Which of the following **is not** part of the advice that Ferraro gives for conducting participant-observation fieldwork?

a. Proceed slowly.
b. Secure permission from the top down in the political hierarchy.
c. Never eat the local food unless you've seen it prepared.
d. Be consistent in how you explain who you are.
ANS: C
PG: 101

18. Project Camelot was conducted

a. with funding from United States anthropologists.
b. in the United States in the 1960s.
c. with funding from the U.S. Army to study the causes of civil violence in countries in Asia, Latin America, Africa, and Europe.
d. as a model for correct ethical behavior on the part of United States anthropologists.
ANS: C
PG: 116

19. A disadvantage of participant-observation is that

a. only a small sample can be studied.
b. nonverbal behavior can be observed.
c. rapport is enhanced.
d. actual behavior can be distinguished from expected behavior.
ANS: A
PG: 103

20. Participant-observation has the advantage of

a. providing a large sample size.
b. ease of recording of data.
c. being an unobtrusive data gathering technique.
d. enabling fieldworkers to distinguish actual from expected behavior.
ANS: D
PG: 102

21. The ethnographic interview is different from the sociological or psychological interview because the

a. interviewer and the subject almost always speak different first languages.
b. ethnographic interview is much more narrow in scope.
c. ethnographic interview always focuses on the experiences of a single individual.
d. ethnographic interview is typically used alone without other sources of data.
ANS: A
PG: 104-105

22. Photography

a. can provide a record of land-use patterns.
b. can document the technology of the culture and how it is used.
c. can provide information on patterns of interaction.
d. all of the above
ANS: D
PG: 107-108

23. Unstructured interviews

a. seldom provide useful or accurate data.
b. should only be used at the end of one's fieldwork.
c. contain open-ended questions and are paced by the interviewees.
d. are all very short in duration.
ANS: C
PG: 104-106

24. Anthropologists have a responsibility to

a. their subjects.
b. their discipline.
c. their colleagues.
d. all of the above
ANS: D
PG: 117

25. Cultural anthropologists use document analysis in addition to interviewing and observation because

a. people can never be trusted to tell the truth.
b. it can produce large quantities of data.
c. it is relatively inexpensive.
d. b and c
ANS: D
PG: 107

26. Culture shock includes the following symptom(s):

a. a sense of confidence about the proper way to behave.
b. a loss of self-esteem.
c. a sense of being accepted by members of the other culture.
d. a feeling of having total control over the situation.
e. all of the above
ANS: B
PG: 112

27. The validity of anthropological data can be checked by

a. never asking more than one person the same question.
b. asking a single individual the same question repeatedly over a period of time.
c. comparing people's answers to questions to their actual behavior.
d. b and c
ANS: D
PG. 106

28. When conducting ethnographic interviews, you should

a. use simple, unambiguous questions
b. obtain informed consent after the interview is completed
c. leave the more controversial questions for the end of the interview
d. a and c only
ANS: D
PG: 106

29. Anthropologists collect information on all the relatives(kin) of the informant by

a. mapping.
b. the genealogical method.
c. proxemic analysis.
d. document analysis.
ANS: B
PG: 107

30. Biculturalism means

a. a loss of understanding of one's own culture.
b. a capacity to function effectively in two or more cultures.
c. an inability to shift gears between one's own and another culture.
d. extreme homesickness.
ANS: B
PG: 112-113

31. Discussions of anthropological field techniques used in research

a. seldom were published before the 1960s.
b. have always been an important part of publications based on field research.
c. always explained how the anthropologist felt about doing their fieldwork.
d. always explained how many people were interviewed and observed.
ANS: A
PG: 94

32. One anthropologist studying the same village at two different times

a. will always have a harder time on her or his second trip because the people will have learned how to avoid the anthropologist.
b. would experience two different fieldwork situations, because both the anthropologist and the people under analysis will have changed.
c. would experience almost identical fieldwork situations if she or he had done good ethnographic research the first time.
d. will always have an easier time on his or her second trip because the people will have learned that the anthropologist is harmless.
ANS: B
PG: 95

33. A researcher's complimenting and touching a Malaysian child on the head

a. violated the sacred part of the child's body.
b. helped the anthropologist establish rapport.
c. invited bad fortune on the child.
d. a and c
ANS: D
PG: 99

34. When teaching, anthropologists should be

a. fair, candid, and nonexploitive in their dealing with students.
b. sure to minimize the importance of ethics in anthropological research.
c. careful to keep students away from their research and writing for publication.
d. a and b
ANS: A
PG: 117

35. An anthropologist decides on which techniques to use based on

a. the nature of the problem being studied.
b. a realistic appraisal of what he/she can get away with.
c. the reception of the people being studied.
d. a and c
ANS: D
PG: 108

36. "Narrative ethnography" is concerned

a. with traditional notions of scientific objectivity.
b. with co-producing ethnographic knowledge by focusing on the interaction between anthropologists and their informants.
c. analyzing informant's information in light of the political structure.
d. with avoiding the influence of the personality of the anthropologist.
ANS: B
PG: 114

37. Ethnographic fieldwork is different from research in a chemistry or physics laboratory because

a. observers must interact with their subjects, which introduces subjectivity.
b. subjects have a free will and can behave in an atypical manner.
c. relationships with ethnographers cam cause informants to behave differently.
d. all of the above.
ANS: D
PG: 114

38. Anthropologists receiving support from their sponsors must

a. reflect upon the purposes of the sponsoring organizations and the potential uses to which the findings will be put.
b. never reveal their sources of information to their sponsors.
c. never accept more money than to meet their research expenses.
d. accept the fact that their sponsors have the right to make all ethical decisions.
ANS: A
PG: 117

39. In her study in Senegal, Renaud worked with registered prostitutes and found that

a. approximately four of every 10 registered prostitutes were HIV positive.
b. almost all prostitutes enforced condom use among their clients.
c. the prostitutes required their boyfriends to use condoms only 71 per cent of the time.
d. all of the above
ANS: D
PG: 104-105

40. Many anthropologists working in foreign countries

a. seldom are able to be as honest with their host government as they could be with their own government.
b. often compromise their professional standards in order to get a research clearance.
c. should be honest with both their own and the host governments.
d. may engage in clandestine research for their own or their host government.

ANS: C
PG: 118

True-False

1. For anthropologists, fieldwork is experiential.
ANS: T
PG: 94

2. After the difficult steps of the research process (collecting data), the interpretation of anthropological findings is easy.
ANS: F
PG: 98

3. The popular image of the cultural anthropologist in the field has often been overly romanticized.
ANS: T
PG: 95

4. Participant-observation requires that anthropologists enter into the daily life of people and forget their own cultures for the duration of their fieldwork.
ANS: F
PG: 100

5. Most anthropologists are very dependent on an interpreter because most native languages are extremely difficult to learn.
ANS: F
PG: 96

6. Anthropologists, unlike other researchers, do not have to develop hypotheses and identify independent and dependent variables.
ANS: F
PG: 97

7. When living in cities, people always put greater emphasis on the nuclear family than on more distant kin.
ANS: F
PG: 99

8. As a general rule, one should start formal data collection immediately when doing fieldwork.
ANS: F
PG: 101

9. As a general rule, structured interviews should be used before unstructured interviews.
ANS: F
PG: 105

10. Since "a picture is worth a thousand words," ethnographers always need to document certain features of a culture by taking photographs.
ANS: F
PG: 107-108

Short Answer

1. What must an anthropologist do to prepare for fieldwork?
ANS: make preparations before leaving home, gain acceptance into the community, select appropriate data-gathering techniques, understand how to operate within the local political structure, take precautions against investigator bias, choose knowledgeable informants, cope with culture shock, learn a new language, re-evaluate findings based on new evidence
PG: 95-96

2. How do ethnographic and survey methods differ?
ANS: ethnographic methods are more holistic, are more likely to be experiential, and are usually used in preliterate societies.
PG: 95

3. What is an independent variable?
ANS: the variable that is capable of affecting change in the other variable
PG: 97

4. What are some general guidelines applicable to most participant-observation fieldwork?
ANS: work one's way down the political hierarchy, select one role and use it consistently, proceed slowly, communicate to the local people that she or he is a student, wanting to learn more about a subject on which they are the experts
PG: 100-102

5. What are some of the disadvantages of participant-observation?
ANS: precludes a large sample size, data are often hard to code or categorize, may be difficult to record notes at the same time as observing, has an obtrusive effect on the thing that is being studied
PG: 103

6. What is the difference between unstructured and structured interviews?
ANS: Unstructured interviews involve a minimum of control, use open ended questions, and allow interviewees to respond at their own pace using their own words. Structured interviews use the same set of questions for all informants, in the same sequence, and preferably under the same set of conditions.
PG: 104-106

7. List four other techniques for the collection of cultural data.
ANS: census taking, mapping, document analysis, genealogies, and photography
PG: 106-108

8. What are the methodological advantages of photography?
ANS: allows us to see without fatigue, not selective - captures everything in any particular frame, easier and less time-consuming mode of data collection than written description
PG: 108

9. What are some of the symptoms of culture shock?
ANS: homesickness, boredom, withdrawal, need for excessive amounts of sleep, compulsive eating or drinking, irritability, marital stress, stereotyping of host nationals, hostility toward host nationals, loss of ability to work effectively, physical ailments, unexplainable fits of weeping, exaggerated cleanliness
PG: 112

10. What is meant by "existential shock?"
ANS: a disorientation about boundaries between life and death.
PG: 111

Essay

1. How important is it for an anthropologist to be able to cope with change and with the unknown? Explain your answer.

2. Why is direct fieldwork so important in cultural anthropology? Why is it important for anthropologists to write about their experiences in the field?

3. What are the characteristics of each of the five basic stages of anthropological research?

4. What must anthropologists do in order to establish good relationships with their host government and the community or population with which they will work?

5. What is participant-observation? What demands does this method make on the anthropologist and the population with which she or he is working?

Chapter 6
Language

Multiple-Choice

1. Human language is found in all cultures

   a. that have writing.
   b. that have had significant contact with Europe.
   c. of the world.
   d. a and b only
   ANS: C
   PG: 122

2. Black English Vernacular is

   a. nothing more than street slang.
   b. incorrect English.
   c. a full fledged linguistic system with its own grammatical structure.
   d. a primitive and inferior language.
   ANS: C
   PG: 134

3. Non-human primates and humans share which features of communication?

   a. non-verbal forms of communication
   b. an open call system
   c. vocal speech
   d. all of the above
   ANS: A
   PG: 124

4. Displacement, a feature of human communication, means

   a. combining one or more sounds to create new meanings.
   b. the capacity to convey information about a thing or event that is not present.
   c. not understanding the meaning of nonverbal communication.
   d. an inability to place all morphemes in their proper grammatical place.
   ANS: B
   PG: 125

5. The number of discrete languages that exist in the world today is approximately

a. 100.
b. 550.
c. 1400.
d. 6000.
ANS: D
PG: 122

6. Research on chimpanzee communication shows that they

a. can communicate subtle shades of meaning.
b. use a closed communication system.
c. can combine one or more sounds to create a large number of meanings.
d. can express opinions about abstract ideas.
ANS: B
PG: 124

7. Which of the following languages is most widely spoken?

a. Russian
b. Mandarin Chinese
c. English
d. Japanese
ANS: B
PG: 123

8. The study of the sound structure of a language is

a. phonology.
b. morphology.
c. the study of grammar.
d. the study of syntax.
ANS: A
PG: 127

9. All the languages of the world have phonemes that number ________.

a. about forty-six
b. about fifty-seven
c. from about thirty to sixty-three
d. from about fifteen to as many as one hundred
ANS: D
PG: 127

10. The smallest units of speech that convey a meaning are

a. phonemes.
b. morphemes.
c. compound words.
d. grammars.
ANS: B
PG: 128

11. The word "hats"

a. contains one morpheme.
b. contains a bound morpheme.
c. does not contain a bound morpheme.
d. contains three morphemes.
ANS: B
PG: 128

12. An example of a free morpheme is __________.

a. ly
b. co
c. tar
d. ist
ANS: C
PG: 128

13. An example of a bound morpheme is __________.

a. art
b. sun
c. paint
d. ist
ANS: D
PG: 128

14. The highly complex set of rules that regulates the formation of morphemes into words and words into phrases and sentences is called

a. grammar.
b. dialogue.
c. phonology.
d. syntax.
ANS: A
PG: 128

15. A lingua franca refers to

a. the French language.
b. a common language.
c. a world-wide language understood by most people in the world.
d. a language with no form of nonverbal communication.
ANS: B
PG: 144

16. Which phrase best characterizes second language competence in the United States?

a. basically monolingual
b. fiercely bilingual
c. accepting of all foreign languages
d. striving toward multilingualism
ANS: A
PG: 146

17. The language(s) most efficient at expressing abstract ideas

a. is Navajo.
b. is Chinese.
c. is German.
d. does not exist, no single language is most efficient.
ANS: D
PG: 132

18. Cell phone technology now enables us to

a. send deceptive or false messages
b. pretend to be somewhere other than where we are
c. pretend that you need to leave a particular meeting.
d. all of the above
ANS: D
PG: 133

19. Cultural emphasis refers to

a. the major nonverbal forms of communication in a society.
b. the favorite forms of argument in a society.
c. the one language most members of society learn better than any other.
d. the words in a language that are considered to be adaptively important in that culture.
ANS: D
PG: 133

20. Standard American English's cultural emphasis is on words referring to

a. technology and occupations.
b. weather.
c. cows and crops.
d. religious artifacts.
ANS: A
PG: 133

21. Doublespeak

a. is a medieval form of language no longer used today.
b. refers to the differences in languages between the wealthy and the commoners.
c. is designed to alter our perception of what is real.
d. is the same as being bilingual.
ANS: C
PG: 136-137

22. Nuer terminology reflects the importance of _________in their society

a. women
b. bracelets and necklaces
c. cattle
d. grain
ANS: C
PG: 133

23. The Sapir-Whorf hypothesis argues that language

a. influences perception.
b. is genetically (biologically) based.
c. is nothing more than a means of communication.
d. helps people adjust to their environment.
ANS: A
PG: 134

24. Which accent carries the highest prestige in the United States?:

a. German
b. Southern U.S.
c. British
d. French
ANS: C
PG: 144

25. Language, according to the Sapir-Whorf hypothesis,

a. is responsible for all peoples of the world to perceive the world in the same way.
b. causes all humans to construct reality in similar ways.
c. establishes in our minds categories that force us to distinguish those things we consider similar from those things we consider different.
d. a and b only
ANS: C
PG: 134-136

26. Opponents to the Sapir-Whorf hypothesis argue that

a. language simply reflects, rather than determines, culture.
b. culture reflects language.
c. culture determines language.
d. language and culture are independent of each other.
ANS: A
PG: 137

27. Sociolinguistics concentrates on variations in language that

a. are likely to become extinct in the next fifty years.
b. do not change over time.
c. have a majority of bilingual speakers.
d. depend upon the social situations or contexts in which the speaker operates.
ANS: D
PG: 140

28. Diglossia refers to

a. nearsightedness found widely in China.
b. an inability to speak.
c. one person's ability to speak two varieties of one language in different social circumstances.
d. the inability of a person to learn more than one language during a lifetime.
ANS: C
PG: 141

29. Nonstandard English is

a. a fully efficient language with its own grammar.
b. grammatically incorrect.
c. unable to express abstract thoughts.
d. suffers from a lack of syntax.
ANS: A
PG: 141-144

30. Nonverbal communication includes

a. hand gestures and touching.
b. communication on a telephone.
c. written communication.
d. all of the above.
ANS: A
PG: 145

31. Which statement about language reflecting a culture's basic values is true?

a. Individualism is reflected in English spoken in the United States.
b. A concern for the good of the larger group is reflected in the Japanese language.
c. Individualism is reflected in both U.S. English and Japanese.
d. a and b only
ANS: D
PG: 138

32. Sociolinguists

a. study the structures (phonology and morphology) of a language.
b. focus on how people actually speak in any given social situation.
c. study language change over time.
d. study language families.
ANS: B
PG: 140

33. In the United States, a single area of cultural emphasis

a. is always easy to identify.
b. is impossible to identify.
c. is higher education, an area of culture that is of great significance to people of all backgrounds.
d. is not always easy to identify; nevertheless, sports tends to be one area of culture that is shared by people from a variety of backgrounds.
ANS: D
PG: 133

34. The way that people hold their bodies often communicates information about

a. emotional states.
b. submissiveness or dominance.
c. sexual intentions.
d. all of the above
ANS: D
PG: 147

35. Which statement best describes the difference in linguistic style between speakers of Japanese and speakers of American English?

a. Japanese is direct while English is indirect.
b. Japanese is indirect while English is direct
c. Japanese tends to use exaggeration.
d. Japanese tends to be confrontational.
ANS: B
PG: 139

36. Which statement about communication among nonhuman primates is true?

a. Gorillas use calls and facial expressions to communicate.
b. Nonhuman primate call systems are inflexible.
c. Nonhuman primates use closed systems of communication.
d. all of the above
ANS: D
PG: 124

37. Language acquisition among children

a. involves imitation.
b. is helped by adults' modification of their normal speech.
c. may involve the use of universal grammar.
d. all of the above
ANS: D
PG: 126-127

38. A language that is "moribund" is one that

a. no longer has any living speakers.
b. has only a handful of people that speak the language.
c. has no speakers that are bilingual.
d. had lost its capacity to communicate nonverbally.
ANS: B
PG: 123

39. The historical study of the Lord's Prayer illustrates changes in

a. phonology.
b. morphology.
c. syntax.
d. all of the above
ANS: D
PG: 129

40. Which statement(s) about cultural emphasis is (are) true?

a. In Standard American English, many words refer to technological gadgetry.
b. The people in the Arctic have large numbers of words for snow, ice, and seals.
c. The Nuer have a large vocabulary to describe and identify their cattle.
d. all of the above
ANS: D
PG: 133

True-False

1. An open system of communication is only capable of sending messages which have been sent before.
ANS: F
PG: 124

2. A major limitation to the development of language among gorillas and chimps is physical because they do not possess the vocal equipment for speech.
ANS: T
PG: 124

3. Syntax is the set of principles guiding how words are arranged into phrases and sentences.
ANS: T
PG: 128

4. The English language has a total of forty phonemes.
ANS: F
PG: 127

5. Every language must follow universal rules for ordering morphemes within a word to give linguistic meaning.
ANS: F
PG: 128

6. Small-scale societies with simple technologies have relatively simple languages.
ANS: F
PG: 132

7. "Communities of Practice" possess their own specialized vocabularies.
ANS: T
PG: 142

8. The Sapir-Whorf hypothesis has not been definitively proven.
ANS: T
PG: 137

9. Language has the power to change how people perceive things.
ANS: T
PG: 136

10. Nonverbal communication can aid in interpreting linguistic messages but cannot carry messages of its own.
ANS: F
PG: 145

Short Answer

1. Define a language family.
ANS: composed of all of the languages that derive from its common protolanguage
PG: 131

2. How many different (mutually unintelligible) languages exist in the world?
ANS: approximately 6,000
PG: 122

3. What is displacement?
ANS: the capacity of human language to convey information about a thing or an event that is not present.
PG: 125

4. When adults in most cultures speak with children, they use which attention-getting devices?
ANS: frequently using the child's name, using exclamations, touching the child, using a high-pitched voice, talking in simple sentences about the here and now
PG: 126-127

5. The introduction of new words into a language parallels what social event?
ANS: the events that shape the language community's history and its relationship with other linguistic groups
PG: 130

6. Which anthropologist (and linguist) stated that no two languages are ever sufficiently similar to be considered as representing the same social reality?
ANS: Edward Sapir
PG: 134-135

7. The extent to which a culture values the individual, as compared to the group, is often reflected in its ____________________.
ANS: its linguistic style
PG: 138

8. On what aspect of language do sociolinguists concentrate?
ANS: variations in language use depending on the social situation or context in which the speaker is operating
PG: 140

9. What is diglossia?
   ANS: a linguistic situation where two varieties of the same language are spoken by the same person at different times and under different social situations
   PG: 141

10. What are three forms of nonverbal communication?
    ANS: hand gestures, eye contact, and touching
    PG: 145

Essay

1. How is language different from non-human ways of communicating? How is language symbolic?

2. Describe how a culture's values are reflected in its language. Be specific.

3. How does vocabulary relate to cultural adaptations? When are precise vocabularies needed?

4. What is the Sapir-Whorf hypothesis? How is it supported and how is it contradicted?

5. What is sociolinguistics? Give some examples of linguistic situations from your own life that would be of interest to a sociolinguist.

6. In what ways has the development of technology over the past two decades changed the way that people in the United States communicate?

7. Looking at your own country of origin, which dialects carry high status and which carry low status?

Chapter 7
Getting Food

Multiple-Choice

1. The food-getting strategy used by humans for most of their existence is

a. cattle herding.
b. intensive agriculture.
c. horticulture.
d. food collection.
ANS: D
PG: 156

2. The government of Kenya has coerced Maasai pastoralists to settle on permanent ranches for which reason?:

a. Because selling cattle on the open market will help the national economy
b. To convert them to agriculture
c. So their herds won't compete with wildlife
d. a and c only
ANS: D
PG: 170

3. A society's environment

a. has no effect on its food-getting strategy.
b. determines the one food-getting strategy that is its best adaptation.
c. influences its food-getting strategy.
d. sets very narrow limits on possible alternative food-getting strategies.
ANS: C
PG: 151-52

4. Food collecting societies usually get most of their diet from

a. the exploitation of wild plants and animals.
b. gardens.
c. domesticated animals acquired in trade with agricultural neighbors.
d. all of the above
ANS: A
PG: 156

5. The carrying capacity of an environment

a. is solely determined by its technology.
b. influences only foraging societies.
c. refers to an upper level on productivity which, when exceeded, has the consequence of damage to the environment.
d. refers only to the amount of wild life in an area.
ANS: C
PG: 154

6. Which statement about "optimal foraging theory" is true?

a. Foragers take only enough food to satisfy their immediate needs.
b. Foragers take those plants and animals from the environment that will maximize their caloric return for searching, killing and preparing food.
c. Foragers seek out food sources based on whether they will be worth the effort.
d. b and c only
ANS: D
PG: 155

7. People frequently do not use all the plentiful and nutritious foods in their environment because

a. they cannot scientifically study their environment.
b. most populations don't know what foods are safe to eat.
c. most populations have a hard time determining how much food is available.
d. foragers pursue those foods that maximize their caloric return for time spent to get it.
ANS: D
PG: 155

8. In today's world, food collectors are found

a. in a few, very dense populations.
b. to be the best nourished people in the world.
c. on land very poorly suited for agriculture.
d. all of the above
ANS: C
PG: 156

9. The Ju/'hoansi of southern Africa

a. are an example of malnourished gatherers and hunters.
b. work many more hours a week at food procurement than farmers.
c. have productive and reliable food-gathering techniques.
d. have a very short life expectancy.
ANS: C
PG: 158

10. The Ju/'hoansi environment

a. has been modified to support agriculture.
b. supports a division of labor in food-procurement based on gender.
c. keeps them teetering on the brink of starvation.
d. supplies much meat but little vegetable food.
ANS: B
PG: 158

11. The Inuit of the Arctic region

a. hunt reindeer but not seals because they believe the latter are sacred.
b. seldom have an adequate protein supply.
c. rely heavily on horticulture.
d. live in one of the most inhospitable environments in the world.
ANS: D
PG: 159

12. Food production became important for humans approximately

a. 1.2 million years ago.
b. 450,000 years ago.
c. 10,000 years ago.
d. 4,200 years ago.
ANS: C
PG: 162

13. Plant and animal domestication first developed in which part of the world?

a. the Fertile Crescent
b. China
c. sub-Saharan Africa
d. Mexico
ANS: A
PG: 162

14. Fertility rates tend to be

a highest in food collecting societies.
b. higher in societies where children make an economic contribution.
c. equal in all human societies.
d. highest in pastoral societies.
ANS: B
PG: 163

15. The Neolithic Revolution stimulated

a. a growth in population size.
b. a greater division of labor.
c. more permanent settlements.
d. all of the above
ANS: D
PG: 163-64

16. The Neolithic Revolution

a. caused all societies which existed at that time to become shifting cultivators.
b. freed people from ties to the land.
c. gave humans a measure of control over their food supply.
d. caused food collecting societies to disappear.
ANS: C
PG: 163

17. Which statement about foraging societies is true?

a. They have fairly dense populations.
b. They are typically sedentary, not nomadic.
c. They occupy some of the world's best farmland.
d. Their basic social unit is the family or band.
ANS: D
PG: 157

18. The development of crop cultivation makes specialization of labor possible because

a. there is little need for more technology.
b. group intelligence improves with a cereal-based diet.
c. since farming is more efficient than food collecting, more people can be freed to engage in an activity other than food production.
d. all of the above
ANS: C
PG: 163

19. Horticulture refers to the type of farming that

a. relies on irrigation systems and fertilizers.
b. uses only human energy and yields are high.
c. uses human and animal energy and yields are high.
d. uses land which is permanently settled.
ANS: B
PG: 164

20. The slash and burn method

a. can destroy large tracts of forest and grassland.
b. cannot support a population with a low density.
c. is one in which land is constantly cultivated.
d. all of the above
ANS: A
PG: 164

21. Which two terms are synonymous (mean the same as) with shifting cultivation?

a. slash and burn farming and pastoralism
b. swidden cultivation and horticulture
c. slash and burn farming and swidden cultivation
d. swidden cultivation and horticulture
ANS: C
PG: 164

22. Nomadic pastoralism

a. prevents people from raising as much livestock as they could if they did not migrate.
b. involves raising of camels and cattle only.
c. has no permanent villages.
d. never includes cultivation of any type of grain.
ANS: C
PG: 167

23. Pastoral people in different parts of the world

a. get all of their food from livestock exclusively.
b. may practice some cultivation.
c. may maintain regular trade relations with neighboring agriculturalists.
d. b and c
ANS: D
PG: 168

24. Pastoralists have social uses of cattle

a. such as compensating the family of a homicide victim.
b. such as legitimizing a marriage.
c. which are insignificant compared to the cattle's economic roles.
d. a and b
ANS: D
PG: 168

25. Most pastoralists need some grains to supplement their diets and regularly procure them by

a. foraging.
b. famine relief.
c. regular trade relations with neighboring agriculturists.
d. growing crops themselves.
ANS: C
PG: 168

26. Which statement about the Maasai is false?:

a. they are being forced to settle on permanent ranches
b. they have been very successful at managing their environment
c. for generations they have supplemented their diet with agricultural products
d. they engage in controlled burning to provide better pasturage for their cattle
ANS: C
PG: 168-70

27. Intensive agriculture

a. has access to a much smaller supply of available energy than that of other food-procurement strategies.
b. has access to more efficient intensive cultivation than horticulture.
c. usually fails to produce surplus food.
d. almost always lacks an adequate supply of labor.
ANS: B
PG: 170

28. Peasant populations

a. are only found in Europe.
b. are tied to larger political units.
c. produce no surplus.
d. provide only a small amount of food for urban populations.
ANS: B
PG: 171

29. Industrialized agriculture

a. ensures the production of cheap food.
b. has eliminated hunger in modern societies.
c. has caused considerable environmental destruction.
d. led to the almost universal improvement of water supplies.
ANS: C
PG: 173

30. Good examples of food collecting societies are the

a. Somali and Swazi.
b. Inuit and the Ju/'hoansi.
c. Inuit and the Bemba.
d. Maasai and the Ju/'hoansi.
ANS: B
PG: 156-162

31. Inuits and other people living in extremely cold climates tend to have

a. tall, thin bodies.
b. long extemities.
c. short, stocky bodies.
d. stocky bodies with long extremities.
ANS: C
PG: 152

32. The Inuit food procurement strategy is based on

a. pastoralism (reindeer herding).
b. horticulture.
c. large scale cooperative hunting.
d. large winter hunting groups and smaller hunting and fishing groups in the summer.
ANS: D
PG: 159-62

33. What was revolutionary about the Neolithic Revolution was that it produced

a. the world's first population explosion.
b. a large increase in the world's death rate.
c. much more egalitarian societies.
d. a decrease in role specialization.
ANS: A
PG: 163

34. People who practice swidden agriculture

a. typically use irrigation systems.
b. must periodically shift their homes when they shift their fields.
c. grow tree crops, seed crops, or root crops.
d. don't shift their fields.
ANS: C
PG: 164

35. The power and status of Bemba chiefs was based upon

a. the amount of service they could extract from their subjects in terms of agricultural labor or military service.
b. their assumed supernatural control over land and property.
c. their own personal material wealth.
d. a and b only

ANS: D
PG: 165-66

36. Which statement about medicinal plants from the Amazon is true?

a. They provide the ingredients for many commercial drugs used today.
b. They are the subject of those cultural anthropologists specializing in ethnobotany.
c. The rapid destruction of the Amazon rain forest is contributing to the extinction of some of these species.
d. all of the above

ANS: D
PG: 174-75

37. Peasants in an agricultural society

a. have an important relationship with the cities.
b. almost always occupy the lowest strata of a society.
c. almost always occupy the middle social and economic strata of a society.
d. a and b only

ANS: D
PG: 171-72

38. When some of the men in a pastoral society move their livestock to seasonal pastures while their families stay in permanent homes, the practice is known as

a. transhumance.
b. nomadism.
c. goat herding.
d. yak pastoralism.

ANS: A
PG: 167

39. Western medical science is just beginning to

a. realize how little local populations know about the tropical rainforests.
b. recognize that local tribal people know a great deal about plants in tropical rainforests used for medicines.
c. recognize that all the scientific knowledge of the peoples of the tropical rainforests has already been lost.
d. study why people of the tropical rainforest have never used plants found in their environment as medicine.

ANS: B
PG: 174

40. Traditional Incans used which farming practice(s)?

a. terracing
b. canal building
c. purposeful tree planting to decrease erosion
d. all of the above
ANS: D
PG: 152

True-False

1. Today, pastoralism and food collecting are found in environments that cannot support agriculture.
ANS: T
PG: 157

2. The carrying capacity of the environment is set by the level of technology and the skill of its inhabitants.
ANS: F
PG: 154

3. The basic social unit among food collecting people is the family or band.
ANS: T
PG: 157

4. The Inuit today use satellite maps to follow movements of wildlife.
ANS: T
PG: 161

5. All pastoralists get all of their food needs from livestock.
ANS: F
PG: 168

6. Invention of the wheel, use of fertilizer and draft animals, and irrigation are all innovations that have made agriculture possible.
ANS: T
PG: 170

7. Intensive agriculture requires a great investment of both labor and capital, but it does support more people per unit of land than horticulture can.
ANS: T
PG: 170

8. Industrialized agriculture requires complex systems of market exchange.
ANS: T
PG: 173

9. Horticulture draws upon irrigation systems, chemical fertilizers, and mechanized equipment
ANS: F
PG: 164

10 The over-fishing of our oceans has been more detrimental to the industrialized nations than to the poorer countries.
ANS: F
PG: 162

Short Answer

1. What part of culture helps people adapt to their specific environment?
ANS: technology
PG: 153-55

2. List the five major food-procurement categories found among the world's populations.
ANS: food collection, horticulture, pastoralism, agriculture, industrialization
PG: 156

3. What is the optimal foraging theory?
ANS: the theory that foragers will take the animals and plant species that tend to maximize their caloric return for the time spent searching, killing, collecting, and preparing
PG: 155

4. Food collection was the main subsistence strategy until what event?
ANS: the Neolithic Revolution approximately 10,000 years ago
PG: 162

5. When and in what area of the world did plant and animal domestication first occur?
ANS: the Fertile Crescent, which includes parts of Jordan, Israel, Syria, southern Turkey, northern Iraq, and western Iran
PG: 162

6. List four consequences of the change to food production.
ANS: increase in population, more sedentary population, a greater division of labor and specialization, decline in overall health, increased social inequality
PG: 163

7. What are two other names for shifting cultivation and what does it involve?
ANS: swidden agriculture or the slash and burn method. Involves clearing the land by manually cutting down the growth, burning it, and planting in the burned area. Land is depleted in two years and allowed to lie fallow to restore its fertility
PG: 164

8. What are two types of pastoralism?
ANS: nomadism and transhumance
PG: 167

9. What makes agriculture different from horticulture?
ANS: Agriculture relies on animal power and technology rather than on human power alone.
PG: 170

10. What are some noticeable changes in food getting since the late eighteenth century?
ANS: Agriculture is largely commercialized, majority of food is sold to nonproducers for currency, and industrialized agriculture requires complex systems of market exchange.
PG: 173

Essay

1. What are the primary products of each of the five major food procurement categories? Which are the most productive strategies? Which are the least harmful to the environment?

2. What is the relationship between environment and food-getting strategy? What factors influence human adaptation to and utilization of the environment?

3. What is the optimal foraging theory? What type of population is influenced by that theory?

4. In what type of environment is pastoralism practiced? Describe the social relations and type of population that can be supported by this strategy.

5. Why are marketing and a high level of technological development necessary for industrialization? How does it transform human relationships with their environments?

6. In what ways have the Maasai of East Africa changed over the past 40 years?

Chapter 8

Economics

Multiple-Choice

1. All societies have a finite amount of vital resources which constrain the productivity of

   a. horticultural societies.
   b. industrialized societies.
   c. pastoralist societies.
   d. all of the above
   ANS: D
   PG: 181

2. Economic anthropologists study production, distribution, and consumption

   a. only in industrialized societies of the world.
   b. only in the non-industrialized societies of the world.
   c. in all of the societies in the world, industrialized and non-industrialized.
   d. only in the pastoral societies of the world.
   ANS: C
   PG: 180

3. Which of the following are limitations to personal property rights in the United States?

   a. right of eminent domain
   b. a person can lose property rights if convicted of a felony
   c. zoning laws
   d. a and c above
   ANS: D
   PG: 181-82

4. Formal economic theory is based on assumptions such as:

   a. the value of a particular commodity decreases as it becomes more scarce.
   b. only occasionally do people maximize their material well-being.
   c. people, when exchanging goods and services, naturally strive to maximize their material. well-being and their profits.
   d. all of the above
   ANS: C
   PG: 180

5. Formal economic theory is based on studies of

a. tribal societies.
b. industrialized societies.
c. European societies since 1995.
d. pre-colonial non-western societies.
ANS: B
PG: 180

6. The notion of personal land ownership is

a. present in all societies.
b. absent in food collecting societies.
c. absent in pastoral societies.
d. both b and c
ANS: D
PG: 182

7. Rules that govern the allocation of resources and how they are used are found in

a. very few societies.
b. only food collecting societies.
c. all societies.
d. all food producing societies.
ANS: C
PG: 181

8. The concept of individual property rights is weakest in

a. societies where intensive agriculture is found.
b. highly industrialized societies.
c. food collecting societies.
d. a and b only
ANS: C
PG: 182

9. In terms of private property rights to land, which statement is true?

a. Food collectors seldom have the notion of personal land ownership.
b. Only elites in pastoral societies own pasture lands.
c. Only chiefs in horticultural societies own the land that is planted.
d. all of the above
ANS: A
PG: 182

10. Food collecting communities' control of land rights

a. is uniform for all food collecting societies.
b. is learned from their contact with their surrounding societies.
c. varies because in some societies territorial boundaries between bands or families is rigorously maintained.
d. is likely to continue long into the future in spite of contact with outside societies.
ANS: C
PG: 182

11. The potlatch, as practiced by the Northwest Coast Indians, served to:

a. confer status on generous givers
b. distribute material goods to a wide range of people
c. maintain regional stability
d. all of the above
ANS: D
PG: 197-199

12. Land is most likely owned by an extended kinship group among

a. food collectors.
b. pastoralists.
c. horticulturalists.
d. intensive agriculturalists.
ANS: C
PG: 183

13. In a number of developing countries today

a. a growing number of children under age 14 engage in wage employment.
b. children only work on household chores.
c. children are prohibited by their religion to work for wages.
d. a decreasing number of children under age 14 engage in wage employment.
ANS: A
PG: 191

14. The definition of property rights is reflected in the Swahili language which

a. clearly distinguishes the ownership of land but not cattle.
b. clearly distinguishes the ownership of cattle but not land.
c. contains no word that would be comparable to the English word "own."
d. has over twenty words that distinguish among different types of "ownership."
ANS: C
PG: 184

15. Obtaining goods from the natural environment and transforming them into usable objects is called

a. distribution.
b. consumption.
c. specialization.
d. production.
ANS: D
PG: 185

16. In most industrialized societies, the basic unit of production is the

a. individual.
b. household.
c. village.
d. private company.
ANS: D
PG: 188

17. Wage employment of children under age 14 is nearly universally condemned because

a. children are often exploited.
b. children often work in unsafe and dangerous conditions.
c. children lose their opportunity for proper education.
d. all of the above
ANS: D
PG: 190-191

18. In most non-industrialized societies, the basic unit of production is

a. the individual.
b. the household.
c. the village.
d. the state.
ANS: B
PG: 188

19. Which statement about tribute, or chiefly redistribution, is true?

a. It is found most often in hunting and gathering societies.
b. It is based on the principle of equitable distribution among the parties.
c. It functions to reaffirm the power of the child and the solidarity of the people.
d. Typically, chiefs had no more material wealth than commoners.
ANS: C
PG: 196

20. Sex and age are the basis for the division of labor in

a. only food collecting societies.
b. only pastoralist societies.
c. only food producing societies.
d. all societies.
ANS: D
PG: 189-191

21. The universal division of labor based on sex may occur because

a. men always have greater strength than women.
b. men are always afraid of taking care of children, unlike women.
c. in terms of reproduction, men tend to be more expendable than women.
d. none of the above
ANS: C
PG: 189

22. In societies, gender roles may be so rigidly followed that

a. women rather than men usually risk their life in food procurement to ensure the group's survival.
b. in all societies men refuse to care for children.
c. females and males are ignorant of the occupational skills of the opposite sex.
d. all of the above
ANS: C
PG: 189-190

23. The Yellow Pages of phone directories in the United States indicates

a. a degree of labor specialization very distinct from that of food collecting societies.
b. that gender equality has been achieved in the United States.
c. social organization in a society where there is no discrimination on the basis of age.
d. all of the above
ANS: A
PG: 191-192

24. Reciprocity refers to an exchange of goods and/or services of

a. unequal value that occurs at the same moment in time.
b. exactly the same value that occurs over a short period of time.
c. relatively equal value between two parties without the use of money.
d. unequal value between elites and commoners in a state society.
ANS: C
PG: 192

25. The Kula Ring of the Trobriand Islanders is an example of

a. generalized reciprocity.
b. balanced reciprocity.
c. negative reciprocity.
d. redistribution.
ANS: B
PG: 194

26. Tribute is a form of redistribution and

a. is illustrated by the tax system found in the United States.
b. can be found in chiefdoms with no standardized currency
c. includes the Kula Ring of the Trobriand Islands.
d. includes market economies.
ANS: B
PG: 196

27. Redistribution, as a principle of exchange, includes

a. big men and feast givers.
b. bridewealth.
c. potlatch.
d. all of the above
ANS: D
PG: 195-199

28. Market exchange systems require

a. heavy face-to-face contact.
b. a nonstandardized currency.
c. a complex division of labor.
d. only a small amount of surplus production.
ANS: C
PG: 199

29. A potlatch host

a. is very humble before his guests.
b. boasts about how much he will give his guests.
c. recognizes his poverty in comparison to the wealth of his guests.
d. a and c
ANS: B
PG: 197

30. People in the United States

a. always maximize their economic well-being
b. rarely maximize their economic well-being
c. have become increasingly willing in recent decades to sacrifice their economic well-being in favor of non-economic considerations (values)
d. almost always vote with their pocketbooks
ANS: C
PG: 181

31. The concept of individual property rights

a. is universally found in all societies.
b. is found only in industrialized societies.
c. may be less important in some societies than flexible territorial boundaries.
d. is relatively weak in the United States.
ANS: C
PG: 182

32. A worker at age 65 receiving a gold watch at retirement is an example of

a. the waning physical and mental strength of the elderly.
b. the allocation of tasks by age.
c. negative reciprocity.
d. gender specialization.
ANS: B
PG: 190-191

33. The type of social solidarity based on an increase in the complexity of labor specialization is known as

a. mechanical solidarity.
b. organic solidarity.
c. industrial solidarity.
d. reciprocal solidarity.
ANS: B
PG: 192

34. Anthropologists who have become involved in market research for companies have introduced which innovative techniques?

a. statistical analysis
b. focus groups
c. open-ended interviews
d. gathering data on what people actually do rather than what they say they do
ANS: D
PG: 200-201

35. People who work in complex, bureaucratic organizations are expected to

a. be particularistic.
b. disregard kinship ties and obligations while at work.
c. be universalistic.
d. b and c
ANS: D
PG: 186-87

36. In a study of hiring practices in two companies in Kenya, it was found that

a. workers were purposefully not recruited on the basis of kinship or ethnic relations with the present workers.
b. ethnic/kinship homogenization damaged the organization efficiency.
c. ethnic/kinship homogenization actually improved organization efficiency.
d. rural migrants were better employees than urban residents.
ANS: C
PG: 186-87

37. People who operate in complex, bureaucratic organizations are expected to behave toward one another in an objective and straightforward manner called

a. individualism.
b. particularism.
c. universalism.
d. generalism.
ANS: C
PG: 186-187

38. A prestige economy refers to economies

a. found in very wealth countries.
b. in which distributing goods also functions to allocate social status.
c. economies that produce high GNP.
d. economies that produce more BMW's than Ford Escorts.
ANS: B
PG: 199

39. Subsistence societies with low population densities and simple technologies are likely to have a division of labor based on

a. little more than sex and age.
b. levels of formal education.
c. religion.
d. strength.
ANS: A
PG: 189

40. Generalized reciprocity is usually played out

a. in highly industrial societies.
b. among labor and management in western corporations.
c. among family members and close friends.
d. in racially segregated societies.
ANS: C
PG: 192-93

True-False

1. Economic anthropologists assume that individuals, as well as corporations, are motivated primarily by the desire to maximize their material well-being.
ANS: F
PG: 180

2. The household is the basic unit of production in most industrialized societies.
ANS: F
PG: 188

3. Women and men have distinct roles only because men have greater body mass and strength.
ANS: F
PG: 189

4. Sex and age are the universal basis for the division of labor.
ANS: T
PG: 189

5. The exchanges between parents and children in the United States are examples of reciprocity.
ANS: T
PG: 192

6. The Kula Ring, an example of negative reciprocity, functioned as a system of exchange of goods.
ANS: F
PG: 194

7. Evidence suggests that during economic downturns family businesses increase.
ANS: T
PG: 195

8. Big men are the formal chiefs of New Guinea societies who control the production of their followers without engaging in similar productive activities.
ANS: F
PG: 196

9. Found among the Indians of the Northwest Coast, the potlatch is a mechanism of both redistribution and social ranking
ANS: T
PG: 197

10. The process of globalization of world economies has had the effect of reducing the gap between the rich and the poor.
ANS: F
PG: 203

Short Answer

1. Along which three key dimensions can economic systems be examined cross-culturally?
ANS: the regulation of resources, production, and exchange
PG: 181

2. Give three reasons for opposing wage employment of children under 14 years of age:
ANS: exploitative working conditions, dangerous and unhealthy working conditions, and lack of access to education
PG: 191

3. What are three types of reciprocity?
ANS: generalized, balanced, and negative
PG: 192

4. What is the system of exchange among the Trobriand Islanders that involves an elaborate and ritualized exchange of shell bracelets and necklaces called?
ANS: the Kula Ring
PG: 194

5. What forms can negative reciprocity take?
ANS: hard bargaining, cheating, out-and-out theft
PG: 195

6. What is barter?
ANS: the exchange of one good or service for another without using a standardized currency.
PG: 199

7. What does the subdiscipline of economic anthropology study?
ANS: production, distribution, and consumption comparatively in all societies of the world, industrialized and non-industrialized alike
PG: 180

8. What are two vital resources for pastoralists to maintain their way of life?
ANS: water and pasturage
PG: 183

9. What is a major negative consequence of globalization?
ANS: the increasing gap between the rich and the poor

PG: 203

10. What is a prestige economy?
ANS: One in which the mechanisms of distribution also allocate social status and prestige.
PG: 199

Essay

1. Describe four aspects of the economic process through which all societies face the challenge of having a finite amount of vital resources. What are the three economic systems they must develop?

2. What are the different concepts of property rights associated with each of the following: food collectors, pastoralists, horticulturalists, and industrialization?

3. What does reciprocity mean? Describe three types recognized by economic anthropologists.

4. What are the major differences between general, balanced, and negative reciprocity? Give examples of each.

5. In addition to distribution by markets, what other forms of distribution of goods are found in other parts of the world?

6. How has the study of nonwestern societies illustrated the weaknesses of the theory of "the tragedy of the commons?"

7. What forms of informal (unregulated) economic activity can you find in industrialized societies like Canada and the United States?

Chapter 9

Marriage and the Family

Multiple-Choice

1. Which of the following is a function of the family?

   a. provides for the material, educational, and emotional needs of children
   b. regulates the sexual division of labor
   c. regulates sexual mating and reproduction
   d. all of the above
   ANS: D
   PG: 211

2. The textbook defines marriage as a socially approved union between a man and a women that regulates

   a. the sexual and economic rights and obligations between them.
   b. primarily the rearing of children.
   c. primarily sexual rights and obligations.
   d. primarily their economic rights and obligations.
   ANS: A
   PG: 209-210

3. According to an official statement of the American Anthropological Association,

   a. same sex marriages are threatening to viable social order
   b. same sex marriages are immoral and should be avoided at all costs
   c. families built on same sex marriages can contribute to stable and humane societies
   d. a and b only
   ANS: C
   PG: 210

4. Ferraro defines marriage as a normally permanent arrangement but recognizes that

   a. the permanence of marriage may vary from society to society.
   b. small-scale societies have higher divorce rates than industrialized societies.
   c. in all non-industrialized societies, marriages last until death.
   d. only in very small-scale societies do marriages last until death.
   ANS: A
   PG: 210

5. The Nayar of southern India

a. have no marital institutions at all.
b. live together as husband and wife only for the first several years of marriage.
c. have no children unless they marry a member of another group.
d. neither cohabit nor economically cooperate as married couples.
ANS: D
PG: 211

6. The prohibition against sexual relations with certain categories of kin is called

a. monogamy.
b. cross-cousin marriage.
c. the incest taboo.
d. endogamy.
ANS: C
PG: 211

7. A nuclear family includes all of the following **EXCEPT**

a. mother.
b. uncle.
c. father.
d. sister.
ANS: B
PG: 230

8. The incest taboo

a. universally prohibits first cousins from marrying.
b. prohibits sexual relations with anyone on the father's side of the family.
c. prohibits sexual relations with certain categories of kin.
d. universally prohibits marriage between clan members.
ANS: C
PG: 211

9. The idea that there is a natural aversion to sexual intercourse among those who have grown up together

a. has received no support from anthropological research.
b. does not explain why there are incidents of incest which occur in families.
c. has received some support from evidence that such an aversion may be developed even if it is not natural or genetic.
d. b and c
ANS: D
PG: 212

10. Polyandry is

a. a man having more than one wife at a time.
b. a woman having more than one husband at a time.
c. a practice that keeps family land intact when there is a land shortage.
d. b and c only
ANS: D
PG: 223

11. According to the family disruption theory, mating within the nuclear family would

a. disrupt the family's function as a unit of economic cooperation.
b. disrupt the family's function as a unit of socialization.
c. create role ambiguity.
d. all of the above
ANS: D
PG: 213

12. Incest avoidance can have positive social advantages by forcing people to marry outside of their immediate family, thereby

a. developing a stronger set of relationships within their own family than a wider network of interfamily alliances.
b. creating relationships with people with whom they are likely to cooperate.
c. creating relationships with more people with whom they are likely to become hostile.
d. a and c
ANS: B
PG: 213

13. Marrying outside a group is

a. polygamy.
b. monogamy.
c. exogamy.
d. endogamy.
ANS: C
PG: 214

14. Castes in India provide a good example of

a. caste endogamy.
b. caste exogamy.
c. free selection of spouses.
d. none of the above
ANS: A
PG: 214

15. Which statement about cousin marriage is FALSE?

a. All states in the U.S. prohibit by law cousin marriage.
b. There is no compelling scientific evidence to support banning cousin marriage.
c. Geneticists have proved that cousin marriage causes serious birth defects.
d. Most European countries prohibit cousin marriage.
ANS: B
PG: 213

16. Which statement about bridewealth is FALSE?

a. It tends to destabilize marriage.
b. It symbolizes the union of two kin groups.
c. It represents compensation to the wife's family.
d. It legalizes marriages and legitimizes children.
ANS: A
PG: 225

17. Cross cousins are defined as the children of

a. your second cousins.
b. your mother's brother or father's sister.
c. your father's brother or mother's sister.
d. your parents' cousins.
ANS: B
PG: 217-218

18. The levirate is a marriage custom in which

a. a widow marries the brother or another close relative of her dead husband.
b. a widower marries the sister or another close relative of his dead wife.
c. a person marries a cross-cousin.
d. a person marries a parallel cousin
ANS: A
PG: 219

19. The sororate is a marriage custom in which

a. a widow is expected to marry the brother or another close relative of her dead husband.
b. a widower is expected to marry the sister or another close relative of his dead wife.
c. a man marries his stepsister.
d. a man takes his brother's widow as a wife.
ANS: B
PG: 219

20. Which practice is found among the Ju/'hoansi of southwestern Africa?

a. bridewealth
b. reciprocal exchange of material goods
c. dowry
d. bride service
ANS: D
PG: 226

21. In the majority of cultures of the world, polygyny is

a. the preferred form of marriage.
b. practiced by the majority of men in the world.
c. less common than polyandry.
d. considered by anthropologists to be less moral than monogamy.
ANS: A
PG: 220

22. The marriage of several brothers to one woman

a. sometimes occurs in Tibet.
b. is called primogeniture.
c. is necessary in pastoral societies.
d. occurs only in hunting and gathering societies.
ANS: A
PG: 223

23. The post-marital residence pattern characterized by the couple living with or near the parents of the bride is called

a. patrilocal.
b. bilocal.
c. matrilocal.
d. neolocal.
ANS: C
PG: 229

24. Which statement about polygyny in Africa is FALSE?

a. Polygyny is a thing of the past.
b. Some traditional women support it.
c. Men generally view polygyny more positively than women do.
d. Opposition to polygyny today comes from younger, well-educated women.
ANS: A
PG: 223

25. Competition among co-wives in a polygynous household is reduced when

a. sororal polygyny is practiced.
b. co-wives all live in the same household and share the same kitchen.
c. they are given separate living quarters.
d. a and c
ANS: D
PG: 222

26. Bride service is practiced

a. only in societies with high levels of material wealth.
b. often in hunting and gathering societies.
c. as compensation to the bride's family for the loss of her economic potential and childbearing capacity.
d. b and c only
ANS: C
PG: 226

27. Nuclear families are found in societies

a. in which there is a great amount of geographic mobility.
b. that have become industrialized.
c. with complex systems of government.
d. which are highly stratified.
ANS: A
PG: 230

28. The monetization of bridewealth

a. has increasingly created the view of marriage as a financial transaction.
b. has reduced the significance of marriage as an alliance between kin groups.
c. has been associated with the postponing of marriage until a later age.
d. all of the above
ANS: D
PG: 225

29. Polyandry

a. is one of the most common forms of marriage in the world today.
b. allows a society to avoid the division of small plots of land among sons.
c. leads to competition and especially sexual jealousy among husbands.
d. is practiced widely in South America.
ANS: B
PG: 223

30. Bridewealth

a. is the price a man pays for a wife.
b. increases the likelihood of a marriage ending in divorce.
c. tends to create bad relations between the families of the bride and groom.
d. legitimizes marriages and transfers rights over children to the father's family.
ANS: D
PG: 225

31. Neolocal residence means

a. changing residence from that of the relatives of the husband to those of the wife approximately every two years.
b. living near the relatives of the husband.
c. living near the relatives of the wife.
d. living in a place of one's own.
ANS: D
PG: 229

32. The decline in the percentage of nuclear families in the United States has been influenced by

a. the acceptance of alternative lifestyles in recent years.
b. the increasing divorce rate.
c. delays in childbearing and marriage.
d. all of the above
ANS: D
PG: 233

33. Although the nuclear family has been the ideal in the U.S. for most of the 20th century,

a. now only slightly more than half of American families are nuclear.
b. families today look like the households portrayed in the 1950s sitcoms.
c. now families are becoming more extended.
d. now only about one household in four is nuclear.
ANS: D
PG: 233

34. In extended family systems,

a. the man's obligation to his wife is more important than his obligations to his brothers.
b. blood ties are more important than ties of marriage.
c. a woman cannot be controlled by another person after she is married.
d. a and b only
ANS: B
PG: 233

35. A marriage in which a man marries women who are sisters is called

a. the levirate.
b. fraternal polyandry.
c. sororal polygyny.
d. fraternal polygyny.
ANS: C
PG: 222

36. In this chapter's Contemporary Issue, arranged marriages by an Iraqi father for his daughters (ages 13 and 14) resulted in

a. the father being convicted of child abuse.
b. the father and the daughter being deported from the United States.
c. the husbands of the two daughters being convicted of statutory rape.
d. a and c only
ANS: A
PG: 218

37. Which statement about Skid Row men is true?

a. They have lost all significant contact with their kin.
b. They actually do have considerable contact with their kin, particularly women.
c. Their kin have no role to play in the rehabilitation process of Skid Row men.
d. In most cases, their kin have thoroughly given up on them.
ANS: B
PG: 214

38. In U.S. society, the typical marital residence pattern is

a. neolocal.
b. patrilocal.
c. avunculocal.
d. matrilocal.
ANS: A
PG: 229

39. In Western societies, mate selection is largely a decision made

a. by the bride and groom's extended families.
b. with attention to the financial stability of the two partners.
c. jointly by the prospective bride and groom.
d. by the family of the bride.
ANS: C
PG: 215

40. Which of the following is **NOT** a cause of the rapidly rising divorce rate in the U.S. today?

a. Industrialization and urbanization have undermined traditional family functions.
b. Americans are less moral today.
c. The rise of individualism has caused people to be less willing to make sacrifice for family members.
d. The law has made it increasingly easier to get a divorce.
ANS: B
PG: 228

True-False

1. Ferraro defines family as a social unit characterized by common residence, economic cooperation, and child rearing.
ANS: T
PG: 209

2. Young people in a number of different cultures are beginning to use matchmaking websites on the Internet to find an appropriate spouse.
ANS: T
PG: 217

3. In U.S. society, the preferred marital residence pattern is patrilocal.
ANS: F
PG: 229

4. Outbreeding, which occurs in human populations with strong incest taboos, has a number of positive genetic consequences.
ANS: T
PG: 212

5. Cultures restrict the choice of marriage partners by such practices as endogamy, the levirate and the sororate.
ANS: T
PG: 214, 219

6. Most societies with arranged marriages assume that marriage is a union of two kin groups, not merely two individuals.
ANS: T
PG: 215-216

7. Parallel cousins are first cousins that are born in the same year.
ANS: F
PG: 219

8. According to most anthropologists, arranged marriages are inherently immoral.
ANS: F
PG: 215-217

9. Bridewealth is the money given by the groom when he wants to buy a wife.
   ANS: F
   PG: 224

10. Many young African women today believe that bridewealth functions to heighten her dignity, increase her husband's gratitude, and reduce the chances of divorce.
   ANS: T
   PG: 226

Short Answer

1. What are three social benefits of marriage?
   ANS: the creation of fairly stable relationships between men and women that regulate sexual mating and reproduction, a mechanism for regulating the sexual division of labor, creates a set of family relationships that provide for the material, educational, and emotional needs of children for a long period of time
   PG: 209

2. In which state of the United States is polygyny most widely practiced?
   ANS: Utah
   PG: 223

3. List the theories that attempt to explain the incest taboo.
   ANS: natural aversion theory, inbreeding theory, family disruption theory, theory of expanding social alliances
   PG: 212-213

4. What are three major types of marriage based on the number of spouses permitted?
   ANS: monogamy, polygyny, and polyandry
   PG: 220

5. What is a critical factor influencing the incidence of polygyny?
   ANS: the extent to which women are seen as economic assets (where they do the majority of labor) or liabilities (where men do the majority of the work)
   PG: 220-221

6. Where is bridewealth most widely found?
   ANS: In Africa
   PG: 224

7. What are some of the functions of bridewealth that anthropologists have identified?
   ANS: security or insurance for the good treatment of the wife, a mechanism to stabilize marriage by reducing the possibility of divorce, a form of compensation to the bride's lineage for the loss of her economic potential and childbearing capacity, a symbol of the union between two kin groups, a mechanism to legitimize traditional marriage, the transference of rights over the children from the mother's family to the father's family, the acquisition by the husband to rights to sex
   PG: 225

8. Societies that cannot accumulate capital practice what form of marriage exchange?
ANS: bride service
PG: 226

9. What is dowry?
ANS: a transfer of goods or money from the bride's family to the groom or to the groom's family
PG: 227

10. What are the five types of post-marital residence patterns?
ANS: patrilocal, matrilocal, avunculocal, ambilocal, and neolocal
PG: 229

Essay

1. Describe and discuss the differences between American style marriage and marriage among any cultural group in Sub-Saharan Africa.

2. What is a good cross-cultural definition of marriage? What are some of the problems that emerge from attempting to apply a single definition across cultures?

3. What are the advantages and disadvantages of polygyny for women in cultures that permit plural marriage?

4. What types of societies allow cousins to marry? In those societies, what types of cousins can marry and why is this arrangement preferred?

5. Compare the custom of giving a future bride a diamond engagement ring with bridewealth.

Chapter 10

Kinship and Descent

Multiple-Choice

1. Human social organization, compared to that of other species, is

   a. unique because only humans live in permanent groups with patterned relationships among other group members.
   b. similar to all mammals because group living is always extremely important.
   c. much more complex.
   d. live in relatively simple groups.
   ANS: C
   PG: 237

2. Kinship refers to those relationships found in all societies that

   a. are based on blood.
   b. include consanguineal relatives.
   c. include affinal relatives.
   d. all of the above.
   ANS: D
   PG: 237

3. Anthropologists, as compared to other social scientists, have spent a great deal of time studying kinship because they have

   a. always focused largely on biological relationships.
   b. concentrated mainly on small-scale societies where kinship relations tend to be important.
   c. always studied fictional relationships.
   d. concentrate on industrial societies where kinship relations tend to be important.
   ANS: B
   PG: 237

4. An "aunt" or "uncle" who has no biological or marital relationship is an example of a/an

   a. cross cousin.
   b. fictive kin.
   c. affine.
   d. parallel cousin.
   ANS: B
   PG: 238

5. The most important factor contributing to social structure is

a. political activities.
b. religious activities.
c. kinship.
d. cultural mythology.
ANS: C
PG: 237

6. In all human societies, kinship is tied to the biological relationships created by human reproduction. However,

a. how different societies sort and categorize kinship relationships is as much a matter of culture as it is of biology.
b. bilateral descent systems are less influenced by culture than others.
c. unilineal descent systems are seldom influenced by cultural definitions of social relationships.
d. ambilateral descent systems are the least influenced by culture than others.
ANS: A
PG: 238

7. The use of the same term "uncle" for our mother's brother and our mother's sister's husband is an example of

a. the lack of consideration of biological links in determining kinship in all societies.
b. the importance of distinguishing between biological relationships found in all cultures.
c. the importance of culture in defining kin relationships in most societies.
d. the fact that some kinship systems are inferior to some others.
ANS: C
PG: 239

8. Cross-culturally, most kinship systems across cultures

a. provide few links between successive generations.
b. provide few ties across a single generation.
c. provide links between successive generations and ties across a single generation.
d. only link successive generations.
ANS: C
PG: 239-240

9. EGO refers to the

a. oldest living relative.
b. oldest living relative on the father's side.
c. person from whose point of view we are tracing the relationship.
d. mother's brother's wife.
ANS: C
PG: 240

10. A kinship diagram of a married couple, their children, and their children's children would include

a. four generations; therefore four rows of kinship figures.
b. three generations; therefore three rows of kinship figures.
c. only affinal relatives.
d. only consanguineal relatives.
ANS: B
PG: 241

11. A kinship diagram of a son, father, grandfather, and great grandfather would include

a. affinal relatives.
b. collateral relatives.
c. two genders.
d. lineal relatives.
ANS: D
PG: 242

12. A kinship diagram of EGO and all of her children and cousins would include

a. the lineal relatives which belong to a clan.
b. collateral relatives.
c. a lineage.
d. lineal relatives.
ANS: B
PG: 241

13. Which statement about the Zumbaguan notion of parenthood is true?

a. Biological connection is the most important factor in determining parenthood.
b. Claims to parenthood are created by adults nurturing and caring for a child over a long period of time.
c. Feeding and sharing food with a child is more important than biological connection when determining parenthood.
d. b and c only
ANS: D
PG: 238

14. Which statement about the Zuni (New Mexico) kinship system is true?

a. They have a bilateral system.
b. Husbands divide their time and allegiances between the lineages of their wives and the lineages of their mothers.
c. Women are the major figures in performing sacred lineage ceremonies.
d. They practice patrilocal residence.
ANS: B
PG: 248

15. Traditional Chinese families are good examples of

a. bilateral kinship.
b. matrilineal kinship.
c. double descent.
d. patrilineal kinship.
ANS: D
PG: 244-146

16. Some societies make distinctions among kinship categories

a. based on whether people are older or younger than EGO.
b. based upon whether EGO is related through his mother's or his father's side.
c. determined by whether people are in EGO's generation.
d. all of the above
ANS: D
PG: 241-43

17. The term *descent* is used by anthropologists to refer to

a. the rules a culture uses to establish affiliations with one's parents.
b. the rules a culture uses to establish affiliations with one's siblings.
c. all blood and marriage relationships that help people distinguish between categories of kin.
d. all marriage relationships that help people distinguish between different categories of kin.
ANS: A
PG: 243

18. Unilineal descent systems

a. establish ambiguous social units.
b. comprise approximately sixty percent of all kinship systems in the world.
c. establish special relationships between EGO and his mother's brother.
d. establish special relationships between EGO and his brother's sister.
ANS: B
PG: 244

19. Patrilineal descent groups

a. are the most common of the unilineal descent groups.
b. are found only in North and South America.
c. trace descent through lines of females; for example, the mother, mother's mother, sister's daughter, and so on.
d. are ones in which a woman's children are members of her descent group.
ANS: A
PG: 244

20. In matrilineal descent systems,

a. women have greater power and authority than men.
b. property and political office pass from one man to another, but through women.
c. women and men have similar power and authority.
d. women control property and political office.
ANS: B
PG: 246-248

21. Unilineal descent systems with moieties

a. always have clans.
b. always have lineages.
c. always have phratries.
d. may or may not have phratries, clans, and lineages.
ANS: D
PG: 255

22. Ancestry is traced, step-by-step, back to a common founder in

a. clans.
b. matrilineages only.
c. patrilineages only.
d. lineages.
ANS: D
PG: 248-249

23. Clans, as unilineal descent groups,

a. are the same organizations as lineages, except that they form parts of chiefdoms and not tribes.
b. claim that they are all related to a common ancestor, but cannot trace that genealogical connection step-by-step.
c. are smaller in size than lineages.
d. control more property than any other type of descent group.
ANS: B
PG: 249-250

24. Unilineal descent groups last over time and have a corporate nature, which means

a. they shape a person's identity in some significant way.
b. they regulate marriage, and kin on both the bride and groom's sides must give approval.
c. they control property such as land and animals.
d. all of the above
ANS: D
PG: 250

25. In a matrilineal society, a boy's father figure is his:

a. maternal grandfather
b. mother's brother
c. father's brother
d. father's sister's husband
ANS: B
PG: 246

26. In societies with a double descent system, members are

a. free to choose to which group they will belong.
b. able to choose whether to belong to the matrilineage on their father's or on their mother's side of the family.
c. able to choose whether to belong to the patrilineage on their father's or on their mother's side of the family.
d. part of both their matrilineage and their patrilineage.
ANS: D
PG: 251

27. Individuals, except for siblings, have a unique kindred in a

a. patrilineal descent system.
b. bilateral descent system.
c. unilineal descent system.
d. a and c
ANS: B
PG: 251

28. The Hawaiian system of kinship classification uses the same term for all relatives of the same

a. sex and generation.
b. age.
c. mother.
d. father.
ANS: A
PG: 252

29. The Omaha and the Crow systems of kinship classification

a. concentrate only on matrilineal descent.
b. are mirror images of each other's concentration on unilineal descent.
c. concentrate on patrilineal descent.
d. have separate categories for father and father's brothers.
ANS: B
PG: 254

30. The Sudanese system of kinship classification

a. is the most descriptive system and makes the largest number of terminological distinctions.
b. is a mirror image of the Iroquois system.
c. only distinguishes between cross and parallel cousins.
d. all of the above
ANS: A
PG: 254-255

31. Though cultural anthropology is interested in all societies of the world, it has, in actual practice, tended to concentrate in small-scale societies where

a. kinship relations have little importance in economic transactions.
b. kinship relations have little importance in transfers of political power.
c. kinship relations tend to be all encompassing.
d. political and economic relationships are usually not played out with kin.
ANS: C
PG: 237

32. Affinal kin include one's

a. father.
b. father-in-law.
c. brother.
d. father's brother.
ANS: B
PG: 238

33. Your father's sister's children and your mother's brother's children are your

a. parallel cousins.
b. patrilineal kin.
c. cross cousins.
d. matrilineal kin.
ANS: C
PG: 242

34. All of the following are criteria used to distinguish between different kin categories except

a. generation.
b. gender.
c. side of the family.
d. level of formal education.
ANS: D
PG: 241-43

35. All unilineal descent groups

a. endure over time and clearly define who is a member and who is not.
b. allow members to decide which descent groups they want to belong to; therefore these groups change membership and size radically from generation to generation.
c. cannot clearly define who is or is not a member, but still manage to endure over time.
d. allow individuals to first identify themselves as individuals and then as members of the kinship group.

ANS: A
PG: 244

36. In bilateral descent, individuals

a. are members of the kinship group their parents have selected for them.
b. are equally related to both the mother's and the father's side of the family.
c. trace descent from both a patrilineage and a matrilineage.
d. can choose with which side of the family they wish to affiliate.

ANS: B
PG: 251

37. In the modern world, kinship

a. no longer has importance.
b. no longer provides close and emotional social ties as it did in the past.
c. has become much more complex because of new reproductive technologies.
d. systems remain unchanged through contact with external forces such as colonization and cultural diffusion.

ANS: C
PG: 258

38. The Navajo (New Mexico) system of kinship

a. is very similar to that which governs students in urban Chicago schools.
b. strictly governs the behavior of members of the same clan
c. requires people to find marriage partners within their own clan.
d. is characterized by clan endogamy

ANS: B
PG: 256

39. Which statement about Finkelstein's study of homeless youth is true?

a. there are about 50,000 run away youth in the U.S. every year
b. most of the youth in this study were from wealthy homes
c. homeless youth tend to find a city they like and then stay there
d. homeless youth have extensive networks of friends who substitute for family

ANS: D
PG: 258-259

40. "Partible paternity," as practiced by the Bari of Venezuela, means that:

a. children can have more than one biological father
b. biological fatherhood is not acknowledged at all
c. a child is raised by his grandfather, not his biological father
d. the biological father is never the social father.
ANS: A
PG: 239

True-False

1. Women are the major decision-makers in a matrilineal society.
ANS: F
PG: 246

2. In all societies, biology is more important than culture to the definition of kinship.
ANS: F
PG: 238

3. Kinship provides social continuity by binding together a number of successive generations.
ANS: T
PG: 239-240

4. The Zuni of New Mexico are patrilineal and patrilocal.
ANS: F
PG: 248

5. The first ascending generation would include EGO's mother, father, and the sisters and brothers of the mother and father.
ANS: T
PG: 241

6. Kindreds are found in both unlineal and cognatic descent systems.
ANS: F
PG: 251

7. The majority of kinship systems found in the world are based on the unilineal principle.
ANS: T
PG: 244

8. Patrilineal societies usually have a higher divorce rate than matrilineal societies.
ANS: F
PG: 248

9. In her study of homeless youth, Finkelstein used an "emic" approach to research.
ANS: T
PG: 258

10. Today it is more difficult to obtain information on your distant relatives than it was in past decades.
ANS: F
PG: 255

SHORT ANSWER

1. What is the kinship term for those people to whom we are related through birth or blood?
ANS: consanguineal relatives
PG: 238

2. What is fictive kinship?
ANS: a kinship term used for individuals who are not related by blood or marriage
PG: 238

3. All kinship systems serve which two important functions for the well being of the total society?
ANS: vertical function and horizontal function
PG: 239-240

4. What is the term for the person from whose point of view kinship relationships are traced?
ANS: EGO
PG: 240

5. What is the term for the rules a culture uses to establish affiliations with one's parents?
ANS: descent
PG: 243

6. Name three recent innovations in reproductive technology that are forcing us to redefine some aspects of kinship
ANS: sperm banks, in vitro fertilization, and surrogate mothers
PG: 257-259

7. Name two broad types of descent
ANS: unilineal descent and cognatic descent
PG: 244

8. What four types of kinship groups are based on the unilineal principle?
ANS: lineages, clans, phratries, and moieties
PG: 248-250

9. List the six basic systems of kinship classification.
ANS: Eskimo, Hawaiian, Iroquois, Crow, Sudanese, Omaha
PG: 252-255

10. What is the major feature of the Eskimo system?
ANS: It emphasizes the nuclear family by using separate terms that are not used outside the nuclear family.
PG: 252

Essay

1. What are the criteria on which principles of kinship classification are based? Describe at least six of the categories that are used by some systems.

2. Why has kinship been the subject of so much anthropological research? Why is it said to be the single most important aspect of social structure?

3. Describe the most common rules of descent.

4. In what specific ways do unilineal descent groups act corporately (i.e., as small corporations)?

5. In a bilateral system, which kinship organization is the most significant to an individual? What types of subsistence patterns are found in association with bilateral descent?

6. Are divorce rates higher in matrilineal or patrilineal societies? Support your answer.

Chapter 11
Sex and Gender

Multiple-Choice

1. The text defines gender as

    a. the biological differences in males and females.
    b. the way members of the two sexes are perceived, evaluated, and expected to behave.
    c. the differences in males and females due to the greater strength of males.
    d. universally recognizable male aggressiveness and female maternalism.
    ANS: B
    PG: 263

2. Margaret Mead's study of three New Guinea societies determined that

    a. males in all three societies were more nurturing than were the women.
    b. men and women's gender roles are not defined in the same ways in all societies.
    c. women in these three groups were fiercely aggressive while men's behavior varied.
    d. all of the above
    ANS: B
    PG: 263

3. Sexual dimorphism is

    a. found in all species of mammals.
    b. a characteristic of humans.
    c. the practice of having two sexual partners.
    d. absent in most Asian and African societies.
    ANS: B
    PG: 263

4. Female soccer players

    a. are not seen as less feminine in the U.S.
    b. have higher levels of testosterone than women who do not play soccer.
    c. are thought of as less feminine in Brazil.
    d. a and c
    ANS: D
    PG: 263-264

5. The Hijra of Hindu India exemplify

a. a gender role that tolerates a wider definition of gender than is found in our own society.
b. a gender role which defines masculinity more rigidly than our own society.
c. a gender role which defines masculinity and femininity almost identically.
d. social deviants who are discouraged in their own society.
ANS: A
PG: 264

6. As a general rule, most societies divide labor by gender so that

a. women clear land and tend crops.
b. men collect firewood, carry water, and clear land.
c. men engage in warfare, trap small animals, and clear land.
d. all of the above
ANS: C
PG: 268

7. Which statement about the cross-cultural study of male homosexuality is true?

a. Sexual preference and sexual activity are the same thing.
b. Approximately 30 percent of all U.S. males prefer homosexuality as a lifestyle.
c. Some societies define male homosexuality as a necessary requirement for heterosexual relationships in adulthood.
d. All societies view male homosexuality as deviant and pathological (sick).
ANS: C
PG: 267

8. Male homosexuality among the Azande of the Sudan

a. is considered a legitimate short-term arrangement while men serve in the military.
b. involves the payment of bridewealth.
c. is not considered to be a long-term (lifetime) arrangement.
d. all of the above
ANS D
PG: 268

9. The theory that, because men have greater body mass and strength, they hunt and females care for children

a. explains the division of labor in all societies.
b. does not explain the division of labor among humans.
c. constitutes only a partial explanation for the division of labor in human societies.
d. has been proven invalid because females hunt in many food collecting societies.
ANS: C
PG: 269-270

10. Gender stratification is found

a. only in food collecting societies.
b. only in horticultural societies.
c. only in pastoralist societies.
d. in all types of societies.
ANS: D
PG: 272

11. Anthropological data on human sexuality in other parts of the world is sparse because

a. sexual activity in all parts of the world is considered to be a private matter.
b. data on women has been ignored by the preponderance of male researchers.
c. questions asked by anthropologists have been narrowly defined.
d. all of the above
ANS: D
PG: 265

12. Cross-cultural research has shown that, when women are economically independent, they

a. may remain subordinate to their husbands in most other respects.
b. never are subordinate to their husbands in most other respects.
c. seldom remain subordinate to their husbands in most other respects.
d. usually dominate their husband in most respects.
ANS: A
PG: 273

13. Iranian women's abandonment and subsequent return to the veil and more traditional female roles illustrates that

a. the status of women in societies is not static.
b. political change seldom changes women's roles.
c. men are universally dominant.
d. *purdah* has no place in the modern world.
ANS: A
PG: 273

14. In North Australia, the Tiwi's exchange of daughters, sisters, and widowed mothers for additional wives for themselves

a. supports the idea that women's social roles have uniform levels of status in any given society.
b. allowed all men in the society to maintain relatively equal status.
c. allowed the mothers and sisters, as older women, roles as behind-the-scenes allies of their sons and brothers.
d. demonstrates that Tiwi women are treated violently by their husbands.
ANS: C
PG: 274

15. The most egalitarian societies (in terms of gender) are

a. industrialized.
b. horticultural.
c. pastoralist.
d. food collectors.
ANS: D
PG: 274

16. Among food collecting societies, the roles performed by women and men

a. are assigned a very different status.
b. are very different but their relative status is not.
c. are almost identical, with very similar status.
d. do not determine the status of each gender, which depends solely on ability to accumulate property.
ANS: B
PG: 275

17. Matriarchies

a. do not and have never existed.
b. are rare but do exist in Africa.
c. are rare but do exist in the Amazon.
d. are those with queens.
ANS: A
PG: 275

18. According to Ernestine Friedl, women are subordinate to men because men

a. are bigger and stronger.
b. control the allocation of scarce resources.
c. have more testosterone.
d. are hunters.
ANS: B
PG: 275-276

19. Sexual asymmetry can be shown through the use of doublets,

a. which demonstrate the inequality of women compared to men in America.
b. which are pairs of words that have the same meaning, but one word is used by men and the other by women.
c. which are found in Standard American English.
d. which always vary in terms of loudness and aggressiveness.
ANS: B
PG: 271

20. Pregnant women in developing countries

a. face malnutrition.
b. face a lack of trained medical personnel to deal with high-risk pregnancies.
c. are 80 to 600 times more likely to die of complications of pregnancy than women in the industrialized world.
d. all of the above

ANS: D
PG: 277

21. "Genderlects" refers to linguistic gender differences in the United States, where

a. women's speech tends to be cooperative in character.
b. women engage in "report-talk" while men engage in "rapport-talk."
c. women emphasize establishing a place in the competitive social hierarchy.
d. men tend to engage more often than women do in "active listening."

ANS: A
PG: 271

22. The preference for male children

a. is universal.
b. doesn't really exist and only appears in the anthropological literature because of the male bias in anthropology.
c. is only found in food collecting (foraging) societies.
d. is much more common than the rare preference for female children.

ANS: D
PG: 278

23. According to Deborah Tannen, which statement best describes the differences in language between men and women in the United States?

a. Men engage in "rapport talk" while women engage in "report talk."
b. Men tend to be more competitive.
c. When men and women are talking together, women tend to talk more than men and interrupt them more frequently.
d. Men tend to listen better than women do.

ANS: B
PG: 271

24. Dowry deaths are found in which part of the world?

a. India
b. Mexico
c. China
d. Kenya

ANS: A
PG: 282-283

25. Female genital mutilation, found in parts of Africa and Asia, is

a. condemned by the World Health Organization.
b. justified by traditionalists as socialization of young girls to become proper women.
c. can be detrimental to a woman's health.
d. all of the above
ANS: D
PG: 283

26. Male gender bias is expressed in

a. female infanticide.
b. "honor killings."
c. nutritional deprivation in female children.
d. all of the above
ANS: D
PG: 280-284

27. While human sexuality varies widely from culture to culture,

a. most societies are quite permissive about premarital sex.
b. all societies regulate sexual conduct.
c. all societies expect married adults to have very active sex lives.
d. no societies consider sexual activity essential for good health.
ANS: B
PG: 265

28. The milk-goat project in Malawi was an attempt to address which basic social problem?

a. toddler malnutrition
b. sexual violence against women
c. starvation across the entire population
d. drought
ANS: A
PG: 272-273

29. Which statement about sexuality in the United States is TRUE?

a. young people are becoming sexually active at an earlier age
b. a greater percentage of young people are becoming sexually active
c. for those who are sexually active, their sexual activity is becoming more frequent
d. all of the above
ANS: D
PG: 266

30. Women in many parts of the world are particularly vulnerable to HIV/AIDS because

a. they have less biological resistance to the disease than men.
b. it is unacceptable in some cultures for women to say "no" to unwanted sex.
c. in some sexually restrictive cultures, women are denied information about the dangers of sexually transmitted diseases.
d. b and c only
ANS: D
PG: 277

31. Which statement about the gap between female and male earnings in the U.S. is true?

a. It has narrowed somewhat over the last 30 years.
b. It remains significant, with women making only 70% of what men make.
c. It holds true for all levels, from executive to grocery clerks.
d. all of the above
ANS: D
PG: 285

32. In the United States, occupational segregation along gender lines

a. has disappeared because of the passage of the Equal Rights Amendment.
b. is still high, with a number of occupations more than seventy percent female or male.
c. has dramatically declined in most areas.
d. has actually become more severe over the last four decades.
ANS: B
PG: 285

33. Which statement about Dr. Patten's role in the Malawi goat project is <u>false?</u>

a. She conducted baseline ethnographic information on the local population.
b. She failed to understand the normal relationships between men and women.
c. She helped convince local men to allow women to control the goat herds.
d. She served as a cultural brokers between the project team and the local population.
ANS: B
PG: 272-273

34. Which statement about the "feminization of poverty" is <u>false</u>?

a. It applies to women all over the world.
b. It had little relationship to gender segregation in the American workforce.
c. Female-headed households with children are much less powerful than families that include a male adult.
d. It is particularly severe for minority women in the United States.
ANS: B
PG: 276-277

35. Susan Scrimshaw, an anthropologist studying family planning clinics in Ecuador, found that

a. Ecuadorian women used these clinics at high rates.
b. women's modesty had important implications for how women felt about attending family planning clinics.
c. the staff of local clinics had little to do with women's decisions about attending the clinic.
d. women at the clinics had very positive attitudes about their bodies.

ANS: B
PG: 280-281

36. Practical recommendations for maximizing the utility of family planning clinics in Ecuador included

a. paying women to attend the clinic.
b. prohibiting all conversation during examinations.
c. prohibition of male physicians from the clinics.
d. acting discretely, giving privacy, and allowing women to maintain their modesty during visits to the clinic.

ANS: D
PG: 281

37. Which statement about violence against women in the U.S. is <u>false</u>?

a. Approximately half of the women murder victims are killed by a current or former husband/boyfriend.
b. Many cases of violence against women go unreported each year.
c. Most rapes are committed by strangers.
d. Most violence against women occurs in the home, not on the street.

ANS: C
PG: 283

38. Men in the U.S. have higher mortality rates than women, because men are more likely to

a. abuse their bodies with tobacco, alcohol, and drugs.
b. engage in high-risk behavior.
c. suffer from greater job related stress.
d. all of the above

ANS: D
PG: 286

39. The World Bank has found that financial credit given to women is good business because

a. women are more reliable than men in terms of paying back the loans.
b. women tend to spend their profits on better nutrition for their children.
c. women tend to spend their profits on their children's education.
d. all of the above

ANS: D
PG: 277-278

40. Which statement about the Minangkabau of West Sumatra is TRUE?

a. The society is a true matriarchy
b. This society tends to emphasize cooperation among men and women
c. This society emphasizes women controlling men
d. This society emphasizes high levels of cometition between men and women
ANS: B
PG 275

True-False

1. Cross-cultural studies of gender have found that some societies have more categories than female and male.
ANS: T
PG: 264

2. Women's roles must always be compatible with pregnancy, breast feeding, and childcare.
ANS: F
PG: 269

3. Approximately 15 percent of all children in Malawi suffer from malnourishment.
ANS: F
PG: 272

4. Two-thirds of all the illiterate people in the world today are women.
ANS: T
PG: 276

5. According to Deborah Tannen, women in the U.S. engage in "report talk" while men engage in "rapport talk."
ANS: F
PG: 271

6. "Genderlects" represent sexual symmetry in language.
ANS: F
PG: 271

7. Women in the U.S. have higher mortality rates than men because they are most often victims of family violence.
ANS: F
PG: 286

8. Despite decades of legislation aimed at reducing gender discrimination in the U.S., the majority of men and women work in gender segregated occupations.
ANS: T
PG: 285

9. The practice of men holding hands is a universally understood sign of male homosexuality.

ANS: F
PG: 268

10. Ecuadorian women were reluctant to use family planning clinics because the staff did little to protect women's privacy.
ANS: T
PG: 280-281

Short Answer

1. What are the significant physiological differences between human males and females called?
ANS: sexual dimorphism
PG: 263

2. What definition of gender is used in your textbook?
ANS: the way members of the two sexes are perceived, evaluated, and expected to behave
PG: 263

3. Why is it difficult to measure gender stratification?
ANS: there are many different dimensions, it changes over time, and it varies within some cultures depending of the age of the women.
PG: 272-73

4. Gender roles are noticeably uniform among the cultures of the world, and men perform which tasks?
ANS: engage in warfare, trap small animals, work with hard substances, clear land, build houses, and fish
PG: 268-269

5. Gender roles are noticeably uniform among the cultures of the world, and women perform which tasks?
ANS: tend crops, gather wild fruits and plants, prepare food, care for children, collect firewood, clean house, launder clothing, and carry water.
PG: 268-269

6. Why is there a growing number of stay at home dads?
ANS: more fathers are between jobs, working at home, or working part time.
PG: 270-271

7. What is meant by the "feminization of poverty?"
ANS: That an increasing percentage of women are living in poverty throughout the world.
PG: 277

8. What are four areas in which the world's women have not faired as well as men?
ANS: education, employment, reproductive health, and finance
PG: 276-278

9. What is gender ideology?
   ANS: a system of thoughts and values that legitimize gender roles, statuses, and customary behavior
   PG: 278

10. List three manifestations of extreme gender ideology.
   ANS: female infanticide, nutritional deprivation, honor killings, female genital mutilation, physical violence, sexual assault, and dowry death.
   PG: 281-283

Essay

1. Are there any universals about gender roles across all societies? Is male dominance universal? Use examples from your reading to support your position.

2. How important are economic factors in the definition of gender in the United States? What factors have pushed women into or out of the work force? How important have family considerations been in women's entry into the paid labor force? Why is there a difference between women and men's wages?

3. How does human sexuality vary across cultures? What impact does the imposition of a practice of postpartum sexual abstinence have on a society? What is the impact of cultural expectations of sexual experience before marriage?

4. What is gender stratification? If women are not allowed to hold important positions in religious activities, does that indicate stratification? Does the prohibition of women from the same economic activities as men always indicate stratification? What is necessary for there to be equality between women and men?

5. Does the rigid definition of gender roles in the Middle East mean that women will always have lower status than men? Can there be any type of equality for women when they have a separate sphere than men? Does veiling itself create inequality? Can the separation of women and men benefit women?

6. Discuss some of the variations in male homosexuality throughout the world.

Chapter 12

Political Organization and Social Control

Multiple-Choice

1. Since all societies must maintain social order; they all have

   a. legislatures.
   b. elected officials.
   c. mechanisms of social control.
   d. permanent armies.
   ANS: C
   PG: 290

2. Societies differ in the degree

   a. to which their political institutions are distinct from economic, kinship or religious structures.
   b. to which they concentrate authority into specific political roles.
   c. of their level of political integration.
   d. all of the above
   ANS: D
   PG: 290

3. Band societies are usually

   a. settled populations.
   b. tightly organized under hereditary leaders.
   c. found to have considerable political integration.
   d. none of the above
   ANS: D
   PG: 290-291

4. An example of a band society is the

   a. Ju/'hoansi.
   b. Nuer.
   c. ancient Egyptians.
   d. Chinese
   ANS: A
   PG: 292

5. The quote "He carries his own load and is as thin as the rest" refers to the leader of a

a. band.
b. chiefdom.
c. tribe.
d. state.
ANS: A
PG: 292

6. Tribal societies are usually associated with

a. food production.
b. horticulturalists.
c. pastoralists.
d. all of the above
ANS: D
PG: 292

7. A pan-tribal mechanism is an organization

a. to which all the men belong.
b. to which all the women belong.
c. cutting across and integrating local segments of the tribe into a larger whole.
d. integrating all tribes from a region into a larger group.
ANS: C
PG: 292

8. The shifting nature of the political structure of tribal societies is demonstrated by

a. pan-tribal mechanisms.
b. hunting and gathering
c. segmentary lineage systems.
d. all of the above
ANS: C
PG: 293

9. A good example of a tribal society is the

a. precolonial Hawaiians.
b. Chinese.
c. Ju/'hoansi
d. Nuer.
ANS: D
PG: 293

10. Which statement about pan-tribal mechanisms is true?

a. They serve to segregate local tribal segments.
b. They serve to integrate local tribal segments.
c. They are the same as extended families.
d. They are permanent political fixtures.
ANS: B
PG: 292

11. The European colonial powers

a. only took colonies in societies with long histories as chiefdoms.
b. never found chiefs to be associated with supernatural powers.
c. eliminated traditional chiefs because they interfered with colonial administration.
d. created chiefs where none had previously existed in order to facilitate administration of local populations.
ANS: D
PG: 294-295

12. An example of a chiefdom is the

a. Ju/'hoansi.
b. Nuer.
c. precolonial Hawaiians.
d. Chinese.
ANS: C
PG: 295

13. Which statement about chiefdoms is true?

a. Chiefs are involved with economic activities through redistribution.
b. Chiefs tend to have centralized power.
c. Chiefs hold permanent positions, often hereditary in nature.
d. All of the above
ANS: D
PG: 294-295

14. As a complex form of political organization, a state society

a. always relies on supernatural sanctions to maintain social order.
b. maintains the exclusive right to use force and physical coercion.
c. maintains its authority by brute force alone.
d. has the least amount of deviation from the norms.
ANS: B
PG: 295

15. The characteristics of state systems of government include

a. specialized political roles.
b. large bureaucratic organizations.
c. organizations with a suprakinship basis.
d. all of the above
ANS: D
PG: 295-296

16. A nation refers to a group of people who share a common

a. symbolic identity.
b. culture.
c. history.
d. all of the above
ANS: D
PG: 298

17. Examples of nation-states comprised of a number of ethnic groups include

a. the United Kingdom.
b. Japan.
c. Russia.
d. a and c
ANS: D
PG: 299

18. All political systems vary along a continuum of

a. distinctiveness of political institutions from kinship.
b. level of political integration.
c. degree of political coerciveness.
d. all of the above
ANS: D
PG: 290

19. Which statement about the rise of state systems of government is FALSE?

a. V. Gordon Childe put forth a voluntaristic theory of state formation.
b. Karl Wittfogel is associated with the hydraulic theory of state formation.
c. Robert Carneiro suggested a coercive theory of state formation.
d. None of the above.
ANS: D
PG: 298

20. Foraging societies are usually

a. state societies.
b. chiefdoms.
c. tribal societies.
d. band societies.
ANS: D
PG: 291

21. The redistributive mode of distribution is predominantly found in

a. band societies.
b. chiefdoms.
c. state societies.
d. segmentary lineage societies.
ANS: B
PG: 294

22. Societies with intensive agriculture are most often

a. state societies.
b. chiefdoms.
c. tribal societies.
d. band societies.
ANS: A
PG: 295

23. What do the Kurds living in Turkey, the French living in Canada, and the Chechens living in Russia all have in common?

a. They all share the same religion.
b. They are all seeking statehood or expanded autonomy.
c. They are all at the same level of economic development.
d. They are all tribal societies.
ANS: B
PG: 299

24. Deviance

a. is an absolute defined in the same way by all cultures.
b. is more likely to occur in acephalous societies than in state societies.
c. refers to the violation of social norms.
d. has nothing to do with social control.
ANS: C
PG: 305

25. The global trend over the last several decades has been toward

a. a greater number of democracies.
b. a greater number of autocracies.
c. fewer free elections of political leaders.
d. greater repression of opposition political parties.
ANS: A
PG: 300

26. Corporate lineages function effectively to maintain social control because

a. they have power to control the economic well being of their members.
b. of their small scale nature.
c. of their diffuse roles.
d. all of the above
ANS: D
PG: 307-308

27. In societies where dead ancestors are considered fully functioning members of the descent group, an especially effective means of social control may be

a. socialization.
b. ancestor worship.
c. public opinion.
d. witchcraft.
ANS: B
PG: 309

28. Age set systems serve as mechanisms of social control because

a. they are associated with a belief that social deviance will cause one to suffer in the afterlife.
b. only members of an individual's own age set have any authority over him.
c. the members always spend a lot of time drinking beer together.
d. individuals' initiations almost always include an intense period of training in the norms and values of the society.
ANS: D
PG: 310

29. The nuclear confrontation between India and Pakistan in 2002 was averted by

a. the president of India.
b. leaders of the information technology industry.
c. the president of Pakistan.
d. U.S. diplomatic efforts.
ANS: B
PG: 302

30. Which statement about the legal system of Canada is TRUE?

a. in some provinces local religious authorities can settle certain civil cases
b. the Islamic community in Canada wants to substitute its own religious laws for the national legal structure
c. it is one of the least accepting of immigrant legal ideas and procedures.
d. it is presently considering outlawing the immigration of Muslims into Canada.
ANS: A
PG: 304

31. The basic features of law include

a. the illegitimate use of physical coercion.
b. allocating official authority to privileged people who are able to use coercion legitimately.
c. the total inability to predict the outcome of disputes.
d. all of the above
ANS: B
PG: 314

32. Social control in small-scale (acephalous) societies is maintained by

a. socialization.
b. degradation ceremonies.
c. corporate lineage structures.
d. all of the above
ANS: D
PG: 306-310

33. A society will go to war when

a. it is threatened.
b. it wants to further its own ends.
c. it is defending a moral position.
d. all of the above
ANS: D
PG: 316-317

34. A Leopard-skin Chief among the Nuer

a. serves as a mediator between a victim's family and the family of a murderer.
b. serves as judge and jury in criminal and civil cases.
c. serves as a judge to determine guilt, but has no authority to determine punishment.
d. has authority to impose a settlement on the disputing parties.
ANS: A
PG: 311-312

35. Moots are

a. found in most Asian societies.
b. formal public courts that decide cases involving the breaking of written laws.
c. formal settlements of disputes involving only kinsmen of the litigants.
d. informal airings of disputes involving kinsmen and friends of the litigants.
ANS: D
PG: 312

36. State systems of government are a significant political development in human history and developed because of

a. military might.
b. a variety of reasons on which there is no consensus.
c. skill in food production which allowed the accumulation of surplus.
d. the need to control irrigation.
ANS: B
PG: 298

37. The voluntaristic theory of state development argues that

a. state societies developed before agriculture.
b. state societies developed before occupational specialization.
c. the introduction of intensive agriculture created food surpluses, which allowed some individuals to engage in new occupational roles.
d. state societies developed because of dependence on irrigation.
ANS: C
PG: 298

38. The hydraulic theory of state formation argues that

a. machinery had to be invented before state systems developed.
b. farmers with irrigation systems came to see benefits in joining together and becoming part of a larger political entity.
c. centralized governments developed out of military power rather than self interest.
d. the plow was the major factor behind the development of state systems of government.
ANS: B
PG: 298

39. In Iran the terms "mediation" and "compromise"

a. have a positive meaning for reaching agreement
b. have a negative meaning for reaching agreement
c. have the same meaning as they do in the United States
d. a and c only
ANS: B
PG: 315

40. The Poarch Creek Indians of southern Alabama

a. tried to achieve official recognition as a Native American group at the suggestion of an anthropologist doing research on their identity.
b. had to demonstrate that they had maintained a continuous existence as a political unit with viable leadership that had authority over its members.
c. found no evidence in the National Archives in Washington, D.C. to help support their claim for official recognition as a Native American group.
d. refused help from an anthropologist who offered to help them gain official recognition

ANS: B
PG: 296-297

True-False

1. Political organization involves cultural arrangements to minimize disruption and maintain order.
ANS: T
PG: 290

2. Leadership roles in band societies tend to be very informal.
ANS: T
PG: 291

3. Pan-tribal associations are permanent political fixtures that cut across and integrate all local segments of a tribe.
ANS: F
PG: 292

4. In some parts of their colonial empire, the British imposed chiefs over tribal societies.
ANS: T
PG: 294-295

5. State systems are large, hierarchical, and organized on a suprakinship basis.
ANS: T
PG: 295

6. State systems of government are supported by intensive agriculture, which is required to support a large number of non-food producing bureaucrats.
ANS: T
PG: 295-296

7. In some societies today, women hold the majority of leadership positions in the government.
ANS: F
PG: 299

8. Societies with a belief in witchcraft accept the idea that misfortunes are the result of natural causes.
ANS: F
PG: 309

9. Leadership in band societies is usually hereditary.
ANS: F
PG: 290-291

10. Kpelle moots are held in the homes of the complainant and all parties sit very close together in a random mixed fashion.
ANS: T
PG: 312

Short Answer

1. On what three dimensions do societies differ in their political organization?
ANS: the extent to which political institutions are distinct from other aspects of the social structure, the extent to which authority is concentrated into specific political roles, the level of political integration
PG: 290

2. What are the four types of political structure?
ANS: band societies, tribal societies, chiefdoms, and state societies
PG: 290

3. List traits common to band societies.
ANS: have the least amount of political integration, political decisions are often embedded in the wider social structure, and leadership roles tend to be very informal
PG: 291

4. What is a major difference between tribes and bands?
ANS: Tribal societies have certain pan-tribal mechanisms that cut across and integrate all of the local segments of the tribe into a larger whole.
PG: 292

5. How do chiefdoms differ from bands and tribes?
ANS: integrate a number of local communities in a more formal and permanent way, chiefs are centralized and permanent officials with higher rank, power, and authority than others in the society, redistribution is the mode of economics
PG: 294

6. On which two important functions does the authority of the state rest?
ANS: holds the exclusive right to use force and physical coercion and maintains authority by means of ideology
PG: 295

7. What is a nation-state?
ANS: a group of people sharing a common cultural background and unified by a political structure that they all consider to be legitimate
PG: 298-299

8. What are three theories of state formation and their major proponents?
ANS: V. Gordon Childe – voluntaristic theory of state formation, Karl Wittfogel – hydraulic theory of state formation, Robert Carneiro – coercive theory of state formation
PG: 298

9. List informal mechanisms of social control.
ANS: socialization, public opinion, corporate lineages, and supernatural belief systems, age organizations
PG: 306-311

10. List formal mechanisms of social control.
ANS: song duels, intermediaries, moots, oaths and ordeals, courts and codified law, warfare
PG: 311-317

Essay

1. What are four levels of political integration recognized by anthropologists? How do they differ?

2. How does distribution of products in chiefdoms and states differ from that of bands and tribes? Do economic factors appear to have significant influence on political organization?

3. Discuss the three major theories of state formation by Childe, Wittfogel, and Carneiro. What are the premises and assumptions of each? Which theory offers the most complete explanation? Why?

4. What formal means of social control are used in non-state societies?

5. Contrast the political organization of chiefdoms and states.

6. How can the distorted sex ratios in India and China lead to an increase in warfare and crime?

Chapter 13
Social Stratification

Multiple-Choice

1. According to Max Weber, there are three major criteria used for measuring social inequality:

   a. wealth, power and prestige
   b. prestige, education, and religion
   c. power, race and religion
   d. wealth, religion, and prestige
   ANS: A
   PG: 321

2. Economic inequality is greatest among

   a. the Ju/'hoansi.
   b. the Inuit.
   c. people of the United States.
   d. the Nuer.
   ANS: C
   PG: 321

3. According to C. Wright Mills and William Domhoff, power is concentrated in the hands of

   a. the majority of people.
   b. a power elite.
   c. Republican and Democratic politicians.
   d. college professors, scientists, and other academic types.
   ANS: B
   PG: 322

4. Prestige in the United States is associated with occupations and

   a. rapidly changes over the decades.
   b. has decreased for corporate CEOs in recent years.
   c. has remained remarkably stable for the past 100 years.
   d. a and b only
   ANS: C
   PG: 322

5. Types of societies based on levels of social inequality are

a. band, tribe, chiefdom, and state.
b. state and acephalous.
c. egalitarian and state.
d. egalitarian, rank, and stratified.
ANS: D
PG: 322

6. In an egalitarian society,

a. there are no individuals who are more highly esteemed than others.
b. the most esteemed individuals have the most tools, therefore the most wealth.
c. there are as many positions of prestige as there are persons capable of filling them.
d. there are always a number of positions of power with no one to fill them.
ANS: C
PG: 323

7. Egalitarian societies

a. are the most highly stratified.
b. allocate wealth, power, and prestige fairly evenly.
c. provide relatively equal access to power and wealth, but not prestige.
d. do not recognize any personal differences in certain skills.
ANS: B
PG: 323-324

8. When egalitarian societies come into contact with state societies

a. they almost always are significantly transformed.
b. they are very resistant to change.
c. they change, but only in terms of their political structures.
d. b and c only
ANS: A
PG: 323

9. In a rank society, high-status positions

a. are available only to the best qualified.
b. often expand to include all qualified candidates.
c. are often filled on the basis of kinship.
d. are constantly expanding.
ANS: C
PG: 324

10. Chiefs in a rank society possess great prestige and accumulate large amounts of tribute which

a. is used for their sons' inheritance.
b. is used for the inheritance of all of their children.
c. they then give away.
d. they keep for their own use.
ANS: C
PG: 324

11. Which statement about the class system in the United States is true?

a. All people have an equal chance of going from rags to riches.
b. The U.S. allows for the least amount of social mobility.
c. Most people stay in the same social class for their entire lives.
d. U.S. society places a higher value on ascribed status than on achieved status.
ANS: C
PG: 330

12. Which statement about occupational ranking is false?

a. Rankings have changed considerably over the past fifty years.
b. Rankings have remained remarkably stable over the past fifty years.
c. Rankings in the U.S. are surprisingly consistent with those in other parts of the world.
d. High level occupations generally require more education and more abstract thinking.
ANS: A
PG: 322

13. Which statement about class differences in the U.S. is true?

a. The years 1945-75 witnessed a widening gap between the various classes.
b. Over the last 60 years there has been a shrinking of class differences.
c. The gap between the "haves" and "have-nots" has widened since 1975.
d. Since 1975 class differences have remained essentially unchanged.
ANS: C
PG: 328

14. _____________ societies developed approximately 5,500 years ago.

a. Egalitarian
b. Rank
c. Stratified
d. Caste
ANS: C
PG: 325

15. Caste and class societies

a. differ in terms of social mobility.
b. have either absolute mobility or a total lack of mobility.
c. differ in terms of ascribed versus achieved status.
d. a and c only
ANS: D
PG: 325

16. ____________ systems are based on achieved status and permit considerable social mobility.

a. Chiefdom
b. Egalitarian
c. Class
d. Caste
ANS: C
PG: 325

17. The upper class in the United States has considerable power because it

a. owns the means of production.
b. controls the media.
c. has enormous political influence.
d. all of the above
ANS: D
PG: 329

18. Your text describes how many social classes in the United States?

a. two - the haves and the have-nots
b. four
c six
d twelve
ANS: C
PG: 327-327

19. Members of the same social class share similar economic levels

a. but very different political views and values.
b. and often similar educational backgrounds and political views.
c but very different occupations and memberships in organizations.
d but very different life chances.
ANS: B
PG: 329

20. In caste societies,

a. no caste has a monopoly on certain occupations.
b. marriage between castes is strictly prohibited.
c all castes have equal access to power, prestige, and wealth.
d social mobility is virtually unrestricted.
ANS: B
PG: 331

21. Caste societies are found

a. in South America and Asia.
b. in Scandinavian countries.
c in several regions of the world, such as Hindu India and central Africa.
d only in Hindu India.
ANS: C
PG: 330

22. The highest of the four major Hindu castes is the *varna* of the

a. warriors.
b. priests and scholars.
c tradesmen.
d cultivators.
ANS: B
PG: 330-331

23. The *jati* (sub-castes) of India

a. have social rankings which vary from one region to another.
b. are local groups that are strictly endogamous.
c. only socialize with members of their own group.
d. all of the above
ANS: D
PG: 331

24. Race refers to

a. a group of people sharing similar cultural traits.
b. a group of people sharing similar beliefs and ideologies.
c. nothing more than a statistical statement about the occurrence of physical traits.
d. three categories: Mongoloid, Negroid, and Caucasoid.
ANS: C
PG: 334

25. Ethnicity

a. refers to cultural traits passed from generation to generation.
b. tends to cut across socioeconomic lines.
c. refers to physical and cultural traits of human populations.
d. a and b
ANS: D
PG: 336

26. During the last 25 years, compensation for CEOs in the U.S. (when compared to other segments of the population) has

a. increased dramatically.
b. decreased somewhat.
c. increased only slightly.
d. remained unchanged.
ANS: A
PG: 328

27. The functionalist interpretation of inequality argues that if people are to make sacrifices necessary to perform vital jobs, they must be
a. adequately rewarded.
b. that the most highly skilled people deserve the most money.
c. that the current system serves to move the best people to fill key jobs into those positions in society.
d. all of the above
ANS: D
PG: 342-343

28. The conflict theory interpretation of inequality argues that

a. if people are to make sacrifices necessary to perform vital jobs, they must be adequately rewarded.
b. the most highly skilled people deserve the most money.
c. the upper levels of the hierarchy exploit those below.
d. all of the above
ANS: C
PG: 343

29. Which statement about per capita gross national income (PNI) is TRUE?

a. three quarters of the countries of the world have a PNI of under $3000.
b. the United States has a PNI of over $34,000.
c. Ethiopia and Tanzania have PNIs of less than $100.
d. all of the above
ANS: D
PG: 345

30. Pluralism

a. describes two or more diverse ethnic groups living in harmony.
b. describes a racial or ethnic minority's absorption into the wider society.
c. describes the political, economic, and social repression of racial and ethnic minorities.
d. is a myth because it doesn't exist anywhere in the world today.
ANS: A
PG: 339

31. Assimilation is best illustrated by

a. Palestinians in Israel.
b. Chechens in Russia.
c. various Pacific Island cultures living in Hawaii.
d. French Canadians living in Quebec.
ANS: C
PG: 339

32. As a scientific concept, race

a. is very significant because it gives us a clearer understanding of human behavior than the concept of culture provides.
b. is seldom, if ever, influenced by people's beliefs.
c. justified the exclusion of some groups from the activities of others.
d. is not very significant because it gives us little insight into human behavior.
ANS: D
PG: 335

33. The capitalist class wields enormous influence (well beyond their numbers) by

a. making large financial contributions to political campaigns.
b. being recruited to serve in powerful government positions.
c. controlling the media.
d. all of the above
ANS: D
PG: 329

34. Comparatively, the lower classes in the U.S. has not done very well in the last three decades because

a. the new post-industrial economy requires increasing amounts of higher education.
b. tax cuts during the Reagan and George W. Bush administrations have helped the wealthy more than the poor.
c. labor unions have been on the decline.
d. all of the above
ANS: D
PG: 329

35. Until the recent changes in South Africa in the 1990s, the repression of Blacks under the apartheid system was an example of

a. assimilation.
b. legal protection of minorities.
c. long-term subjugation.
d. extermination.
ANS: C
PG: 341

36. Which statement about the term *Dalit* is false?

a. It refers to the upper caste in Hindu India.
b. It means literally the "crushed" or "oppressed" people of India.
c. It is a more politically correct term for "Untouchables."
d. It refers to the caste of people relegated to performing the most menial tasks.
ANS: A
PG: 330-331

37. Sanskritization refers to the process in India

a. of moving up the caste ladder.
b. of slowly adding beef to one's diet.
c. of gradually eliminating social mobility from the society.
d. of becoming more Islamic and less Hindu.
ANS: A
PG: 331

38. Which ethnic group in the U.S. grew the fastest during the 1990s?

a. Vietnamese
b. Latinos
c. African-Americans
d. Arabic speaking peoples
ANS: B
PG: 338

39. Which statement about the Latino population in the U.S. is true?

a. Most Latinos do not speak English.
b. Most Latinos do not fully participate in the U.S. economy.
c. Most Latinos are short-timers, planning to return home to their native country as soon as possible.
d. Latinos have a higher labor force participation rate than either Anglos or African-Americans.
ANS: D
PG: 338

40. In order to gather adequate data for the rejuvenation of the park in New Jersey, anthropologist Setha Low

a. used only participant-observation as a method.
b. used a number of techniques including social mapping, having all interested parties. make a sketch plan of the proposed park that reflected their values, interests, and needs.
c. used a standardized survey administered by anthropology students.
d. gathered information about the needs and values of the members of the surrounding neighborhood who had the most power and prestige.

ANS: B
PG: 332-333

True-False

1. All complex societies are stratified.
ANS: T
PG: 321

2. Social inequality occurs in terms of wealth, power, and prestige.
ANS: T
PG: 321

3. In egalitarian societies, a few individuals will always have more wealth than others.
ANS: F
PG: 323

4. Rank societies have unequal access to wealth but not to power or prestige.
ANS: F
PG: 324

5. Caste systems are associated with ascribed status, and class systems are associated with achieved status.
ANS: T
PG: 325

6. Based on our knowledge of genetics, we know that there are no pure races.
ANS: T
PG: 335

7. An example of genocide was the "ethnic cleansing" of the Serbian forces under President Slobodan Milosevic.
ANS: T
PG: 341

8. People who accept the functionalist theory of social inequality argue that societies must pay the best money to the best people.
ANS: T
PG: 342-343

9. The conflict theory of inequality holds that stratification contributes to the overall well being of the society.
ANS: F
PG: 343

10. The measurement of different racial groups in the U.S. by using census data is a relatively easy and straight-forward task.
ANS: F
PG: 337

Short Answer

1. Name the three criteria delineated by Max Weber for measuring levels of social inequality.
ANS: wealth, power, and prestige
PG: 321

2. Define power.
ANS: the ability to achieve one's goals and objectives even against the will of others
PG: 321

3. Define prestige.
ANS: the social esteem, respect, or admiration that a society confers on people
PG: 322

4. Name the three types of societies based on levels of social inequality.
ANS: egalitarian, rank, and stratified societies
PG: 322

5. What are two different types of stratified societies?
ANS: those based on class and those based on caste
PG: 325

6. Define achieved status.
ANS: a status that the individual chooses or has some control over and is a result of personal effort
PG: 325

7. What are common characteristics of caste societies?
ANS: caste membership is directly related to occupation, workloads, and control of resources; members of the same caste share the same social status; each caste has its own set of secret rituals; higher castes are most interested in maintaining the system because they benefit from it the most
PG: 330

8. What is a race?
ANS: an interbreeding population whose members share a greater number of traits with one another than they do with people outside the group
PG: 334-335

9. What is ethnicity?
   ANS: cultural traits that are passed on from generation to generation that may include religion, dietary practices, language, humor, clothing, cultural heritage, folklore, national origins, and a shared ancestry and social experience
   PG: 336

10. List the six forms of intergroup relations.
   ANS: pluralism, assimilation, legal protection of minorities, population transfer, long-term subjugation, and genocide
   PG: 339-342

Essay

1. What determines social ranking across cultures? What type of society is the most egalitarian? What type is the least egalitarian?

2. Give an example of a society with extremely rigid social ranking. What factors function to maintain such an organization?

3. What is the functionalist theory of social stratification? How would a functionalist interpret the difference between the salaries of trash collectors and teachers?

4. What is the conflict theory of social stratification? How would conflict theory explain the organization of an egalitarian society?

5. Can race relations in the United States be better understood through the idea of long-term subjugation or assimilation? Will the growth of minorities in the United States ever cause a reverse assimilation where the current majority population becomes absorbed into a currently minority population?

6. What are some of the methodological problems when trying to measure racial composition in the United States by using census data?

Chapter 14
Supernatural Beliefs

Multiple-Choice

1. While forms of religion may vary, they all are founded upon a belief

   a. in one major deity.
   b. that there is life after death.
   c. in the supernatural.
   d. all of the above
   ANS: C
   PG: 349

2. When we claim that religion, as a belief in the supernatural, is universal, we mean that

   a. every person in the world believes in some type of supernatural.
   b. every person in the world believes in good and evil.
   c. individuals believe in the supernatural but not all cultures contain a belief in the supernatural.
   d. all cultures contain a belief in the supernatural but not all individuals believe in one.
   ANS: D
   PG: 349

3. Which statement is true about the distinction between imitative and contagious magic?

   a. Voodoo dolls are an example of contagious magic.
   b. Contagious magic is the notion that an object having been in contact with a person retains a magical connection to that person.
   c. Imitative magic involves doing harm to a person by performing magic on his finger nail clippings.
   d. all of the above
   ANS: B
   PG: 352

4. Anthony Wallace uses the term "cult" to refer to

   a. religious organizations that brainwash their members.
   b. a form of religion having its own set of beliefs, rituals, and goals.
   c. anti-social religious groups that often encourage their followers to commit mass suicide.
   d. small scale religious groups that are opposed to any form of control from the federal government.
   ANS: B
   PG: 360

5. Both religion and magic

a. are nonrational systems of supernatural belief.
b. deal with one's spiritual relationship with deities.
d. are group, rather than individual, activities.
d. all of the above
ANS: A
PG: 352

6. Magic and religion differ because they do not both

a. deal with major issues of human existence.
b. use prayer and sacrifices to appeal to supernatural powers.
c. use officially recognized functionaries such as priests.
d. all of the above
ANS: D
PG: 352

7. Sorcery, involving the use of potions and medicines, is a/an

a. inborn capacity to harm others.
b. involuntary capacity to harm others.
c. often unconscious capacity to harm others.
d. deliberate attempt to bring about harm through the use of supernatural powers.
ANS: D
PG: 353-354

8. As defined by anthropology, witchcraft

a. is always viewed negatively.
b. can harm through evil thoughts.
c. relies only on psychic power to harm people.
d. all of the above
ANS: D
PG: 353

9. Which statement about religion in the United States is true?

a. liberals are more religious than conservatives
b. people under 40 are more religious than people over 40
c. Blacks are more religious than Whites
d. New Englanders are more religious than Southerners
ANS: C
PG: 367

10. Which statement is true about the belief system called Wicca?

a. Wiccans are found mostly in urban areas.
b. Wiccans use their powers for evil purposes.
c. In North America, Wiccans are comprised of mostly women.
d. a and c only
ANS: D
PG: 354

11. Anthropologists have evidence of religious ideas existing at least ________years ago

a. 10,000
b. 20,000
c. 50,000
d. 100,000
ANS: D
PG: 350

12. Which statement about religion in the US is true?

a. Roman Catholicism is the largest single denomination.
b. The fastest growing groups are Catholics from Mexico.
c. Approximately 24% of all US residents are Jewish.
d. Men are more likely than women to describe themselves as religious.
ANS: A
PG: 367

13. Separatist Christian churches in South Africa played a role in conflict resolution because Black South Africans

a. gained real political power through their churches.
b. created an illusion of power by manipulating their own set of religious symbols and forming their own unique churches.
c. gained real economic power through their churches.
d. expressed their resentment against the apartheid government in their religious activity.
ANS: B
PG: 357

14. Religion intensifies group solidarity because

a. people's shared religious beliefs, practices, and rituals often create powerful social bonds.
b. people share in the mysteries of their belief system.
c. people are separated by their beliefs from others who do not share the same ideas.
d. all of the above
ANS: D
PG: 358

15. Individuals benefit psychologically from religion because it

a. helps explain the unexplainable.
b. gives us answers based upon scientific authority.
c. provides a rational and logical framework for giving meaning to events and experiences.
d. all of the above
ANS: A
PG: 359

16. Which statement about shamanism is false?

a. Shamans are full-time specialists.
b. Shamans are thought to have supernatural powers.
c. Shamans contact spirits while in an altered state of consciousness.
d. Shamans use their powers to heal and tell fortunes of their clients.
ANS: A
PG: 361-363

17. What type of religious organization has groups that perform rites for the community?

a. ecclesiastic
b. communal
c. shamanistic
d. individualistic
ANS: B
PG: 363

18. What type of religious organization has full-time religious specialists?

a. individualistic
b. shamanistic
c. communal
d. ecclesiastic
ANS: D
PG: 366

19. The predominant mode of religious organization practiced among food collectors is

a. ecclesiastical cults.
b. shamanistic cults.
c. communal cults.
d. individualistic cults.
ANS: D
PG: 360-361

20. An individual may become a shaman by

a. having a powerful vision.
b. apprenticing with a practicing shaman.
c. avoiding the use of hallucinogenic drugs through his or her life.
d. a and b only
ANS: D
PG: 362

21. Rites of passage with stages of separation, transition, and incorporation are part of

a. ecclesiastical cults.
b. shamanistic cults.
c. communal cults.
d. individualistic cults.
ANS: C
PG: 363-364

22. Rites of solidarity are directed toward the welfare of

a. the entire community.
b. individual members of the community.
c. the group's shaman.
d. the group's leader.
ANS: A
PG: 364

23. Shamans, among the Reindeer Tungus of Siberia,

a. can be either men or women.
b. can neither control spirits nor stop them from causing harm.
c. never serve as mediums for spirits unlike the shamans of other groups.
d. use no special paraphernalia such as costumes or mirrors.
ANS: A
PG: 362-363

24. The Kikuyu initiation ritual

a. involves no physical operation other than the scarring of women and men's elbows.
b. does not involve the separation of the initiates from their former status.
c. involves the incorporation of the initiate back into the society as a whole.
d. all of the above
ANS: C
PG: 364

25. Religion can play an important part in transforming a society when

a. members of the society are well adapted to their environment.
b. there has been a long period of time without social or cultural change.
c. there is cultural stress brought about by rapid change and foreign domination.
d. there has been a successful rejection of an attack by another society.
ANS: C
PG: 372

26. United States society

a. places a high value on organized religion.
b. has a higher percentage of its population affiliated with a religious organization than in
c. Western European countries.
d. has a church membership that has grown steadily over the last hundred years.
d. all of the above
ANS: D
PG: 366-368

27. Handsome Lake, a New York state Seneca Indian,

a. prescribed new moral principles and rules of behavior.
b. received a vision to stop drinking and started a revitalizing religion.
c. urged the adoption of European agricultural practices.
d. all of the above
ANS: D
PG: 373

28. African-American churches in the US have played an important role as agents of social change in which of the following ways?

a. They have served as rallying places for protestors and community activists.
b. They helped freed slaves on the Underground Railroad.
c. Black Muslims have been a force for change by encouraging autonomous African-American communities.
d. all of the above
ANS: D
PG: 372

29. In an ecclesiastical cult, the laypersons are responsible for

a. performing periodic rituals.
b. performing weekly rituals.
c. supporting the church through their labor and money.
d. engaging in a "vision quest."
ANS: C
PG: 366

30. Liberation theology, which developed during the 1970s and 1980s in South America,

a. is an activist form of Catholicism.
b. merged theology with an activism for social justice for the poor.
c. led many priests and nuns to lose their lives in political conflict.
d. all of the above
ANS: D
PG: 372

31. Myths, which tell stories of the gods, their origins, their activities, and the moral injunctions they teach, are found

a. only in large-scale industrialized societies.
b. only in peasant societies.
c. only in food collecting societies.
d. in every society.
ANS: D
PG: 355-356

32. A myth that conveys morals through the stories of anthropomorphized animals is

a. a profane myth.
b. a "trickster myth."
c. an origin myth.
d. a sacred myth.
ANS: B
PG: 356

33. Which of the following is a major religious trend in the world today?

a. the rise of religious nationalism among Islamic nations
b. the dramatic decline in church membership in the United States in recent years
c. the growth of cyber-churches
d. a and c only
ANS: D
PG: 374-376

34. People perform religious rituals as

a. a way of invoking supernatural beings to control those forces over which they feel they have no control.
b. with as little emotion as possible, because they seldom really believe rituals are effective.
c. a way of demonstrating the strong control they have over their own lives.
d. b and c
ANS: A
PG: 359

35. Marx argued that the working class

a. would use religion to overthrow the owners.
b. understood the nature of their relationship with factory owners because of the lesson of religion.
c. was blinded by religion to the fact that they were being exploited by the ruling class.
d. a and b
ANS: C
PG: 358

36. The Crow vision quest is

a. an example of a nativistic movement.
b. an example of a cargo cult.
c. an example of a millenarian movement.
d. a normal way of dealing with the stresses and strains of everyday life.
ANS: D
PG: 361

37. The Amish of rural Pennsylvania, Indiana, or Ohio are one of the oldest and most visible religious minorities in the United States and

a. they practice strict exogamy.
b. they maintain a highly disciplined church-community and excommunicate and/or shun any erring members.
c. they use modern agricultural techniques while avoiding modern technology within their households.
d. they insist that their children attend Catholic high schools run by Jesuit priests.
ANS: B
PG: 370-371

38. In the *Wisconsin v. Yoder* court case over Wisconsin's requirement that Amish children attend public school beyond the eighth grade, anthropologist John Hostetler explained that

a. Amish teenagers could separate the ideas they learned about society and religion in the public high schools from the lessons learned in their homes.
b. schooling alone would not cause alienation between Amish parents and their children.
c. Amish teenagers would suffer great psychological harm if kept from the public high schools attended by their peers.
d. Amish teenagers would suffer great psychological harm in public high schools, which foster radically different social and religious values from their own.
ANS: D
PG: 370-371

39. Wicca, as practiced in North American cities,

a. has a matriarchal character.
b. emphasizes fertility.
c. does not perceive magical powers as supernatural.
d. all of the above
ANS: D
PG: 354

40. Wicca's contemporary popularity

a. has stimulated book sales.
b. is evident in the teenage market.
c. results from its connection with Satanism.
d. a and b
ANS: D
PG: 354-355

True-False

1. All forms of religion are alike in that they are founded on a belief in the supernatural.
ANS: T
PG: 349

2. When anthropologists study religion they do not attempt to determine which religion is true.
ANS: T
PG: 350

3. Both religion and magic are systems of supernatural belief and are not susceptible to scientific verification.
ANS: T
PG: 352

4. Magic is practiced irregularly in response to specific and immediate problems.
ANS: T
PG: 352

5. Contemporary witches are Satanists.
ANS: F
PG: 354-355

6. Witchcraft and sorcery are only found in small-scale non-Western societies.
ANS: F
PG: 353-355

7. Religion can reduce stress and frustrations that often lead to social conflict.
ANS: T
PG: 357-358

8. Religion never enables people to express their common identity in ways that create powerful social bonds.
ANS: F
PG: 358

9. Rites of passage are important public rituals that mark a change in a person's social position.
ANS: T
PG: 363-364

10. Ecclesiastical cults are found in all types of societies, from small-scale to state, and have both part-time and full-time professional clergy.
ANS: F
PG: 366

11. American Catholics are now "outsourcing" their religious rituals to Catholic priests in India.
ANS: T
PG: 371

12. Generally Europeans tend to be more religious than people in the United States.
ANS: F
PG: 367

Short Answer

1. What features do religion and magic share?
ANS: both are systems of supernatural belief, are not susceptible to scientific verification, and are practiced as a way of coping with the anxieties, ambiguities, and frustrations of everyday life
PG: 352

2. What are five differences between religion and magic?
ANS: religion deals with major issues of human existence, magic toward specific, immediate problems; religion uses prayer and sacrifices, magic practitioners believe they can achieve goals through own efforts; religion tends to be a group activity, magic is more individually oriented; religion usually practiced at specific time, magic practiced in response to specific and immediate problems; religion involves officially recognized functionaries, magic performed by wide variety of practitioners
PG: 352

3. What is sorcery?
ANS: often involves use of materials, potions, and medicines, is the deliberate use of supernatural powers to bring about harm
PG: 353

4. What is the basic distinction between witchcraft and sorcery in the industrialized world?
ANS: distinction between the forms of magic used for beneficial purposes and those used for malevolent purposes
PG: 353-355

5. What is the difference between readers of witchcraft books in the 1980s and 1990s?
ANS: readers in 1980s were baby boomers looking for alternative forms of spirituality, 1990s readers are young women in their teens
PG: 354-55

6. What are two types of myths?
ANS: origin myths and trickster myths
PG: 355-356

7. What are social functions of religion?
ANS: social control, conflict resolution, intensifying group solidarity
PG: 356-358

8. What are two types of psychological functions of religion?
ANS: cognitive function and emotional function
PG: 358-360

9. What four principal patterns of religious organizations were identified by Wallace?
ANS: individualistic cults, shamanistic cults, communal cults, and ecclesiastical cults
PG: 360

10. Van Gennep identified which three distinct phases of rites of passage?
ANS: separation, transition, and incorporation
PG: 363

Essay

1. What is a good way to define religion so that it can be applied across cultures? What does "supernatural" mean?

2. How does magic differ from religion? How is it used?

3. Explain and contrast the social and the psychological functions of religion.

4. What are Wallace's four patterns of religious organizations? How do the simplest and most complex organizations differ in the roles of religious practitioner?

5. Explain what Marx meant by the expression "Religion is the opiate of the masses."

6. Describe and explain the functions of revitalization cults. Give two examples.

7. In what ways in the Internet changing the face of religion?

Chapter 15
Art

Multiple-Choice

1. The five piece work of art by artist Russell Biles makes which political statement?

   a. supporting the war in Iraq
   b. against same sex marriage
   c. anti gun control
   d. none of the above
   ANS: D
   PG: 387-389

2. The anthropological definition of art

   a. is a universal one, accepted by all professionals.
   b. refers to processes, products, and transformation of forms in ways that are aesthetically pleasing to members of the society.
   c. emphasizes permanent material forms of art as the most important.
   d. does not recognize symbolic communication as art.
   ANS: B
   PG: 380-381

3. Anthropologists recognize that art may include

   a. folklore told to young children.
   b. dances that are part of initiation ceremonies.
   c. body decoration.
   d. all of the above
   ANS: D
   PG: 380

4. Professional art critics

   a. are part of the art establishment in the U.S. that determines what constitutes good art.
   b. are found in all societies.
   c. set the standards that determine what constitutes good art in all societies.
   d. are found in the U.S. and Europe only.
   ANS: A
   PG: 381

5. Anthropologists consider the term "primitive"

a. to refer to the art of the more backward non-Western societies.
b. misleading, because it connotes inferiority and evolutionary sequencing.
c. to only refer to non-permanent forms of art.
d. to only refer to the non-material art forms of societies that are organized as bands, tribes, or chiefdoms.

ANS: B
PG: 381-382

6. In complex societies

a. art forms and aesthetic knowledge are uniformly spread across all classes.
b. only members of the upper class have the time, money, and knowledge to be able to produce art objects.
c. aesthetic critics responsible for establishing artistic standards are invariably members of the upper classes or are employed by them.
d. art is more democratic and all people have relatively equal access to it.

ANS: C
PG: 383

7. When displayed in museums, descriptions of non-western art (as compared to western art) often include

a. the specific culture from which it comes.
b. the name of the artist.
c. the materials used to make it.
d. a and c only

ANS: D
PG: 382

8. The art form which has received the greatest amount of anthropological attention is

a. body decoration.
b. dance.
c. music.
d. graphic and plastic arts.

ANS: D
PG: 390

9. Bert, Ernie, and Kermit of Sesame Street, through music,

a. only entertain the bored children of a complex society.
b. are not part of an aesthetic process.
c. are examples of art that educates children about conflict resolution, the fun of learning and race or ethnic relations.
d. a and b

ANS: C
PG: 385

10. Liberation Theater is a form of art that is

a. based on the philosophies of Franz Boas.
b. designed to focus on the involvement of the audience.
c. used for social change.
d. b and c only
ANS: D
PG: 387

11. Navajo sand painting is not only an art form, but also plays a part in Navajo

a. religion.
b. myth.
c. healing practices.
d. all of the above
ANS: D
PG: 383

12. When viewed cross-culturally, artists

a. almost always are anti-establishment.
b. often reinforce the existing sociocultural system, especially in non-western societies.
c. never support the inequalities of the stratification system of a society.
d. a and c
ANS: B
PG: 386-387

13. An Inuit artist carving ivory

a. is producing a craft and not art.
b. mostly works for commissions.
c. is involved in a total act of will, which transforms the ivory into whatever he wants to create.
d. sees his activity as a liberation of whatever form is already in a piece of ivory.
ANS: D
PG: 389-390

14. The Mano "god-spirit" mask, which embodies the spiritual force in Liberia,

a. serves as an agent of social control and conflict resolution, as well as an expression of religious belief.
b. plays only a religious role in the society.
c. serves only as a crude reminder of the dead ancestor.
d. is an important social control mechanism that has little or no religious significance.
ANS: A
PG: 386

15. In the more complex societies, state governments

a. deliberately use art to ensure freedom of expression.
b. always carefully control art to prevent social agitation.
c. always represses artistic forms that criticize national symbols.
d. sponsor art for the sake of instilling obedience and maintaining the status quo.
ANS: D
PG: 386

16. Chilean arpilleristas

a. told the story of political oppression on scraps of cloth.
b. were banned in their own country.
c. attempted to raise the consciousness of their oppressed countrymen to bring about political and social change.
d. all of the above
ANS: D
PG: 387

17. Art collecting

a. occurs in all societies.
b. serves as a symbol of high prestige, because art objects are unique and priceless.
c. is found in state societies.
d. b and c
ANS: D
PG: 387

18. Major concerns of ethnomusicology include interest in

a. how a culture distinguishes between music and nonmusic.
b. the social relationships between musicians.
c. the nature of the musical instruments.
d. all of the above
ANS: D
PG: 391

19. Ethnomusicologists are primarily interested in

a. the study of music in its cultural context.
b. the study of music only as artistic process.
c. the study of how much musical performers get paid.
d. a and c
ANS: A
PG: 390-391

20. Dance

a. has been defined as purposeful and intentionally rhythmical nonverbal body movements.
b. is culturally patterned and has aesthetic value.
c. may be of religious significance but never expresses political concerns.
d. a and b
ANS: D
PG: 393

21. The multiple functions of dance

a. may be performed simultaneously.
b. can express political values and attitudes.
c. hinder rather than educate a generation in cultural values.
d. a and b
ANS: D
PG: 393

22. Cultural Survival is an organization which helps indigenous people

a. gain title to their land
b. avoid exploitation by outsiders
c. develop new sources of revenue
d. all of the above
ANS: D
PG: 390-391

23. Folklore, as a creative form of expression, includes

a. tongue twisters.
b. lullabies.
c. proverbs.
d. all of the above
ANS: D
PG: 394

24. Folktales differ from legends in that legends

a. are always true while folktales are not.
b. exist largely for the purpose of entertainment.
c. attempt to explain the establishment of local customs.
d. all of the above
ANS: C
PG: 396

25. Myths are

a. found only in food collecting societies.
b. designed to explain such issues as where we came from and why we are here.
c. always untrue.
d. not found in western, industrialized societies.
ANS: B
PG: 395

26. Myths are important to anthropologists because

a. they are historically factual.
b. they represent the human search for significance, meaning and truth.
c. they are used to attack a society's social order.
d. they are totally non-religious.
ANS: B
PG: 395

27. The Yanomamo myths of creation

a. are rooted in the Biblical story of Adam and Eve.
b. stress the importance of social order.
c. explain how men and women were created.
d. explain that men were created by women.
ANS: C
PG: 395

28. In Western societies, mythology is

a. universally rejected.
b. still has an appeal, as indicated by the popularity of the characters in the Star Wars movies and the work of Joseph Campbell.
c. is no longer seriously studied.
d. a and c only
ANS: B
PG: 395

29. U.S. baseball players have not been very successful at playing in Japan because

a. they try too hard to overpower the ball.
b. they fail to understand the Japanese concept of *wa*.
c. they are inferior players.
d. b and c only
ANS: B
PG: 398

30. Folktales

a. do not have a plot and character development.
b. can be analyzed in terms of plot, character development, and structure.
c. are generally the recognized works of a specific author.
d. play little or no role in socialization.
ANS: B
PG: 396-397

31. An important difference between folktales and written art forms is

a. that folktales have a single, unchanging structure.
b. that folktales are found only in non-Western societies.
c. the significant artistry involved in the telling of the tales.
d. a and c
ANS: C
PG: 397-398

32. Anthropologists do not use the term "primitive" to refer to art because

a. they cannot agree on a definition for the term.
b. primitive art is a craft, not really an art.
c. of its connotations of both inferiority and evolutionary sequencing.
d. contemporary societies do not make such art at the present.
ANS: C
PG: 382

33. Art is the process and the products of applying certain skills to any activity that transforms

a. matter, sound, or motion into a form deemed aesthetically pleasing to people in a society.
b. only durable matter into a form deemed aesthetically pleasing to people in a society.
c. matter, sound, or motion into a form that must be judged by art critics to be aesthetically pleasing.
d. only sound or motion into a form deemed aesthetically pleasing to people in a society.
ANS: A
PG: 380-381

34. Full-time specialists, including aesthetic critics, emerged after

a. World War I.
b. the American Revolution.
c. the Neolithic Revolution.
d. the invention of oil paints.
ANS: C
PG: 383

35. What do Sergei Eisenstein, Akira Kurosawa, Ingmar Bergman, and Zacharias Kunuk all have in common?

a. They are world class sculptures.
b. They are world class filmmakers.
c. They are world class choreographers.
d. They are world class painters.
ANS: B
PG: 398

36. Alan Lomax's cross-cultural research on music

a. found almost no similarities from one society to another.
b. found some broad correlations between various aspects of music and a culture's level of subsistence.
c. found that music in egalitarian, small-scale societies was essentially similar to music in complex, industrialized societies.
d. found that music in small-scale societies had nonrepetitious texts.
ANS: B
PG: 392

37. The film *The Fast Runner* (2002)

a. is a remake of Robert Flaherty's documentary *Nanook of the North.*
b. portrays modern life in Nunavut in the 21st century.
c. is a film based on a traditional Inuit myth.
d. was filmed by a Hollywood film crew.
ANS: C
PG: 398-399

38. Which statement about music in the 21st century is true?

a. There is increasing collaboration between different art forms throughout the world.
b. There is less collaboration between different art forms throughout the world.
c. Within the next generation or two all traditional forms of music will disappear.
d. b and c
ANS: A
PG: 401

39. Music found in large-scale, stratified societies is characterized by

a. repetitious texts.
b. solo singing.
c. wide melodic intervals.
d. slurred articulation.
ANS: B
PG: 392

40. Harvey Littleton, Dale Chihuly, and Stanislav Lebenski all are internationally known

a. painters.
b. filmmakers.
c. glass artists.
d. choreographers.
ANS: C
PG: 400

True-False

1. According to anthropologists, art should be creative, playful, emotionally evocative, transformational, symbolic, and should reflect technical skill.
ANS: T
PG: 380

2. Societies without professional art establishments still have artistic standards although they tend to be more democratic.
ANS: T
PG: 383

3. The symbolism and creative aspect of art always contradicts mainstream social and political thought and works against social integration.
ANS: F
PG: 385

4. Graphic and plastic arts include painting, sculpture, and architecture but not embroidery, weaving, or tattooing.
ANS: F
PG: 389

5. The death masks of the Mano of northeastern Liberia played an important role in the administration of justice.
ANS: T
PG: 386

6. What one actually hears when listening to music from another culture is influenced by one's own culture.
ANS: T
PG: 390-391

7. Dance is purposeful and intentionally rhythmical nonverbal body movements that are culturally patterned and have aesthetic value.
ANS: T
PG: 392

8. Myths are untrue narratives that result from ignorance of history.
ANS: F
PG: 395

9. Folktales are mostly spiritual and have no particular basis in history.
ANS: F
PG: 396

10. Capoeira is a Brazilian art form combining dance, acrobatics, and martial arts
ANS: T
PG: 393-394

Short Answer

1. What term do anthropologists use instead of "primitive culture?"
ANS: small-scale culture
PG: 382

2. What psychological function does art serve for the artist?
ANS: permits the release of emotional energy in a very concrete or visible way
PG: 384-85

3. What negative impact can art have for the artist and the viewer?
ANS: If the process is not successful, can result in increased frustrations and tension for the artist. Can elicit disturbing or painful emotions that can lead to psychological discomfort for the viewer.
PG: 385

4. The association of art with status symbols is seen in societies with what kind of population?
ANS: ranked populations
PG: 386-387

5. What is liberation theater?
ANS: political theater that focuses on the involvement of the audience in the creation and the performance of the play itself
PG: 387

6. List some of the kinds of forms included in graphic and plastic arts.
ANS: painting, sculpture, printmaking, architecture, weaving, embroidery, tailoring, jewelry making, tattooing, wood carving, metalworking
PG: 389

7. What are the four major concerns of ethnomusicology?
ANS: ideas about music, social structure of music, characteristics of the music itself, and material culture of music
PG: 391

8. How does dance perform a political function within a society?
   ANS: expresses political values and attitudes, shows allegiance to political leaders, and controls behavior
   PG: 393

9. What are folktales (legends)?
   ANS: verbal art forms that are more secular in nature, have no particular basis in history, and exist largely for the purposes of entertainment
   PG: 395-396

10. What is the impact of globalization on art forms?
   ANS: Pure art forms are becoming increasingly difficult to find as the world becomes more interdependent.
   PG: 401-403

Essay

1. What are the characteristics of the art process in state societies? What does socioeconomic class have to do with art in complex societies?

2. Contrast the psychological functions of art for the artist and for the audience. Do those functions always elicit positive emotions?

3. Discuss the impact of both internal and external change on expressive arts. How are they affected by globalization in the twentieth century?

4. What is the relationship between art and the status quo? In what types of societies can art serve as a mechanism of social control?

5. What is ethnomusicology? What are the major ways in which ethnomusicologists have found that music differs across cultures?

6. Discuss a number of different examples of how art can make a political statement.

7. In what ways do films from Hollywood (USA) differ from films made in Bollywood (India)?

Chapter 16

Culture Change and Globalization

Multiple-Choice

1. The 1902 edition of the Sears & Roebuck catalog

a. contains almost none of the material items available for purchase today.
b. provides a nearly total inventory of the material culture of the United States at the beginning of the century.
c. offered only Bibles for sale but no other books.
d. illustrated the principle that ideas change more easily than material objects.
ANS: B
PG: 406

2. Cultural change is caused

a. more by diffusion than by invention.
b. more by invention than by diffusion.
c. by mechanical solidarity.
d. by organic solidarity.
ANS: A
PG: 408

3. Ralph Linton argued that

a. conscious inventors are the most important members of any society.
b. inventions receive more attention than they merit.
c. unintentional inventions get very little attention because they seldom make a significant contribution to culture.
d. over the long run, the unconscious inventor has had a greater impact on culture change than has the conscious inventor.
ANS: D
PG: 407

4. Which statement about innovators is true?

a. Innovators usually are prominent religious and political figures.
b. Innovators are always the inventors as well.
c. Innovators are often marginal people living on the fringes of society.
d. Innovators are usually people from dysfunctional families.
ANS: C
PG: 407

5. ____________ percent of all items within a culture originated there.

a. Seventy-five
b. Forty-three
c. Thirty
d. Ten
ANS: D
PG: 408

6. Human culture has developed rapidly, precisely because

a. of the large number of inventions made by each society.
b. the process of diffusion has enabled humans to pool their creative resources.
c. the process of invention has enabled humans to pool their creative resources.
d. a and c
ANS: B
PG: 408

7. Significant cultural differences exist in the world today because

a. not every cultural item is exchanged when two cultures come into contact.
b. there are a large number of inventions in each culture.
c. there are more inventions in each culture than there is diffusion across cultures.
d. b and c
ANS: A
PG: 408

8. The choice to adopt or ignore a cultural item from another culture is affected by whether or not it

a. is seen to be superior to what already exists.
b. is consistent with existing cultural patterns.
c. is easily understood.
d. all of the above
ANS: D
PG: 408-409

9. The contact of two cultures results in

a. changes only in the weaker culture.
b. a two-way process through which each culture is influenced by the other.
c. the dominance of European cultures because their natural superiority.
d. the eventual disappearance of the weaker culture.
ANS: B
PG: 409

10. The part(s) of culture most likely to be diffused is/are

a. religious beliefs.
b. ideas.
c. items of material culture.
d. behavior patterns.
ANS: C
PG: 410

11. Both diffusion and acculturation always involve

a. a single trait.
b. a dominant and a subordinate culture.
c. culture change as the result of contact with another group.
d. the extinction of one of the cultures that come into contact.
ANS: C
PG: 410

12. The Conference of Berlin in 1884 was aimed at

a. the protection of indigenous peoples.
b. the dividing up of the continent of Africa into European colonies.
c. dividing up of South America into colonies by European nations.
d. protecting cultural anthropologists studying local cultures in Africa.
ANS: B
PG: 419

13. An example of acculturation is the

a. last twenty years of contact between the United States and Japan.
b. last one hundred years of contact between the United States and Great Britain.
c. Spanish conquest of Mexico.
d. all of the above
ANS: C
PG: 410

14. Acculturation refers to

a. learning the culture of a society that you visit.
b. learning the culture of a society from which your ancestors migrated.
c. diffusion that takes place as a result of sustained contact between two societies, one dominant and one subordinate.
d. learning the culture of the society into which you were born.
ANS: C
PG: 410-411

15. The Manus of the South Pacific, according to Margaret Mead, accepted westernization because

a. they were forced to by the United States Army during World War II.
b. they saw American technology during the war and chose freely to adopt it.
c. the Americans had treated the Manus with greater respect than had earlier contacts.
d. b and c
ANS: D
PG: 410

16. The reindeer-herding Skolt Lapps of Finland

a. rapidly adopted snowmobiles because of a key cultural concern with personal mobility.
b. rejected snowmobiles because they frightened the reindeer herds.
c. resisted the attempt to force the introduction of snowmobiles upon them.
d. only adopted snowmobiles after a thirty-year period of trial use.
ANS: A
PG: 411-412

17. The introduction of the TV set in the United States had far-reaching consequences for

a. the family system.
b. the political process.
c. the religious institution.
d. all of the above
ANS: D
PG: 413

18. __________ always opposes the process of culture change.

a. The desire for prestige
b. The desire for economic gain
c. The desire for increased efficiency
d. The conservative force promoting the status quo
ANS: D
PG: 413

19. Maintenance of cultural boundaries

a. strengthens the traditions of one's own culture.
b. discourages cultural borrowing from other groups.
c. facilitates the process of diffusion.
d. a and b only
ANS: D
PG: 413

20. The Quebec language law is an example of

a. modernization.
b. maintenance of cultural boundaries.
c. integration of ethnic groups.
d. acculturation.
ANS: B
PG: 413-414

21. Latrines built by U.S. technicians were not accepted in rural El Salvador because

a. they were of the wrong design.
b. they were built too close to peoples' homes.
c. people believed that they would be bewitched if they used latrines.
d. they already had indoor toilets.
ANS: A
PG: 425

22. Strict rules about eating

a. always disrupt social ties and group solidarity.
b. help to maintain social ties and group solidarity.
c. require people to eat alone and never in groups.
d. a and c only
ANS: B
PG: 414

23. An organization of cultural anthropologists working to help indigenous peoples is

a. the Society for Applied Anthropology.
b. the Brazilians Studies Association.
c. Cultural Survival, Inc.
d. the American Anthropological Association.
ANS: C
PG: 418

24. The average income of North Americans is ______times that of the average Ethiopian

a. 10
b. 35
c. 170
d. 450
ANS: C
PG: 419

25. Which statement about cell phone use in U.S. urban areas is TRUE?

a. It has led to an increase in traffic accidents
b. It has led to an increase in pedestrian accidents
c. It has made city life less civil and less friendly
d. All of the above
ANS: D
PG: 412

26. African-Americans and Korean-Americans have different linguistic styles in that:

a. African-Americans engage in "restraint politeness."
b. African-Americans engage in "involvement politeness."
c. Korean-Americans engage in "involvement politeness."
d. African-Americans are more restrained than Korean-Americans
ANS: B
PG: 415

27. Which statement about the Winnemem Wintu people is FALSE?

a. They are in danger of losing their last remaining ancestral land to the Shasta Dam
b. They have already lost ancestral land to the Shasta Dam
c. They are threatened by being wiped out by HIV-AIDS
d. a and b only
ANS: D
PG: 417

28. The organization called Cultural Survival functions to:

a. help indigenous people against exploitation
b. protect the Constitution of the United States
c. help indigenous people raise money for economic development
d. a and c only
ANS: D
PG: 418

29. What causes the rise of obesity throughout the world

a. people just can't say no to junk food
b. with food becoming more affordable, restaurants are "super-sizing."
c. with fewer people growing their own food, they are buying more fattening processed food
d. b and c only
ANS: D
PG: 422-423

30. Which of the following are negative health consequences of economic development programs?

a. an increase in bacterial parasites
b. an increase in such "industrialized" diseases as diabetes, obesity, and hypertension
c. an increase in contagious diseases in urban areas
d. all of the above
ANS: D
PG: 421

31. According to the world systems theory,

a. LDCs can help themselves only if they emulate western cultures.
b. LDCs need to become modernized.
c. rich and poor countries are different because the rich exploit the poor and keep them poor.
d. all of the above
ANS: C
PG: 419

32. Neocolonialism

a. refers to the control of African countries by European powers during the 16th century.
b. ended when South American and African countries gained independence from Europe.
c. is the control of former colonies by wealthy, former colonial nations through political, financial, and military power.
d. a and b only
ANS: C
PG: 420

33. Anthropological criticism of modernization theory is that it

a. is ethnocentric.
b. assumes that modern traits are superior to traditional ones.
c. assumes that traditional people should adopt more modern ways of thinking and acting.
d. all of the above
ANS: D
PG: 419

34. Multinational corporations

a. sometimes have assets and power greater than those of many governments of lesser developed countries.
b. send most of their profits back to their home country.
c. sometimes directly exploit lesser developed countries.
d. all of the above
ANS: D
PG: 420

35. Programs of economic development

a. always lead to improved nutrition for families.
b. may lead to inadequate nutrition.
c. always leads to improved quality of life and standard of living.
d. always leads to a reduction in such diseases as diabetes and heart disease.
ANS: B
PG: 421

36. A program in El Salvador to build latrines failed because

a. religious objections of the local people
b. the latrines were designed inappropriately
c. the latrines were placed too close to the river
d. all of the above
ANS: B
PG: 425

37. Which statement about globalization is INCORRECT?

a. globalization has both good and bad consequences
b. globalization is an irreversible process
c. globalization involves the rapid growth of free market capitalism
d. globalization involves the rapid growth of regional alliances such as NAFTA and EU
ANS: B
PG: 424-429

38. Globalization

a. is a worldwide phenomenon that has replaced the Cold War system.
b. is driven by closed national markets.
c. involves the increase of tariff barriers worldwide.
d. is thought to have started at the end of WWII.
ANS: A
PG: 425

39. Globalization is defined by

a. a revolution in high-speed information technology.
b. privatizing and deregulating national economies.
c. the lowering of tariff barriers worldwide.
d. all of the above
ANS: D
PG: 425

40. The Ju/'hoansi foragers have experienced changes since the mid-1970s, including

a. planting fields and keeping goats.
b. replacing their skin clothing with manufactured clothing.
c. selling their bows and arrows to tourists.
d. all of the above

ANS: D
PG: 427

True-False

1. Inventions stimulate the greatest amount of change in a culture.
ANS: F
PG: 408

2. Whether a particular cultural item is accepted by a society depends largely on the item's utility and compatibility with already existing cultural traits.
ANS: T
PG: 408-409

3. The terms "inventor" and "innovator" mean the same thing.
ANS: F
PG: 407

4. Sometimes people voluntarily become acculturated because they believe that the adoption of certain technologies or behaviors will increase their adaptation to the environment.
ANS: T
PG: 410

5. The functional interrelatedness of the parts of culture helps it to be open to rapid change.
ANS: F
PG: 415-416

6. Multimillion dollar yachts are made in the PRC (China), but Chinese do not buy and use them.
ANS: T
PG: 410

7. Indigenous peoples are those who receive foreign aid from wealthy countries.
ANS: F
PG: 416

8. According to World Systems Theory, wealthy countries achieve high levels of development by exploiting the poorer countries.
ANS: T
PG: 419

9. Most anthropologists today support the position of modernization theory to bring growth to small-scale societies.

ANS: F
PG: 419

10. Rapid globalization will result in local cultures evolving into hybrid cultures.
ANS: T
PG: 427-428

Short Answer

1. What are three ways that a culture maintains its boundaries?
ANS: language, clothing, eating styles
PG: 413-414

2. What is cultural diffusion?
ANS: the spreading of a thing, an idea, or a behavior pattern from one culture to another
PG: 408

3. List some of the consequences of acculturation.
ANS: The subordinate culture could be come extinct, it could be incorporated as a distinct subculture of the dominant group, or it could be assimilated into the dominant group.
PG: 409-410

4. How does food serve to maintain cultural boundaries?
ANS: What foods are eaten, in what manner, how often, and with whom are all factors that vary from one culture to another. Sharing of food is used to maintain social ties and group solidarity.
PG: 414

5. What is meant by "neocolonialism?"
ANS: The former colonial powers continue to control their former colonies through economic domination.
PG: 420

6. What are some problems brought about by the widespread use of cell phones?
ANS: Increased auto accidents, "padlock," and "pedrage."
PG: 412

7. What event marked the symbolic beginning of the age of globalization?
ANS: the fall of the Berlin Wall
PG: 425

8. What are some of the negative consequences of economic development programs?
ANS: Decline in quality of diet, health, the environment, family life, and an increase in unemployment, air pollution, and stress related disorders.
PG: 422-423

9. What is meant by linked changes?
ANS: A change in one part of a cultures brings about changes in other parts.
PG: 412-413

10. What is world systems theory?
    ANS: the theory that the wealthy countries of the world achieved high levels of development by exploiting other regions, plundering their natural resources, using their people as cheap sources of labor, and dominating their markets.
    PG: 419

Essay

1. Compare and contrast modernization and world systems theory.

2. On which ethnocentric assumptions is the modernization theory based?

3. Is globalization a good thing or a bad thing? Support your answer.

4. What impact does acculturation have on small-scale cultures? Can they choose not to acculturate?

5. Discuss some of the major positive and negative consequences of globalization.

Appendix A

Wadsworth's Case Study Catalogue

WADSWORTH CASE STUDIES IN
ANTHROPOLOGY & ARCHAEOLOGY PROGRAM

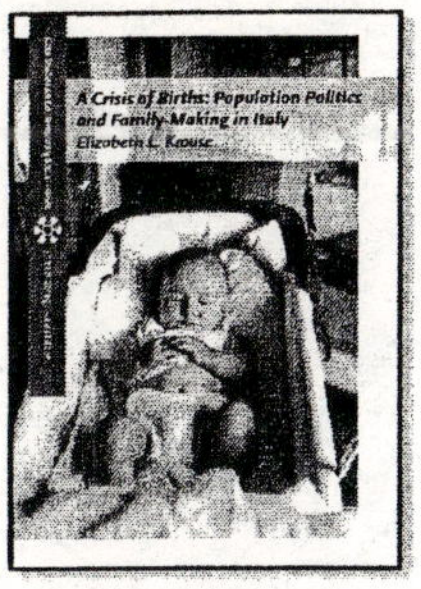

We are pleased to offer a wide and diverse array of case studies in cultural anthropology and archaeology through three exciting series. The program features brief titles on compelling topics that are suitable in any introductory or upper level course. The contemporary topics of recently published case studies show students what anthropologists are doing today, and are ideal complements to a textbook. We have organized the case studies by region but know that you also chose your teaching materials by topics of interest. Turn to pages 28–30 of this catalog for a listing of both print and **TextChoice** print-on-demand case studies organized by topic. Please go to **http://anthropology.wadsworth.com** for a more comprehensive list of case studies by topic.

Knowing that many professors wish to introduce their students to case material but are concerned about cost, Wadsworth offers unique bundle programs at substantial discounts. Contact your Wadsworth/Thomson representative for details about our exciting programs:

1. Bundle two or more case studies (print or **TextChoice** print-on-demand) together at a discount.
2. Bundle one or more case studies at special bundle pricing with one of our Wadsworth textbooks.
3. Bundle a **TextChoice** print-on-demand case study with a Wadsworth textbook at special bundle pricing.

Case Studies on Contemporary Social Issues—Edited by John Young—Each case study examines an issue of socially recognized importance in the historical, geographical and cultural context of a particular region of the world and includes comparative analysis.

The prestigious **Case Studies in Cultural Anthropology—Edited by George Spindler**—continues a tradition of excellence with the introduction of four new cases. The more recent studies in the series provide readable, informative ethnographic treatments of the world's cultures, cultural interactions, and the consequent changes that ensue.

Case Studies in Archaeology—Edited by Jeffrey Quilter—introduces three new cases. These cases provide accessible, concise accounts on a variety of contemporary archaeological topics and sites, and are an excellent resource for illustrating the importance of the archaeological perspective for understanding how the past informs our experiences of the present.

TEXTCHOICE CUSTOM PUBLISHING OFFERS TWO UNIQUE PROGRAMS TO HELP YOU BUILD YOUR COURSE MATERIALS!

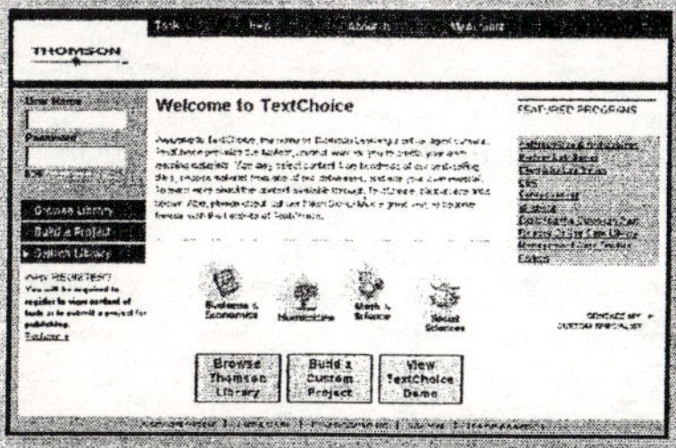

1. Cases marked **TextChoice** in this catalog are available on a print-on-demand basis (10 or more) and are on topics of enduring interest. We are pleased to extend a substantial discount for these cases in a bundle with a Wadsworth textbook.
2. You can create you own customized materials on a topic for your course, using chapters from any of the wide array of case studies available through the **Wadsworth Case Studies in Anthropology & Archaeology Program**.

Titles available exclusively through **TextChoice** are indicated in this catalog with the following icon:

TEXTCHOICE **Exclusively from TextChoice**

Visit **TextChoice.com** for more information.

WADSWORTH CASE STUDIES IN ANTHROPOLOGY & ARCHAEOLOGY PROGRAM

CASE STUDIES ON CONTEMPORARY SOCIAL ISSUES

John A. Young, Series Editor

WITH NO DIRECTION HOME: HOMELESS YOUTH ON THE ROAD AND IN THE STREETS

MARNI FINKELSTEIN, Albert Einstein College of Medicine/Montefiore Medical Center

192 pages. Paperbound. 6-3/8 x 9-1/4. 1-Color. ©2005.
ISBN: 0-534-62649-1.

This book gives voice to the homeless youth and is rich with material on their everyday lives, including living conditions and street experiences. The case study's strength lies in its ethnographic methodology, which combines direct observations and qualitative interviews. Ethnography is particularly important in describing populations and social environments that are hidden from normal observation, and is indispensable when exploring emerging phenomena, such as the formative fictive kin networks among street youth, or new ways of looking at drug addiction. Finkelstein discusses her own experiences with the street kids, including how she was able to develop a rapport within the "street scene."

KEY FEATURES

- The book serves as an urban anthropological study of a contemporary American subculture. It is drawn from the author's two summers of fieldwork among homeless youth in the East Village neighborhood of New York City, and gives a detailed description of the varied life experiences that homeless youth endure. Data is presented qualitatively, with much of the text being in the voices of the youths themselves.
- Two main research questions are addressed: what are the processes that lead youth to the streets and what are the processes that cause them to remain there.
- Finkelstein takes a qualitative, ethnographic approach to the study of homeless youth through interviews with and observations of 50 homeless youth; the data provided by this study helps generate an understanding of their experiences, priorities, concerns, and goals. Street youths themselves are quoted directly throughout the book.
- Poignant images of the youths' lives are presented, serving to enhance the literature of this largely hidden and understudied population.
- Several issues that are uncommon to studies on homeless youth are addressed. For example, Finkelstein is among the first to apply both nomadism and fictive kin theory to the lives of street teens. The youths interviewed in her study are all highly nomadic, often traveling around the country several times in one year, while most prior literature indicates that homeless adolescents don't stray far from "home." Not only did all of the kids in Finkelstein's study travel, they used their mobile lifestyle to self-identify with the nomadic subculture of homeless youth. A complete chapter on nomadic traveling is included in the book.
- Richly descriptive, the book will help generate an understanding of the experiences, priorities, concerns, and goals of homeless youth.

CONTENTS

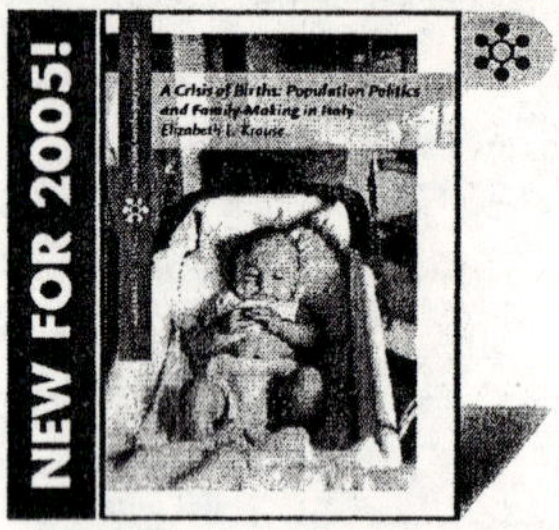

A CRISIS OF BIRTHS: POPULATION POLITICS AND FAMILY-MAKING IN ITALY

ELIZABETH L. KRAUSE, University of Massachusetts, Amherst

192 pages. Paperbound. 6-3/8 x 9-1/4. 1-Color. ©2005.
ISBN: 0-534-63693-4.

This book tells the story of one society's remarkable experience when Italians in the late 1990s attained the lowest birthrate per women of any nation in the world. This case study draws on two years of ethnographic fieldwork over a five year period, to examine the conflicts as well as the possibility that this trend in family-making has created for an otherwise family-centered culture. Krause's innovative project seeks to understand a pressing contemporary issue, and the 'story' she tells takes readers behind the scenes of demographic numbers to reveal what aggregate statistics cannot—a cultural 'politics of population' in which Italians struggle over the meanings of family and children in contemporary society. The reader will gain an in-depth understanding of why Italy's birthrate has fallen so low and what this means for Italians as individuals and Italy as a society and how reproduction has become politicized. The author finds answers in intensely personal dialogues with ordinary people ranging from sweater-makers to counts, and aging bachelors to doting mothers. Their life experiences reveal how a silent revolution against patriarchy reshapes social and sexual morality to create new imperatives for family making. The author hopes to prompt different and critical thinking about populations and the cultural struggles related to the politics of everyday life in modern society.

KEY FEATURES

- In the context of a nationally declining birthrate, this book focuses on the value Italians place on family and children and addresses both the reasons for the decline and the impact it has had on individuals and the society.

- By examining comparative and global perspectives on the cultural politics of population, Krause encourages the reader to think critically and differently about demographics, cultural struggles, and the politics related to everyday life in modern society.
- Grounded in kinship, family, and sexuality, this case study promises to spark interest and debate, as it challenges ethnocentric assumptions about the nature of family and politics in Italy and other European nations.
- Intimate, life history narratives and dialogues support the main themes of each chapter, making the book both intellectually and emotionally appealing to readers.
- Krause challenges the "scientific discourse" of demography by offering cultural interpretations and analysis to achieve deeper understandings of family and sexuality in society.

CONTENTS

BRAVO FOR THE MARSHALLESE: REGAINING CONTROL IN A POST-NUCLEAR, POST-COLONIAL WORLD

HOLLY M. BARKER, Senior Advisor to the Ambassador, Embassy of the Republic of the Marshall Islands (RMI)

192 pages. Paperbound. 6-3/8 x 9-1/4. 1-Color. ©2004.
ISBN: 0-534-61326-8.

Today, instructors are more interested in case studies that reveal the value of the anthropological perspective in addressing today's social problems, including globalization, scarce resource management, biomedical research, environmental degradation, health issues, and changes in the social, economic, and political reality of communities around the world. The new Wadsworth series of *Case Studies On Contemporary Social Issues* edited by John Young, past President of the Society for Applied Anthropology, provides students with highly readable and informative texts that focus on the practical value of anthropology and illustrate the "applied" perspective. The case studies discuss real life situations and contain topics that students will readily relate to, reflecting the changes occurring in a market eager to demonstrate the usefulness of anthropology. Framed around a social issue, each case study draws comparisons from around the world and points to possible alternatives and solutions to the problem(s) addressed and the direction of future research.

Holly Barker's *Bravo for the Marshallese: Regaining Control in a Post-Nuclear, Post-Colonial World,* promises to be of interest to courses beyond the introductory market of Cultural Anthropology, as follows:

- Applied Anthropology
- General Anthropology
- Environmental Anthropology
- Political Ecology
- The Anthropology of Law
- Ethnohistory
- Medical Anthropology
- Language and Culture
- Peoples of the Pacific/Oceania

This case study describes the role an applied anthropologist takes to help Marshallese communities understand the impact of radiation exposure on the environment and themselves, and addresses problems stemming from the U.S. nuclear weapons testing program conducted in the Marshall Islands from 1946-1958. The author demonstrates how the U.S. Government limits its responsibilities for dealing with the problems it created in the Marshall Islands. Through archival, life history, and ethnographic research, the author constructs a compelling history of the testing program from a Marshallese perspective. For more than five decades, the Marshallese have experienced the effects of the weapons testing program on their health and their environment. This book amplifies the voice of the Marshallese who share their knowledge about illnesses, premature deaths, and exile from their homelands. The author uses linguistic analysis to show how the Marshallese developed a unique radiation language to discuss problems related to their radiation exposure—problems that never existed before the testing program. Drawing on her own experiences working with the Government of the Marshall Islands, the author emphasizes the role of an applied anthropologist in influencing policy, and empowering community leaders to seek meaningful remedies.

KEY FEATURES

- The anthropologist draws on 12 years of experience working with the Marshallese government and the communities most affected by the weapons testing program.
- This case study illustrates the importance of linguistic anthropology in helping the Marshallese and others understand the experiences of the nuclear testing program on health and the environment.
- Loss of, damage to, and exile from land have profound implications for the Marshallese people and their way of life. The author uses graphic examples to demonstrate how radiological contamination of land alters the social fabric of Marshallese communities.
- The author's role in helping communities empower themselves to seek restitution is a revealing illustration of the work being done by applied anthropologists today.
- Global comparisons are made to other communities where cultures have been radically affected by radiological contamination.

CONTENTS

CONSERVATION AND GLOBALIZATION: A STUDY OF NATIONAL PARKS AND INDIGENOUS COMMUNITIES FROM EAST AFRICA TO SOUTH DAKOTA

JIM IGOE, University of Colorado, Denver

200 pages. Paperbound. 6-3/8 x 9-1/4. 1-Color. ©2004.
ISBN: 0-534-61317-9.

Today, instructors are more interested in case studies that reveal the value of the anthropological perspective in addressing today's social problems, including globalization, scarce resource management, biomedical research, environmental degradation, health issues, and changes in the social, economic, and political reality of communities around the world. The new Wadsworth series of *Case Studies On Contemporary Social Issues* edited by John Young, past President of the Society for Applied Anthropology, provides students with highly readable and informative texts that focus on the practical value of anthropology and illustrate the "applied" perspective. The case studies discuss real life situations and contain topics that students will readily relate to, reflecting the changes occurring in a market eager to demonstrate the usefulness of anthropology. Framed around a social issue, each case study draws comparisons from around the world and points to possible alternatives and solutions to the problem(s) addressed and the direction of future research.

Jim Igoe's *Conservation and Globalization: A Study of National Parks and Indigenous Communities from East Africa to South Dakota*, promises to be of interest to courses beyond the introductory market of Cultural Anthropology, as follows:

- Applied Anthropology
- General Anthropology
- Environmental Anthropology
- Political Anthropology
- Indigenous Peoples
- Peoples of Africa
- Ethnicity and Class
- Developmental Anthropology

The text can also be used in courses on African Studies, Environmental Studies, Political Ecology, and multi-disciplinary courses on Globalization.

This book makes current issues in political ecology and the question of globalization accessible to undergraduate students, as well as to non-academic readers. It is also empirically and theoretically rigorous enough to appeal to an academic audience.

Conservation and Globalization opens with a discussion of these two broad issues as they relate to the author's fieldwork with Maasai herding communities on the margins of Tarangire National Park in Tanzania. It explores different theoretical perspectives (Neo-Marxist and Foucauldian) on globalization and why both are relevant to the case studies presented. Students are introduced to the practice of multi-sited ethnography and its centrality to the anthropological study of globalization. While drawing on examples from specific Maasai communities, the book is more broadly concerned with the historical and contemporary links between these communities and a global system of institutions, ideas, and money. The ecological incompatibility of Western national park-style conservation with East African savanna ecosystems and Maasai resource management practices are highlighted. The concept of national parks is traced temporally and geographically from Maasai communities to the enclosure movement in 18th century England and westward expansion in 19th century North America. The relationships of parks to Judeo-Christian assumptions about "man's place in nature," colonial ideologies like Manifest Destiny and the Civilizing Mission, and capitalist notions of private property and "The Tragedy of the Commons," are explored. The book also looks at the latest conservation paradigm of "Community-Based Conservation," and explores its connections to the Soviet Collapse, economic and political liberalization, and the global proliferation of NGOs.

KEY FEATURES

- The case study challenges students to critically think about popular notions of conservation, wilderness, and "traditional" indigenous peoples.
- Rather than focusing on other cultures and what makes them seem strange to us, the book emphasizes Western assumptions about nature and our place in the universe, and why these might seem strange to other cultures. It also addresses the ways in which this particular Western worldview has been imposed on other cultures through international conservation and development programs.
- Globalization as a system of discourses and material processes that have impacted peoples' lives in every part of the world—from indigenous communities in Alaska to Zimbabwe—are examined.
- The methodology of multi-sited ethnography allows students to see how distant global processes like the Soviet Collapse, are able to influence something as seemingly unrelated as conservation initiatives in rural African communities.

CONTENTS

NEW CAPITALISTS: LAW, POLITICS, AND IDENTITY SURROUNDING CASINO GAMING ON NATIVE AMERICAN LAND

EVE DARIAN-SMITH, University of California, Santa Barbara

144 pages. Paperbound. 6-3/8 x 9-1/4. 1-Color. ©2004.
ISBN: 0-534-61308-X.

Today, instructors are more interested in case studies that reveal the value of the anthropological perspective in addressing today's social problems, including globalization, scarce resource management, biomedical research, environmental degradation, health issues, and changes in the social, economic, and political reality of communities around the world. The new Wadsworth series of *Case Studies On Contemporary Social Issues* edited by John Young, past President of the Society for Applied Anthropology, provides students with highly readable and informative texts that focus on the practical value of anthropology and illustrate the "applied" perspective. The case studies discuss real life situations and contain topics that students will readily relate to, reflecting the changes occurring in a market eager to demonstrate the usefulness of anthropology. Framed around a social issue, each case study draws comparisons from around the world and points to possible alternatives and solutions to the problem(s) addressed and the direction of future research.

Eve Darian-Smith's *New Capitalists* promises to be of interest to courses beyond the introductory market of Cultural Anthropology, as follows: Native American Peoples; Political Anthropology; Legal Anthropology; Law and Society; Applied Anthropology; and General Anthropology.

There are secondary markets in Sociology, Law and Society Programs, and Native American Studies.

This case study examines the impact of casino gaming on Native American reservations, and also explores why the idea of "rich Indians" and their participation in corporate America disrupts dominant assumptions and attitudes about indigenous peoples, their cultural authenticity, and their place in mainstream urban society.

Taking an anthropological approach to studying gaming on Indian reservations, the case study explores the implications and challenges of historically marginalized peoples now participating in a corporate entertainment industry. The study raises broader questions about the nature of capitalism and the enduring stability of predominant cultural constructs about Indians that have dominated the country's political and economic arenas. By linking gaming with tourism, what is occurring within the United States is comparatively discussed with similar developments in Canada, Australia, and Mexico where native peoples are increasingly demanding greater rights to participate in the formal institutions and governments of modern western societies.

Using extensive interviews with tribal elders, employees of reservation casinos, Las Vegas casino operators, and a broad spectrum of the California public, the book will serve to:

1. Introduce students to the legal, political, economic and cultural tensions surrounding casino operations on Native American reservations.
2. Explore why gaming has become such a politically and emotionally charged issue.
3. Emphasize how these tensions existing between Indian and non-Indian communities are representative of wider cultural conflicts and identity politics increasingly confronting many countries.

KEY FEATURES

- This is a highly relevant and important topic in understanding contemporary Native American issues.
- Laws regarding casinos on reservations are now significant in mainstream party politics.
- The text is written in a very accessible style, designed to stimulate discussion and critical thinking.

CONTENTS

SLAUGHTERHOUSE BLUES: THE MEAT AND POULTRY INDUSTRY IN NORTH AMERICA

DONALD D. STULL, The University of Kansas; and **MICHAEL J. BROADWAY,** Northern Michigan University; Foreword by **ERIC SCHLOSSER**

208 pages. Paperbound. 6-3/8 x 9-1/4. 1-Color. ©2004.
ISBN: 0-534-61303-9.

Today, instructors are more interested in case studies that reveal the value of the anthropological perspective in addressing today's social problems, including globalization, scarce resource management, biomedical research, environmental degradation, health issues, and changes in the social, economic, and political reality of communities around the world. The new Wadsworth series of *Case Studies On Contemporary Social Issues* edited by John Young, past President of the Society for Applied Anthropology, provides students with highly readable and informative texts that focus on the practical value of anthropology and illustrate the "applied" perspective. The case studies discuss real life situations and contain topics that students will readily relate to, reflecting the changes occurring in a market eager to demonstrate the usefulness of anthropology. Framed around a social issue, each case study draws comparisons from around the world and points to possible alternatives and solutions to the problem(s) addressed and the direction of future research.

Stull and Broadway's *Slaughterhouse Blues* promises to be of interest to courses beyond the introductory market of Cultural Anthropology, as follows:

- Applied Anthropology
- General Anthropology
- Social Geography
- Rural Sociology
- Policy Studies
- Food Studies
- American Studies
- Agricultural Economics and Development

Slaughterhouse Blues: The Meat and Poultry Industry in North America draws on more than 15 years of research by the authors, a cultural anthropologist and a social geographer, to present a detailed look at the meat and poultry industry in the United States and Canada. Following chapters on today's beef, poultry, and pork industries, *Slaughterhouse Blues* examines industry impacts on workers and on the communities that host its plants. The book details the authors' efforts to help communities plan for and mitigate the negative consequences of meat and poultry plants as well as community opposition to confined animal feeding operations. The book concludes by exploring alternatives to North America's model of industrialized meat production.

KEY FEATURES

- This case study draws on a rich corpus of ethnographic material, including long-term fieldwork extensive participant observation, and in-depth interviews, in several communities for over more than 15 years.
- The book is well illustrated, rich in detail, and highly readable. It has avoided the ponderous prose that so often characterizes academic writing and many case studies.
- The text traces the historical development of the industrialization of beef, poultry, and pork production and processing in the United States and Canada, and concludes with a careful and highly informed look at possible alternatives and different 'futures'.
- The industrialization of agriculture and its impact on communities is a topic of growing concern to the broad reading public. It complements and expands on the best-selling text by Eric Schlosser, *Fast Food Nation* (one of the top ten most popular books on college campuses today). Schlosser has written the foreword that accompanies the text.

CONTENTS

WADSWORTH CASE STUDIES IN ANTHROPOLOGY & ARCHAEOLOGY PROGRAM

CASE STUDIES IN CULTURAL ANTHROPOLOGY

George D. Spindler, Series Editor

AFRICA

THE DOBE JU/'HOANSI

Third Edition

RICHARD B. LEE, University of Toronto

220 pages. Paperbound. ©2002. **ISBN: 0-15-506333-2.**

This classic, best-selling study of the !Kung San, foragers of the Dobe area of the Kalahari Desert describes relatively recent changes to the !Kung rituals, beliefs, social control, marriage and kinship. It documents their determination to take hold of their own destiny—despite exploitation of their habitat and relentless development—to assert their political rights and revitalize their communities. Use of the name Ju/'hoansi (meaning "real people") acknowledges their new sense of empowerment.

KEY FEATURES

- Includes material from the author's four return trips to the Kalahari this decade.
- Lee documents the increasing changes to Ju/'hoansi rituals, beliefs, kinship system, and social structure.
- Material included on the Ju/'hoansi reactions to government development projects, the AIDS/HIV epidemic, and the eco-tourism movement that brings people into the Kalahari to visit formerly isolated villages.
- Lee has continued to work with archaeologists to excavate historic sites. Material from this work will provide a basis for an expanded discussion on the current "Kalahari debate."
- Every student of cultural anthropology will eventually make the acquaintance of the Dobe. The world has changed, however, and the Dobe Ju/'hoansi are a remarkable people who have changed with the times, finding new ways to subsist in a harsh land.
- Lee uses material from the life histories of elders as well as his own responses to the situation in the Kalahari to present readers with an insightful look at the Dobe Ju/'hoansi.

WATCH AND PRAY: A PORTRAIT OF FANTE VILLAGE LIFE IN TRANSITION

NANCY LUNDGREN, University of Cape Coast, Ghana

178 pages. Paperbound. ©2002. **ISBN: 0-15-505933-5.**

This text is appropriate for courses in Cultural Anthropology and regional courses on Peoples of Africa. It also represents the new case studies in this series that focus on culture change and culture continuity.

The matrilineal Fante are members of one of the most populous ethnic groups in Ghana, the Akan. They are the dominant group in the Cape Coast area and have a long history in the region. They are Fanti speakers, but also speak the national language, which is English. This case study provides an intimate look at the Fante, who now reside in towns and villages, are predominantly Christian and earn their living primarily as traders, farmers and fishing people, but are found in all walks of life including: government officials, teachers, University professors, lawyers and doctors.

The people of Akotokiyr and Abaasa and Nim want readers to know about their villages and the people associated with them because they represent a spirit and a tradition and a collaborative lifestyle that are rapidly changing. The book makes it possible for readers to become participants in the scene—be it in a home, a "palace" of a chief, a church, in the market place, or in the author's own home—where they can see firsthand the ways in which the new is being incorporated into the old. As the Series Editor says, "the blazing sun, the airless rooms with concrete block walls with roofs of sheet iron, the dust, flies, rough streets, the verdant forest, the streams the open, running sewers, all become habitats of our minds as we read of the author's interactions with people in the small villages where she is living and working."

KEY FEATURES

- This ethnography is particularly rich with images and insights of the people, taking the reader right into the villages of Mr. Augustine Ato Baidoo, Akotokyir, and Kim on Cape Coast, Ghana.
- The case study focuses on the rapidly changing traditional lifestyle of the Fante, which is based on a collaborative lifestyle, as well as the ways in which traditional culture has been adapted in the modern world.
- The author is more than a participant-observer in the anthropological tradition: She taught school, contributed money to community projects and helped arrange the necessary resources to complete the projects, and actually became Queen Mother, which is unique in the Fante world.

CONTENTS

A BAGFUL OF LOCUSTS AND THE BABOON WOMAN: CONSTRUCTIONS OF GENDER, CHANGE, AND CONTINUITY IN BOTSWANA

DAVID N. SUGGS, Kenyon College

160 pages. Paperbound. ©2002. **ISBN: 0-15-507038-X.**

This text is appropriate for courses in Cultural Anthropology and regional courses on Peoples of Africa, and will also prove useful in classes on Gender, Culture Change, and Social Organization.

Not since the publication of Lee's case study on the Dobe Ju/'Hoansi and Turnbull's case study on the Mbuti Pygmies, has there been such an interesting addition to the African cases of the *Spindler Case Studies in Cultural Anthropology* series. Set in the sub-Saharan Africa in a contemporary context, this ethnography represents over 12 years of field research that focuses on the popular twin themes of culture change and gender roles amongst the BaKgatla of BaTswana.

KEY FEATURES

- This unique ethnography sketches traditional BaTswana society and culture, and engages students as each chapter opens with a narrative of the author's own experience that in some way highlights a central point to be made in the chapter.
- The material is presented in a way that will be useful to those with differing theoretical orientations, and is intentionally written in plain English for a relatively jargon-free presentation.
- The case analyzes drinking patterns and changing gender roles in BaTswana using the voices of informants, to give a lively presentation on how the BaTswana have redefined roles around gender and age, and reconciled change and continuity to preserve their cultural identity over time.

CONTENTS

1. That Old Man Just Called Me a Monkey!: Of BaTswana and the BaKgatla
2. I'm Very Old For My Age: Women's Life Course
3. The Baboon Woman: Of Coke Cans, Beer, and the Construction of Gender
4. These Young Chaps Think They are Just Men, Too: Constructions of Age Within Masculinity
5. A Bagful of Locusts
6. The Thirst Quencher—Conclusions About Culture Change and Continuity

TEXTCHOICE **Exclusively from TextChoice**

THE RASHAAYDA BEDOUIN: ARAB PASTORALISTS OF EASTERN SUDAN

WILLIAM C. YOUNG, Georgia Southern University

224 pages. Paperbound. ©1996. **ISBN: 0-15-501513-3.**

A supplement to introductory anthropology and cultural anthropology courses, this is the only available book-length study of an Arab Bedouin society that supplements customary observations with data about gender and race. This case study integrates cultural meanings with the pastoral economy in clear, non-technical language. Drawing on the Bedouin notion of habitus, the author points out connections between the cultural organization of space, the sexual division of labor, and gender identity, giving students a strong model of the kind of analysis influential in contemporary anthropology. Extensive pedagogy includes glossaries of Arabic terms and anthropological vocabulary, a current bibliography, diagrams of social relationships, and maps and photographs.

TEXTCHOICE **Exclusively from TextChoice**

THE LUGBARA OF UGANDA

Second Edition

JOHN MIDDLETON, Yale University

128 pages. Paperbound. ©1992. **ISBN: 0-534-96895-3.**

Written by one of the most distinguished ethnographers of African cultures, this edition updates 30 years of research and writing. Middleton's sensitive account dramatizes how this complex sociopolitical society, once reliant on feud or warfare to control competition, became refugees of harassment and victims of famine.

TEXTCHOICE **Exclusively from TextChoice**

THE SEBEI: A STUDY IN ADAPTATION

WALTER GOLDSCHMIDT, University of California, Los Angeles

182 pages. Paperbound. ©1987. **ISBN: 0-534-97147-4.**

The Sebei live on the north slope of a giant extinct volcano, Mount Elgon, in Uganda, in the heart of Africa. This case study is about their adaptation to their environment over time. Cultural evolution is the framework. The shift from pastoralism (cattle herding) to sedentary agriculture and a comparison of two Sebei communities , one pastoral and one agricultural, are highlights.

TEXTCHOICE **Exclusively from TextChoice**

THE SWAZI: A SOUTH AFRICAN KINGDOM

Second Edition

HILDA KUPER, University of California, Los Angeles

187 pages. Paperbound. ©1986. **ISBN: 0-03-070239-9.**

Based upon information collected during half a century of field research in Swaziland, this case study presents rare insight into the dynamics of the country's independence, problems facing traditional leaders, and conflicts of interest and personalities.

TEXTCHOICE **Exclusively from TextChoice**

THE MBUTI PYGMIES: CHANGE AND ADAPTATION

COLIN M. TURNBULL, American Museum of Natural History

161 pages. Paperbound. ©1983. **ISBN: 0-03-061537-2.**

This case focuses on the Mbuti pygmy hunter/gatherers of Zaire and their adaptation to change both before and after independence.

TEXTCHOICE **Exclusively from TextChoice**

THE IGBO OF SOUTHEAST NIGERIA

VICTOR C. UCHENDU, Northwestern University

111 pages. Paperbound. ©1965. **ISBN: 0-03-052475-X.**

This book examines the Igbo social system and view of the world, covers their contact with European culture, and the warfare that raged within the Igbo borders.

TEXTCHOICE **Exclusively from TextChoice**

BUNYORO: AN AFRICAN KINGDOM

JOHN BEATTIE, Oxford University

96 pages. Paperbound. ©1960. **ISBN: 0-534-97128-8.**

This study examines the conflicts that arise when a feudal and bureaucratic administration struggles against the influences of European and traditional standards of behavior.

ASIA

A SINHALESE VILLAGE IN SRI LANKA: COPING WITH UNCERTAINTY

VICTORIA J. BAKER, Eckerd College, Comparative Cultures Collegium

192 pages. Paperbound. ©1998. **ISBN: 0-15-505176-8.**

The most current and detailed case study of South Asia available, this book documents the ways in which the members of a remote agricultural village cope with the dangers that plague them by employing a complex system of ritual practices and beliefs in supernatural forces. The book also addresses topics commonly neglected in other case studies, such as formal education problems in remote areas, the independent and self-confident women of the developing world, and the trials of developmental work in these areas.

TEXTCHOICE **Exclusively from TextChoice**

HIMALAYAN HERDERS

NAOMI H. BISHOP, California State University, Northridge

212 pages. Paperbound. ©1998. **ISBN: 0-534-44060-6.**

This first general case study about the Sherpa people in the Yolmo region of Nepal helps to place the more familiar Sherpa of the Solu-Khumbu region of Mt. Everest in comparative context. This study provides an ethnographic description of a village within the broad context of human adaptation to mountain environments, Tibetan regional cultures, and culture change.

TEXTCHOICE **Exclusively from TextChoice**

ETHNIC IDENTITY IN CHINA: THE MAKING OF A MUSLIM MINORITY NATIONALITY

DRU C. GLADNEY, University of Hawaii, Manoa; East-West Center

176 pages. Paperbound. ©1998. **ISBN: 0-15-501970-8.**

This case study introduces students to the problems of ethnic diversity in China, a modern nation-state that is normally thought of and taught as culturally monolithic. By introducing students to the wide diversity of identity within one nationality, they are exposed to the ethnic complexities as well as to the larger issue of ethnic pluralism in modern nation-states. Students' perceptions regarding other societies, as well as our own, are challenged and broadened.

THE BALINESE

STEPHEN H. LANSING, University of Southern California

148 pages. Paperbound. ©1995. **ISBN: 0-15-500240-6.**

This study of the complex Balinese culture examines Balinese concepts of personhood and society; the integration of art into every aspect of Balinese life; the effects of the Guen Revolution on Balinese agriculture; the ecological role of their water temples in an age-old system of inigrate rice terraces; and the ethnohistory of Bali, including both colonial and Balinese views. The book is organized around four different periods of fieldwork and includes an appendix of available films and videos on the Balinese.

TEXTCHOICE **Exclusively from TextChoice**

CHINA'S URBAN VILLAGERS: CHANGING LIFE IN A BEIJING SUBURB

Second Edition

NORMAN A. CHANCE, University of Connecticut

230 pages. Paperbound. ©1991. **ISBN: 0-534-97156-3.**

This book describes life in a small village within the borders of a large state farm on the outskirts of Beijing. It covers socialization and education, the impact of mechanization and industrialization, efforts at modernization, and the response of the villagers to political realities in a socialist state. This edition incorporates the uprising in China and the tragic events at Tianamen Square.

TEXTCHOICE Exclusively from TextChoice

FRIEND BY DAY, ENEMY BY NIGHT: ORGANIZED VENGEANCE IN A KOHISTANI COMMUNITY

LINCOLN KEISER, Wesleyan University

131 pages. Paperbound. ©1991. **ISBN: 0-03-053332-5.**

This exploration of the blood feuding and its ramifications in Thull, a Kohistani tribal community in the Hindu-Kush Mountains of Pakistan shows how 'mar dushmani' (literally "death enmity") has come to interpenetrate the mountaineer's lives.

TEXTCHOICE Exclusively from TextChoice

GOPALPUR: A SOUTH INDIAN VILLAGE

Fieldwork Edition

ALAN R. BEALS, University of California, Riverside

140 pages. Paperbound. ©1980. **ISBN: 0-03-045371-2.**

From a Western point of view, the problem-solving techniques (including wrestling matches) of the people of Gopalpur seem strange, but this study provides an inside view of Gopalpur's rich and fulfilling life.

TEXTCHOICE Exclusively from TextChoice

A MOUNTAIN VILLAGE IN NEPAL

JOHN THAYER HITCHCOCK

156 pages. Paperbound. ©1980. **ISBN: 0-534-97173-3.**

This village is in Gurkha country, home of the famed fighters that have served everywhere the British have been. Hitchcock describes their way of life focusing on the land and it uses, Godlings and observances, family, marriage and farmstead, kin, and recent change.

CENTRAL & SOUTH AMERICA/MEXICO

AZTECS OF CENTRAL MEXICO: AN IMPERIAL SOCIETY

Second Edition

FRANCES BERDAN, California State University, San Bernardino

192 pages. Paperbound. 6-3/8 x 9-1/4. 1-Color. ©2005. **ISBN: 0-534-62728-5.**

Berdan's book covers the compelling story of a complex, imperial society in Central Mexico during the 15th and 16th centuries. It uses pre- and post-Spanish conquest documents and illustrations, as well as archaeological discoveries, to reconstruct the variety and "feel" of Aztec daily life at various status levels. The strength of Berdan's case study has always been its ethnographic perspective.

NEW TO THIS EDITION

- The extensive archaeological investigations at the Templo Mayor in Mexico City (ancient Tenochtitlan) have unearthed the building stages and more than 100 caches containing thousands of artifacts. These recently-unearthed materials shed new light on Aztec architecture, art, beliefs, attitudes toward earlier history, and tribute. Information available from these excavations is presented throughout the book where appropriate, especially in chapters 1 (Mexico and Mexica), 2 (Economic Organization), 5 (Imperial Politics and Warfare), 6 (Religious Organization and Beliefs), and 7 (Intellectual and Artistic Achievements).
- Archaeological investigations conducted by Michael Smith in Morelos over the past decade have yielded important new data and insights into life in the Aztec provinces. This information provides fascinating comparisons and contrasts with life in the imperial capital, and is usefully incorporated into chapter 4 (Daily Life) as well as chapter 5 (Imperial Politics and Warfare).
- Archaeological investigations on Aztec palaces and "pleasure palaces" provide new insights into the lives of rulers. This new data, excavated by Susan Evans, especially augments and enhances chapters 3 (Social Structure and Dynamics), 4 (Daily Life), and 5 (Imperial Politics and Warfare).
- Two pictorial codices from the eastern realm of the Aztec empire have come to light (through the efforts of Guy Stresser Pean). These documents provide the perspective of the conquered and offer interesting additions, especially to chapters 4 and 5. Additional interpretations of the Aztec written tradition have been published and augment our understanding of Aztec life.
- A new concise discussion on methods is embedded in chapter 1 (Mexico and Mexica). The Aztec civilization came to an abrupt end nearly 500 years ago, and it is important that the reader understand the methods by which the culture has been reconstructed. These methods include archaeology, ethnohistory, ethnographic analogy, and experimental archaeology.
- The Aztecs did not exist by themselves in Mesoamerica. Recent research (by Smith and Berdan) systematically places the Aztecs in a broader network of relations with other groups (such as the Mayans, Zapotecs, and Huaxtecs) in Mesoamerica. This is briefly included, especially in chapter 3 (Economic Organization).
- An updated account of the responses of the Aztecs to the Spanish conquest and its aftermath is provided, including comparisons between native and Spanish accounts.
- New illustrations of recent excavations and artifacts, updated maps, and a new bibliography are included.

KEY FEATURES

- This readable case study makes the culture come alive through the use of real-life enhancements that set it apart from recent books on the Aztecs.
- Complexities of state organization are unraveled in understandable terms, from both anthropological and native perspectives.
- Berdan includes a substantial conclusive chapter on the adaptations of the Aztecs to life under Spanish rule.

CONTENTS

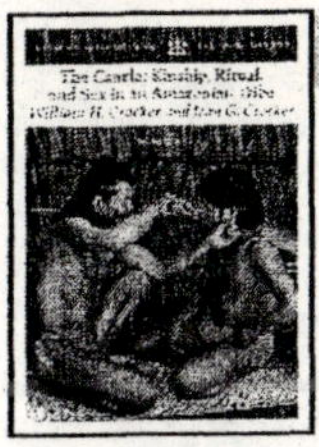

THE CANELA: KINSHIP, RITUAL AND SEX IN AN AMAZONIAN TRIBE

Second Edition

WILLIAM H. CROCKER, National Museum of Natural History, Smithsonian Institution, and
JEAN G. CROCKER

174 pages. Paperbound. 6-3/8 x 9-1/4. 1-Color. ©2004.
ISBN: 0-534-17491-4.

Anthropologists use case studies primarily in undergraduate courses as core material for introductory courses or as supplemental books for textbooks in core introductory courses, as well as adjunct texts in specialized upper-division courses. The classic *Case Studies In Cultural Anthropology* series edited by George Spindler is geared to the sophomore level. Crocker and Crocker's case study is an undergraduate-level cultural ethnography that focuses on their work with the Canela of Brazil. Courses for the book include:

- Cultural Anthropology
- General Anthropology
- Peoples of the World
- Peoples of South America
- Specialty courses on South American Indians, Culture Change, Kinship, Sexuality, or Gender

This text is a case study of one people, the Canela, which traces changes through time, a group uniquely held together by social and sexual bonds, and reveals the ethnographer's fieldwork practices. The authors present much of the material through short narratives and examples and Native points of view are expressed through their diaries. The reader is introduced to the Canela with an account of one of the author's arrivals in the tribe. This is followed by a brief history of the Canela that clarifies how the network of the kinship system holds the society together, and how the unusual sex practices create satisfying bonds among the people. The case study also shows how the practice of rituals affirms the group way of life for the individual. Many contemporary influences have caused the gradual demise of the Canela way of life. The case study concludes with an epilogue on the Canela's future adaptation to Brazilian life.

NEW TO THIS EDITION

- The text is completely rewritten for better clarity and student comprehension.
- New narratives are introduced, including those of females, for a more contemporary approach to engage students.
- The new preface includes more discussion about the career of an anthropologist.
- A new Introduction informs the reader of new aspects of the book.
- A new epilogue helps students consider the Canela's future.
- Approximately 30 new photographs have been included in this edition.
- A new Appendix C provides a grid with locations of comparable materials in the Study Guide, Web site, and Canela video, "Mending Ways."

KEY FEATURES

- Clear organization around three major cultural domains facilitates the student's grasp of the overall sociocultural system.
- Many descriptions of the author's field experiences draw students into the material and illustrate important aspects of fieldwork.
- Many "voices" taken from fieldwork and diary quotations from the Canela themselves, make this group come alive as individuals and highlights their yet-to-be-resolved social problems.
- Accounts of customary extramarital sex and sequential sex open the minds of readers to alternative cultural solutions to social organization.

ANCILLARIES

Mending Ways Video
Available through the *Films for the Humanities and Social Sciences®* video library. Contact your Thomson/Wadsworth representative for more information.

CONTENTS

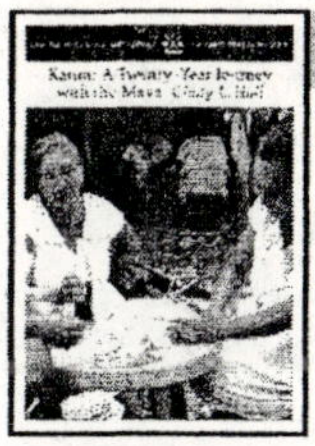

KATUN: A TWENTY-YEAR JOURNEY WITH THE MAYA

CINDY L. HULL, Grand Valley State University

208 pages. Paperbound. 6-3/8 x 9-1/4. 1-Color. ©2004.
ISBN: 0-534-61290-3.

Anthropologists use case studies primarily in undergraduate courses as core material for introductory courses or as supplemental books for textbooks in core introductory courses, as well as adjunct texts in specialized upper-division courses. The classic *Case Studies In Cultural Anthropology* series edited by George Spindler is geared to the sophomore level. Cindy Hull's case study is an undergraduate-level cultural ethnography that focuses on her work with the Maya. Courses for the book include:

- Cultural Anthropology
- General Anthropology
- Peoples of the World
- Peoples of Mesoamerica
- Specialty courses on Mexico, Culture Change, or Gender

The focus of this case study is the changing social and economic structure of the henequen zone in northwest Yucatan, Mexico, with special attention paid to women's economic participation. The henequen zone is unique in that it has been dominated by hacienda and state-controlled monocrop production since the colonial era. In recent years, this system of production has deteriorated. Since the author's first fieldwork in the 1970's, the area has faced economic decline as the henequen (sisal used for the production of binder twine and rope) market has collapsed. Recent national policies have further shaped the current economic and social conditions in the region.

During numerous research periods since that time, the author has been recording the following trends in one village:

- The increase in mixed economic strategies among villagers
- The dramatic expansion of women's economic participation outside of the home and their increased social and political involvement in the village
- Out-migration from the village to Meria, the state capitol, to the resort islands of the Caribbean, and in some cases, outside of the state of Yucatan.

Within these shifting economic and social positions, the text explores how families and communities develop in order to maintain themselves and their culture. The theme of the case study is change and resilience.

KEY FEATURES

- This case study focuses on the themes of culture change and resilience relating to new economic strategies that include women's participation and gives insight into the most significant processes of adaptation taking place in our time.
- This ethnography strives to find a balance between "ethnographic data" and reflexive anthropology, in which the reader can share some of the experiences and concerns, which are embedded in anthropological research.
- The author has provided 38 pictures and 16 outstanding illustrations as an introduction to both the parts and the chapters for visual excitement.
- The text draws from several excerpts from historical documents of the Maya and their conquerors, excerpts from the author's fieldnotes and journals, stories that the author has collected during her twenty years of visiting the village, and ethnographic data which documents the changes in economic and social structure collected and compiled during the years of the author's research.

CONTENTS

FROM THE BUSH: THE FRONT LINE OF HEALTH CARE IN A CARIBBEAN VILLAGE

MARSHA B. QUINLAN, Ball State University

168 pages. Paperbound. 6-3/8 x 9-1/4. 1-Color. ©2004. **ISBN: 0-15-508567-0.**

Anthropologists use case studies primarily in undergraduate courses as core material for introductory courses or as supplemental books for textbooks in core introductory courses, as well as adjunct texts in specialized upper-division courses. The classic *Case Studies In Cultural Anthropology* series edited by George Spindler is geared to the sophomore level. Marsha Quinlan's case study is an undergraduate-level medical ethnography. Courses for the book include:

- Medical Anthropology
- Cultural Anthropology
- General Anthropology
- Ethnobotany
- Peoples of the World

This case study will be the first to deal with a topic in medical anthropology. It explores the world of folk medicine in the Caribbean (Dominica)—local beliefs and practices concerning how the body functions and malfunctions and the home remedies Dominicans use to cure common illnesses. The case study goes beyond discussing the exotic medical system of a developing country (which includes sorcery and folk-illnesses) to discuss how folk medicine flourishes in industrialized countries in a way that is little different than that practiced in Dominica. The theme is that cultural ideas about the body and uses of medicinal plants are deeply intertwined. Ideas about illness direct the consequent medical response. The book's topic is important because knowledge of local ethnomedical practice is essential for the successful development of public health interventions in non-Western settings. This realist ethnography is aimed at any member of the generally educated population.

KEY FEATURES

- This case study presents the actual methods for collecting parallel data in any society, as well as discussing the ethnomedicine of one Caribbean group.
- Plant illustrations are necessary in ethnobotanies so there are 23 plant photographs in this case study. There are also photographs that will familiarize the reader with the setting, introduce the people, and make the book's subject more accessible to students.
- From the Bush also provides a glossary of anthropological and ethnobotanical terms, appendices of Dominican herbal remedies and non-herbal remedies, and a general index.

CONTENTS

TEXTCHOICE **Exclusively from TextChoice**

WAORANI: THE CONTEXTS OF VIOLENCE AND WAR

CLAYTON ROBARCHEK and **CAROLE ROBARCHEK,** both of Wichita State University

214 pages. Paperbound. ©1998. **ISBN: 0-534-44006-1.**

Serving as both a narrative account and a general explanatory framework for understanding violence, this case study on the psychological and cultural dynamics of violence focuses on explaining the roots of violence in Waorani society while developing a theoretical model to explain violence in other societies.

YANOMAMÖ INTERACTIVE: THE AX FIGHT ON CD-ROM

PETER BIELLA, San Francisco State University, **NAPOLEAN A. CHAGNON,** University of California, Santa Barbara, and **GARY SEAMAN,** University of Southern California

©1997. **ISBN: 0-15-505428-7.**

Yanomamö Interactive: The Ax Fight sets a new standard in the teaching of cultural anthropology, using the power of multimedia to enhance and extend the experience of viewing Chagnon and Asch's classics ethnographic film. The CD-ROM includes complete footage of the film, audio narration, maps and graphics, genealogical tables, photos and biographies of the Yanomamö, and important historical and contemporary text analyzing the film. A sophisticated but easy-to-use interface allows users to study the film and supporting documents in a nonlinear fashion, revealing aspects of *The Ax Fight* film in a manner never before possible.

THE YANOMAMÖ
Fifth Edition

NAPOLEAN A. CHAGNON, University of California, Santa Barbara

165 pages. Paperbound. ©1997. **ISBN: 0-15-505327-2.**

Based on the author's extensive fieldwork, this classic ethnography, now in its fifth edition, focuses on the Yanomamö. These truly remarkable South American people are one of the few primitive sovereign tribal societies left on earth. This new edition includes events and changes that have occurred since 1992, including a recent trip by the author to the Brazilian Yanomamö in 1995.

KEY FEATURES

- Chapter 7 examines the author's long-term research in the village of Mishmishimobewei-teri.
- The accompanying CD-ROM includes footage of *The Ax Fight*, providing important genealogies and interpretative narration.

ANCILLARIES

Yanomamö Interactive: The Ax Fight on CD-ROM
ISBN: 0-15-505428-7
See previous listing for details.

CONTENTS

TEXTCHOICE **Exclusively from TextChoice**

THE ISTHMUS ZAPOTECS: A MATRIFOCAL CULTURE OF MEXICO

BEVERLY N. CHINAS, California State University, Chico

133 pages. Paperbound. ©1992. **ISBN: 0-03-055057-2.**

This case study has long been valued for its unique gender role model and focus on the only matrifocal indigenous culture in Latin America. This edition updates historical data and explores new case material on Zapotec attitudes toward gender variations.

TEXTCHOICE **Exclusively from TextChoice**

LIFE UNDER THE TROPICAL CANOPY: TRADITION AND CHANGE AMONG THE YUCATEC MAYA

ELLEN R. KINTZ, State University of New York, Geneseo

170 pages. Paperbound. ©1990. **ISBN: 0-03-032592-7.**

This case study describes how the Maya have lived and benefited from their environment for 13 centuries. An experiment in ethnology and ethnohistory, this text regards culture not as an entity, but as a process enacted in contemporary space in light of past events. This adventure into ethnohistory unravels the impact of time and change on family life, economy, politics and supernatural beliefs.

TEXTCHOICE **Exclusively from TextChoice**

THE ZINACANTECOS OF MEXICO: A MODERN MAYA WAY OF LIFE
Second Edition

EVON Z. VOGT, Harvard University

157 pages. Paperbound. ©1990. **ISBN: 0-03-033344-X.**

This case study explores the Zinacanteco belief system as represented in ceremonies, rituals, and daily life, and discusses how that belief system also serves as a philosophy, cosmology, theology, code of values, and science. This edition includes information obtained by the author and his students in the last ten years. The book begins with explanations of fieldwork methods, followed by detailed descriptions of the cycles encompassing hamlet life, social and domestic relations, and rituals.

TEXTCHOICE Exclusively from TextChoice

YUQUI: FOREST NOMADS IN A CHANGING WORLD

ALLYN MACLEAN STEARMAN, University of Central Florida

164 pages. Paperbound. ©1989. **ISBN: 0-534-97074-5.**

This book examines the effects of 20th century social and cultural changes on the Yuqui, a group of fewer than 100 nomadic foragers who've survived without houses or the ability to produce fire. Recently contacted by missionaries, the Yuqui now face enormous pressures from outside developers and other forces of modernization.

EUROPE

NEW FOR 2005!

SCOTTISH CROFTERS: A HISTORICAL ETHNOGRAPHY OF A CELTIC VILLAGE

Second Edition

SUSAN PARMAN, California State University, Fullerton

192 pages. Paperbound. 6-3/8 x 9-1/4. 1-Color. ©2005.
ISBN: 0-534-63324-2.

This case study focuses on Geall, a community in the Scottish Outer Hebrides. With an understanding gained from an intimate, long-term relationship with Scotland, things Scottish, and the people of the community the author describes Geall as a human community and places it in the wider cultural, historical, economic, and sociopolitical contexts of maintaining relationships to Scotland, England and Europe. This is the first book to look at a Scottish Highland Community and the first ethnography to utilize the semiotic theory of culture, which views history as an act of cultural creation. The book emphasizes the way symbols are used to interpret elements of the culture such as economy, power, mental illness, and religion, by exploring the significant symbols associated with the state, the mechanisms for integrating community and state, and how people define leaders and social role.

NEW TO THIS EDITION

- The revision updates Parman's analysis of crofting, in which she develops the links between crofting, Gaelic-speaking, the "Gaelic Renaissance" of Scotland and Scottish communities abroad, and Scottish nationalism. Parman also updates the status of crofting as a form of land tenure, focusing on the "de-crofting statutes" of the past decade that have sought to bring land out of crofting.
- Assessment of the symbolic significance of the European Union movement to promote crofting as an ecologically sound economic practice that saves the small family farm is provided.
- Changes in the crofting community of Shawbost are outlined, highlighting the crofting activities and the other categories of sociocultural organization described in the first edition. Examples of change include whether or not the week-long communion services are still held, how crofting is integrated into other economic practices, the functioning of political leadership, and the role of the Harris Tweed mills in local leadership.
- New life stories by villagers are incorporated into this edition, providing additional rich commentary on change. Also, close attention is paid to the "exiles," or those who have left the community.

KEY FEATURES

- Aside from being the first book about a Scottish Highland community, the first edition of *Scottish Crofters* was also the first to apply semiotic theory, which views history as an act of cultural creation.
- The second edition continues to explore the relationship between anthropology and history, providing additional resources for interpreting history as socially relevant myth. It introduces the concept of "narratological analysis," and suggests that the historical narratives told by Scottish crofters have a distinctive structure that may be identified as "concretizing and personalizing the historical."
- The role of anthropology in the study of Western (as opposed to non-Western) peoples is explored. The author draws upon thirty years of fieldwork to comment on issues of relevance to all social scientists studying literate communities, such as local history vs. general social science, the use of pseudonyms, and whose story should be told by whom.
- The book is the first to establish "crofting" as a useful socio-economic category of analysis.
- Parman examines Scotland's complex history of economic, political, sociocultural, and linguistic development, and provides an analysis of the relationships among regional, ethnic, national, and transitional processes in the European Union today.
- Emphasis is placed on the use of symbols in interpreting elements of the culture, such as power, mental illness, economic status, and religion. The author identifies significant symbols associated with the state, mechanisms for integrating community and state, and looks at the ways people use these symbols to define leaders and social roles.

CONTENTS

TEXTCHOICE Exclusively from TextChoice

NAZARE: WOMEN AND MEN IN A PREBUREAUCRATIC PORTUGUESE FISHING VILLAGE

JAN BROGGER

148 pages. Paperbound. ©1992. **ISBN: 0-03-043382-7.**

This case study discusses the various gender roles, as well as equalities and inequalities, that exist among a society of people in Portugal.

TEXTCHOICE Exclusively from TextChoice

TOWN AND COUNTRY IN LOCOROTONDO

ANTHONY H. GALT, University of Wisconsin, Green Bay

124 pages. Paperbound. ©1992. **ISBN: 0-03-073327-8.**

This look at peasant and elite cultures of the southern Italian town of Locorotondo focuses on its connection and similarities with Italian society and the ways in which both cultures have changed in the past decades.

TEXTCHOICE Exclusively from TextChoice

VASILIKA: A VILLAGE IN MODERN GREECE

ERNESTINE FRIEDL

Paperbound. ©1962. **ISBN: 0-534-97165-2.**

This case study focuses on Friedl's extensive study of family economics, consumption habits, dowry and inheritance, and the village as a community.

NORTH AMERICA

SKIN AND BONES: THE MANAGEMENT OF PEOPLE AND NATURAL RESOURCES IN SHELL-CRACKER HAVEN, FLORIDA

JANE GIBSON, University of Kansas

192 pages. Paperbound. 6-3/8 x 9-1/4. 1-Color. ©2004. **ISBN: 0-15-508476-3.**

Anthropologists use case studies primarily in undergraduate courses as core material for introductory courses or as supplemental books for textbooks in core introductory courses, as well as adjunct texts in specialized upper-division courses. The classic *Case Studies in Cultural Anthropology* series edited by George Spindler is geared to the sophomore level. Gibson's case study is an undergraduate-level cultural ethnography that focuses on her work in Shellcracker Haven, Florida. Courses for the book include:

- Cultural Anthropology
- General Anthropology
- Peoples of North America
- Cultural Ecology
- Environmental Anthropology
- Environmental History
- Specialty courses on Culture Change and Environmental Studies

Skin and Bones relates the history of Shellcracker Haven, a community pseudonym, to the development of fresh water fish and wildlife management in the state of Florida. It examines the clash of worldviews between community residents who are personally invested and locally sensitive to the ecosystem that has fed their families for several generations, and biologist resource managers who rely on detached science-based models and political sensitivity when making policy decisions. *Skin and Bones* challenges readers to think about the natural world as more than fragile species and ecosystems to be defended against human destruction or as discrete natural resources to be commercially exploited. Through the Knight family of Shellcracker Haven, one learns of the power of emotional investment in the natural world, and the cost to both people and planet when we destroy that relationship.

KEY FEATURES

- The text situates natural resource management in a historical perspective, illuminating the worldview that underpins it and the politics that support it.
- The book depicts the impact of fresh water fishery and wildlife management on resident livelihoods.
- Poverty is explained as the result of a community's failed political struggle to retain control over much needed resources.
- The author describes social and economic adaptations to changing institutional conditions.
- The book suggests an alternative relationship between people and the natural world, one that could advise resource management policy.

CONTENTS

STRANGERS IN A NOT-SO-STRANGE-LAND: INDIAN AMERICANS IN THE GLOBAL AGE

ARTHUR W. HELWEG, Western Michigan University

176 pages. Paperbound. 6-3/8 x 9-1/4. 1-Color. ©2004.
ISBN: 0-534-61312-8.

Anthropologists use case studies primarily in undergraduate courses as core material for introductory courses or as supplemental books for textbooks in core introductory courses, as well as adjunct texts in specialized upper-division courses. The classic *Case Studies In Cultural Anthropology* series edited by George Spindler is geared to the sophomore level. Helweg's case study is an undergraduate-level cultural ethnography that focuses on Asian Indians in the United States. Courses for the book include:

- Cultural Anthropology
- General Anthropology
- Peoples of the World
- Peoples of North America
- Specialty courses on immigration, ethnicity, ethnic relations, multiculturalism, globalization, and transnationalism.

This text is a case study about Asian Indians in the United States. Almost unheard of three decades ago and almost nonexistent in the United States in the 1970s, this community is, on the average, the highest educated and claims the highest average family income of any ethnic community in North America. They are part of and representative of the new kind of immigrant coming to America. This text delves into the subject of immigration by focusing on how the immigration of highly educated and professionally trained migrants, which began in the late 1960s/early 1970s, differs from and challenges the traditional concepts of migration studies. The case study takes a transnational perspective and discusses the role of globalization and the current world system to form a more comprehensive study than those studies that have dominated migration studies and anthropology to date.

KEY FEATURES

- By writing in the first person and avoiding jargon, the author makes the subject of immigration and issues of multiculturalism accessible to students and easy to read and understand.
- The book is written from the perspective of the Asian Indians. It uses quotes and life experiences to enhance discussion of issues and situations for better understanding.
- The book is holistic in perspective. The sending, receiving, immigrant, and relevant diasporic communities are all presented in the narrative and the separate communities are treated together as a unit of analysis.
- The narrative considers the globalization, transnationalism, and world system factors that impact migration.
- By tracing the history of migration, the author provides a framework for understanding the people being studied.

CONTENTS

LIFE IN RIVERFRONT: A MIDDLE WESTERN TOWN SEEN THROUGH JAPANESE EYES

MARIKO FUJITA SANO, Hiroshima University and **TOSHIYUKI SANO,** Nara's Women's University

192 pages. Paperbound. ©2001. **ISBN: 0-15-506421-5.**

Life in Riverfront is a unique case study that offers a fresh approach to ethnography because it looks at American culture as seen through the eyes of Japanese anthropologists. Every cultural anthropology student is introduced to papers on the "Nacirema," a very foreign culture with many daily rituals and a fanaticism for cleanliness, especially as they prepare themselves for work in the morning. In truth, the "Nacirema" is American (spelled backwards), and the lessons learned from seeing one's own culture through the eyes of a 'stranger' illuminate the notion of ethnocentrism in a powerful way. While a major task of anthropology is to make the strange familiar and the exotic or enigmatic understandable, another task is to make the familiar strange so that one can see one's own culture in a new light. This case study accomplishes this and more.

KEY FEATURES

- Informants speak for themselves throughout the book and the authors never lose their interpretive voice, heard throughout as they react to the tales and life histories presented with a constant dialogue between their culture and our own.
- The authors spent four years in middle-America, where they studied the social structure and day-to-day lives of people in a predominately white community in Central Wisconsin. The authors use life histories and 'critical tales' as tools to analyze the cultural assumptions embedded in people's day-to-day lives.
- The authors depict various political disputes attributed to differing religious backgrounds to demonstrate the interconnectedness of various social domains in day-to-day lives, while they also look at individual life stages and gender differences that affect the process of socialization and enculturation.

CONTENTS

SHADOWED LIVES: UNDOCUMENTED IMMIGRANTS IN AMERICAN SOCIETY

Second Edition

LEO R. CHAVEZ, University of California, Irvine

224 pages. Paperbound. ©1998. **ISBN: 0-15-508089-X.**

One of the few case studies of undocumented immigrants available, this insightful anthropological analysis humanizes a group of people too often reduced to statistics and stereotypes. The hardships of Hispanic migration are conveyed in the immigrants' own voices while the author's voice raises questions about power, stereotypes, settlement, and incorporation into American society.

KEY FEATURES

- A section on the history of Mexican migration to the U.S. provides crucial information needed to fully understand contemporary immigration issues and events.
- An updated epilogue contains information on California's Proposition 187 and the new welfare and immigration laws that target immigrants, as well as a look at Operation Gatekeeper on the U.S.-Mexican border and the continued destruction of migrant camps.

TEXTCHOICE Exclusively from TextChoice

PERSONAS MEXICANAS: CHICANO HIGHSCHOOLERS IN A CHANGING LOS ANGELES

JAMES DIEGO VIGIL, The Center for the Study of Urban Poverty, University of California, Los Angeles

208 pages. Paperbound. ©1997. **ISBN: 0-15-503838-9.**

Vigil's impressive case study explores the real-life situations of both suburban and urban Mexican American high school students in 1974 and 1988. The author approaches the study qualitatively so the reader can better understand the subjects, but he also uses a quantitative approach for essential background information.

TEXTCHOICE Exclusively from TextChoice

THE HUTTERITES IN NORTH AMERICA

Fourth Edition

JOHN A. HOSTETLER, Emeritus, Temple University and **GERTRUDE ENDERS HUNTINGTON,** University of Michigan, Ann Arbor

178 pages. Paperbound. ©1996. **ISBN: 0-534-44033-9.**

This case study in cultural anthropology focuses on the day-to-day living patterns of the Hutterites, a German-dialect-speaking Christian sect whose members live communally in the Great Plains of the United States and Canada. The authors describe the Hutterite belief system and how it minimizes aggression and dissention, and protects the members against the outside world.

TEXTCHOICE Exclusively from TextChoice

THE MI'KMAQ: RESISTANCE, ACCOMMODATION, AND CULTURAL SURVIVAL

HARALD E.L. PRINS, Kansas State University,

250 pages. Paperbound. ©1996. **ISBN: 0-03-053427-5.**

Appropriate for courses in North American Indians, American ethnic studies, or introduction to anthropology.

Chronicled here are 500 years of the complex dynamics of Mi'kmaq culture. This text explores the group as a tribal nation—their ordeals in the face of colonialism and their current struggle for self-determination and cultural revitalization.

TEXTCHOICE Exclusively from TextChoice

THE OJIBWA OF BERENS RIVER, MANITOBA: ETHNOGRAPHY INTO HISTORY

A. IRVING HALLOWELL and **JENNIFER S. H. BROWN,** University of Winnipeg

148 pages. Paperbound. ©1992. **ISBN: 0-03-055122-6.**

This case study conveys the essential qualities and patterns of Ojibwa culture. Having spent many years visiting the Berens River Ojibwa communities in Manitoba and northwestern Ontario, Hallowell's finished draft of an ethnography was lost en route to the series editors in 1967—this edition is a revival, heavily edited by Brown, that allows Hallowell's remarkable experiences and insights to finally be shared.

TEXTCHOICE Exclusively from TextChoice

AMISH CHILDREN: EDUCATION IN THE FAMILY, SCHOOL, AND COMMUNITY

Second Edition

JOHN A. HOSTETLER and **GERTRUDE E. HUNTINGTON**

127 pages. Paperbound. ©1992. **ISBN: 0-03-031592-1.**

This case study describes a way of life where families are still stable, people live with a high sense of communal obligation, men and women work with their hands, one hears the clop of horse's hooves rather than the whine of tires, and the school and community are joined. The Old Order Amish schools are taught by teachers who have no more than an eighth grade education, and yet they are doing a good job of teaching the "basics" since Amish children meet state standards in academic performance.

TEXTCHOICE Exclusively from TextChoice

THE INUPIAT AND ARCTIC ALASKA: AN ETHNOGRAPHY OF DEVELOPMENT

NORMAN A. CHANCE, University of Connecticut

241 pages. Paperbound. ©1990. **ISBN: 0-534-44159-9.**

This exciting case study traces accurately the history of the Inupiat Eskimo of Alaska from pre-contact times to the present. Ancient treks and family life are vividly described, while the impact of petroleum and the "Ideology of Progress" are discussed in detail.

THE HURON: FARMERS OF THE NORTH

Second Edition

BRUCE G. TRIGGER, McGill University, Montreal

164 pages. Paperbound. ©1990. **ISBN: 0-03-031689-8.**

This remarkable reconstruction of the sedentary, agricultural, but warlike life of the Huron underscores the importance of studying Huron life, since the Huron were wiped out by other Iroquoians in the 17th Century.

TEXTCHOICE Exclusively from TextChoice

THE GHOST DANCE: ETHNOHISTORY AND REVITALIZATION

ALICE BECK KEHOE, Marquette University

155 pages. Paperbound. ©1989. **ISBN: 0-03-002852-3.**

This classic story of the 1890 Ghost Dance religion and the Wounded Knee Massacre is told in an ethnohistorical context. Comparative chapters describe Black Elk and Sioux religion, the Iroquois Handsome Lake religion, and Navajo Peyotism. The book also discusses theories on several historic American Indian movements.

TEXTCHOICE Exclusively from TextChoice

CHINATOWN: ECONOMIC ADAPTATION AND ETHNIC IDENTITY OF THE CHINESE

BERNARD P. WONG

160 pages. Paperbound. ©1982. **ISBN: 0-534-97137-7.**

This case study analyzes the structural adaptations that Chinese American communities in general, and the New York Chinatown in particular, have made to survive in American society.

TEXTCHOICE Exclusively from TextChoice

LAKOTA OF THE ROSEBUD: A CONTEMPORARY ADAPTATION

ELIZABETH GROBSMITH, University of Nebraska, Lincoln

160 pages. Paperbound. ©1981. **ISBN: 0-03-057438-2.**

This study of the Rosebud Sioux tribe of South Dakota explores the way they meet the challenges of living in the 20th century. They do so by expressing religion and beliefs in a cultural style that mixes native tradition and Christian influence with western technology.

TEXTCHOICE Exclusively from TextChoice

ALEUTS: SURVIVORS OF THE BERING LAND BRIDGE

WILLIAM S. LAUGHLIN, University of Connecticut

151 pages. Paperbound. ©1981. **ISBN: 0-534-9711-99.**

This unusual case study integrates vital data and interpretations to give a complete historical picture of the Aleuts, who have lived for 9,000 years in a remote and inhospitable part of the earth, and whose ancestors are connected with the original human inhabitants of the New World.

TEXTCHOICE Exclusively from TextChoice

THE VICE LORDS: WARRIORS OF THE STREETS

Fieldwork Edition

LINCOLN KEISER, Weleyan University

116 pages. Paperbound. ©1979. **ISBN: 0-534-96931-3.**

This study of a Chicago street gang provides an insightful picture of gangs of similar age and composition operating in depressed areas and ghettos of large American cities.

THE CHEYENNES: INDIANS OF THE GREAT PLAINS

Second Edition

E. ADAMSON HOEBEL, Emeritus, University of Minnesota

137 pages. Paperbound. ©1978. **ISBN: 0-03-022686-4.**

This case study traces the Cheyenne Indians from their first contact with the French explorer LaSalle in 1680. The book then follows their exodus from Minnesota under pressure from the Sioux, Cel, and Ojibwa; their attempt to gain a foothold in eastern South Dakota and the middle Missouri River; and their final movement into the high western plains in the first half of the 19th century.

TEXTCHOICE **Exclusively from TextChoice**

THE URBAN POOR OF PUERTO RICO: A STUDY IN DEVELOPMENT AND INEQUALITY

HELEN ICKEN SAFA

116 pages. Paperbound. ©1974. **ISBN: 0-534-97191-1.**

A study in the shantytown of the San Juan metropolitan area in Puerto Rico that was built by landless agricultural laborers out of the materials at hand. This is not a study of the culture of poverty, though all the conditions of poverty are evident in the shantytown. Los Peloteros contains and nourishes a variety of life styles.

TEXTCHOICE **Exclusively from TextChoice**

HANO: THE TEWA INDIAN COMMUNITY IN ARIZONA

EDWARD P. DOZIER, University of Arizona

114 pages. Paperbound. ©1966. **ISBN: 0-03-075653-7.**

This case study provides a look at Pueblo life as well as the historical forces which shaped the Pueblo communities of today. The author analyzes the relationships of White, Tewa Indians, and Hopi Indians.

PACIFIC OCEANA

THROUGH THE EYE OF THE NEEDLE: A MĀORI ELDER REMEMBERS

MARY KATHARINE DUFFIÉ, University of California, Los Angeles/American Indian Studies Program

224 pages. Paperbound. ©2001. **ISBN: 0-15-506982-9.**

This is a unique ethnography that follows in the tradition of the highly successful book by Marjorie Shostak (*Nisa: The Life and Words of a !Kung Woman.*) Here, the voice of Heeni, a relative of the current Maori Queen, eloquently chronicles the history of the Maori of New Zealand and the adaptations they have made to survive as a group in the modern world.

KEY FEATURES

- The author spent approximately one year in Hamilton, New Zealand collecting the life history of Heeni Wharemaru, a Tainui Maori Elder. Dr. Duffié uses established anthropological methodology to present an edited autobiography of Heeni that clearly shows how the indigenous group retains its quintessential Maoriness at the same time as it forges new relationships with the dominant culture.
- The first half of the book chronicles the aristocratic aboriginal Maori culture, while the second half chronicles the rise of Heeni as a pillar in her community, through her role as deaconess in the Methodist church. The author provides appropriate sociocultural interpretation and the information necessary for the student of cultural anthropology to understand the Maori in their current situation.
- This case study includes the reflexive voice of the author in the text, addressing social change and adaptive processes in the language of the elder herself, making the narrative interesting and human—and therefore particularly useful as an instructional aid.

COLLABORATIONS AND CONFLICTS: A LEADER THROUGH TIME

ANDREW J. STRATHERN and **PAMELA J. STEWART,** both of University of Pittsburgh

176 pages. Paperbound. ©2000. **ISBN: 0-15-502147-8.**

This is a uniquely dramatic account of life in the Papua New Guinea Highlands as told by a well-known leader of the Kawelka people of Mount Hagen. Set into context with a contemporary introduction that discusses the usefulness of biography in anthropology, the case study presents the already well-known autobiography of Ongka, a leader who witnessed the arrival of the first outsiders to the Highlands of New Guinea in the 1930's. By using a life history approach, this ethnographic account serves as a lens through which the anthropology student can view the wider processes of conflict and change brought to the Kawelka people through contact with the outside world.

Capitalizing on the growing awareness of the importance of writing history from an anthropological viewpoint, the book packages Ongka's account in a way that facilitates its use in the teaching of experiential anthropology. The voices of other Kawelka people, including one of Ongka's married daughters, adds new dimensions to the already rich account.

KEY FEATURES

- Unique use of first-hand accounts of early contact with the outside world make concepts come alive.
- The book's lively narrative style appeals to students.
- Theoretical and analytical introduction contextualizes materials for the students.
- The inclusion of a new generation's voice makes text even more interesting for students.
- The book focuses on evolving culture changes brought on by contact with the outside world.

CONTENTS

GRAND VALLEY DANI: PEACEFUL WARRIORS

Third Edition

KARL G. HEIDER, University of South Carolina, Columbia

193 pages. Paperbound. ©1997. **ISBN: 0-15-505173-3.**

This case study examines an isolated tribe in Indonesia, West New Guinea, when tribe members were still using stone axes, bows, arrows, and spears, up to more present times spanning 34 years (1961–1995). The author's long engagement with the Dani results in a wide range of engaging topics as well as coverage of the ethical dilemma he faced as an anthropologist. One immediately acquires a sense of the limitations and strengths of the anthropologist's role in the field.

Heider's 1995 visit to the Dugnm Dani left him less optimistic about the future of the Dani than his 1988 visit. Indonesian Independence Day was celebrated during Heider's stay. The Dani presence was barely acknowledged, while the Indonesian presence was colorfully represented. The past mistakes of foreign occupation of indigenous territory, committed mostly by Western powers, now seem repeated by the Indonesian authorities.

LIVES ON THE LINE: WOMEN AND ECOLOGY ON A PACIFIC ATOLL

ALEXANDRA BREWIS, University of Auckland

85 pages. Paperbound. ©1996. **ISBN: 0-15-501969-4.**

Intended as a supplement to women's studies, human ecology, medical anthropology, or Pacific anthropology courses.

Lives on the Line examines women's issues in Butaritari, an equatorial Pacific atoll 15 kilometers long and a few hundred meters wide. This case study shows how the constraints of ecology and the contingencies of history weave through patterns of human activity on Butaritari Atoll.

TEXTCHOICE **Exclusively from TextChoice**

FROM LONGHOUSE TO VILLAGE: SAMO SOCIAL CHANGE

R. DANIEL SHAW, Fuller Theological Seminary

160 pages. Paperbound. ©1996. **ISBN: 0-15-502561-9.**

The depth of familiarity with Samo life is what gives this case study its special character. Thirty years of change are compactly but meaningfully described and discussed. The effects of population aggregation, from isolated longhouses to villages, are central to the whole process.

TEXTCHOICE **Exclusively from TextChoice**

THE WHITE MAN WILL EAT YOU: AN ANTHROPOLOGIST AMONG THE IMBONGGU OF NEW GUINEA

WILLIAM E. WORMSLEY, Emory University and Georgia State University

135 pages. Paperbound. ©1993. **ISBN: 0-534-44015-0.**

After spending years as an integral part of the Imbonggu community, Wormsley provides special insight into the lives of these people. In this fascinating narrative, readers learn about the Imbonggu's social structure, political process, leadership, social and economic exchange and obligations, bridewealth, religion and magic—as well as what it is like to be an anthropologist.

TEXTCHOICE **Exclusively from TextChoice**

SAMOAN VILLAGE: THEN AND NOW

Second Edition

LOWELL D. HOLMES and **ELLEN RHOADS HOLMES,** both Wichita State University

176 pages. Paperbound. ©1992. **ISBN: 0-534-97120-2.**

Samoan culture, though comparatively stable, is of course changing, and this case study focuses on the way the acceptance of Christianity brought about major changes within the culture. It also gives readers a working knowledge of the basic elements of traditional Samoan culture including subsistence, principles of rank, ceremonies, and the life cycle.

TEXTCHOICE **Exclusively from TextChoice**

SIMBU LAW: CONFLICT MANAGEMENT IN THE NEW GUINEA HIGHLANDS

AARON PODOLEFSKY

166 pages. Paperbound. ©1992. **ISBN: 0-534-97138-5.**

This case study focuses on the various ways conflicts and disputes are managed and ultimately resolved in the Chimbu province of Papua New Guinea.

TEXTCHOICE **Exclusively from TextChoice**

THE MARDU ABORIGINES: LIVING THE DREAM IN AUSTRALIA'S DESERT

Second Edition

ROBERT TONKINSON, University of Western Australia

204 pages. Paperbound. ©1991. **ISBN: 0-534-44087-8.**

Characterized by a simple technology and a complex socioreligious system, the Mardudjara have survived with much of their traditional culture intact. The Mardu culture challenges common assumptions about the relation between technology and progress. This edition describes changes as the Mardu adapt to social, economic, and political realities.

TEXTCHOICE **Exclusively from TextChoice**

SAMOAN PLANTERS: TRADITION AND ECONOMIC DEVELOPMENT IN POLYNESIA

TIM O'MEARA, University of North Carolina, Wilmington

266 pages. Paperbound. ©1990. **ISBN: 0-534-97111-3.**

Vignettes of villagers enliven this exploration into how traditional customs and values influence economic development among Samoan planters. Emphasis on research design and fieldwork combines with an intimate portrayal of a modern Polynesian nation in transition.

TEXTCHOICE **Exclusively from TextChoice**

THE TIWI OF NORTH AUSTRALIA

Third Edition

C.W. M. HART, late of Wayne State University,
ARNOLD R. PILLING, Wayne State University,
and **JANE C. GOODALE,** Bryn Mawr College

179 pages. Paperbound. ©1988. **ISBN: 0-03-012019-5.**

This examination of the colorful Tiwi culture from the late 1920s to the 1980s provides a broad picture of cultural change and modernization in a hunting and food gathering tribe. The first half focuses on marriage contracts and their relationships to other aspects of Tiwi social structure, and the second half examines the Tiwis' response to modern influences.

THE TROBRIANDERS OF PAPUA NEW GUINEA

ANNETTE B. WEINER, New York University

184 pages. Paperbound. ©1988. **ISBN: 0-03-011919-7.**

This re-examination of the Trobrianders of Papua New Guinea, the people described in Malinowski's classic ethnographic work of the early 20th century, provides a balanced view of the society from a male and female perspective, including coverage of new discoveries about the importance of woman's work and wealth in the society.

THE SAMBIA: RITUAL AND GENDER IN PAPUA NEW GUINEA

Second Edition

GILBERT HERDT, University of Chicago

227 pages. Paperbound. ©1987. **ISBN: 0-534-64383-3.**

This cultural and psychological study of gender identity and sexual development in a New Guinea Highlands society includes initiation rites and socialization studies, and contrasts the Sambia with other societies, including our own. Sambia boys experience ritualized homosexuality before puberty and do not leave it until marriage, after which homosexual activity is prohibited. The implications are developed cross-culturally and contextualized in gender literature.

TEXTCHOICE **Exclusively from TextChoice**

'ELOTA'S STORY: THE LIFE AND TIMES OF A SOLOMON ISLANDS BIG MAN

ROGER M. KEESING, The Australian National University

150 pages. Paperbound. ©1983. **ISBN: 0-534-97146-6.**

Keesing supplies a sketch of Kwaio culture, set in the time of 'Elota's life span, and has placed 'Elota's life in this cultural and temporal framework. The text is equally divided between Keesing's presentation of Kwaio culture and 'Elota's own statement, with only minor editing of the latter.

TEXTCHOICE **Exclusively from TextChoice**

THE KAPAUKU PAPUANS OF WEST NEW GUINEA

Second Edition

LEOPOLD POSPISIL, Yale University

142 pages. Paperbound. ©1978. **ISBN: 0-534-97155-5.**

This society, first studied by Pospisil when outside influences were just beginning in 1954-55, is characterized by a form of primitve capitalism, with well-developed trade, money, and legal systems. The Kapauku confront western preconceptions about the nature of "primitive" peoples, and Pospisil develops this theme throughout the text. A chapter on recent change is included.

WADSWORTH CASE STUDIES IN ANTHROPOLOGY & ARCHAEOLOGY PROGRAM

ETHNOGRAPHIES

NEW FOR 2005!

THE GHOSTS OF ICELAND

ROBERT ANDERSON, Mills College

320 pages. Paperbound. 6 x 9. 1-Color. ©2005.
ISBN: 0-534-61052-8.

This ethnography, uniquely set in contemporary Iceland, takes an in-depth look at the way supernatural beliefs and practices (long an important subject of anthropology) thrive as an "unnamed, unpretentious, and quiet, nearly silent, spiritual movement that impacts most of the population either directly or indirectly in deeply personal ways." The author lived and worked in Reykjavik, where friends, acquaintances, students, colleagues and spirit mediums talked with him about their experiences of being in contact with spirits of the dead, including deceased loved ones and spirit doctors. Anderson's book is a primary example of signature anthropology methodology, i.e., ethnographic fieldwork or participant observation. He spent time with spirit mediums, joined in group séances, observed and recorded conversations between the living and the dead, arranged for spirit doctors to treat sick friends, and attended lectures at spiritist schools, and coffee klatches of the 'spirit society.'

KEY FEATURES

- Anderson describes the religious culture of Iceland, a thoroughly Western society, using the same concepts and methods ethnographers have used to portray and interpret the practices of societies around the world.
- The ethnography demonstrates how a predominant state institutionalized religion co-exists with spiritsm, posing little or no conflict for individuals who draw from a 'cultural menu' grounded in Viking lore.
- A strong globalization theme runs throughout the book, as the author compares the modern spiritualism he encountered in Iceland to New Age beliefs and practices in upstate New York and England.
- The book is engaging and lively, providing great examples of the ways individuals interact within social institutions, and how religious groups organize socially and differentiate or imitate one another culturally.
- The author articulates a pragmatic basis for challenging or making sense of truth claims about the immortality of the soul and life after death, and communication with the dead.

CONTENTS

ETHNOGRAPHIC ESSAYS IN CULTURAL ANTHROPOLOGY: A PROBLEM-BASED APPROACH

R. BRUCE MORRISON, Athabasca University; and
C. RODERICK WILSON, University of Alberta

278 pages. Paperbound. ©2001. **ISBN: 0-87581-445-X.**

This collection of ten mini-ethnographies takes a problem-based learning approach, focusing on contextual and cumulative learning to enhance student understanding of the fundamental concepts of cultural anthropology. The problems covered in the text range from questions like how anthropology contributes to an understanding of human similarities and differences and why people believe different things, to inequality, violence, poverty, and death. Each problem is explored in the context of a particular society, including Canada, Ecuador, Indonesia, Kohistan, Tibet, Tonga, the United States, and Sudan.

KEY FEATURES

- Forty-six basic concepts from agricultural society to witchcraft are presented.
- *Ethnographic Essays in Cultural Anthropology* can be used alone or as a supplement to Richard H. Robbins' *Cultural Anthropology: A Problem-Based Approach,* Third Edition, or any cultural anthropology text.

CONTENTS

NEITHER MAN NOR WOMAN: THE HIJRAS OF INDIA

Second Edition

SERENA NANDA, John Jay College of Criminal Justice

208 pages. Paperbound. 6-3/8 x 9-1/4. 1-Color. ©1999.
ISBN: 0-534-50903-7.

This ethnography is a cultural study of the Hijras of India, a religious community of men who dress and act like women. It focuses on how Hijras can be used in the study of gender categories and human sexual variation.

KEY FEATURES

- Serena Nanda, a leading authority on the Hijra, provides access to an important body of knowledge and data on the Hijras of India.
- Explores the relation between gender roles and culture particularly in the relation of both to sexual variation.

ANCILLARIES

Bundle: Text + InfoTrac® College Edition
ISBN: 0-534-16463-3
See *Technology Solutions* section for details.

Researching Anthropology on the Internet, Second Edition
ISBN: 0-534-56793-2
By David L. Carlson. See *Technology Solutions* section for details.

CONTENTS

1. Hijra Roles in Indian Society. 2. Hijras as Neither Man nor Woman. 3. Emasculation Ritual Among the Hijras. 4. Social Organization and Economic Adaptation. 5. Kamladevi: A Prostitute. 6. Meera: A New Guru. 7. Sushila: Achieving Respect. 8. Salima: An Outcast. 9. Hijra Lives in Context. 10. The Hijra in Cross-Cultural Perspective.

Case Studies in Archaeology

WADSWORTH CASE STUDIES IN ANTHROPOLOGY & ARCHAEOLOGY PROGRAM

CASE STUDIES IN ARCHAEOLOGY

Jeffrey Quilter, Series Editor

ETLATONGO: SOCIAL COMPLEXITY, INTERACTION, AND VILLAGE LIFE IN THE MIXTECA ALTA OF OAXACA, MEXICO

JEFFREY P. BLOMSTER, Brandeis University

216 pages. Paperbound. 6-3/8 x 9-1/4. 1-Color. ©2004.
ISBN: 0-534-61281-4.

Anthropologists use case studies primarily in undergraduate courses as core material for introductory courses or as supplemental books for textbooks in core introductory courses, as well as adjunct texts in specialized upper-division courses. The *Case Studies in Archaeology* series, edited by Jeffrey Quilter, is geared to the sophomore level. Courses for Jeffrey Blomster's case study include:

- Introductory Archaeology
- General Anthropology
- Archaeological Fieldwork/Upper Division Field Methods
- History of South America/Mesoamerican Civilizations
- World Prehistory/World Civilizations/Archaeology of Mesoamerica

This case study examines the rise of social complexity and the impact of interregional interaction at the village of Etlatongo, in the Mixteca Alta of Oaxaca. A broad perspective is taken, examining relations with other contemporaneous parts of Mesoamerica, including the Gulf Coast Olmec culture. Methods utilized are examined and critiqued. Innovative approaches to examining interregional interaction are employed, such as neutron activation analysis of fragments of ceramic vessels. Houses and how people lived and died are explored, as is growth of parts of the village through time. The book does not just report what the author did, but why he did it.

KEY FEATURES

- This text discusses innovative approaches in archaeological methods and fieldwork.
- The methods employed in the study are clearly explained and rationalized.
- The text addresses fundamental issues of social complexity as well as relevant theories.
- The author provides an overview of a rarely studied part of ancient Mexico.
- The author's engaging writing style keeps the student interested.
- Key terms are defined, explained and clarified throughoutthe text.

CONTENTS

TROPICAL FOREST ARCHAEOLOGY IN WESTERN PICHINCHA, ECUADOR

RONALD D. LIPPI, University of Wisconsin, Marathon County

168 pages. Paperbound. 6-3/8 x 9-1/4. 1-Color. ©2004.
ISBN: 0-534-61294-6.

Anthropologists use case studies primarily in undergraduate courses as core material for introductory courses or as supplemental books for textbooks in core introductory courses, as well as adjunct texts in specialized upper-division courses. The *Case Studies in Archaeology* series, edited by Jeffrey Quilter, is geared to the sophomore level. Courses for Ron Lippi's case study include:

- Introductory Archaeology
- General Anthropology
- Upper Division Field Methods
- History of South America
- World Prehistory/Archaeology of South America

This case study uniquely covers a tropical forest area in Ecuador. It combines a discussion of the travails of conducting archaeology in the tropical forest and the results of extensive research. Of particular interest are the strategies employed for site survey.

It also explores how present-day descendents of prehistoric peoples and archaeologists can work together to solve environmental problems. This kind of cooperative research promises to bring insight for the future from the two groups that have the greatest personal stake in understanding the ancient past.

KEY FEATURES

- This is the first case study to present specific research methods of doing tropical forest archaeology.
- The text presents an excellent example of cooperative research, i.e. research from the archaeologists as well as from the local descendents of the prehistoric peoples.

- The text discusses how and why people exploited the natural environment and the mistakes that they made and the lessons they have learned.
- The author's engaging style promises to draw students into this captivating study.
- This study can also be used in environmental courses.

CONTENTS

PLANTS AND PEOPLE IN ANCIENT ECUADOR: THE ETHNOBOTANY OF THE JAMA RIVER VALLEY

DEBORAH M. PEARSALL, University of Missouri

200 pages. Paperbound. 6-3/8 x 9-1/4. 1-Color. ©2004.
ISBN: 0-534-61321-7.

Anthropologists use case studies primarily in undergraduate courses as core material for introductory courses or as supplemental books for textbooks in core introductory courses, as well as adjunct texts in specialized upper-division courses. The *Case Studies in Archaeology* series, edited by Jeffrey Quilter, is geared to the sophomore level. Deborah Pearsall's case study focuses on prehistoric ethnobotany and is accessible in style and content to undergraduate students and beginning graduate students. Courses for the book include:

- Introductory Archaeology
- General Anthropology
- Ethnobotany
- Archaeological Methods (Ethnobotany/Archaeobotany)
- Peoples of South America
- World Prehistory/Archaeology of South America

This case study illustrates the contemporary archaeological field of ethnobotany, and explores the interrelationships between the prehistoric residents of a small valley in coastal Ecuador and the dry tropical forest habitat in which they lived. The work has three related objectives: 1. it is an ethnobotany—a work that explores how, through the medium of culture, people shape and are shaped by the environment in which they live, 2. it is a work that synthesizes results of some 10 years of research done by Pearsall during the Jama Archaeological-Paleoethnobotanical project, and 3. it is a work that provides Pearsall with the opportunity to illustrate paleoethnobotanical research methods, an important component of contemporary interdisciplinary archaeology.

Pearsall took as her subject the 3,600-year-old archaeological record of the Jama River valley in northern Manabi, Ecuador, and she determined what plants people selected for food, fuel, building materials, and ritual; evaluated the impact of agricultural activities on the tropical forest environment; and examined the response of populations to volcanic ash fall disasters. Broken into four parts, this case study starts with an introduction to the field of ethnobotany, then goes on to describe Pearsall's experiences doing field work in the Jama River Valley and the results of her research, and concludes with an illustration of how ethnobotany fits into and contributes to archaeology.

KEY FEATURES

- This book is the first to cover ethnobotany in an Archaeology series.
- Over 70 detailed photographs will engage the student.
- The four part organization allows the reader to follow the study from introduction to conclusion of how ethnobotany contributes to archaeology.

CONTENTS

COPÁN: THE RISE AND FALL OF AN ANCIENT MAYA KINGDOM

DAVID L. WEBSTER, Pennsylvania State University; **ANN CORINNE FRETER,** Ohio University; **NANCY GONLIN,** Bellvue Community College

256 pages. Paperbound. ©2000. **ISBN: 0-15-505808-8.**

Webster's case study reconstructs and evaluates the sociopolitical system and culture history of a world-famous Classic Maya Center in the highlands of Western Honduras, whose great temples, palaces, and carved monuments have been investigated since the 1830s. Using material from a series of archaeological excavations begun in 1975 that focused on reconstructing the entire Copán Kingdom, this book presents for the first time an interpretation of the political, demographic, and agricultural history of the entire region. Providing an extensive review of the methods used to reconstruct Copán's history, the book helps students develop a basic understanding of how archaeologists reconstruct ancient social systems.

KEY FEATURES

- This summary of the largest Maya settlement project conducted is a classic topic and an ideal reference point for all anthropology students.
- The case study provides the most current information available on Copán.
- The case study emphasizes two main themes: 1) the research projects and methods that the authors and colleagues used to reconstruct the growth and decline of a major Maya polity, and 2) the specific reconstructed events and culture history derived from this research. The text gives detailed explanations of what the authors know and why they think they know what they do.
- A methodological focus exposes students to a wide array of archaeological methods and directly explores their applications.
- The Copán case study illustrates first-hand how science applies to archaeology. It contains a strong presentation of archaeological methods and theory and instructs students how to apply those methods to test hypotheses.
- Original photographs and maps provide visual explanations of the topics described by authors.
- End-of-chapter summaries highlight the main points of the chapter and re-focus students on the most relevant information covered.

CONTENTS

TEXTCHOICE **Exclusively from TextChoice**

THE PITHOUSES OF KEATLEY CREEK

BRIAN HAYDEN, Simon Fraser University and **JEFFREY QUILTER,** Series Editor

112 pages. Paperbound. ©1997. **ISBN: 0-15-503837-0.**

Brian Hayden's archaeological case study addresses the development of prehistoric and social and economic hierarchies. This archaeology project encompasses a fascinating range of topics making it an ideal case study for all students of archaeology. It also includes a vivid reconstruction of life in one of the largest and most complex Platean communities.

KEY FEATURES

- The text discusses the validity of using a wide variety of data such as stone tools, food remains, and plant remains to provide a coherent picture of cultural complexity.
- The book presents a vivid reconstruction of past life, which helps students understand how data fit together.
- Students are introduced to a wide variety of archaeological techniques such as how population sizes can be estimated.
- The author examines how site formation processes can be established and how site features can reveal information about social organization.

CONTENTS

TEXTCHOICE **Exclusively from TextChoice**

LAMBERT FARM: PUBLIC ARCHAEOLOGY AND CANINE BURIALS ALONG NARRAGANSETT BAY

JORDAN E. KERBER, Colgate University

136 pages. Paperbound. ©1997. **ISBN: 0-15-505190-3.**

The discussion of Kerber's trials, tribulations, and ultimate success in investigating the Lambert Farm site captures what real life archaeology in modern day times is like. This particular case study provides a fascinating review of the evidence for dogs in New World archaeology and prehistoric culture.

PURISIMENO CHUMASH PREHISTORY: MARITIME ADAPTATIONS ALONG THE SOUTHERN CALIFORNIA COAST

MICHAEL A. GLASSOW, University of California, Santa Barbara

180 pages. Paperbound. ©1996. **ISBN: 0-15-503084-1.**

This is the only case study available that focuses on the practice of archaeology in California, prehistory coastal adaptations, and cultural resource management. Unique coverage of the Vandenburg region and Santa Barbara Channel not only introduces students to regional archaeology but also allows them to observe the impact of environmental variations on cultural development. Examples included in the study reinforce relationships between fieldwork, data generation and processing, analysis, and interpretation.

AWATIMARKA: THE ETHNOARCHAELOLOGY OF AN ANDEAN HERDING COMMUNITY

LAWRENCE A. KUZNAR, Indiana University

141 pages. Paperbound. ©1995. **ISBN: 0-15-501528-1.**

This study discusses the use of analogy in archaeology. It examines the practices of modern goat herders in the southern Andes as a means of understanding ancient human and animal behavior at the prehistoric site of Asana. It consolidates and synthesizes 20 years of ethnoarchaeological research in pastoral societies and provides guidelines for interpreting site occupation span and raw material use in pastoral sites.

TEXTCHOICE **Exclusively from TextChoice**

TOWARD A SOCIAL HISTORY OF ARCHAEOLOGY IN THE UNITED STATES

THOMAS C. PATTERSON

191 pages. Paperbound. ©1995. **ISBN: 0-15-500824-2.**

This case study focuses on the forces influencing archaeological intellectual history and the relationship of history to anthropology and scholarship in general within the United States.

TEXTCHOICE **Exclusively from TextChoice**

KHOK PHANOM DI: PREHISTORIC ADAPTATION TO THE WORLD'S RICHEST HABITAT

CHARLES HIGHAM, University of Otago, Dunedin New Zealand, and **RACHANIE THOSARAT,** Thai Fine Arts Departmetn, Bangkok, Thailand

169 pages. Paperbound. ©1994. **ISBN: 0-15-500951-6.**

For the purposes of providing students with an example of how archaeology is done and to what ends, no better example can be found than this account of work conducted in Thailand. The extensive coverage of everything from the initial discovery of the site, to seeking funding, to the final analyses of materials provides ample material for class discussions and lectures.

TEXTCHOICE **Exclusively from TextChoice**

THE CEREN SITE: A PREHISTORIC VILLAGE BURIED BY VOLCANIC ASH IN CENTRAL AMERICA

PAYSON D. SHEETS, University of Colorado, Boulder

172 pages. Paperbound. ©1992. **ISBN: 0-15-567450-1.**

The richness of the archaeological record at Ceren is truly astounding and provides professionals, students, and laymen alike with a more detailed view of the Mayan past. It offers readers previously unavailable knowledge of everyday life by examining the belongings of the common class—pots, tools, food items, and agricultural crops. Sheets also discusses his personal trials and triumphs to give a more human dimension to work in the field.

Cultural Anthropology Case Studies by Topic

Looking for Case Studies to Complement a Thematic Approach?
Bundle a case study with a textbook at a discount or bundle multiple case studies together also at a discount.

Author/Title/ISBN	Page Number	Exclusively from TextChoice	Culture Change/Continuity	Gender/Sexuality	Religion/Spirituality	Environmental/Ecological Issues	Native Americans	Social Organizations/Social Systems	Social Issues	Subsistence/Economic Development	Immigrants/Immigration	Health/Medical Anthropology	Linguistics	Politics/Policy/Law
Baker: **A Sinhalese Village in Sri Lanka: Coping with Uncertainty**, ISBN 0-15-505176-8	9				●							●		
Barker: **Bravo for the Marshallese: Regaining Control in a Post-Nuclear, Post-Colonial World**, ISBN: 0-534-61326-8	3					●			●				●	
Beals: **Gopalpur: A South Indian Village**, ISBN 0-03-045371-2	10	■	●					●						
Beattie: **Bunyoro: An African Kingdom**, ISBN 0-534-97128-8	9	■			●			●						
Berdan: **The Aztecs of Central Mexico: An Imperial Society, 2e**, ISBN 0-534-62728-5	10				●					●				
Bishop: **Himalayan Herders**, ISBN 0-534-44060-6	9	■	●			●				●				
Brewis: **Lives on the Line: Women and Ecology on a Pacific Atoll**, ISBN 0-15-501969-4	20			●		●								
Brogger: **Nazare: Women and Men in a Prebureaucratic Portuguese Fishing Village**, ISBN 0-03-043382-7	14	■		●										
Chagnon: **The Yanomamö, 5e**, ISBN 0-15-505327-2	13								●					●
Chance: **China's Urban Villagers: Changing Life in a Beijing Suburb, 2e**, ISBN 0-534-97156-3	9	■	●					●		●				●
Chance: **The Inupiat and Arctic Alaska: An Ethnography of Development**, ISBN 0-534-44159-9	18	■	●					●		●				●
Chavez: **Shadowed Lives: Undocumented Immigrants in American Society, 2e**, ISBN 0-15-508089-X	17		●								●			
Chinas: **The Isthnus Zapotecs: A Matrifocal Culture of Mexico**, ISBN 0-03-055057-2	13	■	●	●				●		●				
Crocker/Crocker: **The Canela: Kinship, Ritual, and Sex in an Amazonian Tribe, 2e**, ISBN 0-534-17491-4	11			●				●						
Darian-Smith: **New Capitalists: Issues of Law, Politics, and Identity Surrounding Casino Gaming on Native American Land**, ISBN 0-534-61308-X	5						●		●					●
Dozier: **Hano: The Tewa Indian Community in Arizona**, ISBN 0-03-075653-7	19	■	●				●							
Duffié: **Through the Eye of the Needle: A Maori Elder Remembers**, ISBN 0-15-506982-9	19		●		●									
Finkelstein: **With No Direction Home: Homeless Youth on the Road and in the Streets**, ISBN 0-534-62649-1	2			●					●					
Friedl: **Vasilika: A Village in Modern Greece**, ISBN 0-534-97165-2	15	■						●		●				
Galt: **Town and Country in Locorotondo**, ISBN 0-03-073327-8	15	■	●					●						
Gibson: **Skin & Bones: The Management of People and Natural Resources in Shellcracker Haven, FL**, ISBN 0-15-508476-3	15					●			●	●				
Gladney: **Ethnic Identity in China: The Making of a Muslim Minority Nationality**, ISBN 0-15-501970-8	9	■			●									●
Goldschmidt: **The Sebei: A Study in Adaptation**, ISBN 0-534-97147-4	8	■	●		●			●		●				

Looking for Case Studies to Complement a Thematic Approach?
Bundle a case study with a textbook at a discount or bundle multiple case studies together also at a discount.

Author/Title/ISBN	Page Number	Exclusively from TextChoice	Culture Change/Continuity	Gender/Sexuality	Religion/Spirituality	Environmental/Ecological Issues	Native Americans	Social Organizations/Social Systems	Social Issues	Subsistence/Economic Development	Immigrants/Immigration	Health/Medical Anthropology	Linguistics	Politics/Policy/Law
Grobsmith: **Lakota of the Rosebud: A Contemporary Adaptation**, ISBN 0-03-057438-2	18	■	●		●		●						●	
Hallowell/Brown: **The Ojibwa of Berens River, Manitoba: Ethnography into History**, ISBN 0-03-055122-6	17	■	●		●			●						
Hart/Pilling/Goodale: **The Tiwi of North Australia, 3e**, ISBN 0-03-012019-5	21	■	●					●						●
Heider: **Grand Valley Dani: Peaceful Warriors, 3e**, ISBN 0-15-505173-3	20		●					●						
Helweg: **Strangers in a Not-So-Strange-Land: Indian Americans in the Global Age**, ISBN 0-534-61312-8	16		●								●			
Herdt: **The Sambia: Ritual and Gender in Papua New Guinea, 2e**, ISBN 0-534-64383-3	21			●					●					
Hitchcock: **A Mountain Village in Nepal**, ISBN 0-534-97173-3	10	■	●					●						
Hoebel: **The Cheyennes: Indians of the Great Plains, 2e**, ISBN 0-03-022686-4	18						●		●					
Holmes/Holmes: **Samoan Village: Then and Now, 2e**, ISBN 0-534-97120-2	20	■	●					●		●				
Hostetler/Huntington: **Amish Children: Education in the Family, School, and Community, 2e**, ISBN 0-03-031592-1	18	■	●					●						
Hostetler/Huntington: **The Hutterites in North America, 4e**, ISBN 0-534-44033-9	17	■	●					●		●				
Hull: **Katun: A Twenty Year Journey with the Maya**, ISBN 0-534-61290-3	11		●							●				
Igoe: **Conservation & Globalization: A Study of National Parks and Indigenous Communities from East Africa to South Dakota**, ISBN 0-534-61317-9	4					●								
Keesing: **'Elota's Story: The Life and Times of a Solomon Islands Big Man**, ISBN 0-534-97146-6	21	■	●											
Kehoe: **The Ghost Dance: Ethnohistory and Revitalization**, ISBN 0-03-002852-3	18	■			●		●							
Keiser: **Friend by Day, Enemy by Night: Organized Vengeance in a Kohistani Community**, ISBN 0-03-053332-5	10	■			●			●	●	●				●
Keiser: **The Vice Lords: Warriors of the Street**, ISBN 0-534-96931-3	18	■						●						
Kintz: **Life Under the Tropical Canopy: Tradition and Change Among the Yucatec Maya**, ISBN 0-03-032592-7	13	■	●											
Krause: **A Crisis of Births: Population Politics and Family-Making in Italy**, ISBN 0-534-63693-4	2			●					●					●
Kuper: **The Swazi: A South African Kingdom, 2e**, ISBN 0-03-070239-9	8	■	●					●						●
Lansing: **The Balinese**, ISBN 0-15-500240-6	9		●			●								
Laughlin: **Aleuts: Survivors of the Bering Land Bridge**, ISBN 0-534-97119-9	18	■	●			●		●						
Lee: **The Dobe Ju/'Hoansi, 3e**, ISBN 0-15-506333-2	7							●	●	●				
Lundgren: **Watch and Pray: A Portrait of Fante Village Life in Transition**, ISBN 0-15-505933-5	7		●					●						
Middleton: **The Lugbara of Uganda, 2e**, ISBN 0-534-96895-3	8	■	●		●			●						
Nanda: **Neither Man Nor Woman: The Hijras of India, 2e**, ISBN 0-534-50903-7	22			●										
O'Meara: **Samoan Planters: Tradition and Economic Development in Polynesia**, ISBN 0-534-97111-3	21	■						●		●				

Looking for Case Studies to Complement a Thematic Approach?
Bundle a case study with a textbook at a discount or bundle multiple case studies together also at a discount.

Author/Title/ISBN	Page Number	Exclusively from TextChoice	Culture Change/Continuity	Gender/Sexuality	Religion/Spirituality	Environmental/Ecological Issues	Native Americans	Social Organizations/Social Systems	Social Issues	Subsistence/Economic Development	Immigrants/Immigration	Health/Medical Anthropology	Linguistics	Politics/Policy/Law
Parman: **Scottish Crofters: A Historical Ethnography of a Celtic Village, 2e,** ISBN 0-534-63324-2	14				●			●		●				
Podolefsk: **Simbu Law: Conflict Management in the New Guinea Highlands,** ISBN 0-534-97138-5	20	■						●						●
Pospisil: **The Kapauku Papuans of West New Guinea, 2e,** ISBN 0-534-97155-5	21	■	●					●						●
Prins: **The Mi'kmaq: Resistance, Accomodation, and Cultural Survival,** ISBN 0-03-053427-5	17	■	●					●						
Quinlan: **From the Bush: The Front Line of Health Care in a Caribbean Village,** ISBN 0-15-508567-0	12				●				●			●		
Robarchek/Robarchek: **Waorani: The Contexts of Violence and War,** ISBN 0-534-44006-1	12	■	●					●	●					
Safa: **The Urban Poor of Puerto Rico: A Study in Development and Inequality,** ISBN 0-534-97191-1	19	■	●							●				
Sano/Sano: **Life in Riverfront: A Middle Western Town Seen Through Japanese Eyes,** ISBN 0-15-506421-5	16			●				●						
Shaw: **From Longhouse to Village: Samo Social Change,** ISBN 0-15-502561-9	20	■	●		●			●		●			●	
Stearman: **Yuqui: Forest Nomads in a Changing World,** ISBN 0-534-97074-5	14	■	●					●		●				
Strathern/Stewart: **Collaborations and Conflict: A Leader Through Time,** ISBN 0-15-502147-8	19		●						●					
Stull/Broadway: **Slaugherhouse Blues: The Meat and Poultry Industry in North America,** ISBN 0-534-61303-9	5					●			●	●				
Suggs: **A Bagful of Locusts and the Baboon Woman: Constructions of Gender, Change, and Continuity in Botswana,** ISBN 0-15-507038-X	8		●	●										
Tonkinson: **The Mardu Aborigines: Living the Dream in Australia's Desert, 2e,** ISBN 0-534-44087-8	20	■	●		●	●		●						
Trigger: **The Huron: Farmers of the North, 2e,** ISBN 0-03-031689-8	18						●			●				
Turnbull: **The Mbuti Pygmies: Change and Adaptation,** ISBN 0-03-061537-2	8	■	●											●
Uchendu: **The Igbo of Southeast Nigeria,** ISBN 0-03-052475-X	9	■	●					●	●					
Vigil: **Personas Mexicanas: Chicano Highschoolers in a Changing Los Angeles,** ISBN 0-15-503838-9	17	■	●					●						
Vogt: **The Zinacantecos of Mexico: A Modern Maya Way of Life, 2e,** ISBN 0-03-033344-X	13	■	●		●			●		●				
Weiner: **The Trobrianders of Papua New Guinea,** ISBN 0-03-011919-7	21			●				●						
Wong: **Chinatown: Economic Adaptation and Ethnic Identity of the Chinese,** ISBN 0-534-97137-7	18	■	●							●				
Wormsley: **The White Man Will Eat You: An Anthropoligist Among the Imbonggu of New Guinea,** ISBN 0-534-44015-0	20	■	●	●										
Young: **The Rashaayda Bedouin: Arab Pastoralists of Eastern Sudan,** ISBN 0-15-501513-3	8	■		●				●		●				

Author Index

Author Index

Appendix B

InfoTrac College Edition User Guide

InfoTrac College Edition
User Guide
for the Instructor

Contents of the Appendix:

INTRODUCTION

InfoTrac College Edition, a complete Online Research and Learning Center, contains over 10 million full-text articles from nearly 5,000 scholarly and popular periodicals. Covering a broad spectrum of disciplines and topics, this online library is ideal for every type of research. *InfoTrac College Edition*'s articles are updated daily and include research dating back to 1980. In addition to the database, *InfoTrac College Edition* offers InfoWrite, a web-based training tool designed to help develop writing skills. InfoWrite assists students through difficult areas of research writing, such as choosing a topic, composing introductions and conclusions, and crediting sources.

24 Hours a Day

InfoTrac College Edition is accessible 24 hours-a-day, 7 days-a-week from any computer with Internet access. A free 4-month subscription to *InfoTrac College Edition* can be bundled with any Thomson text. Students will not only find an online library, but also online resources with information on financial aid, time management, and exam preparation.

Use it as Part of Your Course

InfoTrac College Edition also does something for you, the instructor. It gives you the flexibility to require outside readings without creating a separate printed reader, something students will appreciate. *InfoTrac College Edition* can be integrated into your course by using the articles to prepare lectures and assignments, or to ignite classroom discussions.

QUICK TIPS FOR THE CLASSROOM

InfoTrac College Edition is an excellent tool to introduce students to researching subjects. You can use it to prepare lectures and outside assignments or to build a reader from the database for your discipline. Students will appreciate the ease of online research, especially when writing papers, preparing class presentations, or researching a key topic. Below are some suggestions on how to incorporate *InfoTrac College Edition in* your classroom.

Writing Assignments

- Provide a topic to your students to research in *InfoTrac College Edition*. Instruct them to choose an article to write a thesis on and construct an outline for.
- Point students to *InfoTrac College Edition* as an excellent reference and information source when preparing their term papers.

Study Questions

- Prepare a list of study questions on a lecture topic and have the students research and answer them using *InfoTrac College Edition*.
- Many Thomson texts include end-of chapter questions. Have your students explore answers using the database.

Reading Assignments

- Select specific articles and assign them to your students for further reading.
- Utilizing the Critical Thinking section in InfoWrite, instruct students to choose an article and evaluate the facts and arguments in that article.

Classroom Activities

- Divide the classroom into groups and provide them with a topic to research and discuss for the next class. Have each group present their discoveries and summary of that topic.
- Set up classroom debates by providing a subject and assigning students to research a pro or con stance to discuss in class.

GETTING STARTED

Registration

Go to www.infotrac-college.com

Step 1

Click on Register New Account.

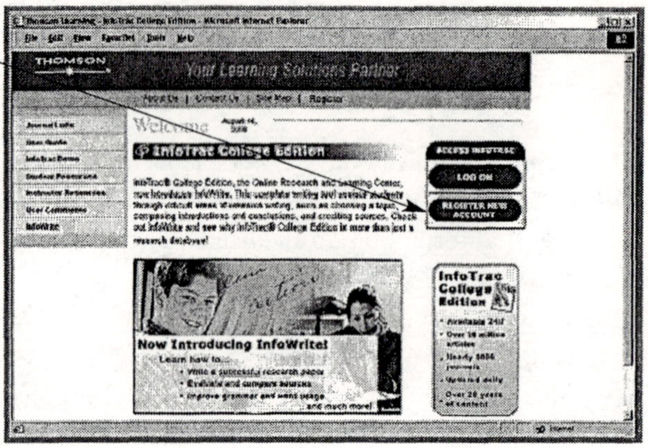

Step 2

Enter passcode and create a username.

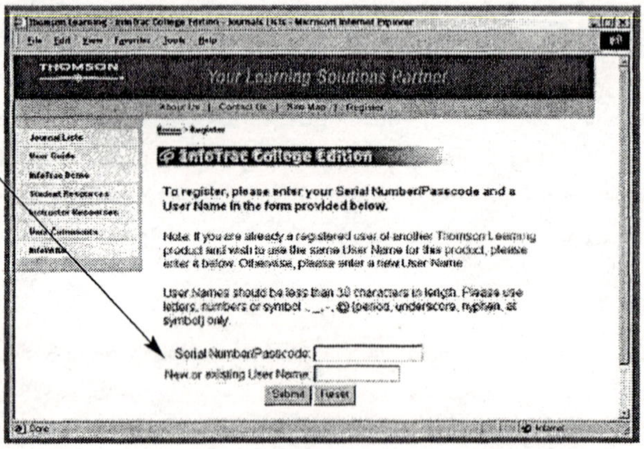

Step 3

Fill out the registration form completely to activate your account.

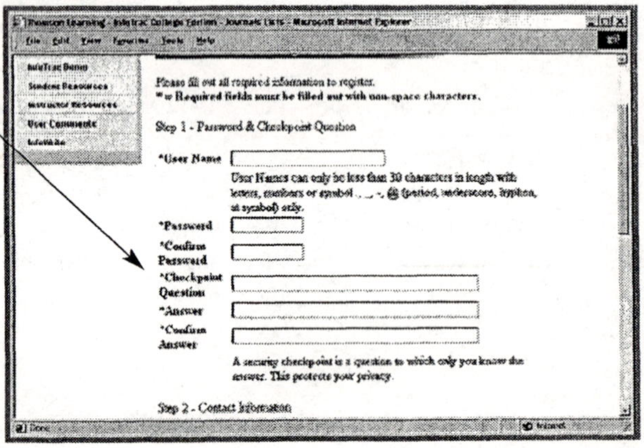

Note: After registration is complete, you will only need your <u>username and password</u> to logon.

USING INFOTRAC COLLEGE EDITION

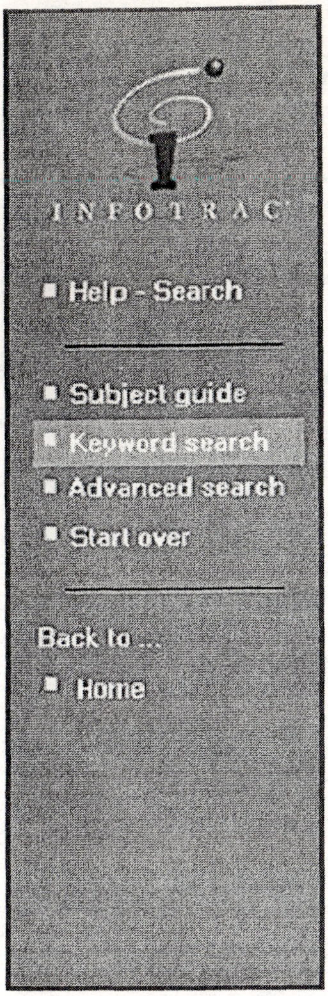

Features

1. The **Help-Search** button will assist you in your current search context.

2. The **Subject Guide** button allows you to search for topics.

3. The **Keyword Search** button allows you to match words in the article itself, not just in the controlled index terms.

4. The **Advanced Search** button allows you to select from the index to narrow your search for that particular term.

5. The **Start Over** button erases your current input and/or search results in the History section.

Subject Guide

Subject Guide allows you to do a broad search on a topic.

Step 1
Type in the term(s) you would like to search.

Step 2- Optional
You may refine your search by specifying dates, journals, and keywords.

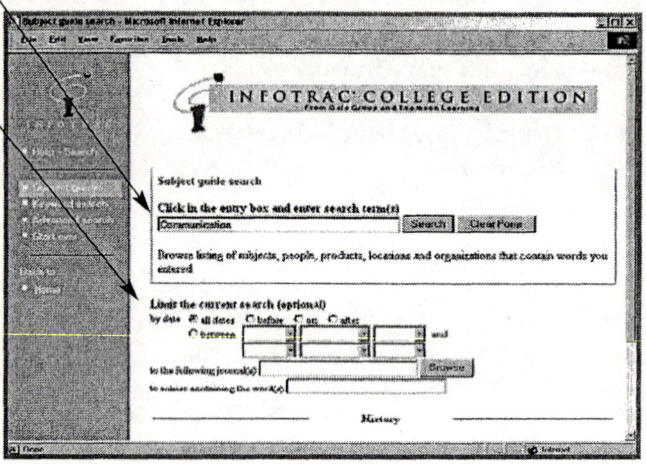

Step 3
A list of all the headings containing your specific topic along with the number of articles found within each heading will appear.

Click on **View** to go to the specific article(s).

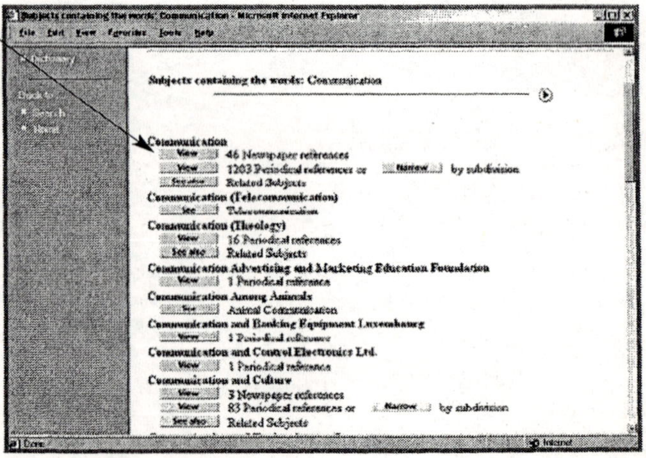

Narrow by Subdivision Results

If you would like to view subdivisions of your topic, click on **Narrow**.

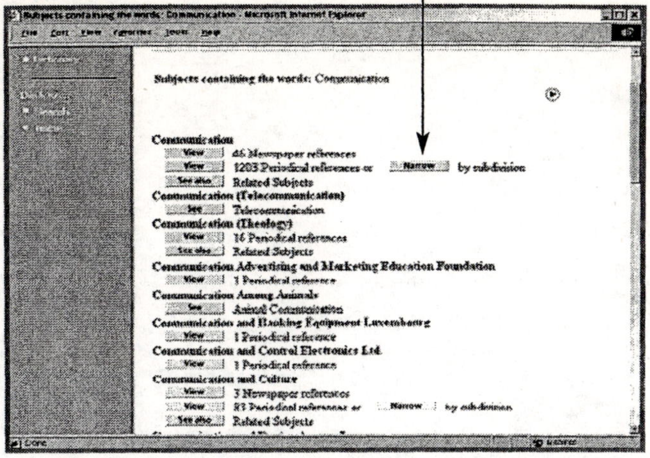

A list of subdivisions will appear. Click on the one that most pertains to your topic.

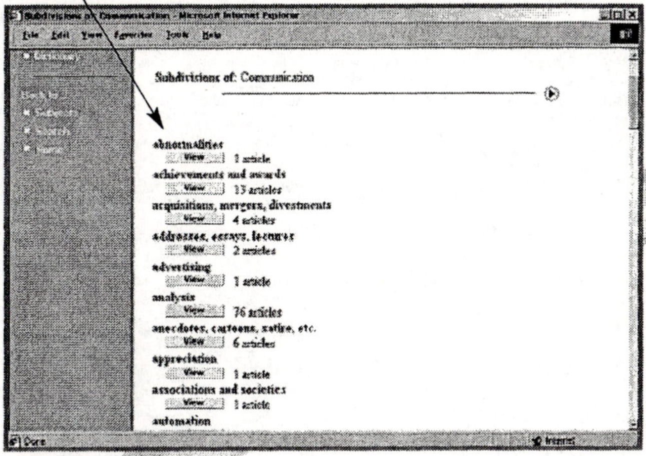

The articles will be listed in reverse chronological order. Click on the title to view.

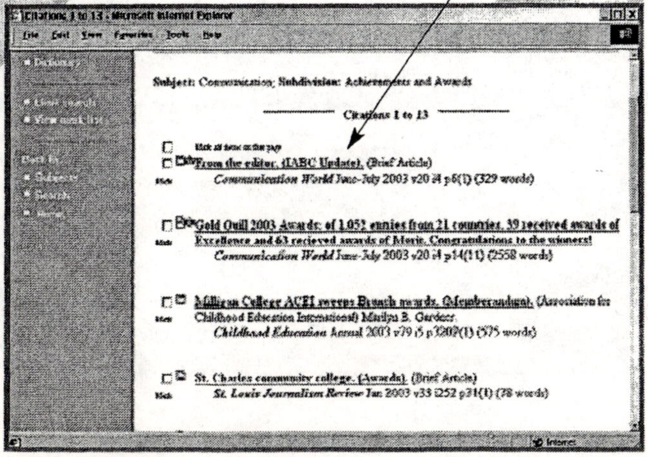

Keyword Search

The **Keyword Search** looks for the word(s) entered. It is more effective when looking for a specific topic, title, author name, or product.

Step 1
Type in the term(s) you would like to search.

Step 2- Optional
You can use logical operators (AND, OR, NOT) to create relationships between search terms.

Step 3- Optional
You may refine your search by specifying dates, journals, and keywords.

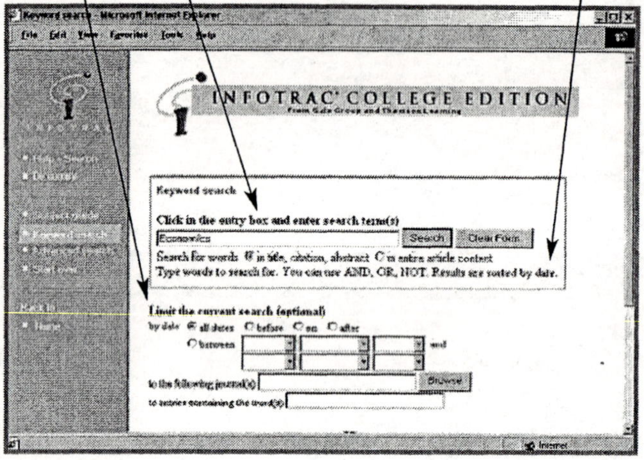

Step 4
The **Keyword Search** will give you a list of articles containing the terms searched. Results are listed in reverse chronological order.

Click on the title to view the full-text article.

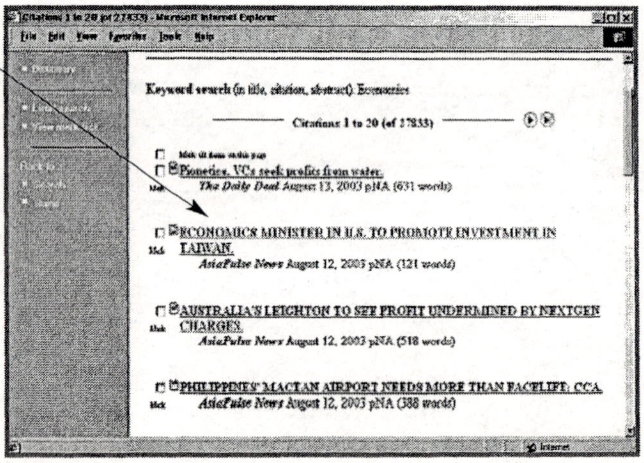

Advanced Search

The **Advanced Search** provides a variety of ways to search the database for articles.

Step 1

Select an index to search by.
What is an index? Each article is indexed by certain variables. These indices include the title, author, publication's name, where and when it was published (see the list on the next page).

Step 2

Type in the term(s) you would like to search.

Step 3- Optional

You may refine your search by specifying dates, journals, and keywords.

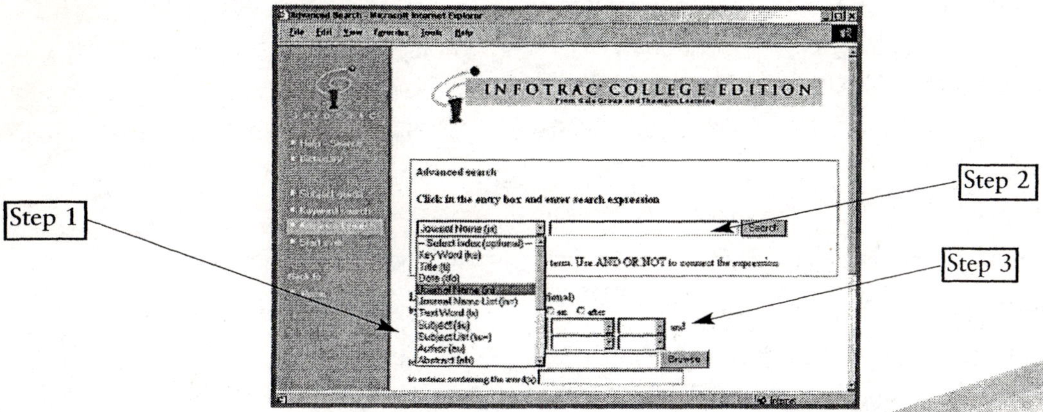

Example Search

If you want to find all the articles from the *Economist,* use the **Advanced Search**.

Step 1

Select the index **Journal Name** and type *Economist* in the **Search** field. Click **Search**.

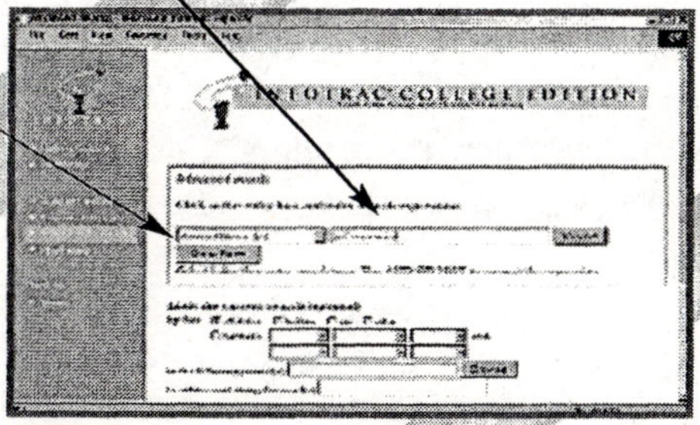

Step 2

Click on **View** to view a list of citations or **Modify** to change your search.

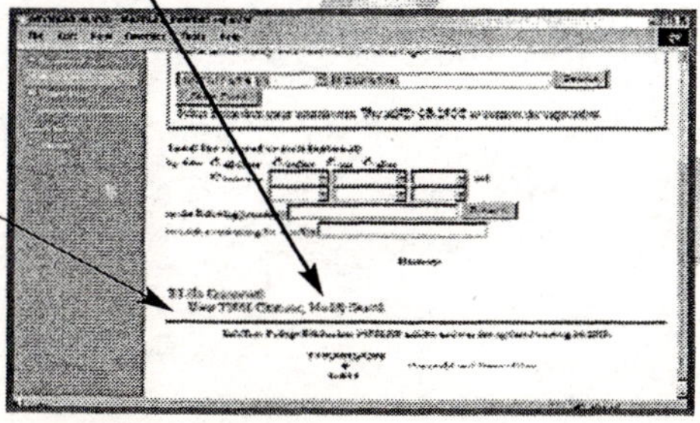

Indexes for Advanced Search

Abstract (ab): Includes words from article abstracts as well as from any author's abstracts.

Author (au): Authors are indexed in surname/given name order; for example, "nelan bruce w." It's best to search in surname-first order. Enter a surname and, optionally, a given name.

Date (da): The date the article was published.

Journal Name (jn): The name of the magazine or periodical.

Journal Name List (jn=): Provides a list of magazines or periodicals in which the search term appears.

Keyword (ke): Words in article titles and authors, as well as subjects, people, companies, products, vocations, events, etc., featured in articles.

Record Number (rn): A full record always includes a unique record number. If you note a record number, you can easily find the record again with the record number index.

Refereed (re): Experts in the same field as the writer review articles in the journal and ensure that the data and methodology has met a high standard. This is also knows as a peer reviewed.

Source (so): Lets you search for records by the type of source from which they're taken (e.g., magazine, journal, or newspapers).

Source List (so=): Lets you browse a list of subjects that contain the word or words you type.

Subject (su): Lets you search for references by the source types under which they are indexed.

Subject List (su=): Provides a list of references by source types.

Text Word (tx): Composed of all words from the body of articles.

Title (ti): The title index is composed of all words in the article.

Volume Number (vo): The volume of the magazine or periodical.

Using Wildcards in the Advanced Search

At times, you might want to find more than just exact matches to a search term. For instance, you might want to find both the singular and plural forms of a word or variant spellings. Wildcards let you broaden your searches to match a pattern.

InfoTrac provides three wildcards:

- An asterisk (*) stands for any number of characters, including none. For example pigment* matches "pigment," "pigments," "pigmentation," etc. The asterisk wildcard can also be used inside a word. For example, colo*r matches both "color" and "colour."
- A question mark (?) stands for exactly one character. Multiple question marks in a row stand for the same number of characters as there are question marks. For example, psych????y matches either "psychology" or "psychiatry", but not "psychotherapy."
- An exclamation point (!) stands for one or no characters. For example, analog!! matches "analog," "analogs" or "analogue" but not "analogous."

If you see a message about a search being invalid, you'll need to add at least one character before one of the wildcards.

Mark List

Clicking on the **Mark Box** allows you to select articles you would like to retrieve for later viewing. The **Mark Box** is available in two ways:

1. *While viewing the citation list.* You may select individual articles or you may select all the items on the page.

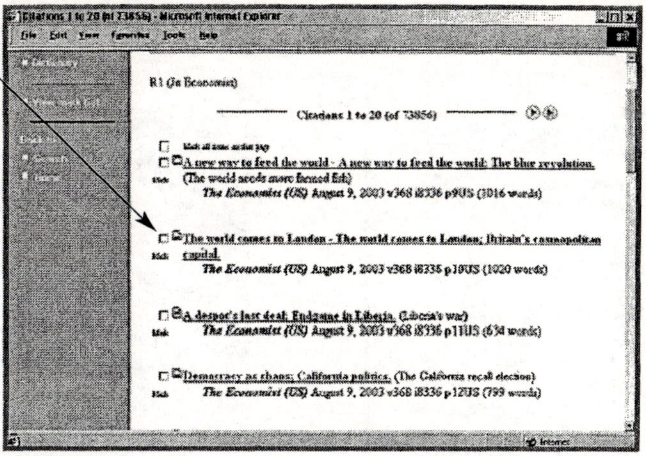

2. *While you are in article view.* Click on the **Mark Box** next to the article citation.

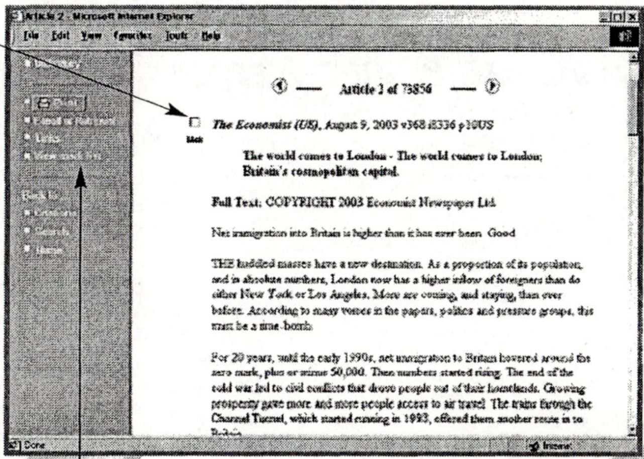

To view selected articles, click on **View Mark List**.

Limit Search

To focus a broad search, you may limit your search by date, journal, or keyword. There are two ways to limit a search:

1. *Limit a search that has already been performed.* To do this, click on **Limit Search** in the left navigation.

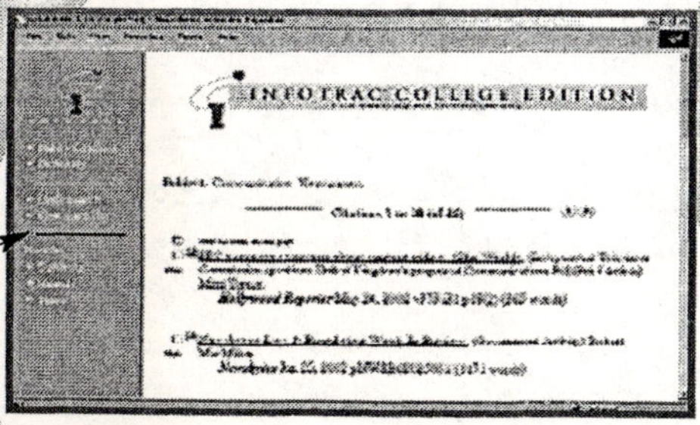

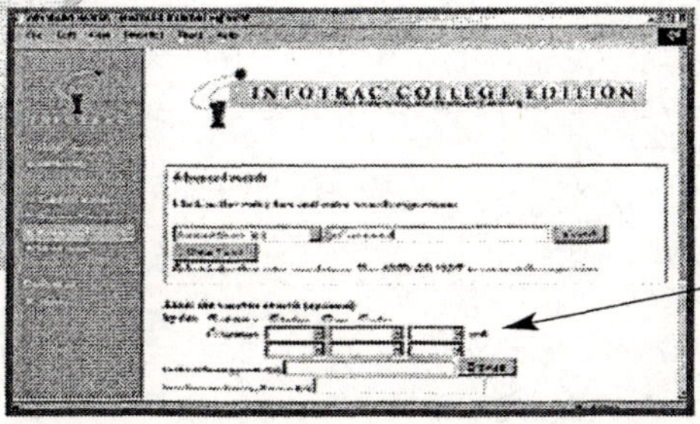

2. *Limit a current search.* To do this, fill out the **Limit Search** box below the search field.

Article Retrieval

There are three article retrieval options available:

- **Browser Print:** Print out the full text article
- **Acrobat Reader:** Review article as a PDF file
- **Email Delivery:** E-mail article to self or others

Click on **Print or Email** to view retrieval options.

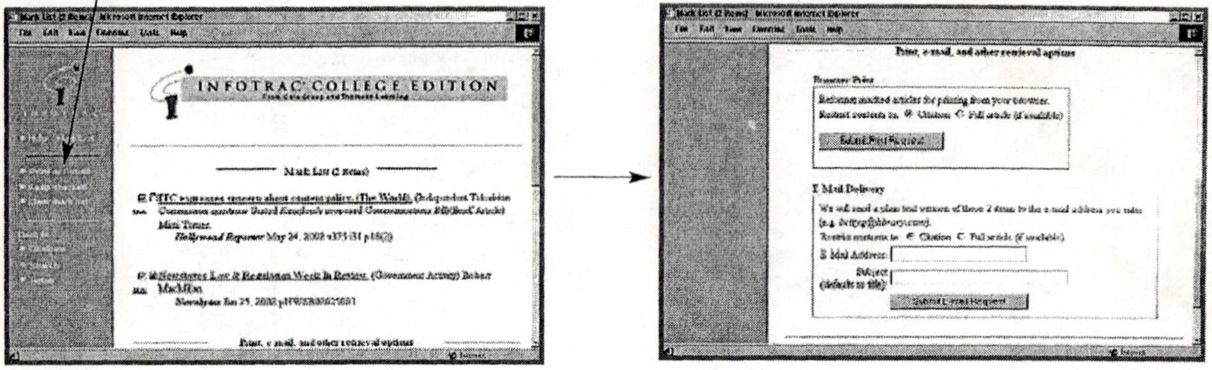

TROUBLESHOOTING & FREQUENTLY ASKED QUESTIONS

If you are experiencing any technical difficulties, you can send a form to Technical Support by clicking **Contact Us** on the *InfoTrac College Edition* homepage, or you can send an e-mail to support@thomsonlearning.com.

Q: *Are there any vowels in my passcode?*
A: There are no vowels in the passcode. If the letter appears to resemble a "U", it is actually the letter "V". If the letter appears to resemble like an "I", it is actually the number "1". If the letter appears to resemble like an "O", it is actually the number "0" (zero).

Q: *How far do the InfoTrac College Edition articles go back in time?*
A: *InfoTrac College Edition* dates back to 1980.

Q: *How often is the database updated?*
A: *InfoTrac College Edition* databases are updated every business day. Daily publications are indexed on a daily basis. Publications will vary by their frequency.

Q: *What if I lose or forget my username/password?*
A: E-mail tech support at the address above and they can help you within 24 hours on business days.

Q: *If I have a problem, what information do I need to provide in my message to InfoTrac College Edition customer service?*
A: Click on the Contact Us button on the welcome screen. You will be prompted for all necessary information.

Q: *How do I access the on-line help file?*
A: Each screen has context sensitive help. Just click on the help button.

QUICK START GUIDE FOR YOUR STUDENTS

The following pages may be duplicated and distributed to your students.

QUICK START GUIDE

InfoTrac College Edition, a complete Online Research and Learning Center, contains over 10 million full-text articles from nearly 5,000 scholarly and popular periodicals. Covering a broad spectrum of disciplines and topics, this online library is ideal for every type of research. *InfoTrac College Edition's* articles are updated daily and include research dating back to 1980. In addition to the database, *InfoTrac College Edition* offers InfoWrite, a web-based training tool designed to help develop writing skills. InfoWrite assists students through difficult areas of research writing, such as choosing a topic, composing introductions and conclusions, and crediting sources.

Registration

Step 1

Go to www.infotrac-college.com and click on **Register New Account.**

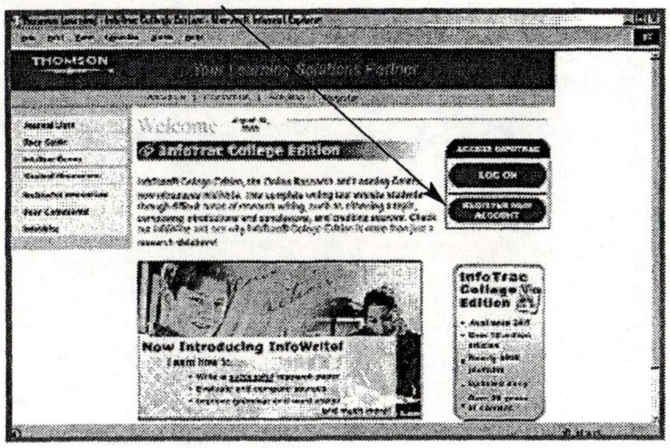

Step 2

Enter passcode and create a username.

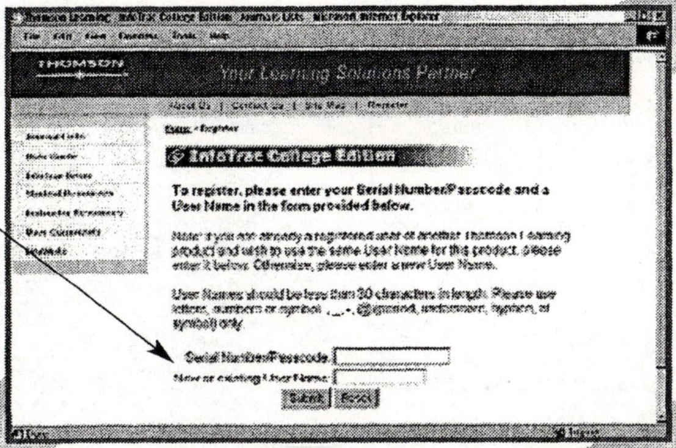

Step 3

Fill out the registration form completely to activate your account.

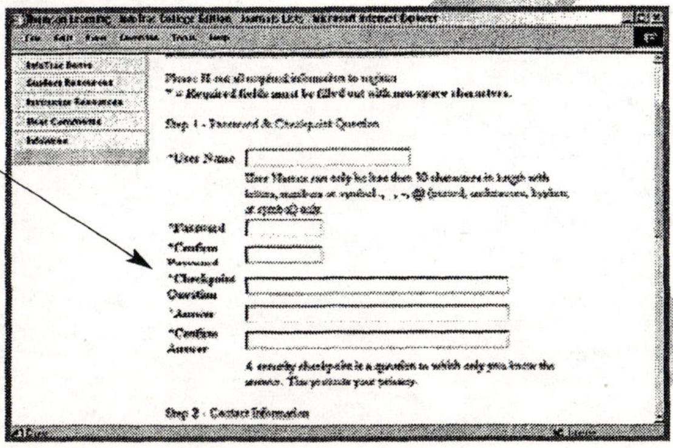

Note: After registration is complete, you will only need your <u>username and password</u> to logon.

USING INFOTRAC COLLEGE EDITION

There are three types of searches:

- Subject Guide Search
- Keyword Search
- Advanced Search

Subject Guide Search

Step 1

Type in the term(s) you would like to search and click **Search**.

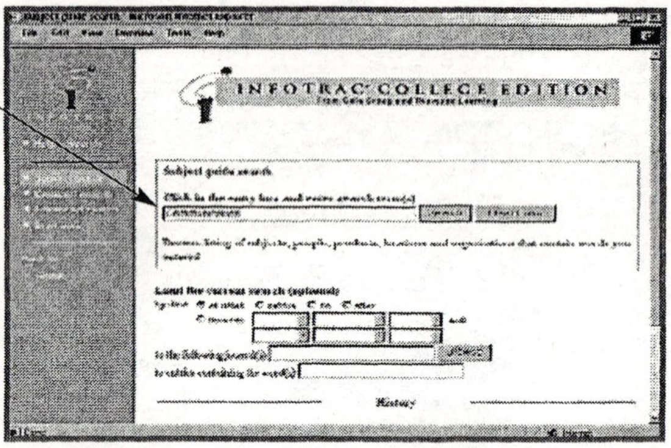

Step 2

After a list of results appear, select an article by clicking on the title. If your search words do not match the Subject Guide database, a list of similar and related subjects will appear. Simply select the subject that most closely matches your topic.

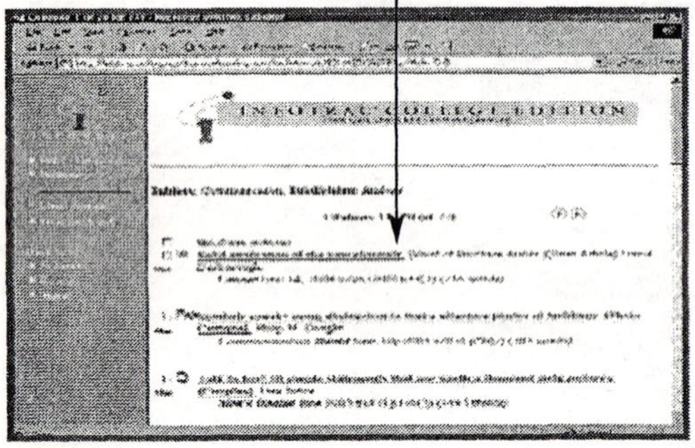

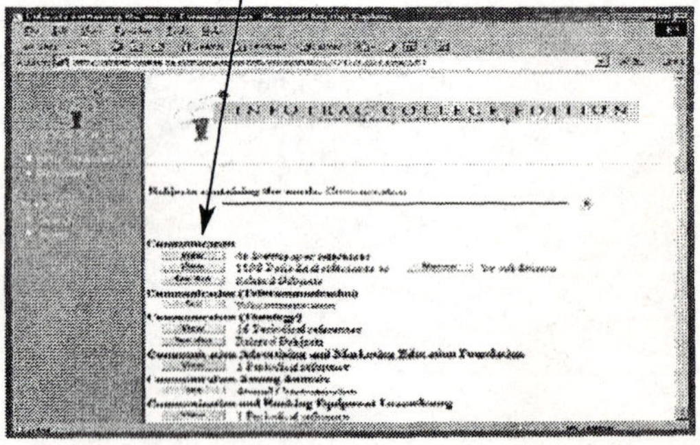

Step 4

A list containing bibliographic information for each article in your search to a maximum of 20 articles per page. To view an article, click on the citation.

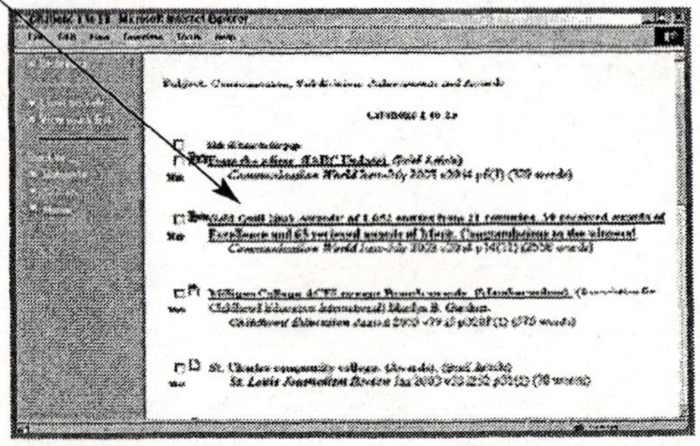

If the term(s) you typed in the **Subject Guide** cannot be found, it will automatically default to the **Keyword Search**.

Keyword Search

The **Keyword Search** looks for the word or words entered. It is more effective when looking for a specific topic, title, author, or product.

Search by **Keyword** just as you would by **Subject Guide.**

The search will return with a list of articles containing the keyword term(s). Results are listed from most recent to oldest publication date.

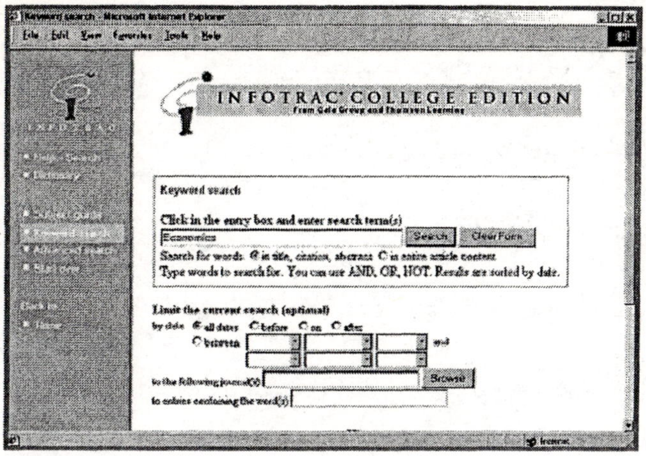

Advanced Search

With **Advanced Search,** a more specific search can be conducted.

Step 1

Select an index to search by. What is an index? Each article is indexed by certain variables. These indices include the title, author, publication's name, where and when it was published (see the list on the next page). Type your search criteria in the entry box to the right.

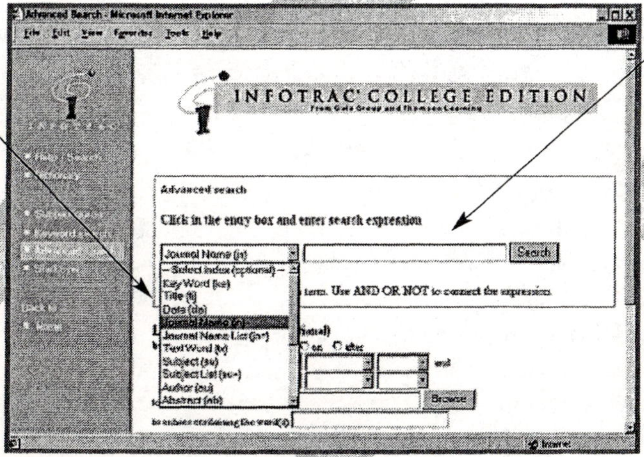

Step 2

If you want to search by multiple criterion, simply repeat the process with an operator between them.

- Logical operators(and/or/not) specify inclusive or exclusive relationships between search terms or result sets.
- Proximity operators (Wn, Nn) specify that two search terms must be within a specific distance (in words) of each other. Proximity operators work only with free text indexes such as keywords, abstracts, text, and titles.
- Range operators (since, before, etc.) specify upper bounds, lower bounds or both searches for numeric data. Numeric indexes include publication dates, number of employees and annual sales.

Indexes for Advanced Search

Abstract (ab): Includes words from article abstracts as well as from any author's abstracts.

Author (au): Authors are indexed in surname/given name order; for example, "nelan bruce w." It's best to search in surname-first order. Enter a surname and, optionally, a given name.

Date (da): The date the article was published.

Journal Name (jn): The name of the magazine or periodical.

Journal Name List (jn=): Provides a list of magazines or periodicals in which the search term appears.

Keyword (ke): Words in article titles and authors, as well as subjects, people, companies, products, vocations, events, etc., featured in articles.

Record Number (rn): A full record always includes a unique record number. If you note a record number, you can easily find the record again with the record number index.

Refereed (re): Experts in the same field as the writer review articles in the journal and ensure that the data and methodology has met a high standard. This is also knows as a peer reviewed.

Source (so): Lets you search for records by the type of source from which they're taken (e.g., magazine, journal, or newspapers).

Source List (so=): Lets you browse a list of subjects that contain the word or words you type.

Subject (su): Lets you search for references by the source types under which they are indexed.

Subject List (su=): Provides a list of references by source types.

Text Word (tx): Composed of all words from the body of articles.

Title (ti): The title index is composed of all words in the article.

Volume Number (vo): The volume of the magazine or periodical.

Using Wildcards in the Advanced Search

At times, you might want to find more than just exact matches to a search term. For instance, you might want to find both the singular and plural forms of a word or variant spellings. Wildcards let you broaden your searches to match a pattern.

InfoTrac provides three wildcards:

- An asterisk (*) stands for any number of characters, including none. For example pigment* matches "pigment," "pigments," "pigmentation," etc. The asterisk wildcard can also be used inside a word. For example, colo*r matches both "color" and "colour."
- A question mark (?) stands for exactly one character. Multiple question marks in a row stand for the same number of characters as there are question marks. For example, psych????y matches either "psychology" or "psychiatry", but not "psychotherapy."
- An exclamation point (!) stands for one or no characters. For example, analog!! matches "analog," "analogs" or "analogue" but not "analogous."

If you see a message about a search being invalid, you'll need to add at least one character before one of the wildcards.

Mark List

Clicking on the **Mark Box** allows you to select articles you would like to retrieve for later viewing. The **Mark Box** is available in two ways:

1. While viewing the citation list, you may select individual articles or you may select all the items on the page.

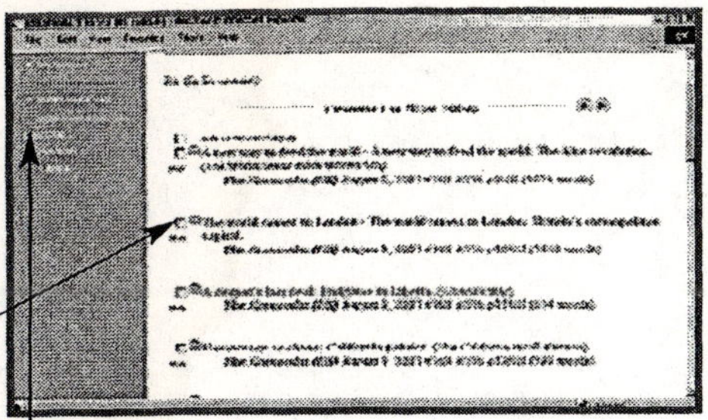

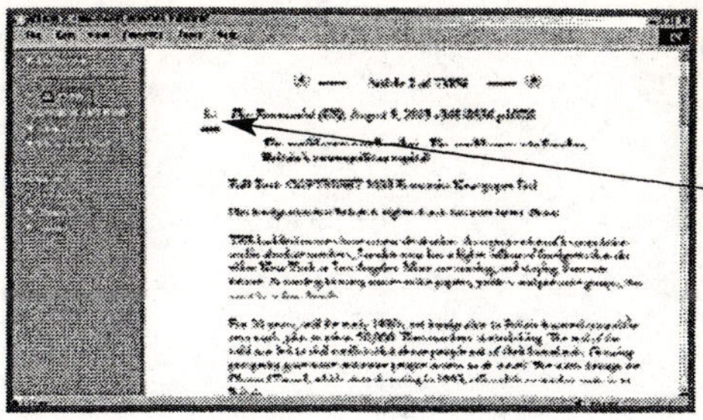

2. Check the **Mark Box** while you are in article view.

Click on **View Mark List** to view selected articles.

Limit Search

You may limit your search if you find yourself immersed in citations or of the citations are too general. Limit your search to dates, specific journals, and keywords. The **Limit Search** function is available in two ways:

1. *Limit a search that has already been performed.* To do this, click on **Limit Search** in the left navigation.

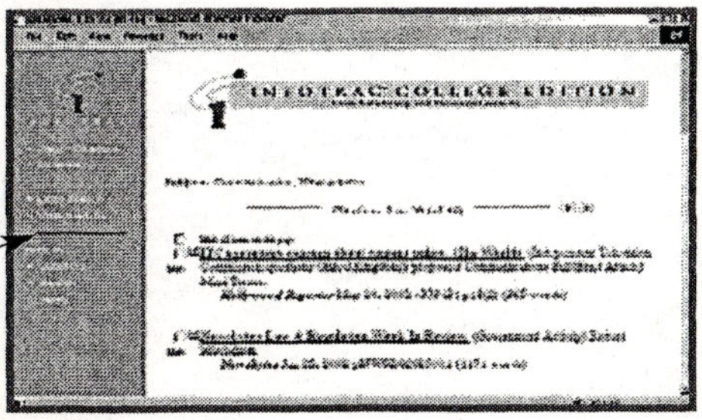

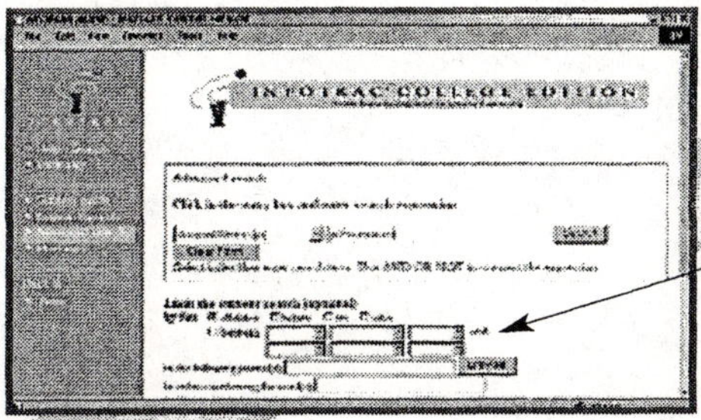

2. *Limit a current search.* To do this, fill out the Limit Search box below the search field.

Article Retrieval

There are three article retrieval options available:

- **Browser Print:** Print out the full text article
- **Acrobat Reader:** Review article as a PDF file
- **Email Delivery:** E-mail article to self or others

Click on **Print or Email** on the left navigation bar while viewing citations.

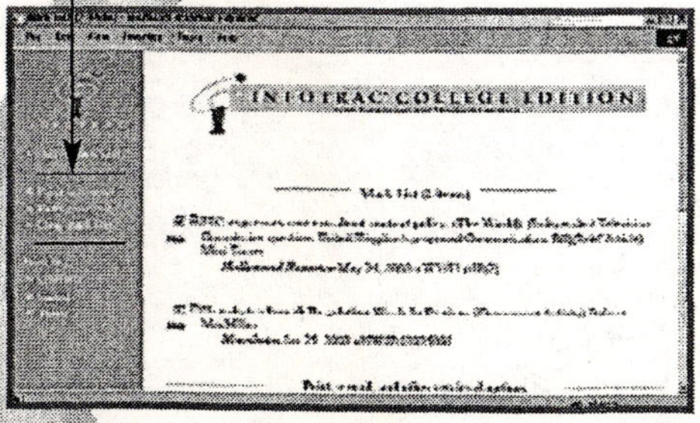

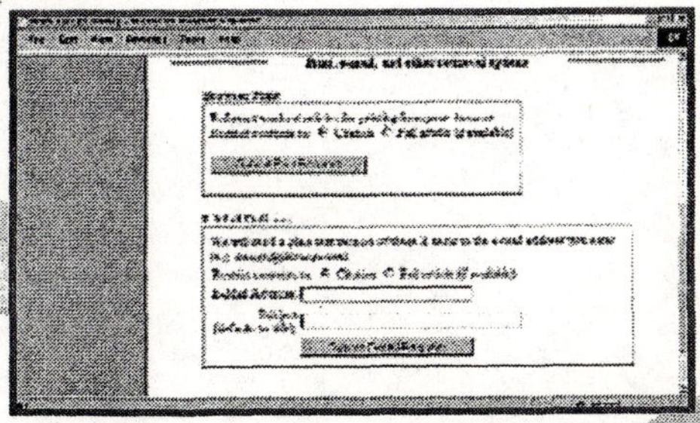

Appendix C

WebTutor™ Integration Tips

WebTutor™ Integration Tips for the Instructor

Contents of the Appendix:

THOMSON

Bb Blackboard www.blackboard.com

Tips for Integrating Thomson's WebTutor™ on Blackboard into your Course

Feature	Description - Benefit
THOMSON PROVIDED CONTENT	
Chapter Summary Materials	Students will be able to view summary material tied directly to their course textbook. These can include, but are not limited to Chapter Outlines, Summaries, internet exercises, interactive games and PowerPoint presentations.
Multimedia Content	Our WebTutor advantage products offer the added advantage of video clips, simulations and/or simulations.
Quizzes	Allow students to practice what they have learned in the textbook. Quiz results are automatically entered into the BB gradebook. Students can take quizzes multiple times, or if the instructor prefers, they can allow only one attempt, set a time limit, or specify a password for students to take a quiz. These quizzes include content not found in the instructor test bank, as well as Internet Activity and InfoTrac College Edition Activity quizzes, and can be edited by the instructor.
Flashcards	Flashcards allow students to review key terms from the textbook. Because students learn in many ways, flashcards (w/audio) allow students to hear the pronunciation of the term and in some cases, the definition. Flashcards are especially beneficial to the ESL or Learning Disabled student.
Web Links	Web links help keep the course current for the instructor and provide numerous opportunities for students to do additional research or project-based activities right on the web. Each WebTutor product comes pre-loaded with web links designed to enhance the course.
Discussion Topics	Threaded Discussion or Bulletin Board systems allow students and instructors to engage in a lively, on going discussion, anytime or anywhere. All Thomson WebTutor products come pre-loaded with suggested discussion topics. Of course, instructors and students can add their own.
PowerPoint Presentations	Many WebTutor products include PowerPoint presentations keyed to the textbook.
InfoTrac College edition	Students have direct, PIN-less, access to InfoTrac College edition offering 24/7 access to millions of articles from scholarly journals and popular periodicals. Students can search by keyword or subject. A must-have resource for any course that involves research.
Bb formatted Test banks	Instructors can request a Blackboard-formatted version of the ExamView testbank files for creation of their own quizzes and tests.
COMMUNICATION TOOLS	
Integrated Calendar	An integrated calendar provides the ability to view information at the institutional, course, and personal level.
Web Mail	Blackboard has third party software embedded in the product to seamlessly link to students existing email accounts.
Virtual Classroom	The Virtual Classroom allows for real-time, communication with the class and combines chat, whiteboard technology and a web browser into a synchronous learning tool. There are many possible uses for chat including virtual office hours, group study sessions or projects, and guest speakers. All chat sessions are logged for the instructor to view - even if they are not an active participant.
Threaded Discussion or Bulletin Board	Threaded Discussion or Bulletin Board systems allow students and instructors to engage in a lively, on going discussion, anytime or anywhere. This tool has many applications including discussion of course topics, debates, or general discussions about course issues. Instructors can create private discussion forums, or allow students to post anonymously. Instructors may assign a student moderator.

THOMSON

Bb Blackboard www.blackboard.com

Group Pages	Group pages allow the instructor to create collaborative learning environment on-line for specific group of students. This is useful for group projects and presentations.
Announcements	An announcement feature allows instructors to post time sensitive information to their class.
STUDENT MANAGEMENT TOOLS	
Course Statistics	Instructors can generate reports on the class or an individual student showing when and how students are accessing their course. Instructors can use this tool to monitor students progress and identify problem areas in a timely manner.
Online Gradebook	Allows instructors to view all students registered in the class and the results of their graded online quizzes and assignments.
Item Analysis	Allows instructor to get detailed item analysis of any quiz or survey item.
Item Tracking	Allows instructor to gather tracking details by student or class on any content item within the course. Report shows number of hits, days and times visited, etc.
T.A or Grader Access	Allows instructor to add a level of access to Teaching assistants or graders for assistance with grading.
Recycle Course	Allows instructors to recycle their courses from term to term without losing their customization. Student rosters, Bulletin Boards, online gradebook, Virtual Classroom archives are reset in preparation for the next term.
CUSTOMIZATION OPTIONS	
Look and feel	Instructors have complete control over the look and feel of their course - they can change button names and colors, add text and images and their school logo if they choose.
Instructor Profile	Instructions can add a profile with contact information for themselves or other key resources such as teaching assistants.
Quizzes	All quizzes are fully editable. Instructors can also create their own quizzes, or pools of questions for additional study or exams. Using the pools feature, instructors can generate randomized quizzes.
Content	Instructors can edit, delete or hide any content provided in the WebTutor product. They can also add their own content as well as re-sequencing the way the current content is presented.
Add additional Blackboard tools	Blackboard provides additional functionality for instructors wanting to take their course to the next level. Here are just a few: a student/instructor dropbox and an Electronic Blackboard for notetaking.
HOSTING OPTIONS	
Locally Hosted - RECOMMENDED	For schools that have Blackboard 5.5 or higher, Thomson will provide the school with an access key so that they can download the content cartridge to their local server. Blackboard provides additional technical support to supplement resources available on campus.
Centrally hosted	For schools that do not have Blackboard 5.5, we provide a hosted option (through Blackboard). All centrally hosted courses include technical support directly from Blackboard.

For additional information, including Frequently Asked Questions, tours, and downloadable Instructor and Student guides, visit us at http://webtutor.thomsonlearning.com

THOMSON

WebCT

Tips for Integrating Thomson's WebTutor™ on WebCT into your Course

Feature	Description - Benefit
THOMSON PROVIDED CONTENT	
Summary Materials	Students will be able to view summary material tied directly to their course textbook. These can include, but are not limited to Chapter Outlines, Summaries, internet exercises, interactive games and PowerPoint presentations.
Multimedia Content	Our WebTutor Advantage products offer the added advantage of video clips, animations and/or simulations.
Quizzes	Allows students to practice what they have learned in the textbook. Quiz results are automatically entered into the WebCT gradebook. Students can take quizzes multiple times, or if the instructor prefers, they can limit the number of times, set a time limit, or specify a specific time when the quiz is available. These quizzes include content not found in the instructor test bank, as well as Internet Activity and InfoTrac College Edition Activity quizzes, and can be edited by the instructor.
Flashcards	Flashcards allow students to review key terms from the textbook. Because students learn in many ways, flashcards (w/audio) allow students to hear the pronunciation of the term and in some cases, the definition. Flashcards are especially beneficial to the ESL or Learning Disabled student.
Web Links	Web links help keep the course current for the instructor and provide numerous opportunities for students to do additional research or project-based activities right on the web. Each WebTutor product comes pre-loaded with web links designed to enhance the course.
Discussion Topics	Threaded Discussion or Bulletin Board systems allow students and instructors to engage in a lively, on going discussion, anytime or anywhere. All Thomson WebTutor products come pre-loaded with suggested discussion topics. Of course, instructors and students can add their own.
PowerPoint Presentations	Many WebTutor products include PowerPoint presentations keyed to the textbook.
InfoTrac College edition	Students have direct, PIN-less, access to InfoTrac College edition offering 24/7 access to millions of full-text articles from scholarly journals and popular periodicals. Students can search by keyword or subject. A must-have resource for any course that involves research.
COMMUNICATION TOOLS	
Integrated Calendar	An integrated calendar can serve as a syllabus tool for instructors and allows them to enter information and key dates for the course. A pop-up window will always notify students when NEW information is placed on the calendar. Instructors can also create a link that will take students directly to a content page (chapter summary, quiz, etc). Students (and instructors) can also use the compile feature to print all assignments for a selected date range. Private entries are also allowed.
e-mail	An integrated e-mail system automatically builds a directory for the course as students create accounts. Students are not required to have an external email account to use WebTutor.
Chat	Chat allows for real-time, synchronous communication with the class. There are many possible uses for chat including virtual office hours, group study sessions or projects, and guest speakers. All chat sessions are logged for the instructor to view - even if they are not an active participant.

Threaded Discussion or Bulletin Board	Threaded Discussion or Bulletin Board systems allow students and instructors to engage in a lively, on going discussion, anytime or anywhere. This tool has many applications including discussion of course topics, debates, or general discussions about course issues. Instructors can create private discussion forums, or allow students to post anonymously.
Whiteboard	A real-time tool that allows you to upload images or presentations for students to view. Instructors or students can draw to the whiteboard.
STUDENT MANAGEMENT TOOLS	
Progress Tracking	Instructors will receive reports on each student that allow them to identify students first and last login, a distribution of hits, percentage of content visited and a complete history of all pages visited. Instructors can use this tool to monitor students progress and identify problem areas in a timely manner.
Participation in Discussion	Instructors will receive information about students participation in the discussion area including the number of items read, the number of original postings and the number of follow up postings. In an online environment, this is a great tool for instructors to measure a student's participation in class.
Student Management - Gradebook	Allows instructors to view all students registered in the class and the results of their graded online quizzes and assignments.
Item Analysis	Allows instructor to get detailed item analysis of any quiz or survey item.
Page Tracking	Allows instructors to see which students have accessed pages of content (from a path) - both the number of times and the time spent. Using this information, instructors can identify where students are spending their time and which areas of the course either need work, or additional reinforcement in class.
Grader Management	Allows the instructor to add graders to the course who have access to quiz information for assistance with grading.
Course RESET	Allows instructors to reset portions of their course for easy transition from term to term without losing their customization. Instructors can reset the student database, e-mail, Bulletin Boards, grader database, chat logs, the calendar tool, and the page-tracking tool.
CUSTOMIZATION OPTIONS	
Look and feel	Instructors have complete control over the look and feel of their course - they can change screen colors, add text and images, counters and their school logo if they choose.
Syllabus Tool	Provides a template for instructors to create their course syllabus. Alternatively, can upload an existing syllabus from a Word, or HTML file.
Quizzes	All quizzes are fully editable. Instructors can also create their own quizzes, or banks of questions for additional study or exams. Randomized quizzes can be created by using the Question Set feature. Additionally quizzes can be set up to prompt students for a password or require that a student is accessing the quiz from a certain IP address.
Content	Instructors can edit, delete or hide any content provided in the WebTutor product. They can also add their own content as well as re-sequencing the way the current content is presented.
Selective Release of Content	Instructors can choose to release content based on certain criteria such as date or time, to a selected group of students, or based on the result of quiz scores.
Add additional WebCT tools	WebCT provides additional functionality for instructors wanting to take their course to the next level. Here are just a few: an assignment dropbox, student presentation areas or homepages, image libraries, audio and video files, and more.

HOSTING OPTIONS	
Locally Hosted ***RECOMMENDED***	For schools that have WebCT, Thomson will provide the school with a content cartridge that they can install on their local server. Instructors and students also receive technical support from WebCT as well as the resources they have available on campus.
Centrally hosted	For schools that do not have WebCT 3.x or higher, we provide a hosted option (through WebCT). All centrally hosted courses include unlimited technical support directly from WebCT for both instructors and students.

For additional information, including Frequently Asked Questions, tours, and downloadable Instructor and Student guides, visit us at http://webtutor.thomsonlearning.com

Appendix D

InfoMarks Professor's Guide

INFOMARKS: MAKE YOUR MARK!

WHAT IS AN INFOMARK?

It's a single-click return ticket to any page, any result, any search from InfoTrac College Edition.

An InfoMark is a stable URL, linked to InfoTrac College Edition articles that you have selected. InfoMarks can be used like any other URL, but they're better because they're stable – they don't change. Using an InfoMark is like performing the search again whenever you follow the link – whether the result is a single article or a list of articles.

HOW DO INFOMARKS WORK?

If you can "copy and paste," you can use InfoMarks.

When you see the InfoMark icon- -on a result page, its URL can be copied and pasted into your electronic document – web page, word processing document or e-mail. Once InfoMarks are incorporated into a document, the results are persistent (the URLs will not change) and are dynamic.

Even though the saved search is used at different times by different users, an InfoMark always functions like a brand new search. Each time a saved search is executed, it accesses the latest updated information. That means subsequent InfoMark searches might yield additional or more up-to-date information than the original search with less time and effort.

CAPABILITIES

InfoMarks are the perfect technology tool for creating:

- Virtual online readers
- Current awareness topic sites- links to periodical or newspaper sources
- Online/distance learning courses
- Bibliographies, reference lists
- Electronic journals and periodical directories
- Student assignments
- Hot topics

ADVANTAGES

- Select from over 15 million articles from more than 5,000 journals and periodicals
- Update article and search lists easily
- Articles are always full-text and include bibliographic information
- All articles can be viewed online, printed, or emailed
- Saves professors and students time
- Anyone with access to InfoTrac College Edition can use it
- No other online library database offers this functionality
- FREE!

How to Use InfoMarks

There are 3 ways to utilize InfoMarks—in HTML documents, Word documents, and Email

HTML Document

1. Open a new document in your HTML editor (Netscape Composer or FrontPage Express).
2. Open a new browser window and conduct your search in InfoTrac College Edition.
3. Highlight the URL of the results page or article that you would like to InfoMark.
4. Right click the URL and click Copy. Now, switch back to your HTML document.
5. In your document, type in text that describes the InfoMarked item.
6. Highlight the text and click on Insert, then on Link in the upper bar menu.
7. Click in the link box, then press the "Ctrl" and "V" keys simultaneously and click OK. This will paste the URL in the box.
8. Save your document.

Word Document

1. Open a new Word document.
2. Open a new browser window and conduct your search in InfoTrac College Edition.
3. Check items you want to add to your Marked List.
4. Click on Mark List on the right menu bar.
5. Highlight the URL, right click on it, and click Copy. Now, switch back to your Word document.
6. In your document, type in text that describes the InfoMarked item.
7. Highlight the text. Go to the upper bar menu and click on Insert, then on Hyperlink.
8. Click in the hyperlink box, then press the "Ctrl" and "V" keys simultaneously and click OK. This will paste the URL in the box.
9. Save your document.

Email

1. Open a new email window.
2. Open a new browser window and conduct your search in InfoTrac College Edition.
3. Highlight the URL of the results page or article that you would like to InfoMark.
4. Right click the URL and click Copy. Now, switch back to your email window.
5. In the email window, press the "Ctrl" and "V" keys simultaneously. This will paste the URL into your email.
6. Send the email to the recipient. By clicking on the URL, they will be able to view the InfoMark.